BC '98

00872435

Baillière's
CLINICAL
HAEMATOLOGY
INTERNATIONAL PRACTICE AND RESEARCH

Editorial Board
C. Hershko (Israel)
A. V. Hoffbrand (UK)
D. C. Linch (UK)
D. Metcalf (Australia)
D. J. Weatherall (UK)

Baillière's

CLINICAL

HAEMATOLOGY

INTERNATIONAL PRACTICE AND RESEARCH

Volume 10/Number 4
December 1997

Gaucher's Disease

A. ZIMRAN MD
Guest Editor

Baillière Tindall
London Philadelphia Sydney Tokyo Toronto

This book is printed on acid-free paper.

Baillière Tindall   24–28 Oval Road
W.B. Saunders   London NW1 7DX, UK
Company Ltd
                     The Curtis Center, Independence Square West,
                     Philadelphia, PA 19106–3399, USA

                     55 Horner Avenue
                     Toronto, Ontario M8Z 4X6, Canada

                     Harcourt Brace & Company
                     Australia
                     30–52 Smidmore Street, Marrickville, NSW 2204, Australia

                     Harcourt Brace & Company
                     Japan Inc
                     Ichibancho Central Building,
                     22–1 Ichibancho, Chiyoda-ku, Tokyo 102, Japan

Whilst great care has been taken to maintain the accuracy of the information contained in this issue, the authors, editor, owners and publishers cannot accept any responsibility for any loss or damage arising from actions or decisions based on information contained in this publication; ultimate responsibility for the treatment of patients and interpretation of published material lies with the medical practitioner. The opinions expressed are those of the authors and the inclusion in this publication of material relating to a particular product, method or technique does not amount to an endorsement of its value or quality, or of the claims made by its manufacturer.

ISSN 0950–3536

ISBN 0–7020–2378–7 (single copy)

© 1997 W B Saunders Company Ltd. All rights reserved.

No part of this publication may be reproduced, stored in a retrieval system, or transmitted in any form or by any means, electronic, mechanical, photocopying, recording or otherwise, without the prior written permission of the Publisher, W B Saunders Company Ltd, 24–28 Oval Road, London NW1 7DX, UK.

Special regulations for readers in the USA. This journal has been registered with the Copyright Clearance Centre, Inc. Consent is given for copying of articles for personal or internal use, or for the personal use of specific clients. This consent is given on the condition that the copier pays through the Center the per-copy fee stated in the code on the first page of the article for copying beyond that permitted by Sections 107 or 108 of the US Copyright Law. The appropriate fee should be forwarded with a copy of the first page of the article to the Copyright Clearance Center, Inc, 27 Congress Street, Salem, MA 01970 (USA). If no code appears in an article the author has not given broad consent to copy and permission to copy must be obtained directly from the author.

This consent does not extend to other kinds of copying such as for general distribution, resale, advertising and promotion purposes, or for creating new collective works, special written permission must be obtained from the Publisher for such copying.

Baillière's Clinical Haematology is published four times each year by Baillière Tindall. Prices for Volume 10 (1997) are:

TERRITORY	ANNUAL SUBSCRIPTION	SINGLE ISSUE
Europe including UK	£108.00 (Institutional) post free	£30.00 post free
	£90.00 (Individual) post free	
All other countries	Consult your local Harcourt Brace & Company office	

The editor of this publication is Gail Greensmith, Baillière Tindall, 24–28 Oval Road, London NW1 7DX, UK.

Baillière's Clinical Haematology is covered in Index Medicus, Current Contents/Clinical Medicine, Current Contents/Life Sciences, the Science Citation Index, SciSearch, Research Alert and Excerpta Medica.

Baillière's Clinical Haematology was published from 1972 to 1986 as *Clinics in Haematology*

Typeset by Phoenix Photosetting, Chatham.
Printed and bound in Great Britain by the University Printing House, Cambridge, UK.

Contributors to this issue

AYALA ABRAHAMOV MD, Senior Lecturer in Paediatrics, Gaucher Clinic, Shaare Zedek Medical Center, Jerusalem, Israel.

JOHANNES M. F. G. AERTS PhD, Associate Professor, Department of Biochemistry, Academic Medical Centre, University of Amsterdam, PO Box 22700, 1100 DE Amsterdam, The Netherlands.

J. A. BARRANGER MD, PhD, University of Pittsburgh Medical Center, Pittsburgh, PA 15261, USA.

BRUNO BEMBI MD, Director of the Centre for Diagnosis and Treatment of Gaucher Disease and Congenital Diseases of Metabolism, Genetica Medica, Istituto di Ricovero e Cura a Carattere Scientifico 'Buro Garofolo', Via dell'Istria 65/1, 34137 Trieste, Italy.

ERNEST BEUTLER MD, Professor and Chairman, Department of Molecular and Experimental Medicine, The Scripps Research Institute, 10550 North Torrey Pines Road, La Jolla, CA 92037, USA.

ROSCOE O. BRADY MD, Chief, Developmental and Metabolic Neurology Branch, National Institute of Neurological Disorders and Stroke, National Institutes of Health, Building 10, Room 3D04, 10 Center Dr MSC 1260, Bethesda, MD 20852-1260, USA.

TIMOTHY M. COX MA, MSc, MD, FRCP, Professor of Medicine, Honorary Consultant Physician, Department of Medicine, University of Cambridge, Level 5, Addenbrooke's Hospital, Cambridge CB2 2QQ, UK.

DEBORAH ELSTEIN PhD, Research Coordinator, Gaucher Clinic, Shaare Zedek Medical Center, PO Box 3235, Jerusalem, 91031 Israel.

ANDERS ERIKSON MD, PhD, Associate Professor, Department of Paediatrics, University of Umeå, S-901 85 Umeå, Sweden.

EDWARD I. GINNS MD, PhD, Chief, Clinical Neuroscience Branch, Clinical Neuroscience Branch, National Institute of Mental Health, NIH, Building 49, Room B1EE16, 49 Convent Drive MSC 4405, Bethesda, MA 20892-4405, USA.

GREGORY A. GRABOWSKI MD, Director, Professor of Paediatrics, University of Cincinnati College of Medicine, Division and Program in Human Genetics, Children's Hospital Medical Center, 3333 Burnet Avenue, Cincinnati, Ohio, 45339-3039, USA.

CARLA E. M. HOLLAK MD, PhD, Internist, Coordinator of Treatment of Gaucher's Disease in The Netherlands, Department of Haematology, F4-222, Academic Medical Centre, University of Amsterdam, PO Box 22700, 1100 DE Amsterdam, The Netherlands.

MIA HOROWITZ PhD, Department of Cell Research and Immunology, Tel-Aviv University, Ramat-Aviv, Israel.

MENACHEM ITZCHAKI MD, Chairman, Department of Orthopaedics, Shaare Zedek Medical Center, Gaucher Clinic, Jerusalem, 91031 Israel.

Editorial Note

The presentation of material in *Baillière's Clinical Haematology* has been updated, and we hope that the changes will make the information in the series more accessible to readers.

Each chapter is now preceded by a short abstract summarizing the content and by keywords that will be used for indexing and abstracting purposes.

Where the author has identified the most important references cited in the chapter, these have been indicated in the reference list with asterisks.

EPHRAT LEVY-LAHAD MD Diplomate ABMG, Director, Medical Genetic Services, Department of Medicine and Gaucher Clinic, Shaare-Zedek Medical Center, Jerusalem, Israel.

S. LUCOT BS, University of Pittsburgh Medical Center, Pittsburgh, PA 15261, USA.

HENRY J. MANKIN MD, Visiting Orthopaedic Surgeon, Massachusetts General Hospital, Director, Harvard Combined Residency Program in Orthopaedics, Harvard Medical School and Edith M. Ashley Professor of Orthopaedics, Department of Orthopaedic Surgery, Massachusetts General Hospital, Boston, Massachusetts, USA.

PRAMOD K. MISTRY BSc, PhD, MBBS, MRCP, Senior Lecturer and Honorary Consultant Physician, Hepato-biliary and Liver Transplant Unit, Royal Free Hospital School of Medicine, Pond Street, London NW3 2QG, UK.

GREGORY M. PASTORES MD, Assistant Professor of Neurology and Paediatrics, Department of Neurology and Paediatrics, New York University School of Medicine, Neurogenetics Laboratory, 400 East 34th Street, IRM RR 311, New York, NY 10016, USA.

RAPHAEL SCHIFFMANN MD, Chief, Clinical Investigation Section, Developmental and Metabolic Neurology Branch, National Institute of Neurological Disorders and Stroke, National Institutes of Health, Bldg, 10, Rm 3D03, 10 Center Drive, Bethesda, MD, 20892-1260, USA.

J. PAUL SCHOFIELD BSc, MB, PhD, MRCP, Lister Research Fellow, Honorary Consultant Physician, Department of Medicine, University of Cambridge, Level 5, Addenbrooke's Hospital, Cambridge CB2 2QQ, UK.

ELLEN SIDRANSKY MD, Chief, Unit of Clinical Genetics, Clinical Neuroscience Branch, National Institute of Mental Health, NIH, Building 49, Room B1EE16, 49 Convent Drive MSC 4405, Bethesda, MA 20892-4405, USA.

ARI ZIMRAN MD, Associate Professor of Medicine, Director Gaucher Clinic, Department of Medicine and Gaucher Clinic, Shaare-Zedek Medical Center, Jerusalem, 91031, Israel.

Table of contents

PREVIOUS ISSUES

Vol. 8, No. 3 1995
Megaloblastic Anaemia
S. N. Wickramasinghe

Vol. 8, No. 4 1995
Multiple Myeloma
F. Mandelli

Vol. 9, No. 1 1996
Acute Myelogenous Leukaemia and Myelodysplasia
B. Löwenberg

Vol. 9, No. 2 1996
Haemophilia
C. A. Lee

Vol. 9, No. 3 1996
Hodgkin's Disease
V. Diehl

Vol. 9, No. 4 1996
Non-Hodgkin's Lymphoma
D. C. Linch

Vol. 10, No. 1 1997
Megakaryocytes and Platelet Disorders
J. P. Caen & Z-C. Han

Vol. 10, No. 2 1997
Chronic Myeloid Leukaemia
J. M. Goldman

Vol. 10, No. 3 1997
Molecular Haemopoiesis
A. D. Whetton

FORTHCOMING ISSUE

Vol. 11, No. 1 1998
Prevention, Diagnosis and Management of Venous Thrombo-embolic Diseases
G. F. Pineo & R. D. Hull

Preface

In 1982, 100 years after Gaucher's original description of the disease that bears his name, Desnick, Gatt and Grabowski edited the first book which was dedicated in its entirety to Gaucher's disease. Two major advances in the past 15 years have revolutionized our ability to diagnose and treat patients with this genetic disorder: the progress made in molecular biology and the introduction of safe and effective enzyme therapy. Modern DNA technology has led to the cloning of the glucocerebrosidase genes and identification of mutations, it has enabled population screening and the creation of animal models as well as the development of future therapeutic modalities involving gene transfer. Enzyme replacement therapy has successfully reversed many of the haematological and visceral manifestations of the disorder and ameliorated other features of the disease, thus significantly improving the quality of life for many patients throughout the world.

Gaucher's disease has become a model for single-gene disorders. Beyond the medical and scientific issues, there are implications for ethical and societal decision-making policies, such as the effective allocation of scarce resources and the controversies regarding large-scale screening for relatively benign/mild diseases. It is within this context that a broad readership of clinical haematologists, general practitioners, geneticists, internists, surgeons, paediatricians, pathologists and others will find the discussions in this issue of interest. I hope this will become a source of information and ideas that stimulate and inspire the next generation of clinicians and researchers.

I have been privileged to invite most of the world experts as contributors to this issue, many with decades of experience in Gaucher's disease. One of the consequences of having multiple authorship is minimal but unavoidable overlap between a few of the chapters. Nevertheless, each chapter stands alone, and the complete issue may hopefully be viewed as a state-of-the-art discussion of Gaucher's disease.

I wish to express my debt to Dr Deborah Elstein (with whom I have worked very closely in both patient care and clinical research) for her help with the editing of this book. I also want to express special thanks to Professor Ernest Beutler who, as my mentor, introduced me in 1986 to

Gaucher's disease. I would like to acknowledge Ms. Gail Greensmith and the team at the publishers, for their efficiency in the preparation of this book. Finally, I wish to applaud the Gaucher patients and the patients' associations from all over the world, for the on-going and enthusiastic support that they have given to the researchers, over many years and in so many different ways, which started long before significant personal benefit could be seen on the horizon.

A. ZIMRAN

1

Gaucher's disease: past, present and future

ROSCOE O. BRADY MD

Chief
Developmental and Metabolic Neurology Branch, National Institute of Neurological Disorders and Stroke, National Institutes of Health, Building 10, Room 3D04, 10 Center Dr MSC 1260, Bethesda, MD 20852-1260, USA

A patient with what is now known as Gaucher's disease was first described by P. C. E. Gaucher in 1882. Fifty years later, Aghion reported that patients with this condition accumulated a sphingoglycolipid called glucocerebroside. Considerably more time was required for the demonstration by Brady and co-workers in 1964 that Gaucher's disease was due to reduced activity of a β-glucosidase called glucocerebrosidase. This information provided the basis for the development of reliable diagnostic tests, detection of most of the carriers of this disorder and the prenatal diagnosis of this condition. Evidence was presented in 1990 and 1991 indicating the highly beneficial effects of enzyme replacement therapy in patients with Gaucher's disease. Gene therapy for Gaucher's disease was initiated in 1995. While little indication of success was obtained in this inaugural attempt, it is expected that improvements in this technology will provide a permanent cure for patients with this disorder.

Key words: glucocerebroside; glucocerebrosidase; sphingolipid; genetic counselling; enzyme replacement therapy; gene therapy.

In 1882, a French medical student named Philippe Charles Ernest Gaucher described a 32-year-old female with an enlarged spleen that he thought was an epithelioma (Gaucher, 1882). He noted the presence of large, unusual cells in the patient's spleen. Reports of additional patients with similar presentations appeared shortly thereafter, and the eponym 'Gaucher's disease' was applied to these individuals. The term 'Gaucher cell' also became commonly used to specify the characteristic engorged cells in the organs of these patients. It was suggested at the beginning of this century that Gaucher's disease was a familial disorder (Brill, 1901). Involvement of the lymph nodes, the liver and the bone marrow was reported 3 years later (Brill, 1904). The first pre-mortem diagnosis of a patient with the disorder was made by a year later (Brill et al, 1905).

It was quickly realized that the age at which the signs and symptoms associated with Gaucher's disease become manifest varied greatly (Collier, 1895; Kraus, 1920; Rusca, 1921). Neurological impairment in an infant

Copyright © 1997, by Baillière Tindall
All rights of reproduction in any form reserved

was first reported 6 years later (Oberling and Woringer, 1927). This phenotype eventually became known as the infantile or acute neuronopathic
form. The nomenclature currently used for such patients is Type 2
Gaucher's disease. Another discrete clinical presentation was described
three decades later (Hillborg, 1959). In the latter patients, neurological
signs appear during the pre-teen and early teen years. This phenotype has
been called the juvenile or chronic neuronopathic form. These patients are
now classified as Type 3 Gaucher's disease. By far, however, the most
frequently encountered patients with Gaucher's disease do not have signs
of central nervous system involvement. Such patients were previously
called adult Gaucher's disease, but now they are generally designated as
Type 1 Gaucher's disease.

Clinical syndromes characteristic of Gaucher's disease gradually
emerged. Patients with Type 1 Gaucher's disease exhibit anaemia,
thrombocytopenia, leukopenia, enlargement and infarctions of the spleen
and liver, undermineralization and fractures of the long bones. These signs
may appear as early as childhood, but in some patients, they become
manifest considerably later in life. The central nervous system is clinically
not involved. Patients with Type 2 Gaucher's disease have hepatosplenomegaly and profound brain impairment. They generally die before 2
years of age. Patients with Type 3 Gaucher's disease have been sub-
classified into 3A and 3B because of differences in their clinical
presentations (Patterson et al, 1993). Patients with Type 3A Gaucher's
disease develop progressive neurological deficits consisting of cognitive
impairment, myoclonic and generalized tonic-clonic seizures, horizontal
supranuclear gaze palsy and mild organomegaly. These patients usually die
from signs associated with brain stem damage. Patients with Type 3B
Gaucher's disease have profound hepatosplenomegaly, anaemia,
oesophageal varices and extensive skeletal damage. The sole neurological
manifestation is horizontal supranuclear gaze palsy. In the past, these
patients usually succumbed to hepatic failure, pulmonary complications or
an uncontrollable haemorrhagic episode (Brady et al, 1997).

RELATIVELY RECENT PAST

Although an increasing number of patients were gradually being identified,
the condition was viewed as extremely rare. Progress in elucidating the
cause of Gaucher's disease in the first part of the 20th century was
inordinately slow. The accumulating material was identified in 1924 by
Lieb as a sphingoglycolipid that he erroneously believed to be galactocerebroside (Lieb, 1924). A decade later, Aghion (1934) demonstrated that
the accumulating material was actually glucocerebroside (Figure 1).
Glucocerebroside is comprised of three components. The first is the
aminoalcohol called sphingosine. A long chain fatty acid is linked to the
nitrogen atom on carbon two of sphingosine forming a complex called
ceramide. A single molecule of galactose is linked by a glycosidic bond to
the oxygen on carbon one of the sphingosine portion of ceramide.

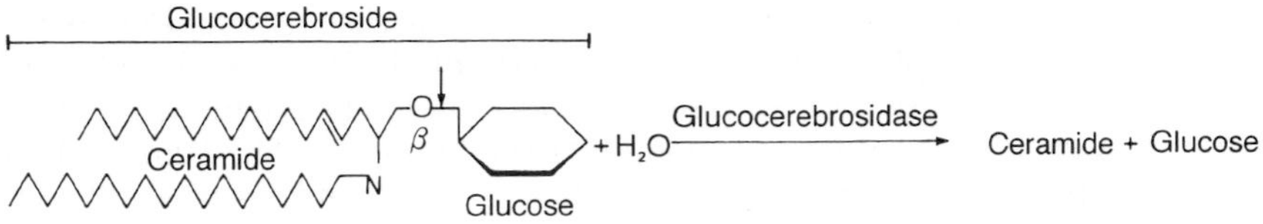

Figure 1. Structure of glucocerebroside that accumulates in Gaucher's disease. the vertical arrow indicates the site of hydrolytic cleavage of glucose catalysed by the enzyme glucocerebrosidase.

Discovery of the metabolic defect in Gaucher's disease

At this point in time, nothing whatsoever was known about the metabolism of sphingolipids. One had to presume that biochemical pathways were available for their formation, but whether they were catabolized catabolism was completely uncertain. I began to explore the cause of Gaucher's disease in 1956. It had been known from the beginning of the 20th century that galactocerebroside was a major lipid component of brain and the spinal cord. There seemed to be two aspects that should be determined during the early phase of our metabolic studies. The first was whether there was an abnormality of carbohydrate metabolism in patients with Type 1 Gaucher's disease that led to the formation of glucocerebroside instead of the more abundant and well-known galactocerebroside. This aspect was eliminated by a simple galactose tolerance test that I performed in a 32-year-old female with Type 1 Gaucher's disease. Disposition of galactose was completely normal. This finding led to the possibility that the pathway of formation of glucocerebroside was altered in Gaucher's disease leading to the production of glucocerebroside instead of galactocerebroside in these patients. This possibility was dispelled in metabolic experiments using surviving slices of spleen tissue obtained from patients undergoing splenectomy, the only remedial procedure that was available for temporary correction of patients' haematological abnormalities. Using [^{14}C]glucose or [^{14}C]galactose as precursors of cerebrosides, I found that either of these substances could be incorporated into both glucocerebroside and galacto-cerebroside. Moreover, I discovered that the rate of formation of glucocerebroside in the splenic tissue of patients with Gaucher's disease was similar to that in control human spleen specimens (Trams and Brady, 1960). Thus, nothing was amiss with the anabolism of glucocerebroside in Gaucher's disease, and I postulated that there may be a defect in the catabolism of glucocerebroside in Gaucher's disease (Trams and Brady, 1960). In order to investigate the biodegradation of glucocerebroside, David Shapiro, Julian Kanfer and I chemically synthesized two preparations of radioactive glucocerebroside. One was labelled with ^{14}C in the fatty acid moiety, and the second with ^{14}C in the glucose portion. We found that all mammalian tissues contain an enzyme that catalyses the hydrolytic cleavage of glucose from glucocerebroside (Brady et al, 1965a). We determined the activity of this enzyme, glucocerebrosidase, in tissues obtained from patients with Type 1 Gaucher's disease. We had expected that if it were the metabolic defect in Gaucher's disease, it might be totally lacking. We found, however, that although markedly diminished from normal, some glucocerebrosidase activity could be demonstrated in patients with Type 1 Gaucher's disease (Brady et al, 1965b; 1966). These experiments indicated clearly that reduced glucocerebrosidase activity was the metabolic defect in Gaucher's disease (Figure 1). The finding that all patients had some detectable enzyme later proved to be extremely important in attempts to treat these patients by enzyme replacement therapy.

Application of this discovery to genetic counselling

For many decades, a definitive diagnosis of Gaucher's disease was made by obtaining a specimen of patients' bone marrow, usually through a sternal puncture. This procedure was greatly disliked by patients. Moreover, the accuracy of this diagnostic procedure was not very satisfactory because of non-uniform distribution of Gaucher cells in the bone marrow and the possibility of confusing these cells with those that occurred in other lipid storage disorders such as Niemann–Pick disease. Knowing that leukocytes contained some enzymes, we performed glucocerebrosidase assays and extracts of these cells. We were gratified to find detectable glucocerebrosidase activity in these preparations, and there was consistently diminished glucocerebrosidase activity in leukocytes obtained from patients with Gaucher's disease (Kampine et al, 1967). A modification of this leukocyte assay for glucocerebrosidase using a fluorgenic glucoside is in worldwide use for the diagnosis of patients with Type 1 Gaucher's disease (Beutler and Kuhl, 1970). Leukocytes can often be used for the detection of heterozygous carriers of Gaucher's disease (Beutler and Kuhl 1970; Brady et al, 1971). However, it is currently estimated that between 15% and 20% of heterozygotes are not accurately identified with this procedure because their glucocerebrosidase levels fall within the spread of normal values. This technology achieved a major additional milestone when the usefulness of glucocerebrosidase assays performed on extracts of cultured skin fibroblasts was demonstrated (Ho et al, 1972).

A major advance in genetic counselling occurred with the demonstration that glucocerebrosidase assays could be used for the prenatal diagnosis of Gaucher's disease (Schneider et al, 1972). This test is most frequently used when the couple is at risk for Type 2 Gaucher's disease, but it has also been applied in pregnancies at risk for the other phenotypes of Gaucher's disease.

The gene for human glucocerebrosidase was localized to human chromosome 1 (Barneveld et al, 1983). It was cloned quickly thereafter (Ginns et al, 1984; Sorge et al, 1985), and many mutations in the gene have been described in patients with the various phenotypical forms of Gaucher's disease (Beutler and Gelbart, 1996). When available, knowledge of the genotype is eminently useful for the identification of heterozygotes.

IMMEDIATE PAST

Development of effective enzyme replacement therapy for Gaucher's disease

Very quickly after the enzymatic defect was demonstrated in Gaucher's disease, consideration was given to the development of therapy for patients with this disorder. Chief among the possibilities were enzyme replacement and gene therapy (Brady, 1966). My colleagues and I quickly embarked on a major effort for enzyme replacement therapy. It was, however, a long and difficult process that required more than two decades to bring to a successful conclusion. I wanted to use a human source of glucocerebrosidase if one could be found in order to minimize the possibility of sensitizing patients to an exogenous protein. It occurred to me that human placenta might contain some glucocerebrosidase, and I was pleased to find it in homogenates of this tissue. We began a long-term effort to obtain it in a highly purified form. Eventually, in 1973, my associate Peter Pentchev was able to isolate small quantities of highly purified glucocerebrosidase (Pentchev et al, 1973). We wished to learn whether the intravenous administration of this enzyme would cause a reduction in the accumulated glucocerebroside. Accordingly, we performed a transcutaneous liver needle biopsy in two splenectomized patients with Gaucher's disease, infused the enzyme, and 2 days later, a second liver biopsy was carried out. In addition, we measured the levels of glucocerebroside in the plasma in these patients. The first recipient was a 15-year-old male with Type 3A Gaucher's disease. We found that the administration of glucocerebrosidase caused a 26% reduction of the glucocerebroside that had been stored in his liver. The second recipient was a 50-year-old female. She had accumulated twice as much glucocerebroside in her liver than the first recipient. She received twice as much enzyme as the boy; and she too, had a 26% reduction of hepatic glucocerebroside (Brady et al, 1974). In addition, the three- to four-fold elevated level of glucocerebroside in the blood returned to a normal value within a 3-day period following infusion of glucocerebrosidase. Perhaps even more encouraging was the very slow re-accumulation of glucocerebroside in the circulation (Pentchev et al., 1975). These observations indicated to us that if we could reduce the accumulated lipid in patients with Gaucher's disease that we might be able to provide concrete benefit to them.

Macrophage targeting of glucocerebrosidase

However, these findings were soon overshadowed by less encouraging observations. We worked for 1 year to obtain additional purified placental glucocerebrosidase. When this was injected into a 19-year-old splenectomized female with Type 1 Gaucher's disease, we saw only an 8% reduction of hepatic glucocerebroside. She had accumulated 20 times more glucocerebroside in her liver than the first recipient and 10 times more than the second. Moreover, there was no decrease of glucocerebroside in the circulation. We reasoned that we had to obtain larger quantities of pure glucocerebrosidase to continue these investigations. We therefore developed a novel procedure to purify the placental enzyme based on its hydrophobic properties (Furbish et al, 1977). Inconsistent reductions of hepatic glucocerebroside were seen when this preparation was infused into patients with Gaucher's disease. At this point, several important pieces of information became available. We had realized that much of the accumulating glucocerebroside originated from membranes of senescent red and white blood cells (Kattlove et al, 1969) and that the catabolism of these materials occurred specifically in macrophages in the spleen, liver and bone marrow. We therefore reasoned that in order for the exogenous placental glucocerebrosidase to be effective, that it had to be delivered to tissue macrophages. To our dismay, we found that most of the new preparation of glucocerebrosidase was taken up by hepatocytes. Hepatocytes do not store glucocerebroside because they are not involved in red or white blood cell catabolism, and they can excrete it via the bile (Tokoro et al, 1987). We embarked on a series of experiments to target glucocerebrosidase to macrophages. We learned that enzymes such as glucocerebrosidase, which had been shown to be concentrated in lysosomes (Weinreb et al, 1968) are glycoproteins (Goldstone and Koenig, 1970). Moreover, it was found that macrophages have a lectin on their surface that interacts avidly with mannose-terminal glycoconjugates (Stahl et al, 1978). We therefore analysed the carbohydrate composition of placental glucocerebrosidase and found that it contained four oligosaccharide chains (Takasaki et al, 1984). Three of these chains were of the complex type terminating in N-acetyl-neuraminic acid (sialic acid). We tried several procedures to increase the mannose content of the enzyme (Brady and Furbish, 1982; Doebber et al, 1982). Although the results of these studies were encouraging, we found the best method to increase the delivery of glucocerebrosidase to macrophages was by the sequential enzymatic removal of N-acetylneuraminic acid, galactose and N-acetylglucosamine with exoglycosidases (Furbish et al, 1981; Brady et al, 1994). This procedure greatly enhanced the delivery of glucocerebrosidase to macrophages (Furbish et al, 1984).

Clinical benefit of macrophage-targeted glucocerebrosidase

Encouraged by the ability to target human placental glucocerebrosidase to macrophages, my colleagues and I initiated a clinical study in which approximately 170 U of this enzyme was injected intravenously into eight patients with Type 1 Gaucher's disease on a weekly basis. Only one of the recipients, a 6-year-old boy who was by far the smallest in the group, appeared to obtain benefit from the enzyme. He received approximately 12 U/kg of body weight. A few months after the injections were begun, his haemoglobin and platelets clearly began to rise (Barton et al, 1990). He reported that he had more energy and he definitely felt better than before receiving the enzyme. We deliberately discontinued the enzyme infusions, and over a period of several months, his haemoglobin and platelet levels gradually decreased to the pre-infusion values. We then reinstated

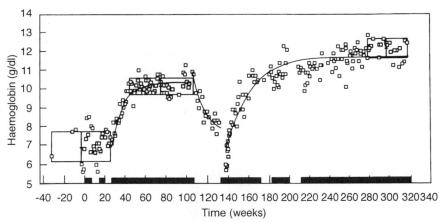

Figure 2. Haemoglobin response to macrophage-targeted human placental glucocerebrosidase in a 5-year-old male with Type 1 Gaucher's disease. The solid horizontal bars on the abscissa indicate periods of enzyme administration.

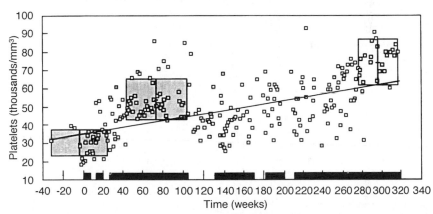

Figure 3. Platelet response to macrophage-targeted human placental glucocerebrosidase in a 5-year-old male with Type 1 Gaucher's disease. The solid horizontal bars on the abscissa indicate periods of enzyme administration.

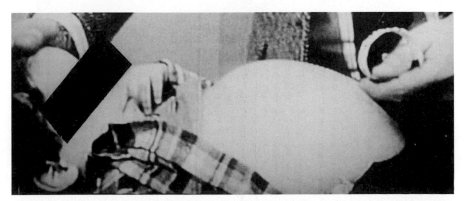

Figure 4. Photograph of the abdomen of the first patient to respond clinically to enzyme replacement therapy before treatment. Note extensive hepatosplenomegaly.

injections of macrophage-targeted human placental glucocerebrosidase at a dose of 30 U/kg of body weight every week. His haemoglobin rapidly rose to the normal range and has remained there ever since (Figure 2). His platelets normalized (Figure 3); there was a great reduction in the size of his liver and spleen (Figure 4), and the damage to his bones improved (Barton et al, 1992). Photographs of this child are shown before (Figure 5) and 2½ years after enzyme replacement therapy (Figure 6).

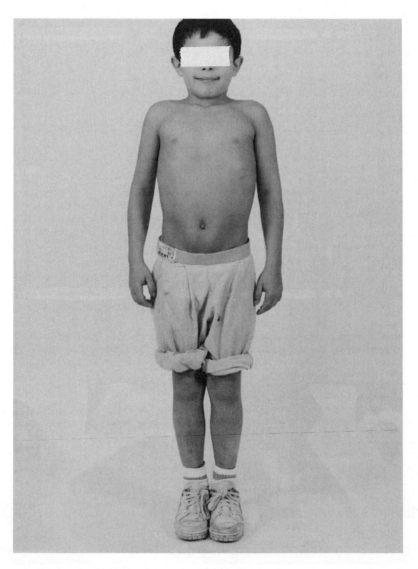

Figure 5. Photograph of the first patient to respond clinically to enzyme replacement therapy 2.5 years after the initiation of treatment showing normalization of abdominal contour.

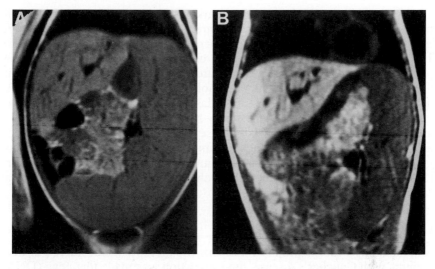

Figure 6. MRI of the abdomen of the first patient to respond to enzyme replacement therapy. (A) Before treatment. (B) Two and one-half years following the initiation of enzyme therapy showing marked reduction of splenomegaly.

We felt that the reason this single child obtained clinical benefit while the other recipients did not was because he had received considerably more enzyme per kg of body weight than any of the others. We therefore conducted a dose–response trial in which we measured the reduction of glucocerebroside in liver biopsy specimens following gradually increasing doses of macrophage-targeted glucocerebrosidase (Brady and Barton, 1994). Consistent reduction of hepatic glucocerebroside was obtained at a dose of 60 U/kg of body weight. We therefore elected to use this dosage in a clinical efficacy trial involving 12 patients with type 1 Gaucher's disease. All of them had remarkably beneficial responses to the enzyme (Barton et al, 1991; Hill et al, 1993; Rosenthal et al, 1995).

The salutary effects of macrophage-targeted glucocerebrosidase have been abundantly confirmed (Beutler et al, 1991; Berthold et al, 1992; Fallet et al, 1992; Mistry et al, 1992; Zimran et al, 1993). Moreover, the bioequivalance of recombinant glucocerebrosidase produced in Chinese hamster ovary cells has been demonstrated (Grabowski et al, 1995). It is anticipated that the recombinant product will eventually completely supplant the use of placental glucocerebrosidase.

PRESENT INVESTIGATIONS

Treatment of patients with neuronopathic forms of Gaucher's disease

One of the major concerns at the time of writing this is whether enzyme replacement therapy is, or can be made, effective in patients with Type 3

Gaucher's disease. Although truly remarkable improvement of the systemic manifestations of Gaucher's disease are seen in these children who are treated with macrophage-targeted glucocerebrosidase (Schiffmann et al, 1997), the effects of this intervention on the neurological manifestations remain problematic. These aspects are discussed more extensively in Chapter 5. It seems probable that technological innovations concerning the delivery of exogenous glucocerebrosidase to the brain will be required in order to make this therapy consistently beneficial for patients with Type 2 and perhaps Type 3 Gaucher's disease. Some encouragement has been achieved in experimental settings in which direct intracerebral infusion of glucocerebrosidase has been carried out under mild hydrostatic pressure (Sanchez et al, 1996). Whether this technique can be adapted to a clinical setting remains to be determined.

Gene therapy

Simultaneous with the proposal that enzyme therapy be considered to treat patients with Gaucher's disease, the suggestion was made that gene (DNA) therapy might also be eventually useful (Brady, 1966). This approach to the therapy of genetic diseases has garnered much attention in the past several years. Because of the storage of glucocerebroside in tissue macrophages, and because these cells are derived from primitive cells in the bone marrow, transduction of stem and progenitor cells has occupied many investigators concerned with gene therapy for Gaucher's disease. We have transduced stem and progenitor cells derived from patients with Gaucher's disease using retroviral vector constructs that contain the human cDNA for gluco-cerebrosidase (Correll et al, 1990; Fink et al, 1990; Medin et al, 1996). CD34$^+$ stem and progenitor cells from patients with Type 1 have been transduced with the retroviral vector and infused back into the patients on single occasions. Although the recipients tolerated the procedure completely satisfactorily, there was little, if any, indication of expression of the glucocerebrosidase gene in patients' leukocytes (Kohn et al, 1997). It is abundantly clear that innovative studies must be carried out to make gene therapy successful for patients with Gaucher's disease. It seems reasonable to surmise, however, that these investigations will proceed rapidly since a much larger number of investigators are involved in trying to develop gene therapy for Gaucher's disease than those who were involved in developing enzyme replacement therapy.

THE FUTURE

Research to develop novel strategies for gene therapy for Gaucher's disease will have to include considerations for the delivery of the gluco-cerebrosidase gene to the brain in patients with the neuronopathic forms of the disorder. Here again, the future looks reasonably auspicious because of the large number of scientists currently involved in this field of research, and I am optimistic about the prospects for this form of intervention.

Several other aspects concerning investigations on Gaucher's disease merit comment. One of these is the possibility of developing enzyme replacement therapy that is much less expensive than that currently available. Because of the high cost, some patients simply cannot obtain the enzyme at this time. This situation is completely regrettable to one who has spent so many years in bringing it to fruition. I hope that innovative technology will quickly be developed so that financial constraint will not preclude any patient with Gaucher's disease from receiving treatment. One of the ways reductions in cost may become feasible is through the production of glucocerebrosidase recombinantly in tobacco plants (Cramer et al, 1995; Murray et al, 1996).

Prophylaxis

The comprehensively verified benefits of macrophage-targeted gluco-cerebrosidase in patients with Gaucher's disease are truly heartening. However, virtually everyone who has worked with patients with Gaucher's disease realize that with this therapy, there is a de-bulking phase during which glucocerebroside that had been accumulated over a number of years must be catabolized. Some of the patients have extensive scar tissue formation in the liver, spleen and bones from infarctions in these organs consequent to glucocerebroside accumulation. Some of this deleterious pathology may take years to reverse if it can be accomplished at all. Because of the relatively slow rate of gluco-cerebroside accumulation, it seems reasonable to me to try to prevent its build up in organs and tissues of patients with Gaucher's disease by prophylactic administration of macrophage-targeted glucocerebrosidase. I believe that a comparatively small amount of enzyme would be required to prevent this daily accumulation. Although the design of an appropriate trial of the prophylactic administration of glucocerebrosidase to patients with Gaucher's disease is inherently difficult, one hopes that eventually the production of a suitable transgenic animal model of Gaucher's disease will enable investigators to determine whether this approach is realistic.

CONCLUDING REMARKS

The saga of Gaucher's disease from the description of the first patient in 1882 through to the discovery of the metabolic defect in 1965 has led the way to the identification of the enzymatic deficiencies in all of the 10 other lipid storage disorders of humans. Hopefully, the development of effective enzyme replacement therapy that has proven to be so beneficial for patients with this condition will also provide an effective paradigm for the treatment of many other metabolic disorders of humans.

REFERENCES

*Aghion E. (1934) La maladie de Gaucher dans l'enfance. In *Thèse*, Faculté de Médecine, Paris, France.

Barneveld RA, Keijzer W, Tegelaers FPW et al (1983) Assignment of the gene coding for human β-glucocerebrosidase to the region q21–q31 of chromosome 1 using monoclonal antibodies. *Human Genetics* **64**: 227–231.

*Barton NW, Furbish FS, Murray GJ et al (1990) Therapeutic response to intravenous infusions of glucocerebrosidase in a patient with Gaucher disease. *Proceedings of the National Academy of Sciences USA* **87**: 1913–1916.

*Barton NW, Brady RO, Dambrosia JM et al (1991) Replacement therapy for inherited enzyme deficiency—macrophage-targeted glucocerebrosidase for Gaucher's disease. *New England Journal of Medicine* **324**: 1464–1470.

Barton NW, Brady RO, Dambrosia JM et al (1992) Dose-dependent responses to macrophage-targeted glucocerebrosidase in a child with Gaucher's disease. *Journal of Pediatrics* **120**: 277–280.

Berthold R, Sieverts H, Benz-Bohm G et al (1992) Response criteria for enzyme replacement therapy in Morbus Gaucher. *Monatschrift vor Kinderheilkund* **140**: 740–744.

Beutler E & Kuhl W (1970) The diagnosis of the adult type of Gaucher's disease and its carrier state by demonstration of a deficiency of beta-glucosidase activity in peripheral blood leukocytes. *Journal of Laboratory and Clinical Medicine* **76**: 747–755.

Beutler E & Gelbart T (1996) Glucocerebrosidase (Gaucher disease). *Human Mutations* **8**: 207–213.

Beutler E, Kay A, Saven A et al (1991) Enzyme replacement therapy for Gaucher disease. *Blood* **78**: 1183–1189.

*Brady RO (1966) Sphingolipidoses. *New England Journal of Medicine* **275**: 312–318.

Brady RO & Furbish FS (1982) Enzyme replacement therapy: specific targeting of exogenous enzymes to storage cells.In Martonosi AN (ed.) *Membranes and Transport,* Vol 2. pp 587–592. New York: Plenum Press.

Brady RO & Barton NW (1994) Enzyme replacement therapy for Gaucher disease: critical investigations beyond demonstration of clinical efficacy. *Biochemical Medicine and Metabolic Biology* **52**: 1–9.

Brady RO, Kanfer J & Shapiro D (1965a) The metabolism of glucocerebrosides. I. Purification and properties of a glucocerebroside-cleaving enzyme from spleen tissue. *Journal of Biological Chemistry* **240**: 39–42.

*Brady RO, Kanfer JN & Shapiro D (1965b) Metabolism of glucocerebrosides. II. Evidence of an enzymatic deficiency in Gaucher's disease. *Biochemical and Biophysical Research Communications* **18**: 221–225.

Brady RO, Johnson WG & Uhlendorf W. (1971) Identification of heterozygous carriers of lipid storage diseases. *American Journal of Medicine* **51**: 423–431.

*Brady RO, Murray GJ & Barton NW (1994) Modifying exogenous glucocerebrosidase for effective replacement therapy in Gaucher disease. *Journal of Inherited Metabolic Disease* **17**: 510–519.

Brady RO, Murray GJ & Barton NW (1997) Glucosylceramide lipidosis: Gaucher disease. In Rosenberg RN, Prusiner SB, DiMauro S & Barchi RL (eds) *The Molecular and Genetic Basis of Neurological Disease*, pp 405–420. Boston: Butterworth–Heinemann.

Brady RO, Kanfer JN, Bradley RM & Shapiro D (1966) Demonstration of a deficiency of glucocerebroside-cleaving enzyme in Gaucher's disease. *Journal of Clinical Investigation* **45**: 1112–1115.

Brady RO, Pentchev PG, Gal AE et al (1974) Replacement therapy for inherited enzyme deficiency: use of purified glucocerebrosidase in Gaucher's disease. *New England Journal of Medicine* **291**: 989–993.

Brill NE (1901) Primary splenomegaly with a report of three cases occurring in one family. *American Journal of Medical Science* **121**: 377–392.

Brill NE (1904) A case of 'splenomegalie primitif': with involvement of the haemopoietic organs. *Proceedings of the New York Pathological Society* **4**: 143–149.

Brill NE, Mandelbaum FS & Libman E (1905) Primary splenomegaly—Gaucher type. Report on one of four cases occurring in a single generation in one family. *American Journal of Medical Science* **129**: 491–504.

Collier WA (1895) A case of enlarged spleen in a child aged six. *Transactions of the Pathological Society of London* **46**: 148–150.

Correll PH, Kew Y, Perry LK et al (1990) Expression of human glucocerebrosidase in long-term reconstituted mice following retroviral-mediated gene transfer into hematopoietic stem cells. *Human Gene Therapy* **1**: 277–287.

Cramer CL, Weissenborn DL & Oishi KK, (1995) Bioproduction of human enzymes in transgenic tobacco. *Abstracts of International Symposium on Engineering Plants for Commercial Products and Applications*, University of Kentucky, October 1–5, 1995.

Doebber TW, Wu MS, Bugianesi RL, et al (1982) Enhanced macrophage uptake of synthetically glycosylated human placental β-glucocerebrosidase. *Journal of Biological Chemistry* **257**: 2193–2199.

Fallet S, Grace ME, Sibille A et al (1992) Enzyme augmentation in moderate to life-threatening Gaucher disease. *Pediatric Research* **31**: 496–502.

Fink JK, Correll PH, Perry LK et al (1990) Correction of glucocerebrosidase deficiency following retroviral-mediated gene transfer into hematopoietic progenitor cells from patients with Gaucher disease. *Proceedings of the National Academy of Sciences USA* **87**: 2334–2338.

Furbish FS, Steer CJ, Krett NL & Barranger JA (1981) Uptake and distribution of placental glucocerebrosidase in rat hepatic cells and effects of sequential deglycosylation. *Biochimica et Biophysica Acta* **673**: 425–434.

Furbish FS, Blair HE, Shiloach J et al (1977) Enzyme replacement therapy in Gaucher's disease: large-scale purification of glucocerebrosidase suitable for human administration. *Proceedings of the National Academy of Sciences USA* **74**: 3560–3563.

Furbish FS, Oliver KL, Zirzow GC et al (1984) Interaction of human placental glucocerebrosidase with hepatic lectins. In Barranger JA & Brady RO (eds) *Molecular Basis of Lysosomal Storage Disorders*, pp 219–232. Orlando: Academic Press.

*Gaucher PCE (1882) De l'épithélioma primitif de la rate. MD Thèse, Faculté de Médecine de Paris.

Ginns EI, Choudary PV, Tsuji S et al (1984) Isolation of cDNA clones for human β-glucocerebrosidase using the λgt11 expression system. *Biochemical and Biohysical Research Communications* **123**: 574–580.

Goldstone A & Koenig H (1970) Lysosomal hydrolases as glycoproteins. *Life Sciences* **9**:1341–1350.

Grabowski GA, Barton NW, Pastores G et al (1995) Enzyme therapy in type 1 Gaucher disease: comparative efficacy of mannose-terminated glucocerebrosidase from natural and recombinant sources. *Annals of Internal Medicine* **122**: 33–39.

Hill SC, Parker CC, Brady RO & Barton NW (1993) MRI of multiple platyspondyly in Gaucher disease: response to enzyme replacement therapy. *Journal of Computer Assisted Tomography* **17**: 806–809.

Hillborg PO (1959) Morbus Gaucher: Norrbotten. *Nordisk Medicin* **61**: 303–306.

Ho MW, Seck J, Schmidt D et al (1972) Adult Gaucher's disease: kindred studies and demonstration of a deficiency of acid β-glucosidase in cultured fibroblasts. *American Journal of Human Genetics* **24**: 37–45.

*Kampine JP, Brady RO, Kanfer JN et al (1967) The diagnosis of Gaucher's disease and Niemann–Pick disease using small samples of venous blood. *Science* **155**: 86–88.

Kattlove HE, Williams JC, Gaynor E et al (1969) Gaucher cells in chronic myelocytic leukemia: an acquired abnormality. *Blood* **33**: 379–390.

Kohn DB, Scheuning F, Dunbar C et al (1997) Early trials of gene transfer for Gaucher disease. In Desnick RJ (ed.) *Advances in Jewish Genetic Diseases*. New York: Oxford University Press, in press.

Kraus EJ (1920) Zur Kenntnis der Splenomegalie Gaucher, insbesondere der Histogenese der Grosszellen Wucherung. *Zeitschrift für Angewandt Anatomie* **7**: 186–234.

Lieb H (1924) Cerebroside Speicherung bei Splenomegalie (typus Gaucher). *Zeitschrift für Physiologische Chemie* **140**: 305–313.

Medin JA, Migita M, Pawliuk R et al (1996) A bicistronic therapeutic retroviral vector enables sorting of transduced CD34+ cells and corrects the enzyme deficiency in cells from Gaucher patients. *Blood* **87**: 1754–1762.

Mistry PK, Davies S, Corfield A et al (1992) Successful treatment of bone marrow failure in Gaucher's disease with low-dose modified glucocerebrosidase. *Quarterly Journal of Medicine* **84**: 541–546.

Murray GJ, Turpen TH, Cameron TI et al (1996) Production of recombinant glucocerebrosidase in plants. *FASEB Journal* **10**: A1126.

Oberling C & Woringer P (1927) La maladie de Gaucher chez la nourrisson. *Revue Français de Pediatrie* **3**: 475–532.

Patterson MC, Horowitz M, Abel RB et al (1993) Isolated horizontal supranuclear gaze palsy as a marker of severe systemic involvement in Gaucher's disease. *Neurology*, **43**: 1993–1997.

Pentchev PG, Brady RO, Gal AE & Hibbert SR (1975) Replacement therapy for inherited enzyme deficiency: sustained clearance of accumulated glucocerebroside in Gaucher's disease following infusion of purified glucocerebrosidase. *Journal of Molecular Medicine* **1**: 73–78.

Pentchev PG, Brady RO, Hibbert SR et al (1973) Isolation and characterization of glucocerebrosidase from human placental tissue. *Journal of Biological Chemistry* **248**: 5256–5261.

Rosenthal DI, Doppelt SH, Mankin HJ et al (1995) Enzyme replacement therapy for Gaucher disease: skeletal responses to macrophage-targeted glucocerebrosidase. *Pediatrics* **96**: 629–637.

Rusca CL (1921) Sul morbo del Gaucher. *Haematologica* (Pavia) **2**: 441–509.

Sanchez OA, Laske DW, Corthèsy M-E et al (1996) High-flow intracerebral microinfusion of modified glucocerebrosidase: a feasibility study for potential therapy of CNS involvement in Gaucher's disease. *Abstracts, 64th Meeting of the American Association of Neurological Surgeons*, April 27–May 2, 1996, Minneapolis, MN pp. 195–196.

Schiffmann R, Heyes MP, Aerts JM et al (1997) Prospective study of neurological responses to treatment with macrophage-targeted glucocerebrosidase in patients with type 3 Gaucher disease. *Annals of Neurology*, in press.

*Schneider E , Ellis WG, Brady RO et al (1972) Infantile (Type II) Gaucher's disease: in utero diagnosis and fetal pathology. *Journal of Pediatrics* **81**: 1134–1139.

Sorge J, Eest C, Westwood B et al (1985) Molecular cloning and nucleotide sequence of human glucocerebrosidase cDNA. *Proceedings of the National Academy of Sciences USA* **82**: 7289–7293.

Stahl PD, Rodman JS, Miller MJ & Schlesinger PH (1978) Evidence for receptor-mediated binding of glycoproteins and lysosomal glycosidases by alveolar macrophages. *Proceedings of the National Academy of Sciences USA* **75**: 1399–1430.

Takasaki S, Murray GJ, Furbish FS et al (1984) Structure of the N-asparagine-linked oligosaccharide units of human placental β-glucocerebrosidase. *Journal of Biological Chemistry* **259**: 10112–10117.

Tokoro T, Gal AE, Gallo LL & Brady RO (1987) Studies of the pathogenesis of Gaucher's disease: Tissue distribution and biliary excretion of ^{14}C-L-glucosylceramide in rats. *Journal of Lipid Research* **28**: 968–972.

*Trams EG & Brady RO (1960) Cerebroside synthesis in Gaucher's disease. *Journal of Clinical Investigation* **39**: 1546–1550.

Weinreb NJ, Brady RO & Tappel AL (1968) The lysosomal localization of sphingolipid hydrolases. *Biochimica et Biophysica Acta* **159**: 141–146.

Zimran A, Hollak CE, Abrahamov A et al (1993) Home treatment with intravenous enzyme replacement therapy for Gaucher disease: an international collaborative study of 33 patients. *Blood* **82**: 1107–1109.

2

Gaucher's disease: molecular, genetic and enzymological aspects

GREGORY A. GRABOWSKI MD

Director, Professor of Paediatrics, University of Cincinnati College of Medicine
Division and Program in Human Genetics, Children's Hospital Medical Center, 3333 Burnet Avenue, Cincinnati, Ohio, 45339-3039, USA

MIA HOROWITZ PhD

Department of Cell Research and Immunology, Tel-Aviv University, Ramat-Aviv, Israel

The molecular, genetic and enzymological abnormalities in Gaucher's disease have been delineated during the past decade. Although our understanding of the primary predisposition to the Gaucher's disease phenotypes has improved, the relationships remain poorly understood between the mutant alleles, the resultant enzyme variants, the saposin C (activator protein) locus and phenotypes. Of the more than 100-disease associated alleles, about 8 to 10 have significant frequencies in various ethnic and demographic groups. The N370S(1226G) allele is very frequent in Caucasian populations, but absent in Asian groups. In the Ashkenazi Jewish population, the N370S homozygosity predisposes to Gaucher's disease, but over 50% of such patients escape medical detection because of their mild to absent involvement, i.e. N370S may be a predisosing polymorphic variant. Clarification of genotype/phenotype relationships and the identification of modifier loci that impact on Gaucher's disease phenotypes remain a critical area for research. Greater understanding of these issues will facilitate genetic counselling and appropriate interventive therapy to prevent the morbid long-term manifestations of Gaucher's disease.

Key words: lysosomal storage disease; inborn errors of metabolism; glycosphingolipid; β-glucosidases; saposins; prosaposin.

Gaucher's disease designates the disparate phenotypes because of the diminished flux of glucosylceramides and other glucosphingolipids (Figure 1) through cells. Mutations at the locus for GBA (a lysosomal hydrolase termed, acid β-glucosidase or glucocerebrosidase (EC 3.2.1.45)) predispose to the development of the phenotypes. Since C. E. Philippe Gaucher's original description of the disease (Gaucher, 1882), asymptomatic splenomegaly, and unusual storage cells in the spleen and bone marrow are recognized as the most common initial findings. Gaucher's disease is the most frequently occurring lysosomal storage disease (Beutler

Copyright © 1997, by Baillière Tindall
All rights of reproduction in any form reserved

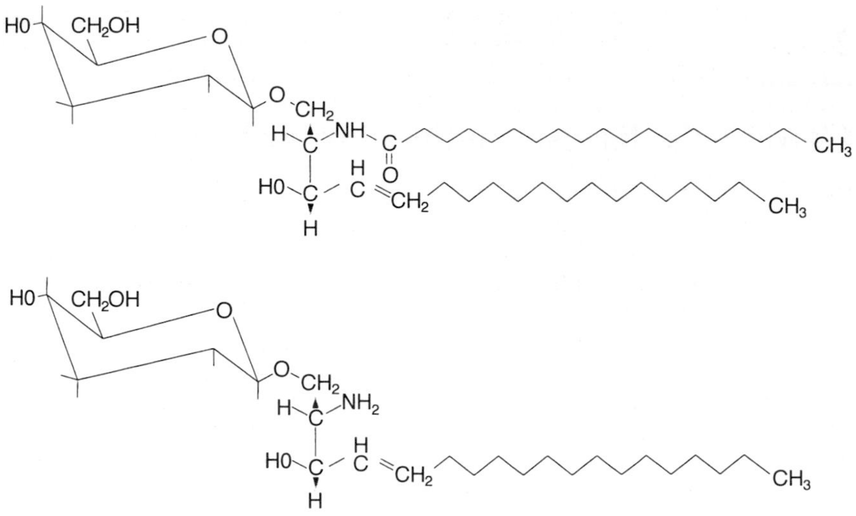

Figure 1. Schematic diagram of glucosylceramide (upper) and its deacylated analogue, glucosyl-sphingosine (lower). The usual unsaturated sphingosyl moiety is about 18 carbons in length. The fatty acid acyl chain can vary from about 16 to >24 carbon bonds in length depending upon the tissue of origin.

and Grabowski, 1995) and has the highest prevalence in the Ashkenazi Jewish population. The delineation of numerous mutations at the GBA locus has provided insight into the molecular basis of the Gaucher's disease predisposition. But, the determinants of genotype/phenotype relationships, the role of activator proteins and the mechanism of acid β-glucosidase action require more complete understanding.

THE STORAGE SUBSTANCES

The major accumulated lipid in Gaucher's disease is N-acyl-sphingosyl-1-O-β-D-glucoside or glucosylceramide, ceramide β-glucoside or gluco-cerebroside (Grabowski, 1993) (Figure 1). The sphingosyl chain is mostly (2S,3R,4E)-2-amino-4-octadecene-1,3-diol (Mislow, 1953; Carter and Fujino, 1956). The fatty acid can vary from 16 to 24 carbons in length (Nilsson and Svennerholm, 1982a; Nilsson et al, 1985). In most mammalian tissues, glucosylceramide is a metabolic intermediate in the anabolic and catabolic pathways of complex glycosphingolipids, i.e, gangliosides or globoside. It is the final intermediate in the degradation of complex glycosphingolipids. Normally, glucosylceramide is resident in cellular membranes. A minor, but pathogenically important, substrate is glucosylsphingosine (Grabowski, 1993) (Figure 1). This derives from the de novo condensation of sphingosine and β-D-glucopyranoside, rather than via deacylation of glucosylceramide.

Plasma, hepatic, splenic and brain glucosylceramide concentrations are increased 2- to 100-fold in affected patients, but the levels do not correlate directly with the type of Gaucher's disease (Kennaway and Woolf, 1968; French et al, 1969; Dawson and Oh, 1977; Nilsson and Svennerholm, 1982a,b; Nilsson et al, 1982; Strasberg et al, 1983; Nilsson et al, 1985; Kaye et al, 1986; Conradi et al, 1991). Glucosylsphingosine is also present in lesser amounts, but normally does not occur in tissues (Nilsson and Svennerholm, 1982b). This toxic sphingoid base may play a major role in the pathogenesis of Gaucher's disease in specific tissues (Grabowski, 1993). Higher concentrations of glucosylsphingosine were found in Types 2 and 3 brains suggesting this lipid's involvement in the pathogenesis of central nervous system (CNS) degeneration (Nilsson and Svennerholm, 1982a,b; Nilsson et al, 1985). Since the amount of residual enzyme activity per cell type remains relatively constant throughout life, the identification of the developmental factors that influence the balance of glucosylceramide and glucosylsphingosine flux through organs remains a research challenge. The identification of these factors have clear practical impact since modification of the substrate flux are sure to influence the phenotype and alter approaches to therapy.

MOLECULAR BIOLOGY

Genomic organization

The loci on human chromosome 1q 21 for acid β-glucosidase and its non-processed pseudogene are densely packed (Figure 2). The mouse locus for acid β-glucosidase maps to mouse chromosome 3 (E3-F1) (Horowitz et al, 1989). In non-human species, the pseudogene is absent. Two other genes, metaxin and thrombospondin 3 (Bornstein et al, 1994), are within ~40 kb 3' of the acid β-glucosidase locus. The metaxin gene is translated convergently to acid β-glucosidase and divergently to thrombospondin 3 (Bornstein et al, 1994). The promoters for metaxin and thrombospondin 3 overlap. These three functional genes are present in human and mouse, but the pseudogenes are absent from the murine genome (Figure 2). Although this dense genomic structure may not directly impact on the expression of Gaucher's disease, large deletions may encompass the acid β-glucosidase

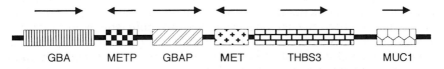

Figure 2. Diagram of the genomic region near the acid β-glucosidase locus (GBA) on chromosome 1. MET, THBS3 and MUC1 are the metaxin, thrombospondin 3 and muc1 oncogene loci, respectively. The METP and GBAP are the MET and GBA pseudogenes. The arrows indicate the direction of transcription of the various genes. The MET and THBS3 genomic loci overlap in the promoter region. The region from GBA to THBS3 is about 40 kb in length.

gene and other genes in this region, and thereby influence the phenotypic expression.

Murine (O'Neill et al, 1989) and canine (Liou and Grabowski, unpublished) acid β-glucosidase genes or cDNAs have been characterized. The positions of the 20 intron/exon junctions in the functional genes are precisely conserved in man and mouse. Compared with the human gene, the canine and mouse genes have exonic nucleotide identities of 88 and 84%, respectively. Relative to the human, these cDNAs predict: (i) 92% (canine) and 87% (murine) amino acid identity. A single amino acid deletion, His 274, was predicted in the mouse sequence. (ii) The cysteines are 100% conserved. (iii) The positions of the five glycosylation sites are strictly conserved and the sequences were identical in the canine and human acid β-glucosidases. Sites 1 and 2 have different amino acid contents in the mouse. Additional phylogenetic amino acid sequence and functional studies would be helpful in identifying conserved domains since acid β-glucosidase is not contained in any glycosidase superfamilies.

Expression of acid β-glucosidase

The expression levels of acid β-glucosidase mRNA and activity vary considerably in different tissues (Reiner et al, 1988a; Reiner and Horowitz, 1988). For example, Northern analyses have indicated that the acid β-glucosidase mRNA varies in cell lines (Reiner et al, 1987; Reiner and Horowitz, 1988; Reiner et al, 1988a; Wigderson et al, 1989) with high, moderate, low and very low levels in epithelial cells, fibroblasts, macrophages and B-cells, respectively. This variation in mRNA and enzyme activity levels have not been consistently concordant in different cell lines (Reiner and Horowitz, 1988; Doll and Smith, 1993). In one study neuronal CNS tumors, U-937 and lymphoblastoid lines had enzyme activity to mRNA ratios of about 1:1 (Doll and Smith, 1993). But in HL60, H4 (neuroglioma) and cultured skin fibroblasts, the ratio was ~5.5:1. In THP-1 monocytes, this ratio was 3:1. These ratios varied independently of either parameter, i.e. high mRNA was associated with high or low activity in various cell types and vis-a-vis. In other cell lines this variation was more concordant (Horowitz, unpublished). This variation of mRNA levels may reflect the repertoire of transcription factors in various cell types rather than the presence or absence of specific factors (see below). Using transgenic retroviral (Xu et al, 1995) or a tetracycline transactivator (Li et al, 1996) systems, discrepancies were also found in the ability of different cells to efficiently translate the mRNA or post-translationally fold the protein into an active conformation. These results are consistent with a several stage control system for the expression of acid β-glucosidase at the transcriptional, translational and post-translational levels. These important control points are not understood and probably have significant import for the molecular pathogenesis of the enzyme deficiency in Gaucher's disease and its treatment.

The 5' region of the functional gene contains two TATA boxes and two possible CAAT-like boxes (Reiner et al, 1988a,b; Horowitz et al, 1989).

Using reporter gene constructs, this region from the functional gene is at least 8–10 times more potent in cell lines than the corresponding pseudogene sequences (Dynan, 1986). Detailed studies of exon 1 and 5′ flanking regions of the human locus reveal several control regions (Figure 3). Relative to the mRNA start site (+1), the TATA box is located at −28 to −25. Except for about 20–30 bp 5′ to the TATA, most of the 5′ region is not necessary for full expression in specific cell lines. Interestingly, an orientation, but not positionally, independent transcriptional enhancer was present within exon 1 between +31 and +79. Specific factors that bind to this region were detected in NIH3T3 and glioblastoma cells. The four transcription factors, OBP (OCT binding protein), AP-1, PEA3 and CBP (CAAT binding protein), had significant promoter activity. The corresponding DNA binding sites were located as follows with reference to the transcriptional start site: OCT (−92 to −99), AP-1 (+70 to +76), PEA3 (near +1) and CBP (−1 to +4) (Moran et al, 1997). There is a TTTAAA consensus binding protein that also participates in the expression of acid β-glucosidase (Horowitz, unpublished). The apparent cellular specificity observed in these studies will require more physiological verification in transgenic animals. But, the up-regulation of OBP and AP-1 in transformed fibroblasts is concordant with the metabolic needs of the cells for turnover of glucosylceramide, the major Gaucher's disease substrate. Thus, the housekeeping function of acid β-glucosidase may be concordantly regulated by the

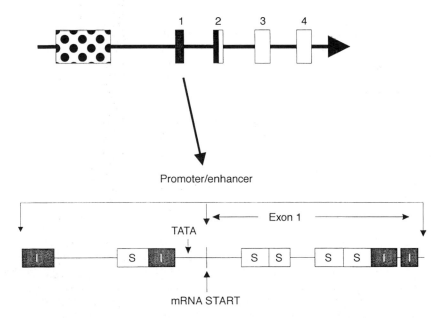

Figure 3. An enlarged view of the 5′ GBA region and flanking sequences. The dotted rectangle in the upper panel represents 5′ flanking promoter regions. The blackened parts of exon 1 and 2 are untranslated. The region below expands the exon 1 and 5′ flanking region to show known in vitro stimulatory (S) and inhibitory (I) sequences.

transcriptional activation that accompanies cell turnover and proliferation. Additional studies are needed to clarify the physiological control of this locus.

Disease mutations

Only a few of the over 108 disease alleles (Table 1) occur with significant frequencies in patients who come to medical attention including: N370S (1226G), 84GG, L444P (1448C) and IVS2$^+$1, D409H (1342C), R496H (1604A) and F213I (754T) (Kawame and Eto, 1991; Beutler et al, 1992; He and Grabowski, 1992; Sibille et al, 1993; Abrahamov et al, 1995; Cormand et al, 1995). The 84GG and IVS2 alleles designate a G insertion immediately 3′ to cDNA base 84G and a A→G substitution at the splice donor site of intron 1, respectively. Rec will be used to designate 'recombinant' alleles, potentially due to genetic rearrangements usually between exons 9 and 10 of the functional and pseudogenes (Figure 4). A

Table 1. Gaucher's disease mutations.

Allele name	cDNA[1]	Exon	Base substitution	AA substitution	Reference
A. *Missense mutations that cause Gaucher's disease*					
G84G	84	2		Gly→Gly	Choy et al, 1993
V15L	160	3	G→T	Val→Leu	Kim et al, 1996
T43I	245	3	C→T	Thr→Ile	Beutler et al, 1995
G46E	254	3	G→A	Gly→Glu	Kim et al, 1996
R48W*	259	3	C→T	Arg→Trp	Miller et al, 1995; Beutler et al, 1995
K74Ter	337	4	A→T	Lys→Stop	Miller et al, 1995
K79N	354	4	G→C	Lys→Asn	Beutler et al, 1996
L105R	431	4		Leu→Arg	Hatton et al, 1997
G113E		4		Gly→Glu	Vilagelin et al, 1997
R120Y		5		Arg→Tyr	Vilagelin et al, 1997
R120W*	475	5	C→T	Arg→Trp	Beutler et al, 1996
R120Q	476	5	G→A	Arg→Gln	Graves et al, 1988
P122S	481	5	C→T	Pro→Ser	Beutler et al, 1992
T134P				Thr→Pro	Vilagelin et al, 1997
D140H	534	5	G→C	Asp→His	Eyal et al, 1991
K157Q	586	5	A→C	Lys→Gln	Latham et al, 1991 Eyal et al, 1991
Q169Ter				Gln→X	Vilagelin et al, 1997
S173Ter	635	6	C→G	Ser→Ter	Beutler et al, 1995
A176D	664	6	C→A	Ala→Asp	Beutler et al, 1994
P178S	649	6	C→T	Pro→Ser	Choy and Wei, 1995
W179Ter	653	6	G→A	Trp→Stop	Miller et al, 1995
P182T	661	6	C→A	Pro→Thr	Beutler et al, 1994
W184R	667	6	T→C	Trp→Arg	Latham et al, 1991
N188S*	680	6	A→G	Asn→Ser	Kim et al, 1996
N188K	681	6	T→G	Asn→Lys	Latham et al, 1991
G189V	683	6	G→T	Gly→Val	Ida and Eto, 1997
V191G	689	6	T→G	Val→Gly	Latham et al, 1991
G195E				Gly→Glu	Vilagelin et al, 1997
S196P	703	6	T→C	Ser→Pro	Hrebicek et al, 1997
G202R*	721	6	G→A	Gly→Arg	Beutler et al, 1994

Y212H	751	6	T→C	Tyr→His	Beutler et al, 1993a
F213I*	754	6	T→A	Phe→Ile	He et al, 1992; Kawame and Eto, 1991
F216V	764	7	T→G	Phe→Val	Horowitz and Zimran, 1994
F216Y	764	7	T→A	Phe→Tyr	Beutler and Gelbart, 1990
T231I	809	7	C→T	Thr→Ile	Kirchhoff et al, 1997
S237F	827	7	C→T	Ser→Phe	Kirchhoff et al, 1997
H255E	882	7	T→G	His→Glu	Kirchhoff et al, 1997
R257Q	887	7	G→A	Arg→Gln	Beutler et al, 1994
R257X				Arg→X	Vilagelin et al, 1997
P266R	914	7	C→G	Pro→Arg	Walley et al, 1995
P266Ter	914	7	C del	Pro→Stop	Lewis et al, 1994
R285C	970	7	C→T	Arg→Cys	Beutler et al, 1994
P289L	983	7	C→T	Pro→Leu	He et al, 1992
Y304C	1028	8	A→G	Tyr→Cys	Kirchhoff et al, 1997
A309V	1043	8	C→T	Ala→Val	Latham et al, 1991
W312C	1053	8	G→T	Trp→Cys	Latham et al, 1991
Y313H	1054	8	T→C	Try→His	Cormand et al, 1996
D315H	1060	8	G→C	Asp→His	Walley et al, 1995
A318D	1070	8	C→A	Ala→Asp	Walley et al, 1995
T323I	1085	8	A→C	Thr→Ile	He et al, 1992
G325R*	1090	8	G→A	Gly→Arg	Eyal et al, 1990; 1991
E326K	1093	8	G→A	Glu→Lys	
C342G	1141	8	T→G	Cys→Gly	Eyal et al, 1990
V352L	1171	8	G→C	Val→Leu	Miller et al, 1995
R359Ter	1192	8	C→T	Arg→Stop	Beutler and Gelbart, 1994
R359Q	1193	8	G→A	Arg→Gln	Kawame et al, 1992
S364N	1208	8	G→A	Ser→Asn	Kirchhoff et al, 1997
S364T	1208	8	G→C	Ser→Thr	Latham et al, 1991
S366G	1213	8	A→G	Ser→Gly	Ida and Eto, 1997
S366N	1214	8	G→A	Ser→Asn	Beutler, unpublished
T369M	1223	8	C→T	Thr→Met	Beutler et al, 1996
N370S	1226	9	A→G	Asn→Ser	Tsuji et al, 1988
N370Ter	1227	9	C→A	Asn→Stop	Kirchhoff et al, 1997
G377S	1246	9	G→A	Gly→Ser	Laubscher et al, 1994
W378G	1249	9	T→G	Trp→Gly	Beutler et al, 1994
D380A	1256	9	A→C	Asp→Ala	Walley and Harris, 1993
D380N	1255	9	G→A	Asp→Asn	Beutler et al, 1994
P387L	1277	9	C→A	Pro→Leu	Morar and Lane, 1996
G389E		9		Gly→Glu	Vilagelin et al, 1997
P391L		9		Pro→Leu	Vilagelin et al, 1997
N392I		9		Asn→Ile	Vilagelin et al, 1997
W393Ter		9		Trp→Stop	Kirchhoff et al, 1997
V394L	1297	9	G→T	Val→Leu	Theophilus et al, 1989b
R395C	1300	9	C→T	Arg→Cys	Kirchhoff et al, 1997
N396T	1304	9	A→C	Asn→Thr	Amaral et al, 1996
V398L	1309	9	G→C	Val→Leu	Seeman et al, 1996
D399N	1312	9	G→A	Asp→Asn	Beutler and Gelbart, 1994
D409H*	1342	9	G→C	Asp→His	Eyal et al, 1990; Theophilus et al, 1989b
D409V	1343	9	A→T	Asp→Val	Thoeophilus et al, 1989a,b
Y412H				Tyr→His	Horowitz et al, 1993
K413Q	1354	9	A→C	Lys→Gln	Ida and Eto, 1997
Q414Ter	1357	9	C→T	Gln→Stop	Beutler et al, 1996
P415R	1361	9	C→G	Pro→Arg	Wigderson et al, 1989
Q414Ter	1357	9	C→T	Gln→Ter	Beutler et al, 1996
F417V	1366	9	T→G	Phe→Val	Choy et al, 1993
Y418C		9		Tyr→Cys	Tuteja et al, 1994
K425E	1390	10	A→G	Lys→Gly	Kawame et al, 1992

Table 1. Gaucher's disease mutations.

Allele name	cDNA[1]	Exon	Base substitution	AA substitution	Reference
L431R				Leu→Arg	
R433G	1413	10	A→G	Arg→Gln	Ida and Eto, 1997
L444P*	1448	10	T→C	Leu→Pro	Tsuji et al, 1987
L444R	1448	10		Leu→Arg	Uchiyama et al, 1994
N462R	1503	10		Asn→Lys	Hatton et al, 1997
R463C	1504	10	C→T	Arg→Cys	Hong et al, 1990
R463Q	1505	10	G→A	Arg→Gln	Ohshima et al, 1993
K466K	1515	11	G→A	Lys→Lys	Kawame et al, 1992
G478S	1549	11	G→A	Gly→Ser	Beutler et al, 1993a
T491I	1584	11	C→T	Thr→Ile	Seeman et al, 1996
R495H	1601	11	G→A	Arg→His	Beutler et al, 1993a
R496C	1603	11	C→A	Arg→Cys	Kawame et al, 1992
R496H	1604	11	G→A	Arg→His	Choy et al, 1997b; Beutler et al, 1993b

B. *Nonsense mutations that cause Gaucher's disease*

72del	72	2	C→C del	Frame shift→Stop	Beutler et al, 1993a
84GG	84	2	G→GG	Frame shift	Beutler et al, 1991
IVS2	IVS2[+1]	2	g→a +1 of Intron 2	Aberrant splicing	He and Grabowski, 1992 Beutler et al, 1992
122CC	122	3	C→CC	Frame shift→Stop	Choy et al, 1997a
203C del	1707	3	C→del	Frame shift	Beutler et al, 1994
500T ins		5			Vilagelin et al, 1997
914del		7	C→del	Frame shift	Beutler et al, 1995
IVS5			g→t	Frame shift	Vilagelin et al, 1997
1098 ins			C→ins		Vilagelin et al, 1997
1098			C→Ca	Stop	Cormand et al, 1996
EX9Δ55*	1263–1317	9	Del	55bpexon 9 Frame shift	Beutler et al, 1993a
1447–1466 del, TG ins				Frame shift	Uchiyama et al, 1994
1451 del AG				Frame shift	
IVS10	IVS[-1]	10	G→A; -1 Intron 10	Aberrant splicing →Stop	Oshima et al, 1993
t ins					Hrebicek et al, 1997
IVS(+2)	Intron 10		T→G	Aberrant splicing	Beutler et al, 1995
Total gene del				N/A	Beutler and Gelbart, 1995

C. *Genetic rearrangements causal to Gaucher's disease*

	Nucleotides involved	Exon	Reference
AZRecTL*	1342–1597	9, 10, 11	Zimran et al, 1990
Complex C**	475–754	5, 6	Latham et al, 1991
Complex A or RecNciI*	1448–1597	10	Latham et al, 1990; Eyal et al, 1990
Complex B or RecTL*	1342–1597	9, 10	Hong et al, 1990; Harzer et al, 1989; Eyal et al, 1990; Latham et al, 1991
	>1255<1263		Eyal et al, 1990; 1991

[1] The cDNA is from Sorge et al, 1985.
[2] The amino acid is from the mature N-terminus.
* Occur in the pseudogene.
** Six of the seven missense mutations in Complex C occur in the pseudogene.

schematic genomic distribution of alleles is shown in Figure 5. The Rec alleles contain 2 to 4 point (missense or conservative) mutations, including L444P, that are also present in the pseudogene sequence (Horowitz et al, 1989). The lack of testing for all substitutions in Rec alleles may lead to misdesignation of an isolated L444P allele. The frequencies for the five

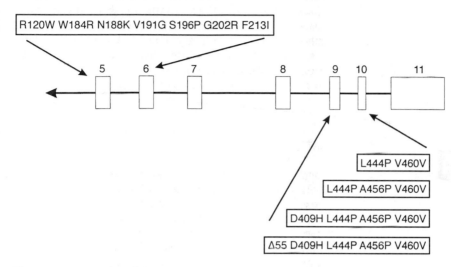

Figure 4. Representation of the complex alleles (Rec) that are associated with Gaucher's disease. Each of the missense mutations, except W184R, and the Δ55 deletion are also present in GBAP.

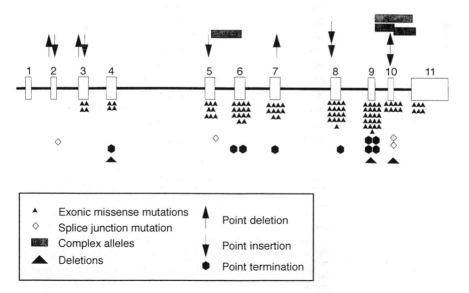

Figure 5. Distribution of the mutations that predispose to the Gaucher's disease phenotypes. There are about 108 mutant alleles with a clustering toward the 3′ half of the gene.

most common alleles in Gaucher's disease type 1 patients are shown in Table 2. The Ashkenazi Jewish Gaucher's disease population has been intensively studied with over 1160 alleles examined world wide (Beutler et al, 1992; He and Grabowski, 1992; Horowitz et al, 1993; Sibille et al, 1993; Horowitz and Zimran, 1994; Lewis et al, 1994; Cormand et al, 1995; Morar and Lane, 1996). About 11% of alleles were not identified by screening for N370S, L444P+Rec, 84GG and IVS2 alleles. In the non-Jewish Caucasian population the frequencies of the N370S and L444P alleles are decreased by ~ 40% and increased by 9-fold, respectively. The 84GG and IVS2 alleles have low frequencies (<0.8%), and ~26% of the alleles are not detected by screening for the above five alleles.

Table 2. Allele distribution in Gaucher's disease Type 1 patients.

Allele	Jewish	Non-Jewish
N370S	71.82	43.6
84GG	11.20	0.2
L444P	2.84	25.6
IVS2	1.72	0.7
Rec	1.42	3.5
Alleles detected	89	73.69
Alleles undetected	11	26.33
Total alleles	1160	419

DNA-based prognostic tests would facilitate medical care of patients who would need intervention to prevent disease progression or modify the disease severity. Most disease alleles in Gaucher's disease lead to dysfunctional enzymes (Grace et al, 1990, 1991, 1994; Ohashi et al, 1991). Thus, various combinations of partially functional and null alleles could lead to different levels or thresholds of residual enzyme activity (Conzelmann and Sandhoff, 1983) and, hence, differing phenotypes. Clinically, homozygosity for L444P or N370S correlate with neuronopathic or milder type 1 variants, respectively, in Caucasian populations (Zimran et al, 1992; Sibille et al, 1993). Homozygotes for L444P in Japanese populations can have non-neuronopathic phenotypes, at least into the 2nd and 3rd decades (Eto et al, 1993). In non-Asian type 1 patients, the N370S/L444P or N370S/'null allele' genotypes have earlier onset and more severe involvement than the N370S homozygotes. The largest such studies were among Ashkenazi Jewish Type 1 patients (Zimran et al, 1992; Sibille et al, 1993) and these correlations appear to provide a basis for genetic counselling and prognostication in controlled settings. However, as the number of Gaucher's disease Type 1 families with greater ethnic diversity has greatly expanded, a disturbingly (potentially expected) greater variation in phenotype is being observed. Thus, while the statistics will continue to support categorical groupings of phenotypic severity, the variations in phenotype are likely to make such data less useful to individual families, particularly for pre-natal diagnosis.

The correlations of genotype and clinical type are summarized in Table 3 for four frequently tested alleles in the Gaucher's disease population as of March 1997. We have attempted to eliminate duplicated reports of patients and to exclude patients without sufficient clinical data to distinguish Type 1 from Type 3. The Swedish Type 3 patients have been excluded since this population has only the L444P allele (Dahl et al, 1990; Latham et al, 1990). These data confirm the initial impression (Theophilus et al, 1989a,b) that the N370S allele, even as a genetic compound with another allele, leads to a non-neuronopathic phenotype. The other alleles found in Gaucher's disease Type 1 are found usually heterozygously with the N370S allele. One patient that was thought to have a neuronopathic phenotype and an N370S allele, but characterization of the alleles showed a D399N/R463C genotype (Tayebi et al, 1996). Thus, to date there are no typical neuronopathic patients who have the N370S allele. The N370S allele, when present, appears to be diagnostic of Gaucher's disease type 1.

Table 3. Frequency of Gaucher's disease alleles among the phenotypes.

Variant	Frequency of mutant allele				
	N370S	L444P	84GG	REC	Other
Type 1	882/1366 (64.5%)	144/1245 (11.56%)	40/578 (6.92%)	22/490 (4.48%)	170/922 (18.4%)
Type 2	0/30	47/99 (47.5%)	—	3/18 (16.7%)	28/50 (56%)
Type 3	0/117	97/142 (68.3%)	0/48	—	27/83 (32.5%)

In comparison, the L444P and Rec alleles occur at significant levels in the neuronopathic patients. L444P homozygosity occurs frequently in Types 2 and 3 disease. One of us (GAG) had postulated that the detection of L444P homozygosity might obscure that existence of a Rec allele that was present heterozygously or homozygously in Type 2 patients, and that the greater protein dysfunction derived from an allele with multiple point mutations (i.e, Rec) may be the basis for Type 2 disease (Latham et al, 1990). There are now examples of Types 2 and 3 arising from L444P homozygosity, so that the original postulate may not generally be applicable. These results and the report of L444P homozygosity in Japanese patients type 1 (Eto et al, 1993) clearly implicate other modifying factors in the evolution of the neuronopathic phenotype. These findings, the highly variable Swedish Gaucher's disease phenotypes, and the existence of late-onset adult neuropathic variants of arylsulphatase A and β-hexosaminidase A deficiencies show the continuing need for careful and detailed follow-up of affected patients to draw genotype/phenotype conclusions that would be useful for genetic counselling.

To improve genotype/phenotype correlations, clinical assessments need standardization and agreement on the measurement of independent parameters. The assessments of hepatic and splenic volumes by magnetic resonance imaging (MRI), computed tomography (CT) or ultrasound images are generally available and should be universal in such studies. In comparison, assessment of bone disease is more difficult, because of the

non-uniform involvement, degree of secondary damage and the insensitivity
of plain radiographs. Also, the quantitative assessment of bone disease
severity is not clearly defined, e.g. are fractures of the vertebral column
more severe than hip fractures? Our inability to effectively treat vertebral
disease, compared with hip disease, does not necessarily reflect the biology
of the disease. The CNS involvement is clearly of distinct biological origin.
Thus, a severity ranking can be developed from the age-at-onset, the hepatic
and splenic volumes and the degree of bone disease (marrow and
trabecular). Additional degrees of severity can be based on the presence of
cirrhosis and/or lung involvement due to Gaucher's disease.

Ascertainment bias clouds genotype/phenotype correlations and the
basis for genetic counselling. In the Ashkenazi Jewish population, the
N370S/L444P or N370S/null allele (i.e. 84GG) genotypes have earlier
onset and more severe involvement than the N370S homozygotes (Zimran
et al, 1992; Sibille et al, 1993). While this is generally true, there is a gross
overestimate of the degree of clinical involvement of N370S homozygotes
because of detection based on clinical presentation. The distribution of
genotypes of clinically affected Ashkenazi Jewish patients with Gaucher's
disease Type 1 is shown in Table 4. This is derived from the world-wide
reports (Table 2). The severity of the phenotypes with N370S/84GG or
L444P genotypes would be sufficient to insure that most of these patients
would come to medical attention, i.e. nearly complete ascertainment.
Screening studies in the Ashkenazi Jewish population (>2000 persons)
showed allele frequencies for N370S and 84GG of 0.0321 (1/31.2) and
0.00217 (1/460.8) (Beutler et al, 1993b). Thus, the N370S/N370S to
N370S/84GG genotype ratio should be ~14.8:1. The observed ratio is
2.207. This means that the observed N370S/N370S genotype in the
Ashkenazi Gaucher's disease patients ascertained by clinical involvement
is ~6.7-fold lower than expected. Assuming homoethnic matings, only
about 30% of the expected N370S/N370S individuals have sufficient
involvement to be ascertained medically. Similar conclusions were
obtained in a smaller study (Beutler et al, 1993b). This implies a gross
overestimate of the degree of 'affectedness' of N370S/N370S patients.
These considerations also clearly show that the N370S/N370S genotype is
a necessary, but not sufficient, condition for Gaucher's disease phenotypes
in the Ashkenazi Jewish population.

Table 4. Genotype frequencies in the Ashkenazi Jewish population.*

Genotype	Observed frequency	Expected frequency*
N370S/N370S	287	871
N370S/84GG	130	130
N370S/L444P or Rec	48	48
N370S/IVS2	20	20
N370S/Other	63	63
Other/Other	32	32
Total	580	1164

* Adapted from Grabowski (1997). Calculated from the gene frequencies
in the Ashkenazi Jewish population (Beutler et al, 1993b).

In the non-Jewish populations of Gaucher's disease Type 1 similar calculations cannot be accomplished nor can the same degree of 'mildness' of the N370S/N370S genotype be assumed. There are no data on the frequency of asymptomatic N370S/N370S patients since large non-Jewish populations have not been screened. In general, composite statistics from various populations will continue to support categorical groupings of phenotypic severity. However, until the modifier genes that determine phenotypic variation are identified such composite data may not be directly useful to individual families, particularly for pre-natal diagnosis and pre-symptomatic enzyme therapy interventions.

ENZYMOLOGY

Acid β-glucosidase is a peripheral membrane glycoprotein composed of 497 amino acids. Except for mutations in Gaucher's disease, the acid β-glucosidase amino acid sequence appears to be invariant; i.e. there are no functional polymorphisms. The enzyme is present in lysosomes of all tissues, and has been purified from natural and recombinant sources (see Beutler and Grabowski, 1995 for references). The enzyme contains 5 glycosylation consensus sequences. Only the first four are normally occupied. Occupancy of the first glycosylation appears to be necessary for the co-translational vectoral folding of the enzyme during synthesis (Berg-Fussman et al, 1993). The enzyme has seven cysteine residues and three disulphide bonds in the monomer. Site-directed mutagenesis of each of the cysteines to serine residues indicates that all cysteine, except for C126, are necessary for activity of the enzyme (Grabowski et al, 1997). C126 is the free cysteine. Because of the very close association of the first four cysteines, the assignment of disulphide structure is yet to be fully elucidated. The nucleophile in catalysis has been identified as E340 by covalent labelling with 2-fluoro-2-deoxy-β-D-glucopyranoside-fluoride (Miao et al, 1994). Conduritol B epoxide, an active site directed covalent inhibitor (Legler, 1990), labelled residue D443, suggests a role for this residue in the catalytic cycle (Dinur et al, 1986). Site-directed mutagenesis and heterologous expression studies of various mutations identified in Gaucher's disease and other random mutations suggest that residues important to the proteolytic stability of acid β-glucosidase are present across exons 5 and 6, and also in exons 9 and 10 (Figure 6). The carboxy terminal end of the enzyme also appears important to catalytic activity, and the final 10 to 20 amino acids may participate in the formation of a lid for the active site similar to the other lipases (Ponce et al, 1994; Grabowski et al, 1997). Extensive kinetic studies have indicated a high degree of specificity of the active site for binding of the glycon head group (see Beutler and Grabowski, 1995 for references). Although glucose itself has low affinity ($K_i = 0.25$ M), the presence of an amino or imino group at C1 or at position 5 in the pyranose ring increases affinity by 10^5 to 10^6 (Greenberg et al, 1990; Legler, 1990). The addition of acyl chains of 10 to 12 carbons

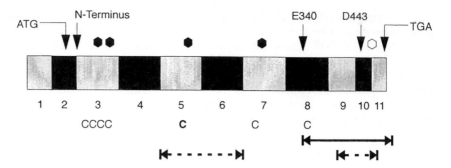

Figure 6. A function map of the acid β-glucosidase protein. The alternating dark and light regions represent exons that are numbered below. The dark and light hexagons are the occupied and un-occupied N-glycosylation consensus sequences. Glycosylation of the first site is essential for proper folding of the enzyme during translation. The Cs are the cysteines with free C129 in bold. All other cysteines participate in disulphide bond formation. The hatched and solid arrows below represent regions important to enzyme stability and catalytic activity, respecively. The three-dimensional structure of acid β-glucosidase has not been solved.

in length to these nitrogen groups further increases the affinity by an additional factor of 10^3 to 10^4 (Greenberg et al, 1990). N-acyl-β-glucosylamines with acyl chains of 10 to 12 carbons in length are the most potent inhibitors known for this enzyme, K_i ~0.1 nM, i.e. these are slow-tight binding inhibitors. These results suggest that the transition state during reaction involves the development of a significant positive charge at carbon 1 of the pyranose ring (Legler, 1990). Like other glycosidases that retain the anomeric configuration of the glycon upon cleavage from a substrate, human acid β-glucosidase probably forms a covalent enzyme/ α-glucose intermediate during the catalytic cycle. Similar kinetic studies with heterologously expressed mutant proteins bearing Gaucher's disease substitutions result in enzymes with diminished catalytic rate constants coupled with decreased proteolytic stability of the enzymes within cells (Grace et al, 1991, 1994; Ohashi et al, 1991). The most common mutation, N370S, also has diminished affinity for certain transition analogues. This suggests a relationship between its diminished catalytic rate constant and the affinity of substrate for the catalytic site (Grace et al, 1994).

Acid β-glucosidase activity requires the interaction of the enzyme, phospholipids and/or a receptor on the inner lysosomal membrane, a specific activator protein (saposin C), and an insoluble substrate glucosyl-ceramide. Numerous papers have detailed the interactions of the enzyme with various components in vitro, but the mechanism of this enzyme's reaction remains poorly understood. In vitro studies of acid β-glucosidase's interaction with negatively charged phospholipids suggested that these lipids conform the enzyme to be ready for catalysis (Berent and Radin, 1981). This basic model has remained unchanged since proposed by Berent and Radin (1981) and direct evidence has been lacking. Recent work in these laboratories (Qi and Grabowski, unpublished), using intrinsic acid β-glucosidase tryptophan fluorescence, show that: (i) acid β-glucosidase is probably a monotopic membrane protein that interacts with phosphatidyl-serine liposomes to a depth of ~7–15 carbon bonds,(ii) the interaction of acid β-glucosidase and phosphatidylserine results in fluorescence shifts that are dependent on the structure of the liposome and its fluidity, and (iii) by circular dichroism, greater α-helical content, i.e. a significant confor-mational change, develops when the enzyme binds to the membrane.

Although essential for enzyme activity, the mechanism of saposin C's interactions with normal or mutant acid β-glucosidases are unclear. Kinetic studies of Ho et al and others, have suggested an interaction of the enzyme directly with saposin C (Ho et al, 1973; Berent and Radin, 1981; Iyer et al, 1983). Vaccaro and coworkers suggested that saposin C fused liposomal membranes, and the fusogenic properties were correlated with the activation of acid β-glucosidase by saposin C (Vaccaro et al, 1993, 1994). Our recent studies (Qi and Grabowski, unpublished) confirm saposin C's interaction with particular negatively charged phospholipid membranes, but in contrast to Vaccaro's suggestion, we concluded that saposin C alters liposomal membrane structure rather than facilitating membrane fusion. Neither model accounts for the specificity of the saposin C's effect on acid β-glucosidase. Our studies (Qi et al, 1996) and those of Weiler et al (1995) strongly implicate residues in the carboxyl terminal half of saposin C that mediate the activation effects and the specificity of saposin C's interaction with acid β-glucosidase. The residues of saposin C or acid β-glucosidase that interact directly, or the actual mechanism for the specificity of this interaction remains to be elucidated. Such detailed background is essential for understanding the aberrant interactions of mutant enzymes, the lysosomal membrane and saposin C. An overall reaction scheme indicating the various conformers of the individual components is shown below.

$$E_{\text{free}} + PS \rightarrow E_m^{*}(PS)_n + Sap\ C \rightarrow E_m^{**}(PS^*)_n\ (Sap\ C)_p \rightarrow E_m^{***}(PS^{**})_n$$
$$(Sap\ C)_p^{*}\ (GC_r \rightarrow E_{\text{free}},\ PS,\ Sap\ C,\ \beta\text{-glucose and ceramide}$$

The above is a proposed overall reaction for acid β-glucosidase (E) cleavage of glucosylceramide (GC) in the lysosome where PS and $Sap\ C$ designate phosphatidylserine and saposin C, respectively. The superscripts * indicate different conformational changes at various steps. The m, n, p and r subscripts refer to the number of molecules of each species involved at a particular step. The stoichiometry at any step is unknown. The final step releases β-glucose and ceramide. This may be accompanied by additional structural changes in E, PS and $Sap\ C$ and/or their dissociation. The amount of $[E]_{\text{free}}$ is unknown, but in many artificial membrane systems $[E]_{\text{free}}$ is probably small.

Clearly, our understanding of the mechanism of reaction, the stability and the structure/function relationships in acid β-glucosidase remain rudimentary. Solving of the crystal structure of the enzyme, and additional physical biochemical studies of the reaction mechanism and its stability should improve our understanding of enzyme function and therapeutic potential. Its complex interaction with the inner lysosomal membrane, saposin C and glucosylceramide membrane substrates have yet to be fully elucidated and are sure to have major impact for improvement in the delivery and stability of active enzyme to the lysosome. In addition, the nature of these interactions requires elucidation to understand the relationships between in vitro, ex vivo and in vivo properties of the normal and mutant enzymes, and disease pathogenesis.

PROSAPOSIN AND SAPOSIN C

Saposin C enhances acid β-glucosidase in vitro activity in the presence of negatively charged phospholipids. Its deficiency causes a Gaucher-like disease (Christomanou et al, 1986). The locus encoding saposin C maps to human chromosome 10 (Fujibayashi et al, 1985; Inui et al, 1985). Importantly, three other sphingolipid hydrolase activator proteins, or saposins are encoded by the same gene in humans (O'Brien et al, 1988; Gavrieli-Rorman and Grabowski, 1989; Nakano et al, 1989), rats (Collard et al, 1988) and mice (Reiner et al, 1989) (Figure 7). The saposins derive from the precursor, prosaposin, by extensive post-translational proteolytic processing through preferential initial pathways in various tissues (Leonova et al, 1996; Vielhaber et al, 1996). Lysosomal localization of prosaposin or derived fragments is via the mannose-6-phosphate dependent and independent pathways in fibroblasts (Vielhaber et al, 1996).

High-levels of prosaposin mRNA expression are found in specific cell types in the postnatal mouse (Sun et al, 1994), particularly in selected regions of the CNS. Sprecher-Levy et al (1993) found increased expression in hindbrain structures in embryos. This expression was limited to the choroid plexus epithelial and the ependymal lining cells. Low level expression is present in the primitive neuroglial tissue during the early to mid-stages of gestation. During later gestation, the developing cortical layers in the cerebrum and cerebellum had increased expression (Sun et al, 1994). In the CNS, the change in level of prosaposin expression may correlate with a switch toward myelination and the different needs for glycosphingolipids in the CNS. This specificity of CNS expression continued to increase in the postnatal period in well differentiated neurons, choroid plexus and ependymal lining cells.

The degrees of cellular specificity, and temporal and spatial distribution have not been appreciated for other lysosomal loci, and suggests an

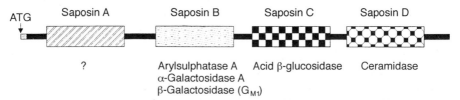

Figure 7. The coding region of the prosaposin cDNA is shown with the homologous domains for the saposins. Each of the saposins is proteolytically clipped from the precursor by proteases in the ER and lysosomes. The latter organelle is primarily responsible for final proteolytic processing. Each saposin has one N-glycosylation site and saposin A has two. The cognate enzymes for the saposins are shown below. The physiological function of saposin A is unknown.

independent regulation of the prosaposin locus. The high levels of expression found in hepatocytes and epithelial cells have no known functions or relationship to development aspects of glycosphingolipid metabolism. Prosaposin also has neurotrophic properties in vitro (O'Brien et al, 1994, 1995; Qi et al, 1996) and in vivo (Kotani et al, 1996b) that are mediated through amino acid sequences in the N-terminal half of saposin C (O'Brien et al, 1995; Kotani et al, 1996a; Qi et al, 1996). Prosaposin also has several different sizes of mRNAs that result from alternative utilization of a cryptic splice site in the saposin B region and incorporation of 6 to 9 bp of additional sequence (Holtschmidt et al, 1991). The alternative forms of the resultant prosaposin may play a role in trafficking the precursor protein to the lysosomes (shorter) or for secretion out of the cell (longer). The role, if any, of transcriptional regulation alternative forms or proteolytic processing variations of prosaposin to the phenotypic expression of Gaucher's disease, remains an unexplored, but potentially important area for research.

REFERENCES

Abrahamov A, Elstein D, Gross-Tsur V et al (1995) Gaucher's disease variant characterized by progressive calcification of heart valves and unique genotype. *Lancet* **346:** 1000–1003.

Amaral O, Pinto E, Fortuna M et al (1996) Type 1 Gaucher disease: identification of N396T and prevalence of glucocerebrosidase mutations in the Portuguese. *Human Mutation* **8:** 280–281.

Berent SL & Radin NS (1981) Mechanism of activation of glucocerebrosidase by co-β-glucosidase (glucosidase activator protein). *Biochimica Biophysica Acta* **664:** 572–582.

Berg-Fussman A, Grace ME, Ioannou Y & Grabowski GA (1993) Human β-glucosidase: N-glycosylation site occupancy and the effect of glycosylation on enzymatic activity. *Journal of Biological Chemistry* **268:** 14861–14866.

Beutler E & Gelbart T (1990) Gaucher disease associated with a unique KpnI restriction site: identification of the amino-acid substitution. *Annals of Human Genetics* **54:** 149–153.

Beutler E & Gelbart T (1994) Two new Gaucher disease mutations. *Human Genetics* **93:** 209–210.

Beutler E & Gelbart T (1995) Erroneous assignment of Gaucher disease genotype as a consequence of a complete gene deletion. *Human Mutation* **4:** 212–216.

*Beutler E & Grabowski GA (1995) Glucosylceramide lipidoses: Gaucher disease. In Scriver CR, Beaudet AL, Sly WS, & Valle D (eds) *The Metabolic and Molecular Bases of Inherited Disease* pp. 2641–2670. New York: McGraw-Hill.

Beutler E, Gelbart T & West C (1993a) Identification of six new Gaucher disease mutations. *Genomics* **15:** 203–205.

Beutler E, Demina A & Gelbart T (1994) Glucocerebrosidase mutations in Gaucher disease. *Molecular Medicine* **1:** 82–91.

Beutler E, Gelbart T, Kuhl W et al (1991) Identification of the second common Jewish Gaucher disease mutation makes possible population-based screening for the heterozygous state. *Proceedings of the National Academy of Sciences USA* **88:** 10544–10547.

Beutler E, Gelbart T, Kuhl W et al (1992) Mutations in Jewish patients with Gaucher disease. *Blood* **79:** 1662–1666.

*Beutler E, Nguyen NJ, Henneberger MW et al (1993b) Gaucher disease: gene frequencies in the Ashkenazi Jewish population. *American Journal of Human Genetics* **52:** 85–88.

Beutler E, Gelbart T, Demina A et al (1995) Five new Gaucher disease mutations. *Blood Cells, Molecules and Diseases* **21:** 20–24.

Beutler E, Gelbart T, Balicki D et al (1996) Gaucher disease: Four families with previously undescribed mutations. *Proceedings of the Association of American Physicians* **108:** 179–184.

Bornstein P, LaMarca ME, McKinney CE et al (1994) Targeted disruption of a novel gene contiguous to both glucocerebrosidase (GC) and thrombospondin (TSP3) results in an embryonic lethal phenotype in the mouse. *American Journal of Human Genetics* **55:** A129.

Carter HE & Fujino Y (1956) Biochemistry of the sphingolipids: IX. Configuration of the cerebrosidases. *Journal of Biological Chemistry* **21:** 879.

Choy FY & Wei C (1995) Identification of a new mutation (P178S) in an African-American patient with type 2 Gaucher disease. *Human Mutation* **5:** 345–347.

Choy FY, Humphries ML, & Ferreira P (1997a) Novel insertion mutation in a non-Jewish Caucasian type 1 Gaucher disease patient. *American Journal of Medical Genetics* **68:** 211–215.

Choy FY, Linsey J & MacLeod PD (1997b) Gaucher disease: Molecular screening of the glucocerebrosidase 1601G and 1601A alleles in Victoria, British Columbia, Canada. *Journal of Medical Genetics* **34:** 83–85.

Choy FYM, Wei C, Applegarth D & Yong S (1993) A new missense mutation in glucocerebrosidase exon 9 of a non-Jewish Caucasian type 1 Gaucher disease patient. *Human Molecular Genetics* **3:** 821–823.

*Christomanou H, Aignesberger A & Linke RP (1986) Immunochemical characterization of two activator proteins stimulating enzymic sphingomyelin degradation in vitro. Absence of one of them in a human Gaucher disease variant. *Biological Chemistry Hoppe-Seyler* **367:** 879–890.

Collard MW, Sylvester SR, Tsuruta JK & Griswold MD (1988) Biosynthesis and molecular cloning of sulfated glycoprotein 1 secreted by rat Sertoli cells: sequence similarity with the 70-kilodalton precursor to sulfatide/GM1 activator. *Biochemistry* **27:** 4557–4564.

Conradi N, Kyllerman M, Mänsson JE et al (1991) Late-infantile Gaucher disease in a child with myoclonus and bulbar signs: neuropathological and neurochemical findings. *Acta Neuropathologica* (Berlin) **82:** 152–157.

Conzelmann E & Sandhoff K (1983) Partial enzyme deficiencies: residual activities and the development of neurological disorders. *Developmental Neuroscience* **6:** 58–71.

Cormand B, Vilageliu L, Burguera JM et al (1995) Gaucher disease in Spanish patients: analysis of eight mutations. *Human Mutation* **5:** 303–309.

Cormand B, Vilageliu L, Balcells S et al (1996) Two novel (1098insA and Y313H) and one rare (R359Q) mutation detected in exon 8 of the β-glucocerebrosidase gene in Gaucher's disease patients. *Human Mutation* **7:** 272–274.

Cremin BJ, Davey H & Goldblatt J (1990) Skeletal complications of type I Gaucher disease: the magnetic resonance features. *Clinical Radiology* **41:** 244–247.

Dahl N, Lagerström M, Erikson A & Pettersson U (1990) Gaucher disease type III (Norrbottnian type) is caused by a single mutation in exon 10 of the glucocerebrosidase gene. *American Journal of Human Genetics* **47:** 275–278.

Dawson G & Oh JY (1977) Blood glucosylceramide levels in Gaucher's disease and its distribution amongst lipoprotein fractions. *Clinica Chimica Acta* **75:** 149–153.

Dinur T, Osiecki KM, Legler G et al (1986) Human acid β-glucosidase: isolation and amino acid sequence of a peptide containing the catalytic site. *Proceedings of the National Academy of Sciences USA* **83:** 1660–1664.

Doll RF & Smith FI (1993) Regulation of expression of the gene encoding human acid β-glucosidase in different cell types. *Gene* **127:** 255–260.

Dynan WS (1986) Promoters for housekeeping genes. *Trends in Genetics* **2:** 196–197.

Eto Y, Kawame H, Hasegawa Y et al (1993) Molecular characteristics in Japanese patients with lipidosis: novel mutations in metachromatic leukodystrophy and Gaucher disease. *Molecular and Cellular Biochemistry* **119:** 179–184.

Eyal N, Wilder S & Horowitz M (1990) Prevalent and rare mutations among Gaucher patients. *Gene* **96:** 277–283.

Eyal N, Firon N, Wilder S et al (1991) Three unique base pair changes in a family with Gaucher disease. *Human Genetics* **87:** 328–332.

French JH, Brotz M & Poser CM (1969) Lipid composition of the brain in infantile Gaucher's disease. *Neurology* **19:** 81–86.

Fujibayashi S, Kao R-T, Jones C et al (1985) Assignment of the gene for human sphingolipid activator protein-2 (SAP-2) to chromosome 10. *American Journal of Human Genetics* **37:** 741–748.

Gaucher PCE (1882) De l'épithélioma primitif de la rate, hypertrophie idiopathique del la rate san leucemie. MD Thesis, Paris.

Gavrieli-Rorman E & Grabowski GA (1989) Molecular cloning of a human co-β-glucosidase cDNA: Evidence the four sphingolipid hydrolase activator proteins are encoded by single genes in humans and rats. *Genomics* **5:** 486–492.

Grabowski GA (1993) Gaucher disease: Enzymology, genetics, and treatment. *Advances in Human Genetics* **21:** 377–441.

Grabowski GA (1997) Gaucher disease: Gene frequencies and genotype/phenotype correlations. *Genetic Testing* (in press).

Grabowski GA, Ponce E, Leonova T & Qi X (1997) Clinical and basic studies of enzyme and gene therapy in Gaucher disease type 1. *Japanese Journal of Inherited Metabolic Diseases* **13**: 283–292.

*Grace ME, Graves PN, Smith FI & Grabowski GA (1990) Analyses of catalytic activity and inhibitor binding of human acid β-glucosidase by site-directed mutagenesis. Identification of residues critical to catalysis and evidence for causality of two Ashkenazi Jewish Gaucher disease type 1 mutations. *Journal of Biological Chemistry* **265**: 6827–6835.

Grace ME, Berg A, He GS et al (1991) Gaucher disease: heterologous expression of two alleles associated with neuronopathic phenotypes. *American Journal of Human Genetics* **49**: 646–655.

Grace ME, Newman KM, Scheinker V et al (1994) Analysis of human acid β-glucosidase by site-directed mutagenesis and heterologous expression. *Journal of Biological Chemistry* **269**: 2283–2291.

Graves PN, Grabowski GA, Eisner R et al (1988) Gaucher disease type 1: cloning and characterization of a cDNA encoding acid β-glucosidase from an Ashkenazi Jewish patient. *DNA and Cell Biology* **7**: 521–528.

Greenberg P, Merrill AH, Liotta DC & Grabowski GA (1990) Human acid β-glucosidase: use of sphingosyl and N-alkyl-glucosylamine inhibitors to investigate the properties of the active site. *Biochimica Biophysica Acta* **1039**: 12–20.

Harzer K, Paton BC, Poulos A et al (1989) Sphingolipid activator protein deficiency in a 16-week-old atypical Gaucher disease patient and his fetal sibling: biochemical signs of combined sphingolipidoses. *European Journal of Pediatrics* **149**: 31–39.

Hatton CE, Cooper A, Whitehouse C & Wraith JE (1997) Mutation analysis in 48 British and Irish Gaucher patients. Identification of two missense mutation and two recombinant alleles. European Working Group on Gaucher disease, May.

He G & Grabowski GA (1992) Gaucher disease: A G(+1) to A(+1) IVS2 splice donor site mutation causing exon 2 skipping in the acid β-glucosidase mRNA. *American Journal of Human Genetics* **51**: 810–820.

He G, Grace ME & Grabowski GA (1992) Gaucher disease: Four rare alleles encoding F213I, P289L, T323I, and R463C in type 1 variants. *Human Mutation* **1**: 423–427.

*Ho MW, O'Brien JS, Radin NS & Erickson JS (1973) Glucocerebrosidase: reconstitution of activity from macromolecular components. *Biochemical Journal* **131**: 173–176.

Holtschmidt H, Sandhoff K, Kwon HY et al (1991) Sulfatide activator protein: alternative splicing that generates three mRNAs and a newly found mutation responsible for a clinical disease. *Journal of Biological Chemistry* **266**: 7556–7560.

Hong CM, Ohashi T, Yu XJ et al (1990) Sequence of two alleles responsible for Gaucher disease. *DNA Cell Biology* **9**: 233–241.

Horowitz M & Zimran A (1994) Mutations causing Gaucher disease. *Human Mutation* **3**: 1–11.

*Horowitz M, Wilder S, Horowitz Z et al (1989) The human glucocerebrosidase gene and pseudogene: structure and evolution. *Genomics* **4**: 87–96.

Horowitz M, Tzuri G, Eyal N et al (1993) Prevalence of nine mutations among Jewish and non-Jewish Gaucher disease patients. *American Journal of Human Genetics* **53**: 921–930.

Hrebicek M, Hodonova K, Cerenkova M et al (1997) Analysis of mutations in the glucocerebrosidase gene in Czech Gaucher patients. European Working Group on Gaucher disease, May.

Ida H & Eto Y (1997) Clinical and genetic features of 47 Japanese patients with Gaucher disease. *American Journal of Human Genetics* **59**: A201.

Inui K, Kao R-T, Fujibayashi S et al (1985) The gene coding for a sphingolipid activator protein, SAP-2 is on chromosome 10. *Human Genetics* **69**: 197–200.

Iyer SS, Berent SL & Radin NS (1983) The cohydrolases in human spleen that stimulate glucosyl ceramide β-glucosidase. *Biochimica Biophysica Acta* **748**: 1–7.

Kawame H & Eto Y (1991) A new glucocerebrosidase-gene missense mutation responsible for neuronopathic Gaucher disease in Japanese patients. *American Journal of Human Genetics* **49**: 1378–1380.

Kawame H, Hasegawa Y, Eto Y & Maekawa K (1992) Rapid identification of mutations in the glucocerebrosidase gene of Gaucher disease patients by analysis of single-strand conformation polymorphisms. *Human Genetics* **90**: 294–296.

Kaye EM, Ullman MD, Wilson ER & Barranger JA (1986) Type 2 and type 3 Gaucher disease: a morphological and biochemical study. *Annals of Neurology* **20**: 223–230.

Kennaway NG & Woolf LI (1968) Splenic lipids in Gaucher's disease. *Journal of Lipid Research* **9:** 755–765.

Kim J, Ponce E, Lai M et al (1996) Gaucher disease: identification of three new mutations in the Korean and Chinese (Taiwanese) population. *Human Mutation* **7:** 214–218.

Kirchhoff U, Schopa F, Albrecht B et al (1997) New missense mutations in the glucocerebrosidase gene in non-Jewish Caucasian Gaucher disease patients: results of a prospective sequencing study. *Human Genetics* (in press).

Kotani Y, Matsuda K, Wen T et al (1996a) A hydrophilic peptide comprising 18 amino acid residues of the prosaposin sequence has neurotrophic activity in vitro and in vivo. *Journal of Neurochemistry* **66:** 2197–2200.

*Kotani Y, Matsuda S, Sakanaka M et al (1996b) Prosaposin facilitates sciatic nerve regeneration in vivo. *Journal of Neurochemistry* **66:** 2019–2025.

Latham T, Grabowski GA, Theophilus BD & Smith FI (1990) Complex alleles of the acid β-glucosidase gene in Gaucher disease. *American Journal of Human Genetics* **47:** 79–86.

Latham TE, Theophilus BD, Grabowski GA & Smith FI (1991) Heterogeneity of mutations in the acid β-glucosidase gene of Gaucher disease patients. *DNA and Cell Biology* **10:** 15–21.

Laubscher K, Glew RH, Lee RE & Okinaka RT (1994) Use of denaturing gradient gel electrophoresis to identify mutant sequences in the β-glucosidase gene. *Human Mutation* **3:** 411–415.

Legler G (1990) Glycoside hydrolases: mechanistic information from studies with reversible and irreversible inhibitors. *Advances in Carbohydrate Chemistry and Biochemistry* **48:** 319–384.

Leonova T, Qi X, Bencosme A, Ponce E et al (1996) Proteolytic processing patterns of prosaposin in insect and mammalian cells. *Journal of Biological Chemistry* **271:** 17 312–17 321.

Lewis BD, Nelson PV, Robertson EF & Morris PC (1994) Mutation analysis of 28 Gaucher disease patients: The Australasian experience. *American Journal of Medical Genetics* **49:** 218–223.

Li B, Xu Y, Grabowski GA & Ponce E (1996) Expression of human acid β-glucosidase (hGC) in CHO cells and murine C2C12 myoblasts: potentials and pitfalls for organoid gene therapy. *American Journal of Human Genetics* **59:** A203

Miao S, McCarter J, Tull D et al (1994) Identification of Glu340 as the active site nucleophile in human glucocerebrosidase by use of electrospray tandem mass spectrometry. *Journal of Biological Chemistry* **269:** 10 975–10 978.

Miller EC, Grace ME & Pastores GM (1995) Identification and expression of rare mutations in acid β-glucosidase causing types 1 and 2 Gaucher disease. *American Journal of Human Genetics* **57:** A246.

Mislow K (1953) The geometry of sphingosine. *American Chemical Society* **74:** 155.

Moran D, Galperin E & Horowitz M (1997) Identification of factors regulating the expression of the human glucocerebrosidase gene. *Gene* **194:** 201–213.

Morar B & Lane AB (1996) The molecular characterization of Gaucher disease in South Africa. *Clinical Genetics* **50:** 78–84.

Nakano T, Sandhoff K, Stumper J et al (1989) Structure of full-length cDNA coding of sulfatide activator, a co-β-glucosidase and two other homologous proteins: two alternate forms of the sulfatide activator. *Journal of Biochemistry* **105:** 152–154.

*Nilsson O & Svennerholm L (1982a) Accumulation of glucosylceramide and glucosylsphingosine (psychosine) in cerebrum and cerebellum in infantile and juvenile Gaucher disease. *Journal of Neurochemistry* **39:** 709–718.

Nilsson O & Svennerholm L (1982b) Characterization and quantitative determination of gangliosides and neutral glycosphingolipids in human liver. *Journal of Lipid Research* **23:** 327–334.

Nilsson O, Håkansson G, Dreborg S et al (1982) Increased cerebroside concentration in plasma and erythrocytes in Gaucher disease: significant differences between type I and type III. *Clinical Genetics* **22:** 274–279.

Nilsson O, Grabowski GA, Ludman MD et al (1985) Glycosphingolipid studies of visceral tissues and brain from type 1 Gaucher disease variants. *Clinical Genetics* **27:** 443–450.

O'Brien JS, Kretz KA, Dewji N et al (1988) Coding of two sphingolipid activator proteins (SAP-1 and SAP-2) by same genetic locus. *Science* **241:** 1098–1101.

O'Brien JS, Carson GS, Seo HC et al (1994) Identification of prosaposin as a neurotrophic factor. *Proceedings of the National Academy of Sciences USA* **91:** 9593–9596.

O'Brien JS, Carson GS, Seo H et al (1995) Identification of the neurotrophic factor sequence of prosaposin. *Federation of American Societies of Experimental Biology* **9:** 681–685.

Ohshima T, Sasaki M, Matsuzaka T & Sakuragawa N (1993) A novel splicing abnormality in a Japanese patient with Gaucher's disease. *Human Molecular Genetics* **2:** 1497–1498.

Ohashi T, Hong CM, Weiler S et al (1991) Characterization of human glucocerebrosidase from different mutant alleles. *Journal of Biological Chemistry* **266**: 3661–3669.

O'Neill RR, Tokoro T, Kozak CA & Brady RO (1989) Comparison of the chromosomal localization of murine and human glucocerebrosidase genes and of the deduced amino acid sequences. *Proceedings of the National Academy Sciences USA* **86**: 5049–5053.

Ponce E, Mear J & Grabowski GA (1994) Gaucher disease: pseudoreversion of a disease mutation's effects—Implications for structure–function and genotype/phenotype correlations. *American Journal of Human Genetics* **55**: A343.

Qi X, Qin W, Sun Y, Kondoh K, & Grabowski GA (1996) Functional organization of saposin C: definition of the neurotrophic and acid β-glucosidase activation regions. *Journal of Biological Chemistry* **271**: 6874–6880.

Reiner O & Horowitz M (1988) Differential expression of the human glucocerebrosidase-coding gene. *Gene* **73**: 469–478.

Reiner O, Wigderson M & Horowitz M (1988a) Structural analysis of the human glucocerebrosidase gene. *DNA* **7**: 107–116.

Reiner O, Wigderson M & Horowitz M (1988b) Characterization of the normal human glucocerebrosidase genes and a mutated form in Gaucher's patient. In Salvayre R, Douste-Blazy L & Gatt S (eds) *Lipid Storage Disorders. Biological and Medical Aspects,* pp. 29–39.New York: Plenum Press.

Reiner O, Dagan O & Horowitz M (1989) Human sphingolipid activator protein-1 and sphingolipid activator protein-2 are encoded by the same gene. *Journal of Molecular Neuroscience* **1**: 225–235.

Reiner O, Wilder S, Givol D & Horowitz M (1987) Efficient in vitro and in vivo expression of human glucocerebrosidase cDNA. *DNA* **6**: 101–108. .

Seeman E, Finckh U, Hoppner J et al (1996) Two new missense mutations in a non-Jewish Caucasian family with type 3 Gaucher disease. *Neurology* **46**: 1102–1107.

*Sibille A, Eng CM, Kim SJ et al (1993) Phenotype/genotype correlations in Gaucher disease type I: clinical and therapeutic implications. *American Journal of Human Genetics* **52**: 1094–1101.

Sprecher-Levy H, Orr-Urtreger A, Lonai P & Horowitz M (1993) Murine prosaposin: expression in the reproductive system of a gene implicated in human genetic disease. *Cellular and Molecular Biology* **39**: 287–299.

Strasberg PM, Warren I, Skomorowski MA & Lowden JA (1983) HPLC analysis of neutral glycolipids: an aid in the diagnosis of lysosomal storage disease. *Clinica Chimica Acta* **132**: 29–41.

Sun Y, Witte DP & Grabowski GA (1994) Developmental and tissue specific expression of prosaposin mRNA in murine tissues. *American Journal of Pathology* **145**: 1390–1398.

Tayebi N, Nerman J, Ginns EI & Sidransky E (1996) Genotype D399N/R463C in a patient with type 3 Gaucher disease previously assigned genotype N370S/R463C. *Biochemical and Molecular Medicine* **57**: 149–151.

Theophilus B, Latham T, Grabowski GA & Smith FI (1989a) Gaucher disease: molecular heterogeneity and phenotype-genotype correlations. *American Journal of Human Genetics* **45**: 212–225.

Theophilus BD, Latham T, Grabowski GA & Smith FI (1989b) Comparison of RNase A, a chemical cleavage and GC-clamped denaturing gradient gel electrophoresis for the detection of mutations in exon 9 of the human acid β-glucosidase gene. *Nucleic Acids Research* **17**: 7707–7722.

*Tsuji S, Choudary PV, Martin BM et al (1987) A mutation in the human glucocerebrosidase gene in neuronopathic Gaucher's disease. *New England Journal of Medicine* **316**: 570–575.

Tsuji S, Martin BM, Barranger JA et al (1988) Genetic heterogeneity in type 1 Gaucher disease: multiple genotypes in Ashkenazic and non-Ashkenazic individuals [erratum Aug;85(15):5708]. *Proceedings of the National Academy of Sciences USA* **85**: 2349–2352.

Tuteja R, Tutega N, Lilliu F et al (1994) Y418C: a novel mutation in exon 9 of the glucocerebrosidase gene of a patient with Gaucher disease creates a new BglI site. *Human Genetics* **94**: 314–315.

Uchiyama A, Tomatsu S, Kondo N et al (1994) New Gaucher disease mutations in exon 10: a novel L444R mutation produces a new NciI site the same as L444P. *Human Molecular Genetics* **3**: 1183–1184.

Vaccaro AM, Tatti M, Ciaffoni F et al (1993) Function of saposin C in the reconstitution of glucosylceramidase by phosphatidylserine liposomes. *Federation of American Societies of Experimental Biology Letters* **336**: 159–162.

Vaccaro AM, Tatti M, Ciaffoni F et al (1994) Saposin C induces pH-dependent destabilization and fusion of phosphatidylserine-containing vesicles. *Federation of American Societies of Experimental Biology Letters* **349**: 181–186.

Vielhaber G, Hurwitz R & Sandhoff K (1996) Biosynthesis, processing and targeting of sphingolipid activator protein (SAP) precursor in cultured human fibroblasts. *Journal of Biological Chemistry* **271:** 32 438–32 446.

Vilagelin L, Cormand B, Gort L et al (1997) Identification of 24 different mutations in 53 Spanish patients and Cosegregation analysis with highly polymorphic markers: implications for counseling. European Working Group on Gaucher disease, May.

Walley AJ & Harris A (1993) A novel point mutation (D380A) and a rare deletion (1255del55) in the glucocerebrosidase gene causing Gaucher's disease. *Human Molecular Genetics* **2:** 1737–1738.

Walley AJ, Ellis I & Harris A (1995) Three unrelated Gaucher's disease patients with three novel point mutations in the glucocerebrosidase gene (*P266R, D315H* and *A318D*). *British Journal of Haematology* **91:** 330–332.

Weiler S, Kishimoto Y, O'Brien JS et al (1995) Identification of the binding and activating sites of the sphingolipid activator protein, saposin C, with glucocerebrosidase. *Protein Science* **4:** 756–764.

Wigderson M, Firon N, Horowitz Z et al (1989) Characterization of mutations in Gaucher patients by cDNA cloning. *American Journal of Human Genetics* **44:** 365–377.

Xu Y, Wenstrup RJ & Grabowski GA (1995) Gene therapy in Gaucher disease: effect of cellular type on expression of active acid β-glucosidase. *Gene Therapy* **2:** 647–654.

Zimran A, Sorge J, Gross E et al (1990) A glucocerebrosidase fusion gene in Gaucher disease. implications for the molecular anatomy, pathogenesis, and diagnosis of this disorder. *Journal of Clinical Investigation* **85:** 219–222.

Zimran A, Kay A, Gelbart T et al (1992) Gaucher disease. Clinical, laboratory, radiologic, and genetic features of 53 patients. *Medicine* **71:** 337–353.

3

Gaucher's disease: clinical features and natural history

TIMOTHY M. COX MA, MSc, MD, FRCP
Professor of Medicine, Honorary Consultant Physician

J. PAUL SCHOFIELD BSc, MB, PhD, MRCP
Lister Research Fellow, Honorary Consultant Physician

Department of Medicine, University of Cambridge, Level 5, Addenbrooke's Hospital, Cambridge CB2 2QQ, UK

Gaucher's disease is an inherited disorder characterized by pathological storage of glycolipid in mononuclear phagocytes: it is a multi-system disease associated with striking variation in its clinical manifestations, severity and course. Although molecular analysis of the glucocerebrosidase gene in patients with Gaucher's disease has permitted broad correlations between genotype and phenotype to be made, with few exceptions genetic variation at this locus does not allow confident prediction of clinical phenotype or prognosis. Partial deficiency of glucocerebrosidase is associated principally with parenchymal disease of the liver, spleen, bone marrow and, in severe cases, the lung, in non-neuronopathic, Type 1, Gaucher's disease: here storage material in macrophages originates from turnover of *exogenous* glycolipids. Severe deficiency of glucocerebrosidase caused by disabling mutations is additionally associated with neurological manifestations that in part reflect a failure to degrade *endogenous* neuronal glycosphingolipids, the so-called neuronopathic, Type 2 and Type 3 disease categories. Here we describe the clinical features, complications and natural history principally of Type 1 Gaucher's disease: emphasis is placed on emerging pulmonary, osseous and other manifestations of obscure pathogenesis that respond poorly to enzyme-replacement therapy.

Key words: Gaucher's disease; systemic; skeletal; phenotypic diversity; neuronopathic; non-neuronopathic; hepatic; splenic; pulmonary; rare manifestations.

The emergence of enzyme replacement for Gaucher's disease and the desire to correlate genotypic variation at the glucocerebrosidase locus with disease phenotype have ensured that the clinical manifestations of Gaucher's disease are well-documented. Although the pathological pathways that lead to clinical disease are uncharacterized, the principal manifestations of this multi-system disorder are familiar. However, with the

Copyright © 1997, by Baillière Tindall
All rights of reproduction in any form reserved

exception of the acute neuronopathic form of infancy (Type 2), disease progression is extremely variable and difficult to predict. Nonetheless, surgical and pharmaceutical interventions alter the course or outcome of at least some manifestations of Gaucher's disease.

No convincing explanation for the clinical variability of Gaucher's disease, that extends to affected sibs with shared genotypes or even affected twin pairs, has been advanced. Recently, asymptomatic individuals with few physical signs or laboratory manifestations of Gaucher's disease have been identified in the population at large; since these subjects are nonetheless homozygous for mutant alleles of glucocerebrosidase, it is clear that genetic determinants are necessary but not sufficient to account for clinical disease. Unknown environmental factors appear to be critical for disease expression.

DISEASE CLASSIFICATION

Disease nosology is of value when it allows outcomes and therapeutic responses to be predicted. Gaucher's disease is thus best resolved into neuronopathic and non-neuronopathic forms. Its division into three types was first proposed in 1962 (Knudson and Kaplan, 1962) (Table 1). The infantile neuronopathic form Type 2 carries a uniquely severe prognosis and may be clearly separated. Type 3 disease originally described in Norrbottnian patients from Sweden (Svennerholm et al, 1982) might best therefore be defined as neuronopathic Gaucher's disease that is not Type 2. Attempts have been made to distinguish additional sub-types of Type 3 Gaucher's disease (Brady et al, 1993) setting strenuous standards of nosology: some patients suffer progressive neuronopathic disease with onset in adolescence (Type 3a) whereas others suffer spectacular hepatosplenomegaly and bone disease but non-progressive oculomotor apraxia (Type 3b). The clinical features associated (so far uniquely) with homozygosity for the D409H mutation have been classed as Type 3c disease. Type 1 disease is reserved for Gaucher's disease without any discernible neuronopathic features (see Chapter 6). Having set out these operational criteria, it should be understood that they are an imperfect representation of a biological continuum (see below).

Table 1. Clinical sub-types of Gaucher's disease.

Manifestation	Type 1	Type 2	Type 3A	Type 3B	Type 3C
Onset	>1 year	<1 year	>10 years	<5 years	2–20 years
Hepatosplenomegaly	++	±	±	+++	+
Bone disease	++	—	—	+++	—
Cardiac valvular disease	—	—	—	—	+++
Progressive brain disease	—	+++	+	—	±
Oculomotor apraxia	—	+	+	+	+
Corneal opacities	—	NT	NT	NT	+
Age at death	60 years*	<3 years	<20 years	~30 years	<20 years

NT, = not formally tested; * Mean age, data from Lee, 1995.

CLINICAL DESCRIPTION

Since neuronopathic Gaucher's disease is described in Chapter 6, only the non-neuronopathic forms will be considered in further detail.

Type 1 (non-neuronopathic disease)

Disease frequency

Gaucher's disease is the most common of the human glycosphingolipid disorders and is thus an important member of the diverse group of lysosomal storage diseases. For these reasons, Gaucher's disease is prominent but it is a relatively rare disorder with an overall frequency globally of about 1 in 200 000 of the population. Precise estimates of its frequency are difficult to obtain because inheritance of the prevalent non-inactivating disease alleles may not be associated with symptoms until late in life; this pertains particularly to the so-called N370S mutation, which occurs with a gene frequency of 0.023 in Jews of Ashkenazi descent. The combined frequency of the two most common mutations (N370S and 84GG) in this population has been found by DNA-based analysis to be 0.0343, which would give an expected incidence of one Gaucher's patient per 855 Ashkenazi Jewish births (Beutler et al, 1993). Since the number of Jews is $\sim 15 \times 10^6$, compared with a world population of $\sim 5 \times 10^9$, the direct contribution of mutant alleles from this ethnic group must be a minor fraction of the global burden of this disease (see below).

Little information is available about the frequency of Gaucher's disease in non-Jewish populations. In the United Kingdom with a population of about 6×10^7, between 200 and 300 cases of Gaucher's disease are known; similarly in The Netherlands with a population of approximately 1.5×10^7, about 100 cases of Gaucher's disease are known. Since World War II, the number of Jews living in Holland has been extremely small. Nonetheless, molecular analysis of DNA has shown that the N370S mutation occurs with a frequency of approximately 40% of mutant alleles in patients of apparently Dutch ancestry. Studies in other European countries where recent mass extermination of Jews has not occurred, such as the United Kingdom, with a Synagogue list of $\sim 3 \times 10^5$, the distribution of mutant alleles of glucocerebrosidase remains the same.

An important study conducted in Portugal determined the frequency of the N370S mutation in an unbiased random sample of 2000 blood cards obtained from the Portugese neonatal population screening programme (Lacerda et al, 1994). The frequency of the allele was found to be 0.0043 predicting ~ 200 N370S homozygotes to exist in the Portugese population. Because only a few disease alleles were detected, the confidence limits of this frequency estimate are wide: nonetheless the estimate exceeds by several-fold that predicted from the number of known patients with Gaucher's disease and supports the idea that many individuals in the population escape ascertainment and remain asymptomatic. It is significant that the haplotype of the Portugese N370S allele is indistinguishable from the Ashkenazi allele, even though most Portugese Jews and their gentile descendants will have been of North African (Sephardic) origin.

The overall burden of disease for Type 1 Gaucher's disease may be estimated crudely: assuming that the frequency of the N370S and 84GG mutations is globally the same in the Ashkenazi population as that determined in American Jews, and that a significant proportion do not become symptomatic, then there would be expected to be between 5000 and 10 000 patients with Gaucher's disease who are of Ashkenazi descent; taking the estimate of the frequency of Gaucher's disease in the non-Ashkenazi global population to be 1 in 200 000, ~30 000 individuals would be affected worldwide. Clearly, robust data concerning the frequency of Gaucher's disease and its world burden are not yet available but the development of disease registers in several countries, including those of the European Union, already indicate that several thousand patients have been diagnosed.

Fortunately, non-neuronopathic Gaucher's disease greatly outnumbers the neuronopathic forms of the disorder: in most surveys, only 5–10% of reported patients have neuronopathic features. Although this generalization is broadly true, it is open to ascertainment bias: (i) severe forms of the disorder are clearly associated with early fatality and so are increasingly subject to DNA analysis for future prenatal diagnosis; and (ii) hydrops fetalis due to Gaucher's disease, the severe neonatal form, and the infantile neuronopathic forms may escape ascertainment and evade diagnosis even at death in a proportion of cases. It is salutary to consider that the neuronopathic form of Gaucher's disease originally reported from Northern Sweden occurs in only a small cluster of patients, with less than 60 individuals identified from two extended pedigrees (see Chapter 6) (Svennerholm, 1982).

CLINICAL DESCRIPTION

Gaucher's disease is an unusual lysosomal storage disorder in that most of the storage material is derived from exogenous membrane components released by phagocytosis of haematopoietic cells (Brady, 1978). Thus the clinical features of the condition mainly reflect the distribution of abnormal macrophages (Gaucher's cells) that are the principal pathological focus and hallmark of this condition (Burns et al, 1977; Lee, 1982). In Type 1 Gaucher's disease, appreciable residual glucocerebrosidase activity is present; only when the genetic defect severely impairs the activity of this enzyme does the endogenous turnover of cellular glycosphingolipids, e.g. in brain neurones, contribute to the storage burden (see below). Sub-total deficiency of glucocerebrosidase thus has a threshold effect on cells in which the turnover of glycosphingolipids is greatest: the components of the mononuclear phagocyte system include the fixed histiocytes of the spleen, liver and bone marrow. Subsidiary sites include the lymph nodes, lung and glomerular mesangium (Beutler and Grabowski, 1995). In Type 1 disease, clinically undetectable foci of perivascular macrophages may occur in the Virchow–Robin spaces of the brain.

Symptoms of Gaucher's disease are usually declared as a result of splenic enlargement: either obvious visceromegaly is noticed or the individual presents with the consequences of hypersplenism (anaemia, a bleeding tendency caused by thrombocytopenia and sometimes accompanied by recurrent bacterial infection related to neutropenia). Visceral enlargement may be first noticed during routine examination. This, or recurrent haemorrhage caused by nosebleeds or bleeding after minor trauma, and surgical procedures including tooth extraction, may prompt blood count and film examination with the suspicion of haematological malignancy (Matoth and Fried, 1965; Kolodny et al, 1982; Zimran et al, 1992; Zevin et al, 1993). Abnormal blood counts combined with hepatomegaly and the presence of serum abnormalities of liver-related tests usually prompt ultrasonic or radiological investigations followed by biopsy examination of bone marrow or hepatic tissue. Growth retardation, sometimes accompanied by skeletal pain is an early manifestation of Type 1 Gaucher's disease in childhood (Zevin et al, 1993). Retrospective enquiry in patients at the time of diagnosis frequently reveals a history of bone pains (attributable to the so-called bone infarction crises) and a diagnosis of osteochondritis especially affecting femoral epiphyses; indeed a prior diagnosis of Perthé's disease is common. Occasionally Gaucher's disease comes to light because of skeletal disease, usually with an episode of avascular necrosis affecting the hip, proximal humerus or associated with painful compression fractures of necrotic vertebrae. Rare manifestations include presentation with solitary plasmacytoma occurring on a background of longstanding asymptomatic Gaucher's disease or with prominent lymph node enlargement.

Patients with Gaucher's disease usually notice longstanding fatigue independent of the symptoms of anaemia. This appears to be associated with abnormal energy metabolism (Barton et al, 1989) and may be a manifestation of the persistent acute phase response characteristic of established Gaucher's disease (see Chapter 8). Pallor and palpitations may result from anaemia and spontaneous bruising may reflect thrombocytopenia with or without associated blood coagulation abnormalities. In patients with

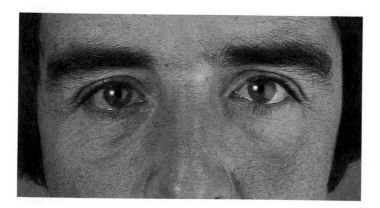

Figure 1. Facial signs in a 30-year-old man with Type 1 Gaucher's disease: note prominent pingueculae and malar vasodilatation.

marked hypersplenism, neutropenia may declare itself as recurrent cutaneous infections or furunculosis. Purpura is unusual unless the platelet count falls below 30×10^9/litre. Haemorrhage may occur at any site: even intracranial haemorrhage may be the defining illness in the patient whose splenomegaly has escaped diagnosis.

CLINICAL EXAMINATION

The patient may be pale with a distended abdomen due to visceromegaly and there may be cutaneous signs of haemorrhagic tendency with purpura or ecchymoses. Children with early-onset Gaucher's disease characteristically show growth retardation and infantilism associated with delayed sexual maturation: successful treatment by bone marrow transplantation or enzyme replacement therapy results in a phase of vigorous catch-up growth and accelerated puberty. Cutaneous manifestations of Gaucher's disease include generalized pigmentation typical of longstanding severe cases, a malar flush and pingueculae (Figure 1). These triangular, yellow-brown deposits occur in the lateral sclerae, a condition reflecting elastosis or breakdown of the collagen fibres in the sclerae rather than deposits of Gaucher's cells at this site (Chu et al, 1984). The malar flush is often present in patients with early onset severe Gaucher's disease and the attendant manifestations of liver infiltration include palmar erythema and spider angiomata. Jaundice may be present, especially where a vicious cycle of transfusion-dependent hypersplenism has been established. In rare patients with pulmonary disease, digital clubbing is observed associated with central cyanosis.

The patient's habitus may be deformed as a result of wasting and osseous disease: vertebral compression fractures may lead to kyphoscoliosis; large joint destruction as a result of epiphyseal foci of avascular necrosis in the proximal humeri and femora, leads to shoulder and hip deformity. Other deformities result from pathological fractures occurring in osteoporotic bone or in regions of focal osteolysis.

Palpation may occasionally reveal non-tender mobile lymphadenopathy especially in the axillae or sub-occipital regions. The lymph nodes have a rubbery texture and rarely exceed 1.5 centimetres in diameter; they were the presenting sign and source of a diagnostic biopsy in one patient in our series of 80 when he was aged 5 years. In cyanosed patients with pulmonary Gaucher's disease, signs of pulmonary hypertension may be present with a raised jugular venous pressure, positive Kussmaul's sign, right ventricular heave and an accentuated pulmonary second heart sound; signs of tricuspid regurgitation may also be detected. Abdominal examination may reveal previous scars resulting from surgical exploration and or splenectomy; modest-to-massive enlargement of the liver and spleen is usually obvious. In patients who have undergone splenectomy in childhood, hepatic enlargement may be very striking and large nodules of surviving parenchyma following previous infarction with fibrosis may be palpable. The signs of portal hypertension are unusual in patients with Gaucher's disease but ascites, with or without peripheral pitting oedema and prominent cutaneous veins in the abdomen may be observed in rare patients in whom recurrent infarction with hepatic scarring or 'cirrhosis' have supervened (James et al, 1981; Aderka et al, 1982). Cyanosis as part of the hepatopulmonary syndrome caused by intra-pulmonary shunting has been observed in several patients with Gaucher's disease. After examining the livers of several patients with portal hyper-tension and severe hepatic scarring, we doubt the existence of a true cirrhosis in Gaucher's disease in the absence of associated hepatitic viral infections.

SPLENIC DISEASE

Clinical evidence of splenic disease is present in at least 95% of patients with Gaucher's disease (Kolodny et al,1982). The spleen may be just palpable below the costal margin or, generally in cases of early onset disease, greatly distend the abdomen and extend into the pelvis. A medial notch may be readily palpable under these circumstances. The spleen may enlarge rapidly during the acute childhood exanthems and especially as a result of EB virus infection in children and young adults (Kolodny et al, 1982). In patients who have not received enzyme-replacement therapy, the progression of splenic disease is usually slow, occurring over many years, but a critical point may be reached where the patient develops transfusion-dependent anaemia. Under these circumstances a vicious cycle of hypersplenism evolves: red cell trans-fusions are accompanied by marked increases in splenic size caused by sequestration and destruction of donor red cells. Rapid institution of enzyme replacement therapy or even splenectomy may be required.

Gaucher's disease may come to light as a result of splenectomy urgently prompted by blunt trauma to the spleen with rupture or subcapsular haematoma. Splenic enlargement may accelerate in pregnant females with Gaucher's disease (see below). Splenomegaly contributes to the abdominal distension related to the enlarging uterus and rapid splenic growth may be shown by ultrasonic examination or magnetic resonance imaging (MRI) scanning under these circumstances. The occurrence of focal lesions, including mixed or hypoechoic lesions in the spleen and liver detected by ultrasonography, may lead to a spurious diagnosis of haematological malignancy or lymphoma (Neudorfer et al, 1997). Splenic nodules with extramedullary haematopoiesis, focal infarcts and vascular malformations are commonly observed in pathological specimens (Lee, 1982).

Splenic infarction

Acute pain in the left hypochondrium or central abdomen heralds the onset of splenic infarction, a frequent accompaniment of the massive splenomegaly associated with Gaucher's disease (Figure 2A). In this set-ting, local pain and tenderness is associated with fever and occasionally abdominal guarding. Pain referred to the left shoulder (Kehr's sign) reflects diaphragmatic irritation. The spleen is often tender with evidence of perisplenitis with or without peritonitis indicated by rebound tenderness and the presence of a friction rub heard during respiration. Provided the infarcted splenic tissue does not become infected as a result of coincidental bacteraemia, the symptoms resolve usually within 2 to 3 weeks, although narcotic analgesia may be required to relieve pain. Large splenic infarcts are frequently accompanied by abnormalities of serum liver-related enzymes and unconjugated hyperbilirubinaemia; there may also be a reduction in the already low platelet count and laboratory indications of consumptive coagulopathy. Infected splenic infarcts are clearly a medical emergency and prompt institution of parenteral antimicrobial therapy is needed to prevent the development of splenic abscesses.

Splenectomy for Gaucher's disease may be needed for acute hypersplenism in the transfusion-dependent phase. Other indications include cytopenias not responding to enzyme therapy and pressure effects including early satiety or left-sided hydronephrosis. Adhesions may result from perisplenitis related to previous infarction. The operation is not hazardous and for this reason partial splenectomy has been considered, especially in infants. However, after partial or total splenectomy, regrowth of splenic tissue or splenunculi has been repeatedly documented, despite the use of enzyme replacement therapy (Zimran et al,1995). The possible influence of splenectomy on the course of skeletal disease is discussed below.

HEPATIC DISEASE

The Kupffer cell or liver histiocyte is a specialized macrophage and microscopic examination indicates that it is an invariable site of abnormal glycolipid storage in Type 1 Gaucher's disease (Figure 2B). Clinical examination shows hepatomegaly in 70–80% of patients with established Type 1 Gaucher's disease. However, clinically significant complications of hepatic disease are rare and occur in less than 5% of affected patients. As shown in the detailed survey of 25 patients by James et al (1981), approximately half the patients show abnormalities of serum liver alkaline phosphatase and glutamate transferase but less than 10% develop portal hypertension with bleeding oesophageal varices.

In 21 patients who were submitted to liver biopsy, 'cirrhosis' was detected in only three although fibrosis (chiefly around centrizonal storage cells) was found in most cases. Fibrous septae were detected in one quarter. In patients with severe septal fibrosis only slight regenerative activity of the hepatocytes were seen. Foci of hepatocyte necrosis, bile duct proliferation and cholestasis were strikingly absent. Microscopic evidence of extramedullary haematopoiesis was observed in five of the 21 biopsies examined.

Hepatic infarction is well-recognized in Gaucher's disease with clinical features resembling those of splenic infarction: fever, pain in the right flank and sub-costal region associated with signs of peritoneal inflammation accompanied by a friction rub are characteristic. Hepatic infarction appears to have been particularly frequent in the past and in our experience this may accompany the rapid increase in peripheral platelet count in the immediate period after splenectomy. Recurrent infarction of the liver appears to cause extensive scarring throughout the organ giving rise to a distorted

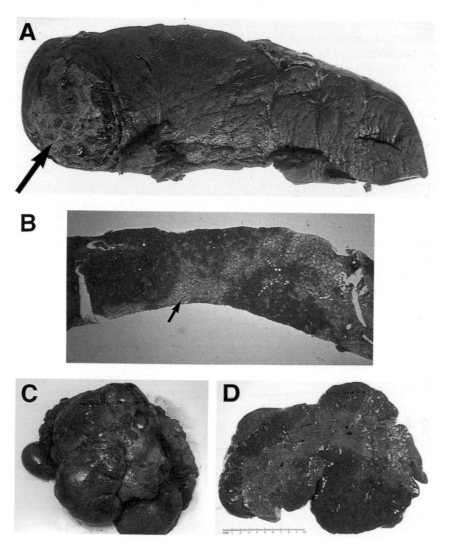

Figure 2. (A) Splenectomy specimen from a 54-year-old man with Type 1 Gaucher's disease with left hypochondrial pain and decreasing platelet count despite enzyme-replacement therapy (alglucerase 45 IU/kg body weight per month, in divided doses) given for 6 months. Arrow indicates large fresh area of infarction with perisplenitis. (B) Low-power micrograph of needle liver biopsy specimen obtained froma 30-year-old man with Type 1 Gaucher's disease: arrow depicts interlobular zone replaced by lightly-staining Gaucher's cells (haematoxylin and eosin stain). (C) Macroscopic specimen of fibrotic liver removed at necropsy from a 42-year-old woman with untreated Type 1 Gaucher's disease. She had variceal dilatation of the oesophages due to portal hypertension and died as a result of sepsis complicated by renal failure; an infected haematoma in the R hip joint was immediate cause of death. Note the gross macronodular appearance and interlobar scarring. (D) Macroscopic section of liver specimen depicted in (C). Note the extensive interlobular scarring associated with Type 1 Gaucher's disease. Microscopic examination showed extensive interconnecting bands of mature collagen with central hyalinization; only scant Gaucher's cells were present in the periphery of the scar tissue.

appearance observed at surgery or at necropsy (Figure 2C and D). Serum liver test abnormalities, with the exception of hypoalbuminaemia indicating hepatocellular failure, may respond to enzyme replacement therapy with alglucerase or imiglucerase; clearly, however, end-stage fibrotic change with established portal hypertension will not respond to enzyme replacement treatment and in a few instances orthoptic hepatic transplantation has been carried out. All seven of the patients with portal hypertension and hepatic scarring known to the authors had undergone splenectomy in childhood.

BONE MARROW DISEASE

Diffuse involvement of the mononuclear phagocyte system including fixed tissue macrophages in the liver spleen and bone marrow, has rendered it difficult to determine the individual effects of Gaucher's cell infiltration on the bone marrow in those patients in whom the spleen remains intact. In established Type 1 Gaucher's disease, the presence of sheets of Gaucher's cells within the marrow space associated with pericellular fibrosis and an increased deposition of reticulin leads to difficulties in aspiration biopsy at diagnosis ('dry tap'), here the diagnosis is facilitated by trephine biopsy. In the presence of a greatly enlarged spleen the contribution of marrow disease to the wide-ranging haematological abnormalities observed in Gaucher's disease is unclear. However, once the spleen has been removed, the intramedullary effects of infiltration by Gaucher's cells become manifest. Characteristically, Gaucher's disease is associated with a mild-to-moderate macrocytic anaemia, reflecting intrinsic marrow disease and associated with thrombocytopenia and leukopenia; splenectomy leads to a great increase in the platelet count and the appearance of target cells, Howell Jolly bodies, lymphocytosis and monocytosis.

In the absence of iron deficiency (possibly related to excess blood loss) or other incidental haematinic deficiencies in patients with Gaucher's disease, development of anaemia in a splenectomized patient immediately suggests bone marrow failure. In this setting skeletal disease is the rule: it is either manifest by local avascular necrosis or more commonly by generalized osteopenia with demineralization leading to osteoporosis in extreme cases, and osteolytic changes may also be evident. Untreated, bone marrow failure carries a severe prognosis in Gaucher's disease but several investigators have observed that anaemia and other cytopenias, usually occurring in adults some years after splenectomy, respond very rapidly to enzyme replacement therapy (Mistry et al, 1992).

BONE DISEASE

The osseous manifestations of Gaucher's disease are major determinants of morbidity and functional outcome (see Table 2) (Herman et al, 1986). Despite the introduction of enzyme replacement, they also present a

Table 2. Principal skeletal effects of Gaucher's disease.

- *Modelling deformity (Erlenmeyer flask)*
  Osteoclastic failure reflected by defective tubulation of long bones.

- *Osteopenia/osteoporosis*
  Osteoclastic overactivity, diffuse, especially affects vertebrae and long bones with generalized demineralization.

- *Expansion of medullary cavity*
  Related to local intramedullary deposits of Gaucher's cells; leads to cortical erosion.

- *Osteolysis*
  Local endosteal destruction of cortex of long bones.

- *Avascular necrosis*
  Mixed lucency and sclerosis due to ischaemic lesions of vertebrae, long bones and pelvis. Typically affect epiphyseal regions of vertebrae, femora, humeri and tibiae and sacro-iliac joint margins.
  Leads to collapse of epiphyses with deformity of humeral or femoral heads, vertebral compression and secondary osteoarthrosis.

---

formidable challenge for diagnosis, monitoring and treatment (Grabowski, 1996) (see Figure 3A–C and Figure 4A–E).

Although much is known about the histopathological changes of skeletal Gaucher's disease at its end point (Lee, 1982), the disturbances of normal bone physiology and growth that result in skeletal complications of Gaucher's disease are ill-understood. Nearly every adult patient with Gaucher's disease develops osseous complications at some point (Stowens et al, 1985) so that in treated patients these remain an important (and painful) cause of illness. A working hypothesis for the cause of bone disease relates to the local infiltration by abnormal macrophages within the bone marrow. Some believe that simple mechanical effects of the Gaucher's tissue lead to an increase in intra-osseous pressure (Beighton and Goldblatt, 1981) which, combined with the local release of hydrolases and possibly cytokines (Stowens et al, 1985), contribute to the bone abnormalities. Generalized disorders of bone including osteopenia, or frank osteoporosis (Pastores et al, 1996), may result from systemic release of cytokines, particularly tumour necrosis factor and interleukin 6, which are known to be increased in some patients with Gaucher's disease and which are important promoters of osteoclastic resorption (Michelakakis et al, 1996; Allen et al, 1997). However, the lytic lesions are closely related to foci of Gaucher's disease in the intramedullary space. Painful bone crises are now known to result from episodes of bone infarction leading ultimately to bone death (avascular necrosis) otherwise known as 'osteonecrosis'. These changes clearly do not result from abnormal osteoclast activity but appear to result from microcirculatory disease of the bone leading to nutrient starvation of living osteones and bone death.

Although the detailed microvascular pathology of bone necrosis in Gaucher's disease has yet to be examined, the analogy between other microcirculatory disorders of bone such as Caisson disease and sickle cell anaemia is inescapable. These are disorders in which microvascular obstruction clearly leads to infarction at the femoral epiphysis, the proximal humoral epiphysis and in the verebral bodies. The best-known skeletal manifestation of Gaucher's disease (the so-called Erlenmeyer flask deformity well-known in the radiological literature) is in fact the least important. This condition occurs in up to 80% of patients and appears to have no prognostic significance in its own right (Kolodny et al, 1982). It affects the distal femur and proximal tibia and represents a clear failure of modelling of the metaphyseal regions leading to a loss of normal development of tubulation during growth. Similar changes may be observed where osteoclast modelling and re-modelling is deficient, as in osteopetrosis. Even though it is a classical feature of Gaucher's disease, the Erlenmeyer flask deformity is of little consequence. It nonetheless serves as a pointer to the effects of Gaucher's disease on cell types such as osteoclasts, which are ultimately derived from the common GM progenitor that gives rise to the pathological macrophage.

Osteopenia and osteoporosis

Adult patients with Gaucher's disease may have a lower bone mass than expected for their age and sex . Generalized demineralization of bone can be detected by densitometric scanning using dual-energy photon methods and diffuse bone loss appears to worsen with age (Pastores et al, 1996). Some patients with Gaucher's disease develop severe demineralization and loss of bone mass early in childhood leading to generalized osteoporosis complicated by frequent pathological fractures (Ostlere et al, 1991) (see Figure 3A and B). There is loss of the trabecular bone and cortical thinning; bisphosphonate therapy appears to be beneficial (Ostlere et al, 1991). These changes are distinct from the local osteolytic lesions or endosteal scalloping defects that appear to relate to the presence of local Gaucher's cell deposits within the intramedullary cavity (Mankin et al, 1990). Caution is needed in interpreting bone mineralization density studies obtained by dual-energy photon quantification since many patients with Gaucher's disease who have avascular necrosis suffer bone collapse and compression fractures especially of the neck of femur and of the vertebrae; this leads to artefactual increases in the apparent bone mineralization density and may obscure a diagnosis of underlying osteoporosis. Quantitative computed tomography (CT) scanning methods for determining bone mineralization density or analysis of uninvolved bone, for example by determining bone mineralization density at the wrist, may avoid this difficulty.

Avascular necrosis

Bone infarction crises have attracted much attention in the popular and medical literature and certainly appear to be one of the most important clinical manifestations of Gaucher's disease in children and adults (Beighton and Goldblatt, 1981). Severe pain develops rapidly. As with other disorders caused by impaired vascular supply to bone, during the attacks of pain local tenderness may be absent although there is low-grade fever and evidence of elevated inflammatory markers including the erythrocyte sedimentation rate, C-reactive protein as well as a polymorphonuclear leukocytosis. Typically the epiphyseal regions of the long bones in the hip, knee and shoulder are affected, but bone infarction crises may affect the verebrae and pelvis with almost equal frequency. In the acute phase, radiographic changes are absent but radiographs taken 4–8 weeks after the pain may reveal local increases in radio-density compatible with infarction. Later, compression fractures, especially in the vertebrae occur. Although compression fractures may heal without overt clinical effects, bone collapse usually produces deformity with kyphoscoliosis or even gibbus formation. Very rarely, spinal root or cord compression may result.

Skeletal scintigrams carried out using radiolabelled bisphosphonates at the time of bone crises show local decreased uptake of the radionucleide during the time of a bone crisis and provide evidence of ischaemia. The diagnostic sensitivity of this procedure appears to exceed 90% (Katz et al, 1991). The development of acute local bone pain ultimately with osteolysis and a local periosteal reaction in a febrile patient with Gaucher's disease may suggest a true septic osteomyelitis; clinical suspicion of osteomyelitis is also heightened in patients with splenectomy or those prone to recurrent infection (Bell et al, 1986). While osteomyelitis may complicate surgical interference with osteonecrotic bone in Gaucher's disease and blood-borne bacteria may proliferate in a nidus of dead bone causing osteomyelitis secondary to avascular necrosis, primary osteomyelitis is a rare complication of Gaucher's disease. For this reason unless there are positive blood cultures or other signs, for example a positive indium-labelled leukocyte scintigram indicating bone infection, surgical interference is to be avoided. Clearly infarcted bone presents an encouraging pabulum for the growth of bacteria and as far as possible even after skeletal trauma from other causes, the insertion of orthopaedic foreign bodies, e.g. metal fixing-pins, is best avoided. In the acute phase, proton MRI scanning may show bone oedema rather than pyogenic cavitation in the ischaemic bone crises of Gaucher's disease. MRI is a useful non-invasive means for evaluation of the disordered bone marrow and osseous disease (Hermann et al, 1993). Recently in a large series of patients with Gaucher's disease from Israel, radiographs of their maxilla and mandible with panoramic dental views have been examined. In 28 patients from an unselected cohort of 266 patients with Type 1 Gaucher's disease, clinically significant bone disease was observed distinct from the osseous complications in long bones. The findings included widening of the marrow spaces, endosteal scalloping in the mandible and evidence of marked resorption of the roots of the teeth with frequent dental loss (Elstein et al, 1997).

Difficulties in understanding the pathogenesis of the diverse skeletal manifestations of Gaucher's disease are compounded by uncertainties as to how best to evaluate and monitor the changes that occur. Whereas skeletal radiographs may show gross changes (resulting from pathological fracture, osteonecrosis, lytic lesions including endosteal scalloping, as well as the mottled appearance representing the lytic and sclerotic changes associated with osteonecrosis), symptomatic disease may occur in the absence of overt radiological changes. Although treatment by enzyme-replacement therapy unequivocally reduces the frequency of bone infarction crises and of bone pain, radiological improvement in the skeleton may not be observed. Usually changes in bone solidity occur after prolonged therapy (Barton et al, 1991).

To avoid radiation exposure associated with repeated conventional radiology, many centres use magnetic resonance imaging to assess the affects of therapy and progression of Gaucher's disease in the long term. This method allows for integrated visceral volumes to be determined as well as allowing differences in the proton MRI signal resulting from parenchymal changes in the viscera to be determined. The intra-medullary proton MRI signal arises from the relative contributions of fat and from water, which has slight differences in resonance frequency. Since Gaucher's infiltration of the bone marrow leads to displacement of the normal adult yellow fat signal or red haematopoietic marrow on T_1-weighted coronal MR images, at least in older children and adults, it is possible to obtain a linear score of the total marrow fat fraction . This has been used for example in the lumbar spine resulting in quantitative chemical shift imaging (Johnson et al, 1992). In young children and infants, however, changes in the fat signal are complicated by the normal replacement of red by yellow fat marrow that occurs normally during development.

Not all centres have been able to quantify the proton magnetic resonance signals usefully, as diverse patterns of MR images are obtained from long bones and vertebrae of patients with Gaucher's disease. In general, Gaucher's disease leads to a decreased signal intensity on T_1 and T_2 weighted images, which appears to reflect pathological infiltration of the marrow cavity with the abnormal macrophages. MRI studies can identify bone marrow infarction and avascular necrosis well before plain radiographs show changes and this may be useful as a guide to enzyme replacement therapy. Except in specialized centres, quantitative chemical shift imaging for determining the amount of triglyceride or fat within the marrow cavity including ^{133}Xe inhalation scans (Castronovo et al, 1993) have not found general favour. Whilst the search must continue for non-invasive and quantitative methods suitable for reliable long-term monitoring, at present most centres would concede that judicious use of skeletal radiographs combined with bone scintigraphy and longitudinal magnetic resonance imaging are at present the best generally available tools for evaluation.

PULMONARY MANIFESTATIONS

The usual cardio-respiratory effects of Gaucher's disease result from compression of the lung caused by massive visceromegaly or thoracic restriction by kyphoscoliosis related to vertebral collapse. Thus restrictive lung disease resulting from extrinsic factors reduces tidal volume and ventilatory flow (see Figure 3B).

The intrinsic pulmonary manifestations of Gaucher's disease have received little attention until recently. Hitherto, sporadic autopsy studies of the rare Type 2 and Type 3 forms of the disease have dominated the literature (Lee, 1982) However, with increasing experience that reflects the use of enzyme-replacement therapy, it appears that all forms of Gaucher's disease may involve the lung. Gaucher's disease may affect pulmonary vasculature and cause pulmonary arterial hypertension. It may otherwise infiltrate the substance of the lung either in the perivascular, peribronchial and septal regions causing interstitial fibrosis (Myers, 1937; Wolfson, 1975) or, usually terminally, by filling alveolar air spaces leading to rapidly progressive lung consolidation. These abnormalities have been principally reported in severely-affected children and young adults examined at necropsy. The radiological changes have included bilateral fine reticular opacification or a reticulo-nodular pattern (Tunaci et al, 1995); terminal alveolar disease is characterized by diffuse hazy opacification (Figure 3D).

In a series of 95 individuals with Type 1 Gaucher's disease, pulmonary function abnormalities were abnormal in up to 68% of patients with a reduction of diffusing capacity in 42%. Abnormalities were observed in 15 individuals of 81 studied by chest radiography (Kerem et al, 1996) . In seven patients, a reduction in diffusing capacity was observed but no clear interactions between Gaucher's disease and smoking were identified. However, mild airways obstruction was seen in about one-fifth of Type 1 Gaucher's patients and although this may reflect peribronchiolar infiltration by Gaucher's cells, the effect of prior smoking could not be excluded. In most adults with Type 1 Gaucher's disease, progression of pulmonary infiltrates appears to be very slow and clinically significant lung disease is rare.

Vascular malformation in the lung has only been recently recognized as a manifestation of Gaucher's disease (Theise and Ursell, 1990). This may manifest as pulmonary hypertension, not attributable to other well-defined causes such as thromboembolic disease or autoimmune vasculitis and portal hypertension. Pulmonary hypertension is defined as a mean pulmonary arterial pressure greater than 25 mmHg and leads to enlarged pulmonary arteries, right ventricular hypertrophy with truncation of the pulmonary vascular tree. Pulmonary function tests are normal, except there may be a slight decrease in diffusion capacity. Echocardiography may reveal right ventricular hypertrophy and Doppler analysis of the tricuspid regurgitant flow can provide an estimate of peak pulmonary arterial pressure. Right heart catheterization may be required to confirm the diagnosis. Ultimately, increasing shortness of breath with cor pulmonale and peripheral oedema may result. Death occurs as a result of inanition and right heart failure with uncontrollable tachyarrhythmias.

'Primary' pulmonary hypertension has been described in siblings with Gaucher's disease and in patients not treated with placental alglucerase (Roberts and Fredrickson, 1967; Smith et al, 1978; Wisch, 1996). Limited histopathological studies usually note the presence of intracapillary Gaucher's cells, although in one case marked thickening of the inner layers of the pulmonary arterioles was identified in the absence of Gaucher's cells. This suggests that the changes resulted from the action of a humoral factor. Pulmonary hypertension is well-recognized after exposure to toxins: it has been described in patients receiving L-tryptophan and haemophiliacs treated with lyophilized crude Factor VIII, individuals exposed to rape-seed oil contaminated with oleoanilide, and in patients who have received appetite suppressant treatment based on amphetamines. Characteristically pulmonary hypertension related to toxins is associated with a common vascular abnormality of the fine pulmonary arterioles in the absence of parenchymal lung disease. Dilatation of the arterioles to form thin-walled sacs that anastomose with alveolar capillaries occurs and the endothelium proliferates to produce a plexiform lesion (Harris and Heath, 1986). A few cases of severe pulmonary hypertension have recently been reported in adult patients receiving alglucerase and the possibility that this potentially fatal condition may be caused by contaminants of this placental product, including human chorionic gonadotrophin or tissue lipid components, requires exclusion (Harats et al, 1997). The absence of lung histology, specifically searching for plexiform dilatation lesions in the pulmonary capillary bed of these patients, does not permit any conclusions about toxic aetiology to be drawn. To date no cases of pulmonary hypertension have been reported in patients receiving the recombinant preparation, imiglucerase.

Sporadic patients with non-neuronopathic Gaucher's disease have presented with a severe hypoxic syndrome associated with widespread intra-pulmonary vascular anastomoses. This usually occurs in combination with established cirrhosis and portal hypertension, 'hepatogeneous cyanosis' (the so-called hepatopulmonary syndrome). Specific features include dyspnoea and cyanosis in the upright position, which are relieved by lying down. This phenomenon reflects the redistribution of blood that normally perfuses the lung apices. The patients usually have finger clubbing and it is likely that failure to metabolize a circulating mediator of dilatation such as nitric oxide in the pulmonary vascular bed, which is normally detoxified in the liver, accounts for this phenomenon. Despite the cyanosis and clubbing and intra-pulmonary vascular dilatation leading to desaturation, hypoxia can usually be overcome by the administration of inhaled oxygen. Because of this, specific imaging tests to identify intrapulmonary shunts may be overlooked. Hepatic transplantation may relieve this condition (see below).

Rare adult patients with Gaucher's disease have been reported with high-grade pulmonary arterial hypertension and extensive arteriovenous shunting in the lung. Several have been treated with high-dose placental-derived alglucerase and have not deteriorated. Indeed a few patients in whom intra-pulmonary vascular shunts with associated pulmonary hypertension were documented, improved as a result of enzyme replacement treatment given intensively over 2 to 3 years (Beutler et al, 1991; Pelini et al, 1994). Other sporadic reports have described marked improvement following vigorous enzyme replacement therapy.

Although the number of cases of pulmonary hypertension in Gaucher's disease is very small, observations of patients with primary disease indicate that, once established, median survival from the time of diagnosis is very short (D'Alonzo et al, 1991). The influence of vigorous enzyme replacement therapy, either with the recombinant agent imiglucerase, or with other specific agents such as endothelin analogues designed to modify pressor responses in the pulmonary arterial and capillary bed has much promise, but is yet to be evaluated. Clearly it is desirable to establish as complete a picture of the pulmonary manifestations of Gaucher's disease as possible in any individual patient, despite the difficulties involved in its clinico-pathological definition. Suspected pulmonary hypertension with or without intrapulmonary shunting should prompt consideration of arterial blood gas measurements, computerized tomograms of the thorax, pulmonary angiography, cardiac (Doppler) echosonography and right heart catheter studies. Open lung biopsy and hepatic biopsy may however be dangerous and offer little added value to the management of critically-ill patients. Successful heart and lung transplantation has not yet been reported in this syndrome, but in at least one patient with Gaucher's disease and 'cirrhosis' associated with the hepatopulmonary syndrome, pulmonary arterial pressures returned to normal after liver transplantation (Carlson et al, 1990). Improvement after transplantation has been reported in other patients with hepatopulmonary syndrome complicating cirrhosis (Krowka and Cortese, 1990; Scott et al, 1993; Koneru et al, 1994).

OTHER RARE NON-NEURONOPATHIC MANIFESTATIONS OF GAUCHER'S DISEASE

Gaucher's disease in association with homozygosity for the D409H mutation

An unusual clinical syndrome of Gaucher's disease in consanguineous Arab patients from an extended family living in Israel, in patients from Spain and in Japanese patients, has been described (Uyama et al, 1992; Abrahamov et al, 1995; Chabas et al, 1995). The disorder occurs in association with mild neuronopathic manifestations and is compatible with survival to the third decade. It has thus been termed Type 3C. Non-progressive oculomotor apraxia was the original presenting finding. Slight to moderate enlargement of the spleen was noted but no hepatomegaly or skeletal manifestations have been detected in patients up to the age of 20 years. Clinical inspection has revealed bilateral corneal opacification with white opacities at their highest concentration in the deep corneal layers. Visual acuity is not impaired and the abnormalities are identified only on slit lamp examination.

In this syndrome, the heart is characteristically affected. There is with progressive thickening and calcification of mitral and aortic valves associated with a clinically significant mitral regurgitation, mild aortic insufficiency or severe aortic stenosis, requiring surgery. Heavy calcification of the valve leaflets in the absence of Gaucher's cell infiltration has been demonstrated. Some patients have died suddenly of presumed cardiac tachyarrhythmias before surgery for aortic valve disease. Cranial CT scans show dilatation of lateral ventricles with brachicephaly in all patients. Several patients with this disorder have survived cardiac surgery and have little evidence of systemic or neurological progression of their disease (Abrahamov et al, 1995).

The explanation for this phenomenon is as yet unknown and the extent to which the corneal opacification and cardiac manifestations occur in other severe forms of Gaucher's disease has not been examined systematically, however, sporadic reports of cardiac disease exist in the literature (Saraclar et al, 1991) and lone opacification of the cornea has been noted (Tsutsumi, 1982). The suggestion that this variant of Type 3 Gaucher's disease represents a contiguous gene syndrome seems highly improbable because the consistent clinical features have been reported in three distinct populations and in all are associated with homozygosity for a missense mutation in the glucocerebrosidase gene. It seems more likely that the mutation interferes with the function of a specific region of the intact glucocerebrosidase molecule that is responsible for subsidiary catalytic activities of the enzyme. In this respect, homozygosity for the D409H mutant allele of glucocerebrosidase resembles acid β-galactosidase deficiency in which particular mutations may be associated with either GM1 gangliosidosis or the mucopolysaccharidosis syndrome, Morquio B disease. In the authors' view, the D409H variant of Gaucher's disease in all probability represents an overlap syndrome with many features (e.g. corneal opacification and valvular disease) typical of the connective tissue manifestations of a mucopolysaccharidosis. It seems likely that other genotypes at the glucocerebrosidase locus will eventually be found to share this fascinating clinical presentation. Untreated, the course of the new variant appears uniformly fatal as a result of progressive calcific valvular heart disease; the long-term influence of enzyme replacement after surgery and on neurological outcome has yet to be determined.

OTHER RARE MANIFESTATIONS OF GAUCHER'S DISEASE

Renal

Although occasional Gaucher's cells have been identified histologically in the kidney at autopsy and on renal biopsy within the mesangium or renal glomerulus, very few instances of clinically significant renal disease, in the absence of amyloidosis, have been reported. At least one case of acute glomerulonephritis with heavy proteinuria has been identified. In an African-American woman, fatal Gaucher's disease associated with cardiac, renal and pulmonary infiltration was identified; there were myocardial deposits as well as deposits in the glomerulus (Smith et al, 1978). The influence of enzyme replacement therapy and clinical course of patients with Gaucher's disease affecting the kidney has not been studied. In general, this appears to be pathological curiosity occurring in severe end-stage systemic disease.

Pericarditis

Several patients have been reported with pericarditis, which may be recurrent and occasionally associated with pericardial calcification and constriction (Roberts and Frederickson, 1967; Harvey et al, 1969; Tamari et al, 1983). In at least one case, this was associated with EB virus infection, which may provoke presentation of symptomatic Gaucher's disease in genetically-predisposed individuals (Kolodny et al, 1982).

Parkinson's disease

Several case reports from France and Israel describe Parkinson's disease in association with patients with Type 1 Gaucher's disease (Neudorfer et al, 1996). In one patient the Parkinsonian manifestations were accompanied by cerebellar lesions and dementia. The mean onset of Parkinson's syndrome, which runs a relatively severe course, is between the fourth and the sixth decade of life. In six patients from Israel this was found to be at a mean of 47.5 years, which is significantly different from the mean age of onset of symptoms of Parkinson's disease in Ashkenazi Jews in the absence of Gaucher's disease (61 years). At present, it is by no means clear whether Gaucher's disease and the Parkinson syndrome share a cause-and-effect relationship, but the unusual features of the Parkinsonian syndrome and its apparent resistance to conventional therapy in the existing reports are note-worthy. In 80 patients with Type 1 Gaucher's disease we have encountered only one man with Parkinson's disease, which was diagnosed at 60 years.

Colitis

One patient has been reported with profuse colonic haemorrhage in association with Gaucher's disease (Henderson et al, 1991). Histological examination of the colonic mucosa revealed diffuse infiltration by Gaucher's cells suggesting local inflammatory manifestations as a cause of the bleeding rather than the more usual explanation of gastrointestinal haemorrhage in association with a generalized haemorrhagic tendency. In the light of this well-documented report it may be that further cases of gastrointestinal Gaucher's disease will be identified.

Neonatal Gaucher's disease

More than 20 cases of infantile Gaucher's disease presenting in the neonatal period or with premature labour have been reported. In about half of these, hydrops fetalis occurred with maceration of the fetus (Sidransky et al, 1992). In other cases severe congenital ichthyosis was observed associated with abnormal membrane structures within the stratum corneum resulting in loss of skin integrity and excess fluid loss (Sherer et al, 1993). At birth, massive hepatosplenomegaly has been observed in many fetuses in association with acute neuronopathic features and arthrogryphosis. The unusual translucency and skin texture of those infants that escape maceration has led to the descriptive term 'colloidon infants' (Lui et al, 1988). It appears that the abnormal skin integrity results from complete absence of glucocerebrosidase activity since a similar lethal syndrome was observed in transgenic mice homozygous for a disrupted glucocerebrosidase allele. It is now known that free ceramides (products of glucocerebrosidase) are important for the maintenance of normal cutaneous hydration and structural integrity (Holleran et al, 1994).

Lymphoproliferative disease

As reported in Chapter 8, abnormalities of serum immunoglobulins and other manifestations of disturbed B-cell function are frequently observed in patients with Gaucher's disease (Pratt et al, 1968; Schoenfeld et al, 1980; Allen et al, 1997). The long-term presence of Gaucher's cells that accompany adult cases of Type 1 Gaucher's disease appear to be most closely associated with evidence of lymphoproliferation: oligoclonal banding may be seen in up to 85% of patients with Type 1 Gaucher's disease beyond the age of 50 years. Further evidence of chronic B cell stimulation is provided by reports of amyloidosis in adult patients with Type 1 Gaucher's disease (Hanash et al, 1978).

Gaucher's disease has also been associated with an increased risk frequency for neoplastic disease of the lymphoid system. The most common neoplasm is the B cell malignancy, multiple myeloma (Miller et al, 1982): of the 463 patients with Type 1 Gaucher's disease reported from the University of Pittsburgh Registry of Gaucher's disease, 40 patients died of neoplastic conditions and of these *five* suffered multiple myeloma (Lee, 1995). There are numerous other reports of multiple myeloma complicating Gaucher's disease and occasionally coming to light as the presenting feature of Gaucher's disease (Figure 5). The University of Pittsburgh Registry also records four patients with lymphoma and three with chronic lymphatic leukaemia which, together with Hodgkin's disease, have all been reported independently as complications of Gaucher's disease. Although the explanation for the prevalence of lymphoproliferative disorders of the B cell type in Gaucher's disease is unclear, the recent finding of abnormal cytokine profiles, particularly of interleukin 6 and other macrophage products that influence the development of acute-phase responses and B-cell growth, suggests that these factors may be responsible (Allen et al, 1997).

Sphingolipid activator protein deficiency (Sap-C)

A few cases of severe Gaucher's disease have been reported with deficiency of the β-glucocerebroside activator Sap-C, otherwise known as Sap-2. This is a severe phenotype with marked visceromegaly evident in the first year of life and neuronopathic manifestations with dementia, ataxia, proximal weakness and irregular pigmentation in the optic fundi. In the first case, death occurred at the age of 14 and in a second patient with milder mental retardation, death occurred at 15½ years of age accompanied by seizures and spastic quadriparesis (Christomanou et al, 1986). Point mutations in the Sap-C gene were identified after enzymatic assay revealed a partial deficiency of glucocerebrosidase. In a further well-studied patient, consanguinity was present in the parents, who were fourth cousins.

Pronounced muscular contractions in their hypotonic infant were noted soon after birth (Harzer et al, 1989). A bone marrow smear at the age of 5 weeks revealed abundant pathological macrophages and glucosylceramide and ceramide were elevated in liver tissue. Biochemically the patient had partial deficiencies of β-galactocerebrosidase, β-glucocerebrosidase and ceramidase in fibroblast extracts. The diagnosis of atypical Gaucher's disease caused by deficiency of Sap-2 (Sap-C) was confirmed by absent immunostaining. Similar abnormalities were shown in tissue extracts obtained from a sibling fetus aborted after pre-natal biopsy. The propositus died at 15 weeks of age. Thus severe infantile and less severe neuronopathic forms of atypical Gaucher's disease appear to be associated with Sap-C deficiency. This is a diagnosis that is suggested by the presence of normal, or a partial deficiency of glucocerebrosidase with or without accompanying deficiencies of β-galactocerebrosidase and ceramidase. Affected patients show increased lysosomal storage of glycolipids, which may be confirmed ultrastructurally; lipid analysis indicates generalized disturbances of ceramide metabolism.

THE NATURAL HISTORY OF GAUCHER'S DISEASE

Although the ability to detect mutations at the glucocerebrosidase gene locus that cause Gaucher's disease has encouraged correlations between genotype and phenotypic manifestations to be made, the course of Gaucher's disease is incompletely documented. The least well documented form of Gaucher's disease is the Type 1 non-neuronopathic variant: this shows the greatest clinical variability and is the most common form encountered. The effects of diverse treatments, including enzyme replacement, splenectomy and orthopaedic procedures clearly influence the disorder and are likely to affect its outcome. However, in the absence of rigorous means to quantify and record these influences in the long-term follow-up of patients, the effects of these interventions on the course and progression of the disease remain uncertain. Clearly the development of comprehensive disease registers, including wide-ranging data-sets that will allow critical analysis, is to be encouraged both within and between collaborating centres in different countries.

The neuronopathic forms of Gaucher's disease are more severe and this clinical severity is associated with an increasing conformity of prognosis; the infantile neuronopathic form is associated with inevitable death within the first 3 years of life and appears to be resistant to all forms of treatment apart from supportive measures. Type 3 Gaucher's (neuronopathic non-Type 2 disease) has a more variable course (see Chapter 6). It is appropriate to note that unambiguous deterioration in neuronopathic Type 3 Gaucher's disease may follow total or even partial splenectomy (Kyllerman et al, 1990) Such an interaction appears to be restricted to patients with established neuronopathic disease and it has been suggested that the elevation of plasma glucosylceramide following the procedure leads to

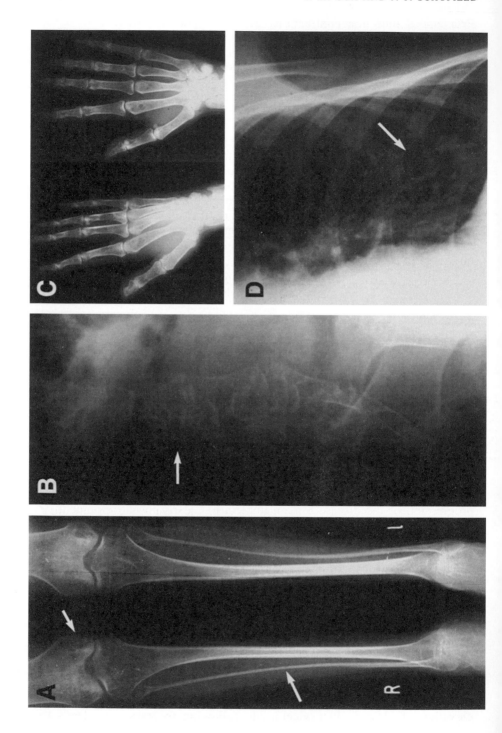

enhanced uptake and glycolipid storage by the perivascular cells in Virchow–Robin spaces with consequential ischaemia (Erikson, 1986).

Although some patients carrying the same DNA mutations may have similar clinical courses in Type 1 Gaucher's disease, others, even those belonging to the same pedigree, may show wide variation in disease manifestations. It is thus clear that clinical expression of the disease (and by inference, the prognosis) cannot be accurately predicted by mutation analysis alone (Boot et al, 1997). However, several generalizations can be made in the light of molecular analysis of the glucocerebrosidase gene in Type 1 Gaucher's disease. The presence of at least one copy of the missense mutation, N370S, is associated with Type 1 Gaucher's disease only and precludes neuronopathic involvement (Beutler and Gelbart, 1996). This may appear to be explained by the presence of appreciable residual enzymatic activity. In patients homozygous for the N370S mutation, the widest variation in clinical expression is observed: individuals may have complete absence of signs and symptoms of the disease, whereas others may have mild, moderate or even severe crippling skeletal deformity with early enlargement of the spleen. Homozygotes for the L444P mutation, which is found in the Swedish Norrbottnian population of patients, generally predicts neuronopathic Type 3 disease, which may show variable clinical severity in terms of visceral and mental impairment. However, homozygosity for the L444P mutation has been identified in patients with severe, progressive infantile neuronopathic disease as well as individuals with Type 1 Gaucher's disease with complete absence of neuronopathic involvement. In Japanese and British patients, as well as others reported from Poland and elsewhere, homozygosity for L444P may be observed in patients without neuronopathic features of the disease. L444P homozygotes generally show severe systemic manifestations with rapidly progressive visceromegaly, haematological abnormalities and early onset skeletal destruction. Thus homozygosity for the L444P mutation generally produces more severe, early-onset disease, which is rapidly progressive in its untreated form; this appears to reflect the low residual catalytic activity associated with this unstable enzyme variant. Finally the occurrence of the D409H mutation in its homozygous form in the Spanish, Japanese and

---

Figure 3. (A) Radiographs of tibia and fibulae of a 35-year-old female with severe untreated Type 1 Gaucher's disease homozygous for the L444P allele of glucocerebrosidase. Note the Erlenmeyer modelling deformity, lytic lesions in the proximal tibiae (arrows) and extreme thinning of the fibulae, that is accompanied by generalized osteoporosis. (B) Lateral radiograph of lumbo-sacral spine of a 28-year-old man with Type 1 Gaucher's disease complicated by generalized osteoporosis and pathological fractures. Note kyphoscoliosis due to extensive vertebral compression fractures. (Patient originally described by Ostlere et al (1991). Liver scarring, complicated by portal hypertension and variceal bleeding and the cyanotic hepatopulmonary syndrome has subsequently developed. (C) Radiograph of hands of a 33-year-old woman with untreated Type 1 Gaucher's disease and osteoporosis associated with multiple pathological fractures. Note lytic lesions and abnormal trabecular bone pattern in phalanges, representing extensive intramedullary Gaucher's infiltration and severe myeloid disease. (D) Selective views of chest radiograph showing hemithorax of a 18-year-old man with severe Type 1 Gaucher's disease, hepatic scarring associated with growth retardation. Splenectomy had been carried out in early childhood. Arrows depict pulmonary Gaucher's disease with reticulo-nodular opacification especially at the lower zones of (both) lungs.

Israeli Jenin Arab populations is associated consistently with mental retardation, non-progressive oculomotor ataxia, corneal opacification and progressive calcific valve heart disease (Abrahamov et al, 1995). Splenomegaly appears not to be florid or progressive in most cases.

Although the means for quantifying the multisystem manifestations of Gaucher's disease are imperfect, the development of a facile severity score index (SSI) by Zimran et al (1992), has allowed simple correlations between disease expression and other variables to be recorded. The SSI is determined according to the age at the first signs or symptoms of condition, the severity of cytopenias, the degree of hepatosplenomegaly, the presence and age at which splenectomy had been carried out and the presence or absence of skeletal disease or other evidence of organ involvement. The SSI emphasizes the widely-held view that early onset of visceromegaly and other manifestations of Gaucher's disease carries a bad prognosis and is an indication of disease severity; the presence of growth retardation in children affected by non-neuronopathic Gaucher's disease is also a clear and measurable indicator of disease severity and provides a useful means to monitor the effects of therapy in the long term. To standardize future studies of the natural progression of Gaucher's diease, a clinical rating scale that reflects both the signs and the symptoms of the disorder is required. It may be that refinements to the existing SSI should be developed and validated with a uniform scoring system so that the natural history of the disorder can be elucidated with improved precision. Clearly, however, the diverse aspects of skeletal disease are particularly difficult to assess.

With the knowledge of the prevalent mutation responsible for Type 1 Gaucher's disease in different populations, some generalizations can be made:

1. Type 1 Gaucher's disease shows great variability of expression in patients of Ashkenazi origin. The prevalence of the N370S mutation in this population confers greater phenotypic variability so that individuals with mild or absent disease who are homozygous for this mutation may be observed. Neuronopathic disease appears to be proportionately less represented in the Ashkenazi population.
2. In the unusual isolate of Gaucher's disease in Norrbotten, Sweden, homozygosity for the L444P mutation is seen with all clinical phenotypes of the disease but in this region very severe clinical phenotypes with progressive fulminating disease are observed. In other non-Ashkenazi populations, although the severity is variable, in general, more severe disease accompanied by progressive skeletal lesions with or without parenchymal disease of the liver and lungs and requiring early splenectomy is associated with this genotype.
3. Having now recognized that the need for early splenectomy prompted either by massive enlargement or life-threatening cytopenias may be taken as an index of the severity of the disorder, it will be inconsistent to suggest that splenectomy aggravates the skeletal manifestations of Gaucher's disease. Indeed in our own series, and that of Lee (1982), the frequency of bone disease is approximately equal in patients who have

been splenectomized and those who had not been splenectomized. Similar findings are reported by Zimran et al (1992) and all large series of patients with Type 1 Gaucher's disease include individuals whose disease was first diagnosed after investigation for painful bone manifestations.

4. The progressive nature of pulmonary disease complicated by life-threatening pulmonary hypertension and/or widespread arteriovenous shunting remains in all reported studies. Significant pulmonary disease appears to be associated with the rare fibrotic liver complications of cirrhosis, which occur in less than 5% of patients with Type 1 Gaucher's disease, but which again carries an adverse prognosis (James et al, 1981). Although patients with portal hypertension and liver scarring have usually had severe manifestations of Type 1 Gaucher's disease since early childhood or infancy, the possibility that some of the pulmonary manifestations can result from lipid or other contaminants of placental derived enzyme preparations has not yet been entirely excluded. Were this to be the case, plexogenic pulmonary vasculopathy may come to light with more frequency over the next few years during the follow-up of patients with Type 1 Gaucher's disease who have received enzyme therapy. Untreated, pulmonary sequelae of Gaucher's disease appear to be fatal within 1 year of diagnosis. Two patients, recently reported, were confirmed to carry the genotype N370S/84GG (Harats et al, 1997).

Disease registry

The most complete data available from an American series of patients with Type 1 Gaucher's disease (that is likely to contain a relatively high proportion who are homozygous or compound heterozygotes for the N370S mutation) have been published by Lee et al (1982, 1995). The records of 524 patients in the Pittsburgh University Registry of Gaucher's disease have been obtained from medical centres in the United States and Canada. Of the 463 patients with Gaucher's disease of the non-neuronopathic Type 1 phenotype, there have been 95 deaths at a mean age of 60 years. Of the severe neuronopathic Type 2 form, there were 46 patients of whom 44 had died at the time of the last published data of February 1995 with a mean age of 11 months, and of 16 patients classified as Type 3 neuronopathic disease there have been seven deaths with a mean age of 13 years.

These data predominantly represent the outcomes of patients reported before the widespread use of enzyme replacement therapy and elsewhere it has been commented on that the high frequency of malignant neoplasia is a cause of death in 42 of the Type 1 patients. It is salutary to examine data analysed from the same Registry 13 years earlier (Lee, 1982) when 35 patients out of a total of 239 with Type 1 disease had died. Sixteen of these had no malignant tumours and died at an average age of 46 years. Of the 19 with malignant tumours, the mean age of death was 59 years. Since the interval between these two periods was not accompanied by widespread use of enzyme therapy, it appears that the general prognosis for Gaucher's disease has improved. This may represent improved standards of diagnosis and general supportive therapy. Of 15 patients reported in 1995 by Lee who were described as young patients with Type 1 disease, five had died with the consequences of cirrhosis, three with sepsis, three in the post-operative situation, and three with pulmonary disease. Only one of the 15 had a malignant condition. A breakdown of the magnitude of splenic enlargement versus the age of 100 patients arranged at 5-year intervals indicates quite clearly that the relative magnitude of splenic enlargement with age decreases, which reflects the milder disease present in older patients with Type 1 Gaucher's disease (Lee, 1982). This has been borne out by all further series.

Overwhelming sepsis is a prominent cause of death in Gaucher's disease. Although this may well represent the consequences of post-splenectomy sepsis with the previously inadequate antimicrobial and immunization, it is clear that patients with Gaucher's disease may have qualitative and reversible defects of neutrophil migration as well as other predisposing factors to septic disease (Zimran et al, 1993). In the authors' series, one patient died of Gram-negative sepsis incurred during prolonged labour and in another a 20-year-old man with infantilism that had responded to treatment with enzyme therapy, developed fulminant septicaemia and shock due to *Haemophilus influenzae*. This patient, who had had the spleen removed in early childhood, was taking penicillin V prophylaxis and had been immunized with multivalent pneumococcal vaccine. Three patients suffer chronic multifocal osteomyelitis following orthopaedic surgery.

To summarize, patients with Type 1 disease show a variable prognosis: those with florid early manifestions, including marked splenic enlargement in infancy, suffer a more severe course of illness and appear to be at greater risk for the development of parenchymal disease of the liver and lungs; rapidly progressive skeletal disease with avascular necrosis also appears to be prevalent in this group. Patients with milder disease may survive to the fifth and sixth decades but are at greater risk from the development of malignant neoplasia. In this group, lymphoproliferative disorders are over-represented.

Effects of treatment

In all series, many patients with adult Type 1 Gaucher's disease have undergone multiple and sometimes repeated orthopaedic procedures to replace joints (Grigoris et al, 1995). These are compromised as a result of avascular necrosis that particularly affects the epiphyses of long bones. Joint replacement surgery, often in the second and third decade of life, carries attendant risks in relation to coagulation abnormalities and thrombocytopenia, as well as post-operative sepsis in patients who have been treated by splenectomy. Nonetheless, good qualities of life and functional outcomes may be achieved; revision procedures may be required as the natural life of the joint prosthesis expires.

Recent data from the International Collaborative Group on the treatment of Gaucher's disease is that the frequency of bone infarction crises is reduced by 90–95% in patients receiving enzyme replacement therapy. No

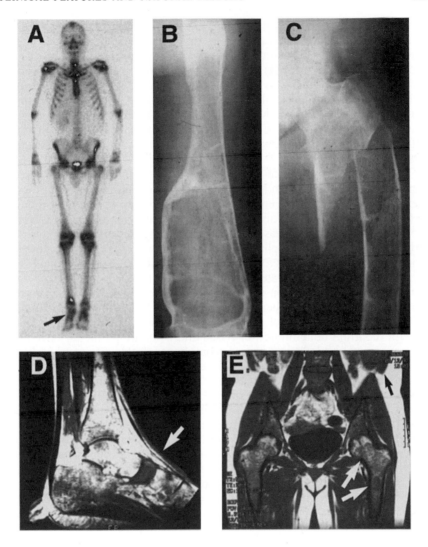

Figure 4. (A) Anterior whole-body ^{99}Tc-pertechnecate bone scintigram of a 26-year-old woman with skeletal Gaucher's disease. Note regions of high isotopic uptake in distal regions of long bones, especially humeri, radii, femora and tibiae. The patient experienced severe pain in the ankles, especially on the right; note 'hot spots' of isotopic activity in right calcaneum and navicular. (B) Radiograph of expansile intramedullary form of Gaucher's disease associated with cortical thinning in distal femur of a 30-year-old woman, 'Gauchoma'. (C) Pathological fracture of upper femoral shaft in a 27-year-old woman with Type 1 Gaucher's disease. Note focal cortical bone lysis in region of fracture. (D) Sagittal T_1-weighted magnetic resonance image of left foot of a 52-year-old man with Type 1 Gaucher's disease. Arrows indicate heterogeneous intramedullary signal in calcaneum and pathological loss of signal in the navicular. (E) T_1-weighted magnetic resonance anterior image of pelvis of a 28-year-old woman with Type 1 Gaucher's disease. Arrows indicate abnormal marrow signal in hips; note tip of spleen shown by arrow extending beyond pelvic brim. This spleen weighed 4 kg when removed surgically.

clear relationship between the frequency and amount of enzyme therapy can be drawn at present. Enzyme therapy, however, does not lead to a complete correction of osseous disease and has no effect on pre-existing necrotic lesions. In patients with osteopenia and osteoporosis a general increase in cortical thickness and bone solidity has been observed Barton et al (1991). Uncontrolled studies in isolated patients who receive bisphosphonate treatment with or without enzyme-replacement therapy suggests that bone mineralization and strength may be improved in those that have suffered pathological fracture or the conseqences of demineralization (Ostlere et al, 1991).

The reported experience of enzyme-replacement therapy in Type 1 Gaucher's disease is currently about 7 years. Enzyme-replacement therapy clearly improves visceral enlargement and haematological abnormalities of Gaucher's disease with an attendant benefit in symptoms and decreased surrogate markers of disease activity, including serum markers such as tartrate-resistant acid phosphatase activity, chitotriosidase and angiotensin-converting enzyme. Objective improvements in visceral size have been clearly demonstrated but categorical evidence of improved life expectancy is not yet available (Barton et al, 1991). Improvement in bone symptoms may take many years to become evident but there are well-documented examples in the literature of patients with progressive bone marrow failure or with recurrent bone infarction crises and cyanotic pulmonary disease in whom enzyme-replacement therapy has been clearly life-saving. All the evidence suggests that enzyme replacement has the potential to prolong life in patients with Gaucher's disease because it ameliorates life-threatening complications of the condition (Beutler et al, 1991, 1995). It thus seems likely that alglucerase, and especially imiglucerase, will favourably modify the natural course and progression of Gaucher's disease in the long-term follow-up of the large cohort of patients (about 2000 at the time of writing) that are receiving this agent (Grabowski, 1996). Evidence that enzyme treatment also improves the qualitative neutrophil chemotactic defect and corrects the coagulation abnormalities that accompany active Type 1 disease provides additional grounds for optimism (Zimran et al, 1993).

Obstetric and gynaecological complications

Procreation and pregnancy provide a particular focus of attention in the course of Type 1 Gaucher's disease (Goldblatt, 1985). Many women with Type 1 Gaucher's disease have borne children, and with the attendant complications of the condition, especially in relation to blood coagulation abnormalities and added weight strain on already compromised joints, they have been the subject of intense examination but have largely escaped review in the literature.

In the first instance, it is necessary to consider the effects of Gaucher's disease on the pregnancy and secondly the influence of pregnancy itself on the course of Gaucher's disease. There is anecdotal evidence that patients with active Type 1 Gaucher's disease, especially those with marked enlargement of the spleen and persistent anaemia and evidence of a sustained acute phase response, have impaired fertility. In 35 of 53 patients, Type 1 Gaucher's disease appeared to be associated with delayed menarche beyond 14 years of age and did not greatly impair subsequent fertility (Granowsky-Grisaru et al, 1995). Twenty-two out of 52 menstruating patients reported heavy menstrual losses and in 102 spontaneous pregnancies, 25 appear to end in spontaneous first trimester abortion.

During pregnancy thrombocytopenia and anaemia may be prominent features but in most cases ante-partum blood transfusion is not required; haemorrhage and fever was frequent after caesarian and vaginal deliveries and possibly complicated by sub-clinical coagulation abnormalities. Other reports over many years have reported accelerated enlargement of the liver and spleen during pregnancy (Goldblatt, 1985; Zlotogora et al, 1989) and although the use of enzyme replacement therapy is not recommended by the manufacturer during pregnancy, evidence of progressive visceral enlargement may give grounds for reconsidering this. In limited experience of giving enzyme replacement therapy during pregnancy no adverse affects have been recorded on either mother or infant (Granowsky-Grisaru et al, 1995)

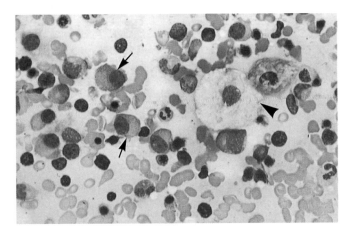

Figure 5. Myelomatosis complicating Gaucher's disease (Leishmann stain). High-power micrograph of bone marrow aspiration sample obtained from a 62-year-old man with Type 1 Gaucher's disease (N370S homozygote). Large Gaucher's cells are indicated by arrow heads; fine arrows point to abundant infiltrating plasma cells. Gaucher's disease was diagnosed after presentation with a solitary plasmacytoma of the tibia.

After pregnancy, anaemia and thrombocytopenia tend to improve. In more than 20% of women, it was judged that the skeletal manifestations of Gaucher's disease (in particular episodes of non-traumatic bone necrosis) were exacerbated during pregnancy. The principal complications of Gaucher's disease in pregnancy include an enhanced blood transfusion requirement because of peri- and post-partum haemorrhage. The effects of enzyme replacement therapy on gynaecological and obstetric complications are too early for evaluation, but where required, limited data in a few patients so far treated indicate no adverse effect on the pregnancy or infant (Granowsky-Grisaru et al, 1995). In our experience, four women had had a diagnosis of primary infertility in association with untreated Gaucher's disease; in each instance, splenectomy alone or in combination with enzyme replacement therapy rapidly led to successful pregnancy. In one further woman with primary infertility, prior enzyme replacement led to conception within 2 months of completing therapy given over 1 year. Seven pregnancies in four women, despite visceral enlargement and thrombocytopenia were carried to term without the need for concurrent enzyme therapy. Three out of the seven pregnancies were complicated by post-partum haemorrhage requiring transfusion of blood products but in no case was surgical evacuation required and the eventual outcome was satisfactory.

Acknowledgements

We thank Mrs Joan Grantham for preparing the manuscript and for her unstinting services to the management of our patients, and Philip Ball for preparing the figures. The assistance and support of the Helen Manuel Foundation and Gauchers Association of the United Kingdom is gratefully acknowledged.

REFERENCES

*Abrahamov A, Elstein D, Gross-Tsur V et al (1995) Gaucher's disease variant characterised by progressive calcification of heart valves and unique genotype. *Lancet* **346**: 1000–1003.

Aderka D, Garfinkel D, Rothem A & Pinkhas J (1982) Fatal bleeding from oesophageal varices in a patient with Gaucher's disease. *American Journal of Hematology* **77**: 838–839.

D'Alonzo GE, Barst RJ, Ayres SM et al (1991) Survival in patients with primary pulmonary hypertension. *Annals of Internal Medicine* **115**: 343–349.

Allen MJ, Myer BJ, Khokher AM et al (1997) Pro-inflammatory cytokines and the pathogenesis of Gaucher's disease: increased release of interleukin-6 and interleukin-10. *Quarterly Journal of Medicine* **90**: 19–25.

Barton D, Ludman M, Benkov K et al (1989) Resting energy expenditure in Gaucher's disease type 1: effect of Gaucher cell burden on energy requirements. *Metabolism* **38**: 1238–1243.

*Barton NW, Brady RO, Dambrosia JM et al (1991) Replacement therapy for inherited enzyme deficiency—macrophage-targeted glucocerebrosidase for Gaucher disease. *New England Journal of Medicine* **324**: 1464–1468.

Beighton P & Goldblatt J (1981) Bone involvement in Gaucher disease. *Progress in Clinical and Biological Research* **95**: 617–624.

Bell RS, Mankin HJ & Doppelt SH (1986) Osteomyelitis in Gaucher disease. *Journal of Bone and Joint Surgery* **68**: 1380–1388.

Beutler E & Gelbart T (1996). Mutation update. Glucocerebrosidase (Gaucher disease). *Human Mutation* **8**: 207–213.

Beutler E, Kay A, Saven A et al (1991) Enzyme replacement therapy for Gaucher disease. *Blood* **78**: 1183–1189.

Beutler E, Nguyen NJ, Henneberger MW et al (1993) Gaucher disease: gene frequencies in the Ashkenazi Jewish population. *American Journal of Human Genetics,* **52**: 85–88.

Beutler E & Grabowski GA (1995) Gaucher disease. In Scriver CR, Beaudet A, Sly WS & Valle D (eds) *The Metabolic and Molecular Bases of Inherited Disease*, 7th edn, pp 2641–2670. New York: McGraw-Hill.

Beutler E, Demina A, Laubscher K et al (1995) The clinical course of treated and untreated Gaucher disease: a study of 45 patients. *Blood Cells and Molecular Disease* **21**: 86–108.

Boot RG, Hollak CEM, Verhoek M et al (1997) Glucocerebrosidase genotype of Gaucher disease patients in the Netherlands: limitations in prognostic value for expression of the disease and response to therapy *Human Mutation* (in press).

Brady RO (1978). Glucosyl ceramide lipidosis: Gaucher's disease. In Stanbury JB, Wyngaarden JB & Fredrickson DS (eds) *The Metabolic Basis of Inherited Disease*, 4th edn, pp 731–746. New York: McGraw-Hill.

Brady RO, Barton NE & Grabowski GA (1993) The role of neurogenetics in Gaucher's disease. *Archives of Neurology* **50**: 1212–1224

Burns GF, Cawley JC, Flemans RJ et al (1977) Surface marker and other characteristics of Gaucher cells. *Journal of Clinical Pathology* **30**: 981–988.

Castronovo FP Jr, McKusick KA, Doppelt SH & Barton NW (1993) Radiopharmacology of inhaled ^{133}Xe in skeletal sites containing deposits of Gaucher cells. *Nuclear Medicine and Biology* **20**: 707–714.

Carlson DE, Busuttil RW, Giudici TA & Barranger JA (1990) Orthotopic liver transplantation in the treatment of complications of type I Gaucher disease. *Transplantation* **49**: 1192–1194.

Chabas A, Cormand B, Grinberg D et al (1995) Unusual expression of Gaucher's disease: cardiovascular calcifications in three sibs homozygous for the D409H mutation. *Journal of Medical Genetics* **32**: 740–742.

Christomanou H, Aignesberger A & Linke RP (1986) Immunochemical characterization of two activator proteins stimulating enzyme sphingomyelin degradation in vitro. Absence of one of them in a human Gaucher disease variant. *Hoppe Seylers Journal of Biological Chemistry* **367**: 879–890.

Chu FC, Rodrigues MM, Cogan DG & Barranger JA (1984) The pathology of pingueculae in Gaucher's disease. *Ophthalmic Paediatrics and Genetics* **4**: 7–11.

Elstein D, Lebel E, Hadas-Halpern I et al (1997) Skeletal involvement in a cohort of 266 patients with type I Gaucher disease. *Proceedings Second European Working Group for the Study of Gaucher's Disease*, May, 1–3. Castle Vaeshartelt, Maastricht, The Netherlands.

Erikson A (1986) Gaucher disease—Norrbottnian type (III). Neuropaediatric and neurobiological aspects of clinical patterns and treatment. *Acta Paediatrica Scandinavia* **75 (supplement 326)**: S1–S41.

Goldblatt J (1985) Obstetric aspects of Gaucher's disease. *British Journal of Obstetrics and Gynaecology* **92**: 145–149.

Grabowski GA (1996) Current issues in enzyme therapy for Gaucher disease. *Drugs* **52**: 159–167.

*Granowsky-Grisaru S, Aboulafia Y, Diamant YZ et al (1995) Gynecologic and obstetric aspects of Gaucher's disease: a survey of 53 patients. *American Journal of Obstetrics and Gynecology* **172**: 1284–1290.

*Grigoris P, Grecula MJ & Amstutz HC (1995) Hip arthopathy for femoral head osteonecrosis in Gaucher's disease. *Hip International* **5**: 25–30.

Hanash SM, Rucknagel DL, Heidelberger KP & Radin NS (1978) Primary amyloidosis associated with Gaucher's disease. *Annals of Internal Medicine* **89**: 639–641.

Harats D, Pauzner R, Elstein D et al (1997) Pulmonary hypertension in two patients with type I Gaucher disease while on alglucerase therapy. *Acta Hematologica* (in press).

Harris P & Heath D (1986) *The Human Pulmonary Circulation*. Edinburgh: Livingstone.

Harvey PKP, Jones MC & Anderson EC (1969) Pericardial abnormalities in Gaucher's disease. *British Heart Journal* **31**: 603–606.

Harzer K, Paton BC, Poulos A et al (1989) Sphingolipid activator protein deficiency in a 16 week-old atypical Gaucher disease patient and his fetal sibling: biochemical signs of combined sphingolipidoses. *European Journal of Pediatrics* **149**: 31–39.

Henderson JM, Gilinsky NH, Lee EY et al (1991) Gaucher's disease complicated by bleeding oesophageal varices and colonic infiltration by Gaucher cells. *American Jouranl of Gastroenterology* **86**: 346–348.

Hermann G, Shapiro RS, Abdelwahab IF & Grabowski G (1993) MR imaging in adults with Gaucher disease type I: evaluation of marrow involvement and disease activity. *Skeletal Radiology* **22**: 247–251.

Hermann G, Goldblatt J, Levy RN et al (1986) Gaucher's disease type I: assessment of bone involvement by CT and scintigraphy. *American Journal of Roentgenology* **147**: 943–948.

Holleran WM, Ginns EI, Menon GK et al (1994) Consequences of β-glucocerebrosidase deficiency in epidermis. Ultrastructure and permeability barrier alterations in Gaucher disease. *Journal of Clinical Investigation* **93**: 1756–1764.

688   T. M. COX AND J. P. SCHOFIELD

*James SP, Stromeyer FW, Chang C & Barranger JA (1981) Liver abnormalities in patients with Gaucher's disease. *Gastroenterology* **80:** 126–131.

Johnson LA, Hoppel BE, Gerard EL et al (1992) Quantitative chemical shift imaging of vertebral bone marrow in patients with Gaucher disease. *Radiology* **182:** 451–455.

Katz K, Mechlis-Frish S, Cohen IJ et al (1991) Bone scans in the diagnosis of bone crisis in patients in patients who have Gaucher disease. *Journal of Bone and Joint Surgery* **73:** 513–517.

Kerem E, Elstein D, Abrahamov A et al (1996) Pulmonary function abnormalities in Type I Gaucher disease. *European Journal of Respiratory Disease* **9:** 340–345.

*Kolodny EH, Ullman MD, Mankin HJ et al (1982) Phenotypic manifestations of Gaucher disease: clinical features in 48 biochemically verified type I patients and comment on type 2 patients. In Desnick RJ, Gatt S & Grabowski GA (eds) *Gaucher Disease: A Century of Delineation and Research*, pp 33–65. New York: Alan R. Liss.

Koneru B, Ahmed S, Weisse AB et al (1994) Resolution of pulmonary hypertension of cirrhosis after liver transplantation. *Transplantation* **58:** 1133–1135.

Knudson AG & Kaplan WD (1962) Genetics of the sphingolipidoses. In Aronson SM & Volk BW (eds) *Cerebral Sphingolipidoses*, p 395. New York: Academic Press.

Krowka MJ & Cortese DA (1990) Hepatopulmonary syndrome: an evolving perspective in the era of liver transplantation. *Hepatology* **11:** 138–141.

Kyllerman M, Conradi N, Månsson JE et al (1990) Rapidly progressive type III Gaucher disease: deterioration following partial splenectomy. *Acta Paediatrica Scandinavia* **79:** 448–453.

Lacerda L, Amaral O, Pinto R et al (1994) The N370S mutation in the glucocerebrosidase gene of Portugese type I Gaucher patients: linkage to the Pvu II polymorphism. *Journal of Inherited Metabolic Disease* **17:** 85–88.

*Lee RE (1982) The pathology of Gaucher disease. In Desnick RJ, Gatt S & Grabowski GA (eds) *Gaucher Disease: A Century of Delineation and Research*, pp 177–217. New York: Alan R. Liss.

Lee RE (1995) The natural history and pathology of Gaucher's disease. Technology Assessment Conference, February 27–March 1st, National Institutes of Health, Bethesda Maryland USA, pp 23–25. See also: *Journal of American Medical Association* (1996) **275:** 548–553, and Lee RE (1982) above.

Lui K, Commens C, Choong R & Jaworski R (1988) Colloidon babies with Gaucher's disease. *Archives of Diseases of Childhood* **63:** 854–856.

*Mankin HJ, Doppelt SH, Rosenberg AE et al (1990) Metabolic bone disease in patients with Gaucher's disease. In Avioli LV & Krane SM (eds) *Metabolic Bone Disease*, pp 730–752. Philadelphia: WB Saunders Co.

Matoth Y & Fried K (1965) Chronic Gaucher disease. Clinical observations on 34 patients. *Israel Journal of Medical Science* **1:** 521–530.

Michelakakis H, Spanou C, Kondyli A et al (1996) Plasma tumor necrosis factor-α (TNF-α) levels in Gaucher disease. *Biochimica et Biophysica Acta* **1317:** 219–222.

Miller W, Lamon JM, Tavassoli M et al (1982) Multiple myeloma complicating Gaucher's disease. (Specialty Conference) *Western Journal of Medicine* **136:** 122–128.

Mistry PK, Davies S, Corfield A et al (1992) Successful treatment of bone marrow failure in Gaucher's disease with low-dose modified glucocerebrosidase. *Quarterly Journal of Medicine* **84:** 541–546.

Myers B (1937) Gaucher's disease of the lungs. *British Medical Journal* **2:** 8–10.

Neudorfer O, Giladi N, Elstein D et al (1996) Occurrence of Parkinson's syndrome in Type I Gaucher's disease. *Quarterly Journal of Medicine* **89:** 691–694.

Neudorfer O, Hadas-Halpern I, Elstein D et al (1997) Abdominal ultrasound findings mimicking hematological malignancies in a study of 218 Gaucher patients. *American Journal of Hematology* (in press).

*Ostlere L, Warner T, Meunier PJ et al (1991) Treatment of Type I Gaucher disease affecting bone with aminohydroxypropylidene bisphosphonate (Pamidronate). *Quarterly Journal of Medicine* **79:** 503–515.

Pastores GM, Wallenstein S, Desnick RJ & Luckey MM (1996) Bone density in Type I Gaucher Disease. *Journal of Bone and Mineral Research* **ii:** 1801–1807.

Pelini M, Boice D, O'Neil K et al (1994) Glucocerebrosidase treatment of type I Gaucher disease with severe pulmonary involvement. *Annals Internal Medicine* **121:** 196–197.

Pratt PW, Estern S, Serkochwa S (1968) Immunoglobulin abnormalities in Gaucher's disease. Report of 16 cases. *Blood* **31:** 633–640.

Roberts WC & Fredrickson DS (1967) Gaucher's disease of the lung causing severe pulmonary hypertension with associated acute recurrent pericarditis. *Circulation* **35:** 783–789.

Saraclar M, Atalay S, Kocak N & Ozkutlu S (1991) Gaucher's disease with mitral and aortic involvement: echocardiographic findings. *Pediatric Cardiology* **13:** 56–58.

Schoenfield Y, Berliner S, Pinkhas J & Beutler E (1980) The association of Gaucher's disease and dysproteinemias. *Acta Haematologica* **64:** 241–243.

Scott V, De Wolf A, Kang Y et al (1993) Reversibility of pulmonary hypertension after liver transplantation: a case report. *Transplantation Proceedings* **25:** 1789–1790.

Sherer DM, Metlay LA, Sinkin RA et al (1993) Congenital ichthyosis with restrictive dermatopathy and Gaucher disease: a new syndrome with associated prenatal diagnostic and pathology findings. *Obstetrics and Gynaecology* **81:** 842–844.

Sidransky E, Sherer DM & Ginns EI (1992) Gaucher disease in the neonate: a distinct Gaucher phenotype is analagous to a mouse model created by targeted disruption of the glucocerebrosidase gene. *Pediatric Research* **32:** 494–498.

Smith RL, Hutchins GM, Sack GH et al (1978) Unusual cardiac, renal and pulmonary involvement in Gaucher's disease. *American Journal of Medicine* **65:** 352–360.

Stowens DW, Teitelbaum SL, Kahn AJ & Barranger JA (1985) Skeletal complications of Gaucher disease. *Medicine* (Baltimore) **64:** 310–322.

Svennerholm L, Dreborg S, Erickson A et al (1982) Gaucher disease of the Norrbottnian type (type III). Phenotypic manifestations. In Desnick RJ, Gatt S & Grabowski GA (eds) *Gaucher Disease: A Century of Delineation and Research*, pp 67–94 New York: Alan R. Liss.

Tamari I, Motro M & Neufeld HN (1983) Unusual pericardial calcification in Gaucher's disease. *Archives of Internal Medicine* **143:** 2010–2011.

Thiese ND & Ursell PC (1990) Pulmonary hypertension and Gaucher's disease: logical association or mere coincidence? *American Journal Pediatric Haematology and Oncology* **12:** 74–76.

Tsutsumi A (1982) A case of Gaucher's disease with corneal opacities. *Ganka Rhinshoiho* **76:** 1730–1733.

Tunaci A, Berkmen YM & Gokmen E (1995) Pulmonary Gaucher's disease: high-resolution computed tomographic features. *Paediatric Radiology* **25:** 237–238.

Uyama E, Takahashi K, Owada M et al (1992) Hydrocephalus, corneal opacities, deafness, deformed toes and leptomeningeal fibrous thickening in adult siblings: a new syndrome associated with β-glucocerebrosidase deficiency and a mosaic population of storage cells. *Acta Neurologica Scandanavica* **86:** 407–420.

Wisch JS (1996) Siblings with pulmonary hypertension and Gaucher disease. *Gaucher Clinical Perspectives* **4:** 10–12.

Wolson AH (1975) Pulmonary findings in Gaucher's disease. *American Journal of Roentgenology, Radiation Therapy and Nuclear Medicine* **123:** 712–715.

Yosipovitch Z & Katz K (1990) Bone crisis in Gaucher disease—an update. *Israeli Journal of Medical Science* **26:** 593–595.

Zevin S, Abrahamov A, Hadas-Halpern I et al (1993). Adult-type Gaucher disease in children: genetics, clinical features and enzyme-replacement therapy. *Quarterly Journal of Medicine* **86:** 565–573.

*Zimran A, Kay A & Gelbart T (1992) Gaucher disease. Clinical, laboratory, radiologic and genetic features of 53 patients. *Medicine* (Baltimore) **71:** 337–353.

Zimran A, Abrahamov A, Aker M & Matzner Y (1993) Correction of neutrophil chemotaxis defect in patients with Gaucher disease by low-dose enzyme replacement therapy. *American Journal of Hematology* **43:** 69–71.

Zimran A, Elstein D, Schiffman R et al 1995) Outcome of partial splenectomy for type I Gaucher disease. *Journal of Pediatrics* **126:** 596–597.

Zlotogora J, Sagi M, Zeigler M & Bach G (1989) Gaucher's disease in pregnancy. *American Journal of Medical Genetics* **32:** 475–477.

4

Plasma and metabolic abnormalities in Gaucher's disease

JOHANNES M. F. G. AERTS PhD

Associate Professor
Department of Biochemistry, Academic Medical Centre, University of Amsterdam, PO Box 22700, 1100 DE Amsterdam, The Netherlands

CARLA E. M. HOLLAK MD, PhD

Internist, Coordinator of Treatment of Gaucher's Disease in The Netherlands
Department of Haematology, F4-222, Academic Medical Centre, University of Amsterdam, PO Box 22700, 1100 DE Amsterdam, The Netherlands

An overview of the most important plasma abnormalities that can be found in Gaucher's disease is presented in this chapter. Attention is focussed on their practical applications and possible clinical relevance. In addition, the result of studies on metabolic alterations in Gaucher's disease are reviewed.

Key words: biochemistry; glucosylceramide; glucocerebroside; acid phosphatase; hexosaminidase; chitotriosidase; cytokines; macrophages; energy expenditure

The primary metabolic defect in Gaucher's disease is an inherited deficiency in activity of glucocerebrosidase, a lysosomal hydrolase that is responsible for the degradation of the natural glycosphingolipid glucosyl-ceramide (glucocerebroside) into ceramide and glucose (Brady et al, 1965; Patrick, 1965). Although glucocerebrosidase is present in almost all cell types, the excessive accumulation of glucosylceramide in symptomatic Gaucher patients seems to be restricted to macrophages, at least in the viscera (Beutler and Grabowski, 1995). This is probably explained by the fact that the lysosomal apparatus of macrophages may become particularly stressed with glucosylceramide following endocytotic uptake of apoptotic and senescent blood cells that are rich in this glycosphingolipid and its precursors. The characteristic lipid-laden macrophages, Gaucher cells, may be present in all organs, but usually there is a preferential accumulation in spleen, liver and bone marrow. It is generally thought that the occurrence of Gaucher cells in tissues and organs underlies the common symptoms in Gaucher patients, such as hepatomegaly, splenomegaly, pancytopenia and skeletal deterioration (Beutler and Grabowski, 1995). In Gaucher's disease

Copyright © 1997, by Baillière Tindall
All rights of reproduction in any form reserved

a number of abnormalities in lipid and protein levels can be found in tissues and plasma. The detection and serial measurement of these factors may have several clinical implications. Some of the factors may be directly produced by the storage cells and their precursors, and thus reflect to some extent the body burden on Gaucher cells and/or activity of disease. Other factors, for example cytokines, might influence the clinical manifestations of the disease by their biological actions.

In this chapter we will review the most important plasma abnormalities that have been identified today and address their role in the monitoring of the disease manifestations and their possible pathophysiological implications. In this connection are also discussed the abnormalities in energy expenditure and glucose metabolism that are commonly encountered in Gaucher patients but have so far received little attention.

TISSUE ABNORMALITIES

The abnormal accumulation of storage cells in tissues of Gaucher patients, and the associated fibronecrotic lesions and splenic fibrovascular nodules (Lee, 1996), may result in marked changes in biochemical tissue composition. Most striking in this respect is the observed 10- to 1000-fold increased glucosylceramide concentration in spleens from Gaucher patients (Suzuki, 1982; Barranger and Ginns, 1989). Markedly elevated glucosylceramide concentrations have also been documented for the bone marrow (Suzuki, 1982) and liver (Barranger and Ginns, 1989), as well as brain (Svennerholm et al, 1982) of neuronopathic Gaucher patients. Furthermore, two- to 10-fold increased levels of several acid hydrolases (e.g. β-hexosaminidase, β-glucuronidase, galactocerbrosidase, tartrate-resistant acid phosphatase and non-specific esterase) have been detected in spleens from patients (Aerts et al, 1990).

PLASMA ABNORMALITIES

Glucosylceramide

Several studies have revealed that the plasma concentration of glucosylceramide is significantly increased in clinically affected Gaucher patients (Ullman and McCluer, 1977; Dawson et al, 1982; Nilsson et al, 1982; Strasberg et al, 1983). The average increase is about twofold, being far less spectacular than that in tissues. Considerable variation exists in plasma glucosylceramide concentration among controls, and in some Gaucher patients no clear elevation in plasma lipid concentration is demonstrable. More pronounced elevations are usually noted for the more severely affected neuronopathic Gaucher patients. The measurement of plasma glucosylceramide concentration is tedious and requires considerable expertise. As an alternative the measurement of glucosylceramide content of erythrocytes rather than plasma is prefered by some researchers (Erikson et al, 1993). Glucosylceramide levels in erythrocytes and plasma are usually elevated to a similar extent. Although it is very probable that the elevation in plasma (and erythrocyte) glucosylceramide is related to the presence of storage cells in tissues and organs, there is no insight into the precise nature of the involved lipid exchange mechanism. It remains therefore unclear as to what extent the elevation in plasma (or erythrocyte) glucosylceramide forms a reflection of the total body burden of Gaucher cells or alternatively is largely determined by a subset of the storage cells in particular body locations. Despite these limitations, the monitoring of plasma (and erythrocyte) glucosylceramide levels during enzyme therapy has been advocated since it is thought to render at least some insight in the effects of the intervention on the number of storage cells. Significant decreases or downward trends in glucosylceramide concentrations have been noted in patients with various Gaucher phenotypes in response to enzyme therapy (Barton et al, 1991; Erikson et al, 1995).

Cholesterol

The concentration of total plasma cholesterol as well as low-density lipo-protein (LDL) and high-density lipoprotein (HDL) cholesterol is reduced in a large proportion of Gaucher patients (Ginsberg et al, 1984; Le et al, 1988). The reductions in LDL and HDL cholesterol seem associated with reduced amounts of these lipoprotein particles, as suggested by the decreased plasma concentrations of apoproteins B and A-1, respectively. It has been suggested that this phenomenon is in part caused by increased catabolism of LDL and HDL by macrophages in Gaucher patients (Le et al, 1988). Interestingly, an increase in plasma apoprotein E concentration has also been documented, being associated with a fraction of large HDL particles (Mahley, 1988). This suggests that a stimulated reverse cholesterol transport from tissues to the liver may also contribute to the observed reduction in plasma cholesterol. In this connection, it is of interest to note that in bile of Gaucher patients, markedly increased glucosylceramide concentrations have been observed (Pentchev et al, 1981), which might be because of increased reversed transport of the glucosylceramide similar to that of cholesterol. Furthermore, it has been noted that after intravenous administration of a metabolically inert steroisomer of the naturally occurring D-glucosylceramide to rats, a significant part of this glycolipid was recovered in faeces (Tokoro et al, 1987). It is as yet unknown to what extent the removal of glucosylceramide via biliary excretion is quantitatively important in normal subjects and whether this process is upregulated in Gaucher patients. To date no detailed reports have been published on the effects of enzyme therapy on plasma concentrations of cholesterol and apoproteins.

Liver enzymes

In Gaucher's disease, increases in patients' plasma alkaline phosphatase and transaminase activities are commonly found (Zimran et al, 1992). These abnormalities are clearly related to the size of the liver and can be explained by the damage to the hepatocytes and obstruction of the intra-hepatic biliary system caused by the massive infiltration with Gaucher cells. Liver function, however, is usually preserved. Enzyme supplementation therapy usually results in a decrease or normalization of liver enzymes, concomittantly with a decrease in liver size.

Transcobalamin and ferritin

Increased plasma transcobalamin II has been detected in association with Gaucher's disease and correction has been observed following enzyme therapy (Gilbert and Weinreb, 1976). It is not known whether the abnormality in vitamin B12 capacity is of clinical importance. Another common abnormality in serum of symptomatic Gaucher patients are increased ferritin levels. In several studies this phenomenon has been noted for a large proportion of the patients investigated (Zimran et al, 1992; Niederau et al, 1996). It has been suggested that high levels of ferritin may be released by Gaucher cells or their monocyte precursors (Bassan et al, 1985), however the precise value of serum ferritin abnormalities as a marker of storage cells, remains so far unclear. The presence of high levels of iron (and ferritin) in Gaucher cells has been documented for a very long time. The serum ferritin elevation in Gaucher's disease may be not without physiological relevance. It has been speculated that the elevated ferritin may interfere with normal T lymphocyte functioning and as such contribute to the increased incidence of certain malignancies among Gaucher patients (Bassan et al, 1985). Although detailed reports are still lacking, it is known that, as in our own experience, reductions in serum ferritin concentrations may occur in Gaucher patients during succesful intervention by enzyme therapy.

Lysosomal hydrolases, angiotensin-converting enzyme and lysozyme

The levels of some common lysosomal hydrolases are generally elevated in sera of symptomatic Gaucher patients (Moffit et al, 1978; Hultberg et al, 1980). The best example in this connection forms β-hexosaminidase activity. Most, but not all, patients show a twofold increase in total β-hexosaminidase activity in sera, the activity of β-hexosaminidase B being usually relatively greater than that of β-hexosaminidase A (see e.g. Natowicz et al, 1992). In the more severely affected Gaucher patients clear elevations in α-mannosidase and β-glucuronidase activity also often occur (Chitayat et al, 1987). Several studies have documented that serum angiotensin-converting enzyme (ACE) levels are often elevated in Gaucher patients; however a marked interindividual variation in the enzyme levels exists that may range from normal to more than 10-fold the median control value (Lieberman and Beutler, 1976; Silverstein and Friedland, 1977; Silverstein et al, 1980; Zimran et al, 1992). Increased levels of serum lysozyme activity in affected Gaucher patients have also been noted (Silverstein and Friedland, 1977).

The exact origin of the excessive amounts of β-hexosaminidase, ACE and lysozyme in sera of Gaucher patients is unclear. The fact that the abnormalities are, at least in part, rapidly corrected by therapeutic inter-vention suggests that the enzymes are directly released by lipid-laden Gaucher cells or by cells that are closely related. The remarkable inter-individual differences in the extent of elevations in the various enzymes does, however, not point to a single source.

Tartrate resistant acid phosphatase (TRAP)

It has been known for a long time that the activity of the tartrate-resistant acid phosphatase (TRAP) is markedly increased in sera of most Gaucher patients (Tuchman et al, 1959). The particular isoenzyme of acid phosphate that is elevated is isoenzyme 5B (Lam and Desnick, 1982; Lord et al, 1990). Demonstration of the markedly increased plasma TRAP activity can support the diagnosis of Gaucher's disease; however, it should be realized that such an abnormality is not unique for this disorder. Furthermore, the assay routinely used to measure TRAP activity is not completely specific for the relevant isoenzyme. A more specific assay can be performed in the presence of the reducing agent mercapto-ethanol (Chambers et al, 1977; Magelhaes et al, 1984). More recently monoclonal antibodies have been generated that specifically recognize the isoenzyme 5B, allowing an accurate measurement of the plasma level of the appropriate TRAP activity (Chamberlain et al, 1995). While interpreting plasma TRAP levels in Gaucher patients it has to be taken in mind that the normal levels are strongly age-dependent, being much higher in children than in adults (Magelhaes et al, 1984). The fact that TRAP is synthesized by osteoclasts has stimulated the idea that plasma TRAP levels may specifically correlate with the extent of skeletal disease in Gaucher patients. However, it seems more likely that the plasma TRAP in Gaucher patients originates from Gaucher cells and their precursors in various body locations. Immunocytochemical analysis of the spleen from a Gaucher patient has suggested that not only the typical large Gaucher cells but also their small mononuclear precursors are enriched in TRAP (Schindelmeiser et al, 1991). Moreover, splenectomy is known to result in a rapid and marked reduction in plasma TRAP activity in Gaucher patients (Rosenthal, 1982). Given the complex origin of TRAP in sera of Gaucher patients it is questionable whether this parameter serves as a specific marker for the extent of skeletal disease in this disorder. Enzyme therapy has been found to lead to a relatively rapid, but often only partial reduction in plasma TRAP activity (see e.g. Barton et al, 1991).

Chitotriosidase

The above-mentioned abnormalities in plasma analytes of Gaucher patients are neither universal nor very pronounced. These shortcomings have prompted us to search for novel markers of Gaucher's disease mani-festation. An ideal disease marker would be a protein that is specifically released by Gaucher cells and that could be sensitively detected in the circulation. Comparative analyses of sera of Gaucher patients and normal controls, as well as analyses of proteins secreted by cultured macrophages, have led to the discovery of a novel enzyme in man. The identified enzyme, named chitotriosidase after its ability to hydrolyse the artificial fluorogenic substrate 4-methylumbelliferyl-chitotrioside (4MU-GlcNac3), can be considered a hallmark of Gaucher's disease manifestation (Hollak et al, 1994). Plasma levels of chitotriosidase are dramatically increased in symptomatic Gaucher patients. In our initial study with 32 untreated Type 1 Gaucher patients, the median value of plasma chitotriosidase activity was found to be more than 600 times that of control subjects. The abnormality in plasma chitotriosidase is far more striking than that of any other known parameter. Our present experience with about 700 symptomatic Gaucher patients with various phenotypic manifestations indicates that the striking abnormality in plasma chitotriosidase is a very common feature. The vast majority of the clinically affected individuals show an enzyme level that is at least 100-fold elevated and in some cases may reach values more than 4000 times the median normal value. However, in asymptomatic Gaucher patients no or only very slight elevations in plasma chitotriosidase activity occur (Hollak et al, 1994). About 6% of all Gaucher patients, as noted for control subjects, completely lacks plasma chitotriosidase activity (Hollak et al, 1994). This is the result of a recessively inherited defect in the chitotriosidase gene. Very recently, the nature of the genetic defect that prevalently underlies the chitotriosidase deficiency has been elucidated by us (in preparation). A single mutation in the chitotriosidase gene occurs in various ethnic populations with an incidence of carriers as high as 30–40%, suggesting an ancient origin. Since among control subjects, carriers for this chitotriosidase mutation show on average half the plasma chitotriosidase levels of individuals that do not carry the defect, it is likely that the extent of plasma chitotriosidase elevation in Gaucher patients is also influenced by their chitotriosidase genotype. Demonstration of a markedly increased plasma chitotriosidase activity is a helpful tool in bio-chemical confirmation of Gaucher's disease. However, it should be kept in mind that false negative results are obtained in the case of chitotriosidase deficiency and for asymptomatic individuals. On the other hand, relatively modest elevations in plasma chitotriosidase elevations are also encountered in some other pathologies, such as some distinct lysosomal lipid storage disorders, sarcoidosis and visceral leishmaniasis (Hollak et al, 1994, Guo et al, 1995).

There is compelling evidence that the dramatic plasma chitotriosidase abnormality in symptomatic Gaucher patients is directly related to the occurrence of Gaucher cells. First, a marked abnormality in plasma chitotriosidase level is not detected in pre-symptomatic Gaucher patients (Hollak et al, 1994). Second, isolated splenic Gaucher cells have been found to be extremely rich in chitotriosidase and the concentrations, of glucosylceramide (Gaucher cells) and chitotriosidase correlate nicely in spleens of Gaucher patients. Third, in situ hybridization experiments have shown that Gaucher cells in spleen, liver and bone marrow produce high levels of chitotriosidase mRNA (Aerts et al, unpublished results). Finally,

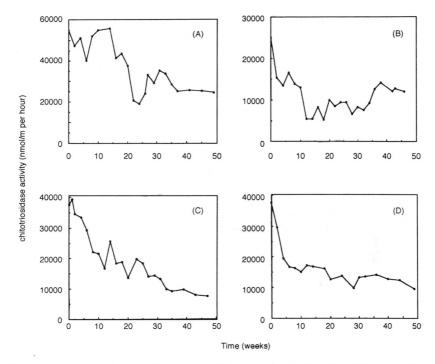

Figure 1. Decrease in plasma chitotriosidase activity over time in four Type 1 Gaucher's disease patients (A–D) treated with enzyme therapy. From Hollak et al (1994, *Journal of Clinical Investigation* **93**: 1288–1292), with permission.

plasma chitotriosidase levels in Gaucher patients rapidly decrease upon succesful intervention by enzyme therapy (Hollak et al, 1994). Generally, no complete correction in plasma chitotriosidase is reached and after the first year of treatment there are no further marked reductions in enzyme level. More recently it has been reported that succesful bone marrow transplantation of Gaucher patients also results in a correction in plasma chitotriosidase activity (Young et al, 1997).

Recently the enzyme chitotriosidase has been characterized by us in some detail (Boot et al, 1995; Renkema et al, 1995, 1997). The hydrolase has been isolated from spleen of a Gaucher patient. It has been observed that pure chitotriosidase is also able to cleave artificial chitobioside (GlcNac2) and chitotetraoside (GlcNac4) substrates and is active towards chitin, the natural polymer of N-acetylglucosamine. In this aspect, and with respect to its sensitivity for inhibition by allosamidin, chitotriosidase is similar to chitinases from various species. Using 4-methylumbelliferyl-chitotetraoside as substrate markedly increased enzyme activities in plasma of symptomatic patients have also been reported (Den Tandt et al 1988), as well as a rapid reduction following initiation of enzyme therapy (Den Tandt and van Hoof, 1996). The cloned chitotriosidase cDNA also indicates that the enzyme should be considered to be the human analogue of chitinases belonging to family 18 of glycosylhydrolases (Boot et al, 1995).

In view of the well-known function of chitinases in various non-vertebrate species in the defence against and/or degradation of chitin-containing pathogens such as fungi, it is presently attractive to speculate that a similar role is fulfilled by chitotriosidase in man. There is, however, to our knowledge no information yet available about a reduced susceptibility of Gaucher patients for fungal infections. Actually no clear differences have so far been noted with respect to the clinical manifestations in Gaucher patients with a several thousand-fold elevated plasma chitotriosidase level compared with chitotriosidase-deficient patients. This suggests that the elevated plasma chitotriosidase activity itself does not markedly effect the clinical course of the disease.

It has become clear that plasma chitotriosidase levels do not reflect one particular clinical symptom, but are rather a reflection of the total body burden of storage cells. Gaucher cells in various locations probably contribute relatively differently to the plasma enzyme level. For example, it seems that the enzyme secreted by the splenic storage cells is most probably cleared very efficiently during its first pass through the liver, and consequently contributes relatively little to the plasma steady state level. On the other hand, Gaucher cells in the liver seem to add quite considerably to the plasma chitotriosidase level.

Since conceptually the target of enzyme supplementation therapy is the correction and/or prevention of formation of Gaucher cells, monitoring of plasma chitotriosidase activity during therapy is of interest. Presently a very large number of Gaucher patients have been analysed by us with respect to changes in plasma chitotriosidase levels following enzyme therapy. Two findings made during the ongoing investigation are of particular interest. First, with every dosing regimen a marked inter-individual difference in the extent of plasma chitotriosidase correction is seen. Second, the average correction in plasma chitotriosidase is more rapid and pronounced for patients receiving a higher dose of enzyme. It may be envisioned that monitoring of plasma chitotriosidase levels in Gaucher patients is attractive for a number of reasons. First, the onset of a marked increase in plasma chitotriosidase concentration may prove to be a harbinger of clinical manifestation of disease. Second, monitoring of changes in plasma chitotriosidase level during therapy may help to identify those patients in which the number of storage cells is not significantly changed despite the intervention. Moreover, monitoring of plasma chito-triosidase levels might be helpful in decision-making about dose adaptations made during maintenance of the enzyme therapy. Further extensive matching of plasma chitotriosidase levels with clinical data will have to substantiate the potential value of chitotriosidase as a marker in the above-mentioned respects.

Abnormalities in clotting and fibrinolytic factors

A number of reports on deficiencies of several clotting factors can be found in the literature. A Type 1 Gaucher's disease patient has been described with a deficiency in factor V and VIII before splenectomy, which normalized completely after removal of the spleen (Vreeken et al, 1967). It was suggested that low grade intravascular coagulation within the spleen was responsible for the deficiencies, based on the presence of fibrin deposits in the spleen after surgery. A deficiency in factor IX in 11 patients with Gaucher's disease has also been reported (Boklan and Sawitsky, 1976). The presence of a plasma factor, that hampers the normal measurement of factor IX has been suggested (Boklan and Sawitsky, 1976). A recent study in nine patients with Gaucher's disease, however, did not confirm the presence of factor IX deficiency, but low levels of factor XI, II, V and VIII were found in some patients (Billet et al, 1996). Isolated factor XI deficiencies have been reported earlier in some cases of Gaucher's disease (Freedman and Puliafito, 1988, Berrebi et al, 1992). It has been established that factor XI deficiency occurs frequently in the Askenazi Jewish population, independent of the presence of Gaucher's disease (Seligsohn et al, 1976).

We performed a detailed study of parameters of coagulation and fibrinolysis in 30 Type 1 Gaucher patients, of whom 14 were splenectomized, before and after treatment with enzyme supplementation therapy (Hollak et al, 1997b). Pre-treatment activated partial thromboplastin time (APTT), and prothrombin time (PT) were prolonged in 42% and 38% of patients, respectively. Serious deficiencies (<50%) of coagulation factors XI, XII, VII, X, V and II and II were observed in 30–60% of the patients. Some coagulation factors, like factor V, were especially very low in patients with massive splenomegaly, indicating that the spleen might play an important role in the clearance of these factors. The presence of low coagulation factors in most splenectomized patients points out that the spleen cannot be the only factor responsible for the abnormalities. In addition, markers for activation of coagulation (thrombin–antithrombin (TAT)-complex) and fibrinolysis (plasmin–α2 antiplasmin (PAP)-complex, fibrin cleavage product D-dimer) were significantly elevated, especially in splenectomized patients. After 12 months of enzyme supplementation therapy partial correction occurred. These data indicate ongoing activation of coagulation and fibrinolysis. It is hypothesized that these processes may be induced by macrophage derived cytokines. Although bleeding tendency is usually related to the degree of thrombocytopenia, the presence of low levels of coagulation factors may contribute to haemorrhagic diathesis. Therefore, when surgical procedures have to be performed, it seems reasonable to supply patients with coagulation factors in case of severe abnormalities.

Immunoglobulin abnormalities

Gaucher's disease is associated with an increased prevalence of monoclonal and oligoclonal gammopathies (see e.g. Pratt et al, 1968). Often polyclonal hypergammoglobulinaemias are found. It has been suggested that aspecific stimulation of B cells, possibly by macrophage derived cytokines, might underly these abnormalities (see section below). In this

respect it is not surprising that Gaucher's disease is incidentally complicated by the occurrence of B cell malignancies (Fox et al, 1984), multiple
myeloma (Garfinkel et al, 1982) and amyloidosis (Hanash et al, 1978;
Hrebicek et al, 1996). The effects of enzyme therapy on changes in
immunoglobulin patterns have so far not been reported. It is also unknown
whether treatment may prevent the occurrence of the malignancies.

CYTOKINES AND MACROPHAGE ACTIVATION MARKERS

Macrophages play an essential role in host physiology and in pathogenesis
of inflammatory and immunologic response (Rutherford et al, 1993). They
interact with their environment through a complicated repertoire of plasma
membrane and secretory molecules. The key role of macrophages in the
pathogenetic process underlying Gaucher's disease has led to many
speculations with respect to the presence of elevated levels of especially
pro-inflammatory cytokines and their possible role in the pathophysiology
of Gaucher's disease (Beutler and Grabowski, 1995). Surprisingly,
relatively few studies have addressed this issue: two very recent reports and
the study from our group. The next section will give an overview of the
main findings on cytokine patterns in Gaucher's disease and their potential
clinical implications.

Pro-inflammatory cytokines: IL-1, IL-6, IL-8, IL-10 and TNF-α

The first study on the potential role of cytokines in Gaucher's disease was
reported in 1981 (Gery et al, 1981). Murine macrophages that were in vitro
challenged with glucosylceramide, showed increased production and
secretion of lymphocyte activating factor (LAF, later named IL-1) upon
stimulation with LPS. It was hypothesized that storage of the lipid in
Gaucher's disease 'primed' the macrophages, facilitating the release of
cytokines to other stimuli. Michelakakis and co-workers were the first to
report on elevated levels of a pro-inflammatory cytokine in Gaucher's
disease (Michelakakis et al, 1996). In this study, slightly increased concentrations of TNF-α were found in plasma samples of Type 1 Gaucher's
disease patients and higher levels were observed in Type 2 and 3 patients.
In the recent work of Allen and co-workers no elevations in TNF-α
concentrations in Type 1 disease could be established (Allen et al, 1997).
These researchers also measured levels of IL-1β, IL-6 and IL-10 and found
that the latter two were elevated in most patients. Interestingly, the
abnormally elevated levels of IL-6 were studied in relation to the
prevalence of monclonal or biclonal gammopathies. It was found that the
higher IL-6 concentrations indeed occurred in the patients showing a clonal
expansion of B cells. This may not be surprising since IL-6 is a well-known
stimulator of cells of the B cell lineage (see e.g. van Oers et al, 1993) and
a high prevalence of diseases associated with clonal expansion, such as
gammopathies (Pratt et al, 1968), multiple myeloma (Garfinkel et al, 1982)
and chronic lymphocytic leukaemia (CLL) (Fox et al, 1984), have been

reported in association with Gaucher's disease. In addition, since IL-6 and IL-10 may influence bone metabolism (Manolagas and Jilka, 1995), the authors investigated the cytokine levels in relation to bone disease. No difference was found in patients with and without radiographic evidence of bone disease. Another feature of Gaucher's disease that may be explained by the involvement of pro-inflammatory cytokines is the increase in both energy expenditure and glucose production (van der Poll et al, 1991; Corssmit et al, 1995; Stouthard et al, 1995). More detailed results of these metabolic investigations will be discussed in another section of this chapter. Table 1 gives a hypothetical relation between established clinical features of Gaucher's disease and the involved cytokines.

Table 1. Possible biological effects of cytokines in Gaucher disease.

Established clinical phenomena	Cytokines
Osteopenia	IL-1β, IL-6, TNF-α, M-CSF
Activation of coagulation	IL-1β, IL-6, TNF-α
Hypermetabolism	IL-1β, IL-6, TNF-α
Gammopathies and multiple myeloma	IL-10, IL-6
Hypolipoproteinaemias	M-CSF

Our group studied levels of IL-6, IL-8 and TNF in Gaucher plasma (Hollak et al, 1997c). Again inconsistent results with the other two reports were established. We found that levels of neither IL-6 nor TNF were elevated. The most plausible explanation for the differences in results with respect to the levels of TNF and IL-6 is the interassay variability. Differences in sensitivy, especially when minor elevations are expected, may easily result in inconsistent outcome. We also measured levels of IL-8. Interleukin 8 is a cytokine, produced by monocytes, macrophages, endothelial cells, hepatocytes and other cell-types, which has specific chemotactic and activating effects on neutrophils (Baggiolini et al, 1989). The concentrations of IL-8 were increased to a variable extent, and were especially high in splenectomized patients. The relevance of the elevation of IL-8 in Gaucher's disease remains obscure. The role of this cytokine in chemotactic actions would suggest the presence of increased attraction and activation of leukocytes. Since Aker and others observed that neutrophil chemotaxis is impaired in Gaucher's disease (Aker et al, 1993), it seems that long-term elevation of IL-8 may have a more complicated effect on neutrophil chemotaxis.

Macrophage colony stimulating factor

Macrophage colony stimulating factor (M-CSF, formerly known as CSF-1), which belongs to the group of haematopoietic growth factors, was found to be elevated 2- to 5-fold in plasma of most Type 1 Gaucher's disease patients in our study (Hollak et al, 1997c) M-CSF regulates the growth and differentiation of the monocyte–macrophage lineage from progenitors to mature cells (Stanley and Heard, 1977). Many cell types besides the monocytes and macrophages are capable of producing M-CSF in response to activating agents such as TNF-α, IFN-γ, granulocyte–macrophage (GM)-CSF and other factors (for review see Munn and Cheung, 1992). The cytokine is detectable in several body fluids under steady-state conditions and elevated plasma and/or tissue levels have been reported in different pathological conditions. M-CSF exerts multiple biological effects. It maintains survival of mature macrophages and stimulates several processes that are important for immunological defence mechanisms including the production of pro-inflammatory cytokines. In osteopetrotic mice that lack the production of normal M-CSF, the infusion of the cytokine cured the disease, which implies that M-CSF is involved in the generation of osteo-clasts (Antoniolo Corboz et al, 1992). Also several studies indicate a role for M-CSF in the clearance and metabolism of lipoproteins and cholesterol (Ishibashi et al, 1990). These observations are of interest with respect to Gaucher's disease: M-CSF activities might add to the pathophysiology of osteopenia (Mankin et al, 1990) and increased bone resorption (Harinck et al, 1984) and also to the low levels of lipoproteins.

In addition to cytokines, we found that the plasma of many Gaucher's disease patients contains up to sevenfold increased concentrations of the monocyte/macrophage activation marker soluble CD14 (sCD14). CD14 is a monocyte/macrophage differentiation antigen that is attached to the membrane through a glycosyl-phosphatidylinositol anchor (Haziot et al, 1988). Not very long ago the molecule was found to be the receptor for lipopolysaccharide–lipopolysaccharide · binding proteins (LPS–LBP) complexes and thus may have an important function in activation signalling (Wright et al, 1990). The soluble form of CD14 is shed from activated monocytes and macrophages (Landmann et al, 1992; Schütt et al, 1992) and production of sCD14, or the expression of CD14 on the cell surface and subsequent release from the cell membrane, occurs also upon induction of phagocytosis. Levels of sCD14 are found to be elevated in several disease states such as in sepsis, malignancies and sarcoidosis (Gadducci et al, 1995; Landmann et al, 1995; Striz et al, 1995). The finding of elevated levels of sCD14 in Gaucher's disease supports the idea that activation of macro-phages occurs, although it may also reflect the presence of the enormous mass of macrophages.

The levels of M-CSF and sCD14 relate positively with the severity of the disease as judged by the severity scoring index (SSI) (Zimran et al, 1992) (Figure 2) and may therefore prove to be useful in the monitoring of the disease. In addition, M-CSF and sCD14 levels decrease significantly upon enzyme supplementation therapy, providing an additional response marker.

METABOLIC EFFECTS

Resting energy expenditure (REE)

Increased resting energy expenditure (REE) was first described by Barton and co-workers in 1989 (1989). They found an increase in REE over the predicted value of 44% in 25 Type 1 Gaucher's disease patients, mainly

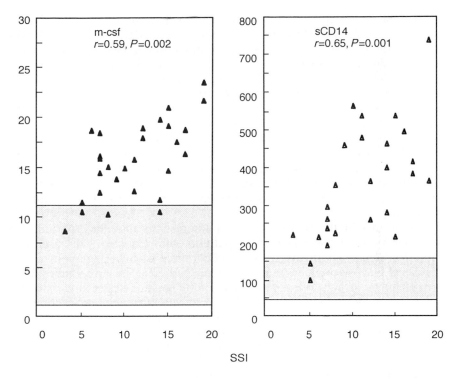

Figure 2. Levels of M-CSF and sCD14 in relation to SSI. ☐ Normal range. From Hollak et al (1997, *Blood, Cells, Molecules and Diseases* **23**: 201–212), with permission.

children. Based upon assessments of liver and spleen volumes and the decrease in REE after splenecomy, they postulated a relation between the increase in energy requirement and Gaucher cell mass.

Our group investigated REE and parameters of glucose metabolism in relation to enzyme therapy (Corssmit et al, 1995; Hollak et al, 1997a). The study was initiated after the observation that most patients, all adults, gained weight during treatment, despite a reduction in organ volumes. REE was measured by indirect calorimetry in 12 adult Type 1 Gaucher's disease patients and in seven healthy matched control subjects before and during enzyme supplementation therapy. Patients were treated according to the protocol used in the Netherlands, which aims to find the lowest effective dose (Hollak et al, 1995). Measurements of liver and spleen volume and body composition were obtained before and after 6 months therapy. In 7 of the 12 patients parameters of glucose metabolism were investigated by primed continuous infusion of [³H]glucose. For comparison, glucose metabolism was studied in seven healthy subjects. There were no statistical significant differences between the patients with Gaucher's disease and the healthy controls with respect to weight, height fat free mass and fat mass. In the patients, the observed REE before treatment was increased by ~29% compared with the predicted REE and by ~25% compared with the controls. After 6 months of therapy, there was a significant increase in weight of 1.7 ± 0.8 kg. Analysis of the body composition revealed that this was mainly because of an increase in fat mass, with a mean of 1.6 ± 1.5 kg. This increase in bodyweight was associated with a decrease of 9% in the observed REE. Glucose production was increased by approximately 30% in patients compared with controls ($P < 0.01$), although plasma glucose concentrations and net glucose oxidation were not different. The differences in basal glucose production were not related to differences in plasma concentrations of insulin or other glucoregulatory hormones. Surprisingly, during 6 months of alglucerase treatment the increased hepatic glucose production and glucose clearance remained unchanged. Liver and spleen volumes decreased by ~10% and ~20% respectively. No correlation between decrease in organ volumes and decrease in REE could be established.

The results of these studies are of interest because they provide an explanation for the weight gain of patients with Gaucher's disease. The precise mechanisms involved in the occurrence of hypermetabolism and increased glucose production are, however, not clear. In vitro studies have provided evidence that glucose production by hepatocytes is modulated by paracrine interaction with liver macrophages through production of adenosine, prostaglandins and cytokines (Casteleijn et al, 1988; Decker, 1985; Kuiper et al, 1989; Decker, 1990). In vivo observations also provide support for the hypothesis that paracrine mechanisms are involved in hepatic glucose production (Corssmit et al, 1993; 1994). We speculate that the activity of macrophages, especially in the liver, is changed in Gaucher's disease, as is discussed in the section on cytokines. This altered paracrine macrophage–hepatocyte interaction may then result in increased glucose production (Corssmit et al, 1995). Consequently, the increase in glucose production might be a reflection of an alteration in the function of the hepatic Gaucher macrophages rather than of an increase in hepatic Gaucher macrophage mass. The fact that enzyme supplementation therapy does not influence the manifestations of Gaucher's disease equally, is again illustrated by the difference in effect of treatment on REE and on glucose production. The lack of correlation between the increase in REE and the organomegaly, together with the relatively time-consuming and burdensome measurement of REE, stresses that regular measurement of REE or parameters of metabolism seem not to be very effective for monitoring the efficacy of enzyme therapy.

PRACTICAL CONSIDERATIONS AND FUTURE RESEARCH

The enormous diversity in plasma abnormalities in Gaucher's disease that may even differ greatly inter-individually, hampers the unequivocal interpretation of these markers in relation to the clinical manifestations. It is, however, useful to formulate some practical considerations with respect to the relevance of the measurement of these factors for diagnostic and therapeutic purposes. First, with the possible exception of chitotriosidase and glucosylceramide levels, neither of the plasma markers is pathognomonic for Gaucher's disease. It should be emphasized that a diagnosis of Gaucher's disease has always to be confirmed by the demonstration of deficient glucocerebrosidase activity or by DNA-analysis. Second, some plasma markers may be useful for the early detection of onset of symptoms and disease progression. Of particular value may be the monitoring of chitotriosidase levels in asymptomatic Gaucher's disease patients: as a direct marker for the presence of Gaucher cells, an increase in chitotriosidase levels may indicate an increase in the number of storage cells, even before clinical progression is apparent. This is particularly relevant since enzyme supplementation therapy is currently no longer exclusively applied for severely affected patients but is now also considered for prophylactic treatment. Thus, chitotriosidase monitoring may contribute in decision making with respect to the initiation of therapy. In the same manner, chitotriosidase levels may be used for the monitoring of the response of the number of storage cells to the therapeutic intervention. In our experience the decrease in chitotriosidase levels in response to treatment is, however, not always clearly related to the extent of improvement in other parameters such as reductions in liver and spleen volumes. Nevertheless it seems logical to be alert for a suboptimal response in those patients that do not show the common therapy induced changes in chitotriosidase. In our view plasma chitotriosidase forms a reflection of the number of mature Gaucher cells. In this respect, the identification of sensitive markers for developing Gaucher cells may have additional value since such factors may serve as more specific markers of disease progression rather than of a mature Gaucher cell mass.

The practical value of regular measurements of other plasma abnormalities in Gaucher patients is presently difficult to assess. Most markers differ greatly, both inter- and intra-individually and the precise relationship with the presence of storage cells is at present unclear. To enhance our insight into the relationship of the plasma markers with Gaucher cells, more specific knowledge as to the source of these factors is needed. In addition, detailed information for the various markers is needed about the factors that determine the steady state plasma levels, such as production and clearance. For example knowledge is needed on the influence of gross splenomegaly and liver dysfunctioning on the clearance of these markers.

Explanations for specific complications of Gaucher's disease may be provided by further insight into the role of the various plasma abnormalities, in particular macrophage derived cytokines. It is very attractive to speculate that the potential influence of enzyme supplementation therapy on the pattern of these biologically active factors may eventually alter the long-term outcome of Gaucher's disease.

REFERENCES

Aerts JMFG, Donker-Koopman WE, Brul S et al (1990). Comparative study on glucocerebrosidase in spleens from patients with Gaucher disease. *Biochemical Journal* **269**: 93–100.

Aker M, Zimran A, Abrahamov A et al (1993) Abnormal neutrophil chemotaxis in Gaucher disease. *British Journal of Haematology* **83:** 187–191.

*Allen MJ, Myer BJ, Khokher AM et al (1997). Pro-inflammatory cytokines and the pathogenesis of Gaucher's disease: increased release of interleukin-6 and interleukin-10. *Quarterly Journal of Medicine* **90:** 19–25.

Antoniolo Corboz V, Cecchini MG, Felix R et al (1992) Effect of macrophage colony-stimulating factor on in vitro osteoclast generation and bone resorption. *Endo* **130:** 437–442.

Baggiolini M, Waltz A & Kunkel SL (1989) Neutrophil activating peptide 1/interleukin 8, a novel cytokine that activates neutrophils. *Journal of Clinical Investigation* **87:** 1045–1049.

Barranger JA & Ginns EI (1989) Gaucher disease. In Scriver CR, Sly WS & Valle D (eds) *The Metabolic Basis of Inherited Disease* pp. 1677–1698. New York: McGraw Hill.

Barton D, Ludman M, Benkov K et al (1989). Resting energy expenditure in Gaucher's disease type 1: Effect of Gaucher cell burden on energy requirements. *Metabolism* **38:** 1238–1243.

Barton NW, Brady RO, Dambrosia JM et al (1991) Replacement therapy for inherited enzyme deficiency—macrophage targeted glucocerebrosidase for Gaucher's disease. *New England Journal of Medicine* **324:** 1464–1470.

Bassan R, Montanelli A & Barbui T (1985) Interaction between a serum factor and T lymphocytes in Gaucher disease. *American Journal of Hematology* **18:** 381–384.

Berrebi A, Malnick SDH, Vorst EJ & Stein, D (1992) High incidence of factor XI deficiency in Gaucher's disease. *American Journal of Hematology* **40:** 153–161.

Beutler E & Grabowski G (1995) Gaucher disease. In Scriver CR, Sly WS & Valle D (eds) *The Metabolic Basis of Inherited Disease* pp. 2641–2670. New York: McGraw-Hill.

Billet HH, Rizvi S & Sawitsky A (1996) Coagulation abnormalities in patients with Gaucher's disease: effect of therapy. *American Journal of Hematology* **51:** 234–236.

Boklan BF & Sawitsky A (1976) Factor IX deficiency in Gaucher disease. *Archives of Internal Medicine* **136:** 489–492.

*Boot RG, Renkema GH, Strijland A et al (1995) Cloning of a cDNA encoding chitotriosidase, a human chitinase produced by macrophages. *Journal of Biological Chemistry* **270:** 26252–26256.

Brady RO, Kanfer JN & Shapiro D (1965) Metabolism of glucocerebrosides. II. Evidence of an enzymatic deficiency in Gaucher's disease. *Biochemical Biophysical Research Communications* **18:** 211–215.

Casteleijn E, Kuiper J, van Rooij H et al (1988) Hormonal control of glycogenolysis in parenchymal liver cells by Kupffer and endothelial liver cells. *Journal of Biological Chemistry* **263:** 2699–2703.

Chamberlain P, Compston J, Cox TM et al (1995) Generation and characterization of monoclonal antibodies to human type-5 tartrate-resistant acid phosphatase: development of a specific immunoassay of the isoenzyme in serum. *Clinical Chemistry* **41:** 1495–1499.

Chambers JB, Aquino L, Glew RH et al (1977) Determination of serum acid phosphatase in Gaucher's disease using 4-methylumbelliferyl phosphate. *Clinica Chimica Acta* **80:** 67–77.

Chitayat DJ, Nakagawa S, Marion RW et al (1987) Elevation of serum beta-hexosaminidase and alfa-D-mannosidase in Type 2 Gaucher disease: a clinical and biochemical study. *Inherited Metabolic Diseases* **10:** 111–114.

Corssmit E, Romijn J, Endert E et al (1993) Indomethacin stimulates basal glucose production in humans without changes in concentrations of glucoregulatory hormones. *Clinical Science* **85:** 679–685.

Corssmit E, Romijn J, Endert E et al (1994) Pentoxifylline inhibits basal glucose production in humans. *Journal of Applied Physiology* **77:** 2767–2772.

Corssmit E, Hollak C, Endert E et al (1995) Increased basal glucose production in type 1 Gaucher disease. *Journal of Clinical Endocrinology and Metabolism* **80:** 2653–2657.

Dawson G, Kwok BCP, Nishigaki M & Shen BW (1982) Role of serum lipoproteins in the pathogenesis of Gaucher disease. In Desnick RJ, Gatt S & Grabowski GA (eds) *Gaucher Disease: a Century of Deliniation and Research* New York: Alan R Liss.

Decker K (1985) Eicosanoids, signal molecules of liver cells. *Seminars of Liver Diseases* **5:** 175–190.

Decker K (1990) Biologically active products of stimulated liver macrophages (Kupffer cells). *European Journal of Biochemistry* **192:** 245–261.

Erikson A, Johansson K, Mansson JE & Svennerholm L (1993) Enzyme replacement therapy of infantile Gaucher disease. *Neuropediatrics* **24:** 237–238.

Erikson E, Astrom M & Mansson J (1995) Enzyme infusion therapy of the Norrbottnian type (type 3) Gaucher disease. *Neuropediatrics* **26:** 203–207.

Fox H, McCarthy P, Andre-Schwartz J et al (1984) Gaucher's disease and chronic lymphocytic leukemia. Possible pathogenetic link between Gaucher's disease and B-cell proliferations? *Cancer* **54:** 312–314.

Freedman S & Puliafito C (1988) Peripheral retinal vascular lesions in a patient with Gaucher disease and factor XI deficiency. *Archives of Ophthalmology* 1351–1352.

Gadducci A, Ferdeghini M, Castellani C et al (1995) Serum levels of tumor necrosis factor (TNF), soluble receptors for TNF (55- and 75-kDa sTNFr) and soluble CD14 (sCD14) in epithelial ovarian cancer. *Gynaecological Oncology* **58:** 184–188.

Garfinkel D, Sidi Y, Ben-Bassat M et al (1982) Coexistence of Gaucher's disease and multiple myeloma. *Archives of Internal Medicine* **142:** 2229–2230.

Gery I, Zigler JSJ, Brady RO & Barranger JA (1981) Selective effects of glucocerebroside (Gaucher's storage material) on macrophage cultures. *Journal of Clinical Investigation* **68:** 1182–1189.

Gilbert HS & Weinreb N (1976) Increased circulating levels of transcobalamin ii in Gaucher's disease. *New England Journal of Medicine* **295:** 1096–1101.

Ginsberg H, Grabowski GA, Gibson JC et al (1984) Reduced plasma concentrations of total, low density and high density lipoprotein cholesterol in patients with Gaucher type 1 disease. *Clinical Genetics*, **26:** 109–116.

Guo Y, He W, Boer AM et al (1995) Elevated plasma chitotriosidase activity in various lysosomal disorders. *Journal of Inherited Metabolic Diseases* **18:** 717–722.

Hanash SM, Rucknagel DL, Heidelberger KP & Radin NS (1978) Primary amyloidosis associated with Gaucher's disease. *Annals of Internal Medicine* **89:** 639–641.

Harinck HI, Bijvoet OL, van der Meer JW et al (1984) Regression of bone lesions in Gaucher's disease during treatment with aminohydroxypropylidene bisphosphonate (letter). *Lancet* **2:** 513.

Haziot A, Chen S, Ferrero A et al (1988) The monocyte differentiation antigen, CD14, is anchored to the cell membrane by a phosphatidylinositol linkage. *Journal of Immunology* **141:** 547–552.

*Hollak CEM, van Weely S, van Oers MHJ & Aerts JMFG (1994) Marked elevation of plasma chitotriosidase activity. A novel hallmark of Gaucher disease. *Journal of Clinical Investigation* **93:** 1288–1292.

Hollak CEM, Aerts JMFG, Goudsmit R et al (1995) Individualized low dose alglucerase therapy for type 1 Gaucher disease. *Lancet* **345:** 1474–1478.

*Hollak C, Corssmit E, Aerts JMFG et al (1997a) Differential effects of enzyme supplementation therapy on manifestations of type 1 Gaucher disease. *American Journal of Medicine* (in press).

Hollak CEM, Levi M, Berends F et al (1997b) Coagulation abnormalities in type I Gaucher disease are due to low grade activation and can be partly restored by enzyme supplementation therapy. *British Journal of Haematology* **96:** 470–476.

Hollak CEM, Evers L, Aerts JMFG & van Oers MHJ (1997c) Elevated level of M-CSF, sCD14 and IL8 in type 1 Gaucher disease. *Blood Cells, Molecules and Diseases* **23:** 201–212.

Hrebicek M, Zeman J, Musilova J et al (1996) A case of type 1 Gaucher disease with cardiopulmonary amyloidosis and chitotriosidase deficiency. *Virchows Archives* **429:** 305–309.

Hultberg B, Isaksson A, Sjöblad S & Ockerman PA (1980) Acid hydrolases in serum from patients with lysosomal disorders. *Clinica Chimica Acta* **100:** 33–38.

Ishibashi S, Inaba T, Shimano H & et al (1990) Monocyte colony stimulating factor enhances uptake and degradation of acetylated low density lipoproteins and cholesterol esterification in human monocyte derived macrophages. *Journal of Biological Chemistry* **265:** 14 109–14 117.

Kuiper J, Zijlstra FJ, Kamps JAAM et al (1989) Cellular communication inside the liver. Binding, conversion and metabolic effect of prostaglandin D2 on parenchymal liver cells. *Biochemical Journal* **262:** 195–201.

Lam KW & Desnick RJ (1982) Biochemical properties of the tartrate-resistant acid phosphatase activity in Gaucher disease. In Desnick RJ, Gatt S & Grabowski GA (eds) *Gaucher Disease: a Century of Deliniation and Research*, pp. 267–278. New York: Alan R Liss.

Landmann R, Fisscher AE & Obrecht J-P (1992) Interferon-gamma and interleukin-4 downregulate soluble CD 14 release in human monocytes and macrophages. *Journal of Leukocyte Biology* **52:** 323–330.

Landmann R, Zimmerli W, Sansano S et al (1995) Increased circulating soluble CD14 is associated with high mortality in Gram-negative septic shock. *Journal of Infectious Diseases* **171:** 639–644.

Le NA, Gibson JC, Rubinstein A et al (1988) Abnormalities in lipoprotein metabolism in Gaucher Type 1 disease. *Metabolism* **37:** 240–245.

Lee RE (1996) Necrotic lesions in Gaucher disease: a perspective in the era of enzyme therapy. *Gaucher Clinical Perspectives* **4:** 5–10.

*Lieberman J & Beutler E (1976) Elevation of serum angiotensin-converting enzyme in Gaucher's disease. *New England Journal of Medicine* **294:** 1442–1444.

Lord DK, Cross NC, Bevilacqua MA et al (1990) Type 5 acid phosphatase. Sequence, expression and chromosomal localization of a differentiation-associated protein of the human macrophage. *European Journal of Biochemistry* **189:** 287–293.

Magelhaes J, Pinto R, Lemos M et al (1984) Age dependency of serum acid phosphatase in controls and Gaucher patients. *Enzyme* **32:** 95–99.

Mahley R (1988) Apolipoprotein E: cholesterol transport protein with expanding role in cell biology. *Science* **240:** 622–630.

Mankin HJ, Doppelt SH, Rosenberg AE & Barranger JA (1990). Metabolic bone disease in patients with Gaucher's disease. *Metabolic Bone Disease and Clinically Related Disorders*. Philadelphia: WB Saunders.

Manolagas SC & Jilka RL (1995) Bonemarrow, cytokines and bone remodelling emerging insights into the pathophysiology of osteoporosis. *New England Journal of Medicine* **332:** 305–311.

*Michelakakis H, Spanou C, Kondyli A et al (1996) Plasma tumor necrosis factor (TNF-α) levels in Gaucher disease. *Biochemica et Biophysica Acta* **1317:** 219–222.

Moffit KD, Chambers JP, Diven WF et al (1978) Characterization of lysosomal hydrolases that are elevated in Gaucher's disease. *Archives of Biochemistry and Biophysics* **190:** 247–260.

Munn DH & Cheung NV (1992) Preclinical and clinical studies of macrophage colony-stimulating factor. *Seminars in Oncology* **19:** 395–407.

Natowicz MR, Prence EM & Cajolet A (1992) Marked variation in blood beta-hexosaminidase in Gaucher disease. *Clinica Chimica Acta* **203:** 17–22.

Niederau C, Birkhahn A, Ehlen C & Haussinger D (1996) Facts and fiction of modern diagnosis of type 1 Gaucher disease. The German experience in 1996. *Gaucher Clinical Perspectives* **2:** 5–14.

Nilsson O, Månsson JE, Håkansson G & Svennerholm L (1982) The occurrence of psychosine and other glycolipids in spleen and liver from the three major subtypes of Gaucher's disease. *Biochimica et Biophysica Acta* **712:** 453–463.

van Oers MHJ, van Zaanen HC & Lokhorst HM (1993) Interleukin-6, a new target for therapy in multiple myeloma? *Annals of Hematology* **66:** 219–223.

Patrick AD (1965) Short communications: A deficiency of glucocerebrosidase in Gaucher's disease. *Biochemical Journal* **97:** 17C–18C.

Pentchev PG, Gal AE, Wong R et al (1981) Biliary excretion of glycolipid in induced or inherited glucosylceramide lipidosis. *Biochimica et Biophysica Acta* **665:** 615–618.

van der Poll T, Romijn JA, Endert E et al (1991) Tumor necrosis factor mimics the metabolic response to acute infection. *American Journal of Physiology* **261:** E457–E465.

Pratt PW, Estern S & Kochwa J (1968) Immunoglobulin abnormalities in Gaucher's disease: report of 16 cases. *Blood* **31:** 633–640.

*Renkema GH, Boot RG, Muijsers A et al (1995) Purification and characterization of human chitotriosidase, a novel member of the chitinase family of proteins. *Journal of Biological Chemistry* **270:** 2198–2202.

*Renkema GH, Boot RG, Strijland A et al (1997) Synthesis, sorting and processing into distinct isoforms of human macrophage chitotriosidase. *European Journal of Biochemistry* **244:** 279–285.

Rosenthal RL (1982) Serum acid phosphatase in Gaucher disease before and after splenectomy. In Desnick RJ, Gatt S & Grabowski GA (eds) *Gaucher Disease: a Century of Deliniation and Research*, pp. 279–284. New York: Alan R. Liss.

Rutherford MS, Witsell A & Schook LB (1993) Mechanisms generating functionally heterogeneous macrophages: chaos revisited. *Journal of Leukocyte Biology* **53:** 602–618.

Schindelmeiser J, Radzun HJ & Munstermann D et al (1991) Tartrate resistant purple acid phosphatase in Gaucher cells of the spleen. Immuno- and cytochemical analysis. *Pathology, Research and Practice* **187:** 209–213.

Schütt C, Schilling T, Grunwald U et al (1992) Endotoxin-neutralizing capacity of soluble CD14. *Research in Immunology* **143:** 71–78.

Seligsohn U, Zitman D, Many A & Klibansky C (1976) Coexistence of factor XI (plasma thrombo-plastin antecedent) deficiency and Gaucher's disease. *Israel Journal of Medical Science* **12:** 1448–1452.

Silverstein E & Friedland J (1977) Elevated serum and spleen angiotensin converting enzyme and serum lysozyme in Gaucher's disease. *Clinica Chimica Acta* **74:** 21–25.

Silverstein E, Pertschuk LP & Friedland J (1980) Immunofluorescent detection of angiotensin-converting enzyme (ACE) in Gaucher cells. *American Journal of Medicine* **69:** 408–410.

Stanley ER & Heard PM (1977) Factors regulating macrophage production and growth. Purification and some properties of the colony stimulating factor from medium conditioned by mouse L-cells. *Journal of Biological Chemistry* **252:** 4305–4312.

Stouthard J, Romijn J, van der Poll T et al (1995) Endocrinologic and metabolic effects of interleukin-6. *American Journal of Physiology* **268:** 813–819.

Strasberg PM, Warren I, Skomorowski MA & Lowden JA (1983) HPLC analysis of neutral glycolipids: an aid in the diagnosis of lysosomal storage disease. *Clinica Chimica Acta* **132:** 29–41.

Striz I, Zheng L, Wang YM et al (1995) Soluble CD14 is increased in bronchoalveolar lavage of active sarcoidosis and correlates with alveolar macrophage membrane-bound CD14. *American Journal of Respiratory and Critical Care Medicine* **151:** 544–547.

*Suzuki K (1982) Glucosylceramide and related compounds in normal tissues and in Gaucher disease. In Desnick RJ, Gatt S & Grabowski GA (eds) *Gaucher Disease: a Century of Deliniation and Research*, pp. 219–230. New York: Alan R Liss.

Svennerholm L, Håkansson G, Månsson JE & Nilsson O (1982) Chemical differentiation of the Gaucher subtypes. In Desnick RJ, Gatt S & Grabowski GA (eds) *Gaucher Disease: a Century of Delineation and Research*, pp. 231–252. New York: Alan R Liss.

Den Tandt WR & van Hoof F (1996) Plasma methylumbelliferyl-tetra-N-acetyl-β-D-chitotetraoside hydrolase as a parameter during treatment of Gaucher patients. *Biochemistry and Molecular Medicine* **57:** 71–72.

Den Tandt WR, Inaba T, Verhamme I et al (1988) Non-identity of human plasma lysozyme and 4-methylumbelliferyl-tetra-N-acetyl-beta-D-chitotetraoside hydrolase. *International Journal of Biochemistry* **20:** 713–719.

Tokoro T, Gal AE, Gallo LL & Brady RO (1987) Studies on the pathogenesis of Gaucher's disease: Tissue distribution and biliary excretion of (^{14}C)L-glucosylceramide in rats. *Journal of Lipid Research* **28:** 968–972.

*Tuchman LR, Goldstein G & Clyman M (1959) Studies on the nature of the increased acid phosphatase in Gaucher's disease. *American Journal of Medicine* **27:** 959–962.

Ullman MD & McCluer RH (1977) Quantitative analysis of plasma neutral glycosphingolipids by high performance liquid chromatography of their perbenzoyl derivatives. *Journal of Lipid Research* **18:** 371–378.

Vreeken J, Meinders AE, Keeman N & Feltkamp TEW (1967) A chronic clotting defect with some characteristics of excessive intravascular coagulation in a patient with Gaucher's disease. *Folia Medica Neerlandica* **10:** 180–185.

Wright SD, Ramos RA, Tobias PS et al (1990) CD14, a receptor for complexes of lipopolysaccharide (LPS) and LPS binding protein. *Science* **249:** 1431–1433.

Young E, Chatterton A, Vellodi A & Winchester B (1997) Plasma chitotriosidase activity in Gaucher disease patients who have been treated either by bone marrow transplantation or enzyme replacement therapy with alglucerase. In *Second EWGGD Workshop* p. 88: Maastricht.

Zimran A, Kay A, Gelbart T et al (1992) Clinical, laboratory radiologic and genetic features of 53 patients. *Medicine* **71:** 337–353.

5

Neuronopathic forms of Gaucher's disease

ANDERS ERIKSON MD, PhD

Associate Professor
Department of Paediatrics, University of Umeå, S-901 85 Umeå, Sweden

BRUNO BEMBI MD

Director of the Centre for Diagnosis and Treatment of Gaucher Disease and Congenital Diseases of Metabolism
Genetica Medica, Istituto di Ricovero e Cura a Carattere Scientifico 'Burlo Garofolo', Via dell'Istria 65/1, 34137 Trieste, Italy

RAPHAEL SCHIFFMANN MD

Chief, Clinical Investigation Section, Developmental and Metabolic Neurology Branch, National Institute of Neurological Disorders and Stroke
National Institutes of Health, Bldg. 10, Rm 3D03, 10 Center Drive, Bethesda, MD, 20892-1260, USA

Neuronopathic Gaucher patients may have a wide variety of clinical manifestations and natural history, and can present with a range of degrees of severity of systemic disease and neurological deficit. The brain pathology of these patients has been well described, but the mechanism by which glucocerebrosidase deficiency leads to neuronal dysfunction is not yet understood. The almost 20 different mutations of the glucocerebrosidase gene that have been described in Type 2 and 3 Gaucher patients poorly predict the phenotype of individual patients. Enzyme replacement therapy (ERT), often at high doses, has been shown to reverse most of the systemic manifestations of this disease, but can rarely reverse the neurological deficits. Therefore, other forms of treatment, such as gene therapy or a more efficient and direct enzyme delivery to neurons, are being devised.

Key words: brain; child; glucosylceramidase; administration; glucosyceramide; enzymes; therapeutic use; treatment outcome; Gaucher's disease; therapy; mutation; bone marrow transplantation.

Patients with Gaucher's disease (GD) and neurological signs have been reported since the early 1920s (Rusca, 1921). Subsequently, most reported patients were infants rather than older children or adults with neurological signs. Since then, three phenotypes of GD have been delineated (Knudson and Kaplan, 1962): chronic, infantile cerebral, and juvenile and adult cerebral GD. This classification is still used, but is frequently designated as Type 1 or non-neuronopathic, Type 2 or acute neuronopathic and Type 3 or chronic neuronopathic, respectively. Initially, the only large group of Type

Copyright © 1997, by Baillière Tindall
All rights of reproduction in any form reserved

3 patients was reported from northern Sweden (Hillborg, 1959; Frederickson and Sloan, 1972).

CLINICAL MANIFESTATIONS

Type 2 (acute neuronopathic)

Type 2 Gaucher's disease, a rare form with no ethnic predilection, is an acute neuronopathic form of the illness presenting during infancy. There is some heterogeneity in this group of patients but not as much as in GD Type 3. In addition to typical systemic signs of GD, a characteristic neurological syndrome develops that includes dysphagia, persistent head hyper-extension, paralytic strabismus because of abducens nerve paresis, trismus, generalized spasticity and psychomotor regression. Laryngospasm and apneic spells often occur in the later stages of the disease. Some patients develop myoclonus and generalized tonic-clonic seizures. Death usually occurs by 2 years of age as a result of progressive brainstem dysfunction. Some patients have a later onset and slower disease course but with the same symptoms and outcome (Kyllerman et al, 1990; Beutler and Grabowski, 1995; Brady, 1996). A very rare and severe form exists that can be called congenital GD, and is characterized by skin abnormalities and hydrops fetalis at birth, with death rapidly ensuing. These symptoms are similar to those occurring in the knock-out Gaucher mouse with null mutation (Sidransky et al, 1992).

Type 3 (subacute or chronic neuronopathic)

Type 3 Gaucher's disease is a chronically progressive neuronopathic form of the illness that presents during infancy, childhood, adolescence or adulthood. The clinical features of this phenotype are more variable than those observed in Type 2 Gaucher's disease. At least four subtypes are distinguishable on clinical grounds; the most thoroughly characterized group of patients presents with progressive myoclonic epilepsy in con-junction with a horizontal supranuclear gaze palsy. Dementia, ataxia and spasticity develop as the illness progresses over several years. Systemic signs of GD tend to be mild with death occurring as a result of progressive neurological deterioration (Winkelman et al, 1983). Initially, somato-sensory evoked potentials in these patients show giant cortical potentials (Figure 1) that reflect decreased inhibitory input in the cerebral cortex. Subsequently, the EEG becomes frankly epileptogenic.

The Norrbottnian isolate in Northern Sweden represents another carefully studied group of patients with Type 3 Gaucher's disease. Presentation typically occurs in childhood with aggressive systemic disease and a slowly progressive heterogeneous neurological syndrome. Most common is horizontal supranuclear gaze palsy and a slowly increasing dementia. Other manifestations include convergent squint due to abducens nerve palsy, retinal infiltrates, ataxia, mild spasticity in the legs and epilepsy (myoclonic

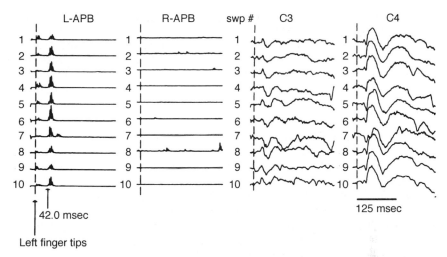

Figure 1. Somatosensory evoked potential in a Gaucher patient with clinical myoclonus. Repetitive finger taps to the left hand. Giant evoked potential is recorded over the right hemisphere after each stimulation. Electromyographic recording registered a myoclonic muscle contraction that was time-locked to the stimulus and to the giant cortical evoked potential (courtesy of Dr Camilo Toro). APB: abductor pollicis brevis; swp: sweep.

or complex partial seizures). Ataxia and spasticity were seen in the Norrbottnian patients as late signs only, developing several years after splenectomy (Dreborg et al, 1980; Erikson, 1986). Some patients have an early onset of symptoms followed by a rapid course and death by the age of 2–3 years. Other patients have a much slower course and live into their 40's. A representative untreated group succumbed at a median age of 12 years.

In our experience, the most common subtype of Type 3 Gaucher's disease is characterized by the following (Patterson et al, 1993): (i) presentation in infancy or childhood with aggressive systemic disease leading to death in adolescence from complications of portal or pulmonary hypertension; (ii) early development of horizontal supranuclear gaze palsy as the major neurological sign of the illness; and (iii) infrequent seizures, usually as agonal events. Detailed neurological evaluation of our case material (Patterson et al, 1993) revealed a variable combination of EEG abnormalities, abnormal brainstem auditory evoked potentials and mild cognitive impairment. Prior to the development of ERT, clear progression of the neurological syndrome could not be demonstrated because patients succumbed to systemic disease. The estimated incidence is less than 1 case per 100 000 people in the general population. Recently, patients presenting with mild systemic disease and horizontal supranuclear gaze palsy as the only neurological manifestation have been described (Abrahamov et al, 1995; Chabas et al, 1995). This phenotype is specifically associated with homozygosity for a rare point mutation, D409H (Pasmanik-Chor et al, 1996).

Although the separation of GD patients into Type 2 and 3 is still useful, it has been increasingly clear that the phenotypes of neuronopathic Gaucher represent a continuum from the most severe congenital Gaucher's disease to the mildest form of chronic neuronopathic Type 3 patients with very mild horizontal supranuclear gaze palsy. We have observed Gaucher patients with Type 2 features able to walk and live well beyond the expected life-span. In addition, there are patients with severe systemic disease with isolated supranuclear gaze palsy who developed progressive myoclonic encephalopathy (Schiffmann et al, 1997). Although it has been thought that the genotype of these patients plays an important role in determining the natural history of the brain involvement (Beutler, 1995a; Mistry, 1995), the extent and mechanism by which a defined genotype leads to a particular phenotype is not known.

Recently, a number of GD patients with parkinsonism or early onset Parkinson's disease that is poorly responsive to L-dopa treatment were described (Neudorder et al, 1996). However, no brain pathology of such patients is available, and it is not known whether there is a causal relationship between the glucocerebrosidase deficiency and the parkinsonism.

GENOTYPES THAT CAN LEAD TO NEURONOPATHIC FORMS

Mutations leading to neuronopathic Gaucher's disease (Beutler, 1995b; Choy and Wei, 1995; Seeman et al, 1996; Tayebi et al, 1996) are described in Table 1. As a general rule, these mutations lead to a residual enzyme activity that is below 15% of normal. However, the genotype of a particular patient is not a useful predictor of the extent of neurological involvement. It is likely that modifiers such as other unknown mutations of the gluco-cerebrosidase gene, other genes and the environment contribute to the phenotype. The pathogenesis of neuronal dysfunction in GD is not under-stood.

Table 1. Mutations of the GD gene leading to neuronopathic phenotype.

	Base substitution in cDNA (from 5′ ATG)	Amino acid mature protein	Phenotype
1	T1448C	L444P	3, 2, 1 Most common in the Norrbottnian type, present in all ethnic groups
2	A586C	K157Q	2
3	C1361G	P415R	2
4	G1312A	D399N	2
5	T1141G	C342G	2
6	G1090A	G325R	2
7	C1192T	R359Stop	2, 1
8	C649T	P178S	2
9	T754A	F213I	3
10	G1297T	V394L	3, 1
11	G1342C	D409H	3, 1
12	A1343T	P415R	3
13	A1390G	K425E	3
14	C1504T	R463C	3
15	G1505A	IVS463, R→H	3

NEUROPATHOLOGY

Microscopic abnormalities are found in the brain of both Type 2 and 3 patients (Conradi et al, 1984; Kaye et al, 1986). The most striking feature is the perivascular accumulation of Gaucher cells in the Virchow–Robin spaces (Figure 2A). This accumulation is also seen in Type 1 patients, but to a lesser extent. The brain parenchyma surrounding these Gaucher cell infiltrates shows astrogliosis and local neuronal loss. This loss is wide-spread in the brain of Type 2 patients especially in the basal ganglia, nuclei of the midbrain, pons and medulla oblongata. In the cerebral cortex of Type 2 patients with Gaucher cell infiltration, gliosis and neuronal loss of the third and fifth cortical layers have been found at autopsy and brain biopsy. Free Gaucher cells have been found in the cortex; in a Swedish Type 2 patient with late onset, there was a continuous band of Gaucher cells in the occipital and temporolateral cortices corresponding to the fourth cortical layer (Conradi et al, 1991) (Figure 2B). In Type 3 patients, there were few changes other than perivascular infiltrations. In a Swedish study of four Type 3 patients, a collagen and reticulum membrane was found between the Gaucher cell infiltrations and astrogliosis in the brain. Focal loss of neurons and minor loss of axons were also apparent (Conradi et al, 1988).

NEUROCHEMISTRY

In a group of Type 3 patients, glucosylceramide level in the cerebral cortex was 10-fold higher than the levels of controls in both splenectomized and non-splenectomized patients. In the cerebellum and cerebral subcortical white matter, the level was elevated but similar to non-splenectomized patients, while it was higher in those who had been splenectomized. There seemed to be a positive correlation between the lifespan post-splenectomy and the level of stored glucocerebroside (Conradi et al, 1984).

The fatty acid composition of glucosylceramide identifies its origin. In cerebral gray matter from Type 2 patients, it appeared to be of cerebral origin. In the white matter of Type 3 patients, there are indications that the glucocerebroside has its origin in the peripheral circulation (Erikson, 1986). The cytotoxic compound glucosylsphingosine has been found within the cerebral and cerebellar cortex of Type 2 and 3 patients. The level was highest in Type 2 patients (Nilsson and Svennerholm, 1982). The residual glucocerebrosidase activity in the same areas was lower in Type 2 than in Type 3 patients.

PATHOGENESIS OF NEURONAL DYSFUNCTION IN GAUCHER'S DISEASE

The mechanism by which the glucocerebrosidase deficiency in some GD patients leads to neurological disease is not understood. The presence of cerebral perivascular Gaucher cells and gliosis as the only pathological

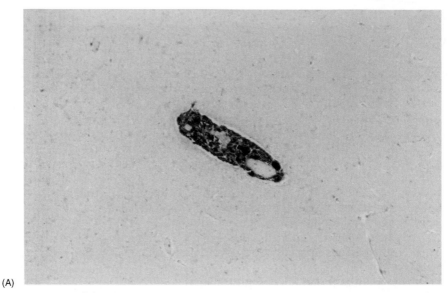

(A)

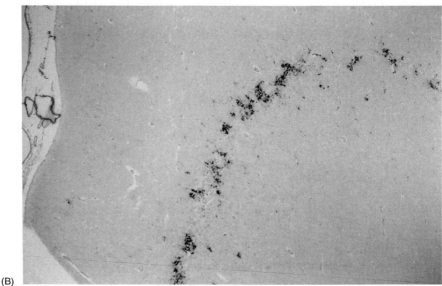

(B)

Figure 2. Brain of a Gaucher Type 2 patient stained with anti-macrophage antibody Kp-1 by an immunoperoxidase method. (A) Perivascular staining representing Gaucher cells (×40). (B) Selective Gaucher cells infiltrates in layer IV of cortex; magnification ×20 (courtesy of Dr David Katz).

abnormality in some brains of Type 3 patients led to the hypothesis that toxic metabolic factors extrinsic to the neuron induce neuronal dysfunction. Although these changes can also be seen in Type 1 Gaucher patients (Soffer et al, 1980), intraparenchymal accumulation of Gaucher cells in lamina IV with accompanying gliosis has been described only in patients with neuronopathic GD. Indirect supporting evidence is the fact that in Norrbottnian Type 3 patients, the storage material seemed to increase in splenectomized patients and was associated with a more rapid progression of dementia in these patients. Ataxia and spasticity appeared several years after splenectomy only (Erikson, 1986). However, it is probable that the enzyme deficiency in neurons plays a major role in neuronal dysfunction. Selective vulnerability of certain inhibitory neurons may contribute to the myoclonic encephalopathy. Toxic damage by glucosylsphingosine has been implicated in causing brain pathology and neurological symptoms (Nilsson and Svennerholm, 1982). The possible role of glucosylsphingosine in brain dysfunction is suggested by the fact that its levels are higher in Type 2 than in Type 3 brains. Interestingly, in three patients with Type 3 Gaucher's disease, there were no increased spinal fluid glucosylsphingosine levels (Schiffmann et al, 1997).

TREATMENT

Splenectomy

Splenectomy has long been the treatment of choice to avoid severe hypersplenism or to relieve compression of neighbouring organs. The question whether splenectomy does or does not have an overall positive impact on the course of the disease has been a matter of debate through the years (Shiloni et al, 1983; Ashkenazi et al, 1986; Zimran et al, 1995). In the Norrbottnian group of patients, ataxia and spasticity and intellectual regression were only seen among splenectomized patients (Erikson, 1986). However, since the need for splenectomy in these patients may simply reflect a more severe phenotype, the role of splenectomy in the pathogenesis of brain involvement in GD remains unclear.

Partial splenectomy may decrease the risk of severe bacterial infections. However, it requires a greater surgical expertise and may not prevent subsequent bone complications (Zimran et al, 1995). At present, splenectomy is indicated only as an adjunct to ERT, in patients in whom the enlarged spleen causes a compression syndrome or severe hypersplenism and who do not respond to high doses of ERT.

Bone marrow transplantation

Children with Gaucher's disease Type 3 have been treated with allogenic bone marrow transplantation (Hobbs et al, 1987; Ringden et al, 1995). The haematological and visceral results were excellent, e.g. the children's body growth normalized and their general well-being improved. Additionally, no further neurological or mental deterioration were noticed in these Norrbottnian patients. However, this group of patients is relatively small and definite conclusions concerning neurological effect cannot be made. Furthermore, the significant morbidity and mortality of bone marrow transplantation limits its use. The effect of bone marrow transplantation on patients with progressive myoclonic epilepsy is not known. Bone marrow transplantation in Type 2 patients has not, to our knowledge, been attempted.

Enzyme replacement therapy

Type 3 Gaucher patients

Intravenous infusion of macrophage-targeted glucocerebrosidase of human placental or of recombinant origin has become the standard treatment for moderate-to-severe Type 1 Gaucher's disease (Barton et al, 1991). This treatment reverses the haematological abnormalities, decreases liver and spleen size as well as the skeletal involvement, especially in children. There is still no consensus concerning dosage and dose intervals.

Most of the Type 3 Gaucher patients who were treated with ERT had severe systemic involvement without progressive myoclonic epilepsy. All treated patients had beneficial systemic responses identical to similarly affected non-neuronopathic Gaucher patients. In the Norrbottnian Type 3 Gaucher patient population, similar results were obtained (Erikson et al, 1995). The children in this series were initially treated with enzyme dosage ranging from 200 to 250 U/kg per 4 weeks given as biweekly infusions. Subsequent dose reduction was monitored by levels of circulating glucosylceramide (plasma and red blood cells) and chitotriosidase, a macrophage enzyme whose activity is greatly elevated in the plasma of GD patients (Hollak et al, 1994). Follow-up of these patients is presently 3–5 years. So far, there has been no further neurological deterioration. In fact, their IQ test scores have somewhat improved. The ataxia in four adult patients decreased with treatment. However, the follow-up is still too short to draw conclusions to determine if the treatment can prevent or even reverse the neurological impairment of patients in this Swedish isolate. The increased IQ scores might have been secondary to the patients' improved well-being.

Bembi and his collaborators (Bembi et al, 1994; Carrozzi et al, 1995), treated three Type 3 patients with severe systemic involvement; the age range at onset was 1.3 to 8.5 years. These patients received enzyme doses of 30 to 120 U/kg per 4 weeks, given every 1 or 2 weeks for 6 years. The neurological responses in this group of patients was variable. One patient developed myoclonic epilepsy on treatment, another developed an epileptogenic EEG, and a third remained stable. IQ scores paralleled the neurological course.

At the National Institutes of Health in Bethesda, Maryland, 12 patients with similar phenotype received ERT for 2 to 6 years. Most patients were homozygous for the L444P mutation. Treatment started at ages ranging from 6 months to 8.5 years at a dosage of 120–480 U/kg per 4 weeks. All but one patient responded systemically to the treatment. Liver and spleen volumes were followed using magnetic resonance imaging (MRI) (Erikson et al, 1995). Liver volume decreased by 42 to 60%, and spleen volume decreased by 35 to 82%. Four patients underwent a partial splenectomy before the start of ERT. Two patients developed radiological evidence of interstitial lung disease during treatment, but remained without overt respiratory symptoms. All but two patients had enlarged axillary and hilar lymph nodes at treatment onset. There was no appreciable decrease in the size of these nodes in any of these patients. Neurological responses were not uniform. Two patients deteriorated neurologically under treatment. One patient developed progressive myoclonic encephalopathy 1.5 years after onset of treatment, and the other patient developed a paralytic strabismus and an abnormal EEG after 2 years of treatment. Both patients had one or two alleles with an unknown mutation of the glucocerebrosidase gene. The other patients remained stable including one patient who showed improved saccadic eye movements after 6 years of treatment. Sequential cerebrospinal fluid (CSF) samples obtained during the first 3 years of treatment in three patients were analysed for biochemical markers of disease burden (Schiffmann et al, 1997). Glucocerebrosidase delivery to the spinal fluid compartment was minimal and was significant only with an infusion of 120 U/kg of body weight of Ceredase®. No elevation of glycosyl-sphingosine, interleukin-1, transforming growth factor-β1, nitrites and interleukin-1 receptor antagonist in CSF was found. However, elevated chitotriosidase and quinolinic acid were found in two of the three patients. A progressive decrease in chitotriosidase and quinolinic acid CSF levels was observed in those patients with ERT; such a decrease in the CSF levels of these two macrophage markers during the 3 years of treatment implies a decreased number of Gaucher cells in the cerebral perivascular space. Similar changes were not observed in the patient who had a poor neurological outcome. These results were further supported by the finding that quinolinic acid levels and the number of perivascular Gaucher cells were decreased in the brains of treated Type 2 and 3 GD patients compared with the brain of an untreated Type 2 patient (Schiffmann et al, 1997). Glucocerebroside was not found to be elevated in any of the CSF samples from these patients. From this collective experience, it is clear that Type 3 patients with early disease onset and with greatly enlarged spleens require high doses of enzyme to effectively reverse the systemic manifestation of the disease. This reflects a relatively severe glucocerebrosidase deficiency and rapidity of glucocerebroside accumulation. Patients with progressive myoclonic epilepsy who have mild-to-moderate systemic involvement were treated by several investigators (Bembi et al, 1994) at doses ranging from 30 to 120 U/kg per 4 weeks. Although their anaemia and organomegaly reversed with treatment, myoclonic epilepsy continued to progress.

In summary, ERT is very effective in reversing most of the systemic manifestations of patients with Type 3 Gaucher's disease. It prolongs their lifespan (Patterson et al, 1993) and increases its quality (Verderese et al, 1993). However, the enzyme apparently does not effectively penetrate the lymphatic and pulmonary tissue of these patients, and the long-term consequences of this limitation remain to be established. Although there is evidence that in some patients the number of cerebral perivascular Gaucher cells decreases with treatment, the net effect of ERT on neurological disease progression requires more extensive follow-up. It is possible that some aspects of brain involvement such as tremor and supranuclear gaze palsy can be ameliorated or prevented by ERT. Other complications such as progressive myoclonic encephalopathy seem to be refractory to ERT.

Type 2 Gaucher's disease

Several patients with Gaucher Type 2 disease received ERT. Intravenous enzyme infusions partially reversed the anaemia and organomegaly in these patients, but did not reverse the pulmonary involvement (Bove et al, 1995). It is possible that ERT prolonged the lives of individual patients, but it does not alter the ultimate dismal neurological outcome. Type 2 Gaucher patients receiving ERT and maximum supporting therapy can live past the age of 5 years. In addition, patients who undergo placement of a tracheostomy tube tend to live longer, and this represents a confounding factor. Therefore, ERT is currently not recommended for this form of the disease.

In an attempt to deliver enzyme directly to neurons and arrest or reverse the neurological progression in Type 2 Gaucher patients, Bembi and his collaborators (Bembi et al, 1995; Carrozzi et al, 1995) infused Ceredase® directly into the CSF of three patients with Type 2 Gaucher's disease. The infusions were given intraventricularly through an Omaya reservoir in two patients and intrathecally in a third patient. Dosage was 5–20 U/kg per 4 weeks given as a continuous infusion with a peristaltic pump. Patients received concurrently intravenous Ceredase® infusions at a dose of 240 U/kg per 4 weeks. Treatment was begun at 1, 8 and 9 months of age, and lasted 53 days to 10 months. The intraventricular infusion caused no side-effects but the intrathecal infusion seemed painful to the patient. Only one patient showed reduction in tone, in the frequency of laryngospasm episodes, and in trismus. However, dysphagia and myoclonus epilepsy worsened. The other two patients continued to deteriorate. Two patients died at ages 4 and 15 months. One patient is still alive at 5 years of age. We feel that such heroic measures are not useful in the treatment of Type 2 Gaucher's disease. It is probable that systemic delivery of enzyme across an intact blood–brain barrier and into neurons will be required to effectively treat the cerebral manifestations of this disease.

Gene therapy

Effective gene therapy in GD is not yet available. Since successful bone marrow transplantation cures the systemic manifestations of the disease, the prospects of gene transfer to autologous haematopoietic stem cells is an attractive therapeutic approach (Correll and Karlsson, 1994; Xu et al, 1994). A number of phase I studies in non-ablated Gaucher patients are currently being conducted (Dunbar and Kohn, 1996). Such 'corrected' bone marrow stem cells are expected to generate normal macrophages from their progeny. These macrophages should progressively replace the systemic and cerebral perivascular Gaucher cells and possibly some of the intraparenchymal cerebral microglia (Krivit et al, 1995). Since it is probable that the neurological deficit is mostly caused by neuronal gluco-cerebrosidase deficiency, correcting the haematopoietic cell lineages is likely not to be enough to effectively treat all the neurological mani-festations of GD. Direct delivery of the normal gene to neurons will probably be required.

Acknowledgement

We thank D. G. Schoenberg, M.S., for help in manuscript editing.

REFERENCES

Abrahamov A, Elstein D, Gross-Tsur V et al (1995) Gaucher's disease variant characterised by progressive calcification of heart valves and unique genotype [see comments]. Lancet 346: 1000–1003.

Ashkenazi A, Zaizov R & Matoth Y (1986) Effect of splenectomy on destructive bone changes in children with chronic (Type I) Gaucher disease. European Journal of Pediatrics 145: 138–141.

Barton NW, Brady RO, Dambrosia J et al (1991) Replacement therapy for inherited enzyme deficiency—macrophage-targeted glucocerebrosidase for Gaucher's disease [see comments]. New England Journal of Medicine 324: 1464–1470.

Bembi B, Zanatta M, Carrozzi M et al (1994) Enzyme replacement treatment in type 1 and type 3 Gaucher's disease. Lancet 344: 1679–1682.

Bembi B, Ciana G, Zanatta M et al (1995) Cerebrospinal fluid infusion of alglucerase in the treatment of acute neuronopathic Gaucher's disease. Pediatric Research 38: 425 (Abstract).

*Beutler E (1995a) Gaucher disease, a paradigm for single gene defects. Experientia 51: 196–197.

*Beutler E (1995b) Gaucher disease. Advances in Genetics 32: 17–49.

Beutler E & Grabowski GA (1995) Gaucher disease. In Scriver CR, Beaudet AL, Sly WS & Valle D (eds) The Metabolic and Molecular Bases of Inherited Disease, pp. 2641–2670. New York: McGraw-Hill.

Bove KE, Daugherty C & Grabowski GA (1995) Pathological findings in Gaucher disease type 2 patients following enzyme therapy. Human Pathology 26: 1040–1045.

*Brady RO (1996) Gaucher disease. In Moser HW (ed.) Handbook of Clinical Neurology, pp. 123–132. Amsterdam: Elsevier Science.

Carrozzi M, Zanatta M, Scabar A & Bembi B (1995) Enzyme replacement therapy for Gaucher's disease type 1, 2, and 3. In Di Donato S, Parini R & Uziel G (eds) Metabolic Encephalopathies, pp. 123–130. London: John Libbey Company Ltd.

Chabas A, Cormand B, Grinberg D et al (1995) Unusual expression of Gaucher's disease: cardio-vascular calcifications in three sibs homozygous for the D409H mutation. Journal of Medical Genetics 32: 740–742.

Choy FY & Wei C (1995) Identification of a new mutation (P178S) in an African-American patient with type 2 Gaucher disease. Human Mutation 5: 345–347.

Conradi NG, Kalimo H & Sourander P (1988) Reactions of vessel walls and brain parenchyma to the accumulation of Gaucher cells in the Norrbottnian type (type III) of Gaucher disease. Acta Neuropathologica (Berlin) 75: 385–390.

*Conradi NG, Sourander P, Nilsson O et al (1984) Neuropathology of the Norrbottnian type of Gaucher disease. Morphological and biochemical studies. Acta Neuropathologica Berlin 65: 99–109.

Conradi N, Kyllerman M, Mansson JE et al (1991) Late-infantile Gaucher disease in a child with myoclonus and bulbar signs: Neuropathological and neurochemical findings. Acta Neuropatho-logica (Berlin) 82: 152–157.

*Correll PH & Karlsson S (1994) Towards therapy of Gaucher's disease by gene transfer into hematopoietic cells. European Journal of Hematology 53: 253–264.

Dreborg S, Erikson A & Hagberg B (1980) Gaucher disease—Norrbottnian type. I. General clinical description. European Journal of Pediatrics 133: 107–118.

Dunbar C & Kohn D (1996) Retroviral mediated transfer of the cDNA for human glucocerebrosidase into hematopoietic stem cells of patients with Gaucher disease. A phase I study. *Human Gene Therapy* **7:** 231–253.

*Erikson A (1986) Gaucher disease—Norrbottnian type (III). Neuropaediatric and neurobiological aspects of clinical patterns and treatment. *Acta Paediatrica Scandinavica*, **326:** S1–S42.

Erikson A, Astrom M & Mansson JE (1995) Enzyme infusion therapy of the Norrbottnian (type 3) Gaucher disease. *Neuropediatrics* **26:** 203–207.

Frederickson DS & Sloan HR (1972) Glucosylceramide lipidoses: Gaucher disease. In Stanbury JB, Wyngaarden JB & Frederickson DS (eds) *The Metabolic Basis of Inherited Disease*, pp. 730–759. New York: McGraw-Hill.

Hillborg PO (1959) Morbus Gaucher in Norbotten. *Nordisk Medicin* **61:** 303–313.

Hobbs JR, Jones KH, Shaw PJ et al (1987) Beneficial effect of pre-transplant splenectomy on displacement bone marrow transplantation for Gaucher's syndrome. *Lancet* **1:** 1111–1115.

Hollak CE, Van Weely S, van Oers MH & Aerts JM (1994) Marked elevation of plasma chitotriosidase activity. A novel hallmark of Gaucher disease. *Journal of Clinical Investigation* **93:** 1288–1292.

Kaye EM, Ullman MD, Wilson ER & Barranger JA (1986) Type 2 and Type 3 Gaucher disease: a morphological and biochemical study. *Annals of Neurology* **20:** 223–230.

Knudson AG Jr & Kaplan WD (1962) Genetics of the sphingolipidoses. In Aronson SM & Volk BW (eds) *Cerebral Sphinolipidoses*, pp. 395–411. New York: Academic Press.

*Krivit W, Sung JH, Shapiro EG & Lockman LA (1995) Microglia: the effector cell for reconstitution of the central nervous system following bone marrow transplantation for lysosomal and peroxisomal storage diseases. *Cell Transplantation* **4:** 385–392.

Kyllerman M, Conradi N, Mansson JE et al (1990) Rapidly progressive type III Gaucher disease: deterioration following partial splenectomy. *Acta Paediatrica Scandinavica* **79:** 448–453.

Mistry PK (1995) Genotype/phenotype correlations in Gaucher's disease [comment]. *Lancet* **346:** 982–983.

Neudorder O, Giladi N, Elstein D et al (1996) Occurrence of Parkinson's syndrome in type I Gaucher disease. *Quarterly Journal of Medicine* **89:** 691–694.

Nilsson O & Svennerholm L (1982) Accumulation of glucosylceramide and glucosylsphingosine (psychosine) in cerebrum and cerebellum in infantile and juvenile Gaucher disease. *Journal of Neurochemistry* **39:** 709–718.

Pasmanik-Chor M, Laadan S, Elroy-Stein O et al (1996) The glucocerebrosidase D409H mutation in Gaucher disease. *Biochemical and Molecular Medicine* **59:** 125–133.

*Patterson MC, Horowitz M, Abel RB et al (1993) Isolated horizontal supranuclear gaze palsy as a marker of severe systemic involvement in Gaucher's disease. *Neurology* **43:** 1993–1997.

Ringden O, Groth CG, Erikson A et al (1995) Ten years' experience of bone marrow transplantation for Gaucher disease. *Transplantation* **59:** 864–870.

Rusca CL (1921) Sul morbo del Gaucher. *Hematologica* **2:** 441.

*Schiffmann R, Heyes MP, Aerts JM et al (1997) Prospective study of neurological responses to treatment with macrophage-targeted glucocerebrosidase in patients with type 3 Gaucher disease. *Annals of Neurology* **42:** 613–621.

Seeman PJ, Finckh U, Hoppner J et al (1996) Two new missense mutations in non-Jewish Caucasian family with type 3 Gaucher disease. *Neurology* **46:** 1102–1107.

Shiloni E, Bitran D, Rachmilewitz E & Durst AL (1983) The role of splenectomy in Gaucher's disease. *Archives of Surgery* **118:** 929–932.

Sidransky E, Sherer DM & Ginns EI (1992) Gaucher disease in the neonate: a distinct Gaucher phenotype is analogous to a mouse model created by targeted disruption of the glucocerebrosidase gene. *Pediatric Research* **32:** 494–498.

Soffer D, Yamanaka T, Wenger DA & Suzuki K (1980) Central nervous system involvement in adult-onset Gaucher's disease. *Acta Neuropathologica* (Berlin) **49:** 1–6.

Tayebi N, Herman J, Ginns EI & Sidransky E (1996) Genotype D399N/R463C in a patient with type 3 Gaucher disease previously assigned genotype N370S/R463C. *Biochemical and Molecular Medicine* **57:** 149–151.

Verderese CL, Graham OC, Holder-McShane CA et al (1993) Gaucher's disease: a pilot study of the symptomatic responses to enzyme replacement therapy. *Journal of Neuroscience Nursing* **25:** 296–301.

Winkelman MD, Banker BQ, Victor M & Moser HW (1983) Non-infantile neuronopathic Gaucher's disease: a clinicopathologic study. *Neurology* **33:** 994–1008.

Xu L, Stahl SK, Dave HP et al (1994) Correction of the enzyme deficiency in hematopoietic cells of Gaucher patients using a clinically acceptable retroviral supernatant transduction protocol. *Experimental Hematology* **22**: 223–230.

*Zimran A, Elstein D, Schiffmann R et al (1995) Outcome of partial splenectomy for type I Gaucher disease. *Journal of Pediatrics* **126**: 596–597.

6

Gaucher's disease: the best laid schemes of mice and men

ELLEN SIDRANSKY MD

Chief, Unit of Clinical Genetics

EDWARD I. GINNS MD, PhD

Chief, Clinical Neuroscience Branch

Clinical Neuroscience Branch, National Institute of Mental Health, NIH, Building 49, Room B1EE16, 49 Convent Drive MSC 4405, Bethesda, MA 20892-4405, USA

The creation of animal models of Gaucher's disease, the inherited deficiency of the enzyme glucocerebrosidase, has led to new clinical insights and to a new appreciation of the complexity of the glucocerebrosidase gene locus. Murine embryonic stem cells with targeted modifications in the glucocerebrosidase gene were used to generate mouse models of Gaucher's disease, the first having a null glucocerebrosidase allele. The resulting knock-out mice have no glucocerebrosidase activity and die within 12 hours of birth. Ultrastructural studies of liver, spleen, brain and bone marrow demonstrate the characteristic storage material seen in Gaucher patients. In the nervous system, storage of lipid increased in a rostral–caudal distribution. Analysis of skin from the knockout mice revealed histological, ultrastructural and biochemical abnormalities. The null allele Gaucher mice are analogous to neonates with Type 2 Gaucher's disease who present with hydrops foetalis and/or congenital ichthyosis. Moreover, the epidermal changes seen in Type 2 mice are also found in Type 2 patients and may provide a means to pre-symptomatically discriminate Type 2 from Type 1 and 3 Gaucher's disease. Another targeted modification in the murine glucocerebrosidase gene locus led to the discovery of a contiguous gene, metaxin. Closer analysis of the glucocerebrosidase gene locus, including sequencing of 75 kb of genomic DNA, reveals that this is a gene-rich region coding for seven genes and two pseudogenes. Further study of these closely arrayed genes may contribute to our understanding of the clinical variation encountered among patients with Gaucher's disease.

Key words: Gaucher's disease; glucocerebrosidase; murine; knockout models; epidermal; metaxin.

'The best laid schemes of mice and men gang oft a-gley' Robert Burns *To a Mouse.*

The generation of animal models of Gaucher's disease, the inherited deficiency of the lysosomal enzyme glucocerebrosidase (EC 3.2.1.45),

Copyright © 1997, by Baillière Tindall
All rights of reproduction in any form reserved

continues to be a challenging endeavour. To paraphrase Robert Burns, our best laid schemes have led to directions never anticipated. The strategies designed to create mouse models of Gaucher's disease have resulted in new and unexpected insights into this autosomal recessively inherited disorder. The mice generated have provided new clinical perspectives and an appreciation of the complexity of the entire glucocerebrosidase locus.

Gaucher's disease, first described in 1882 by Phillipe Gaucher (Gaucher, 1882), is characterized by vast phenotypic variation. Generally, patients with Gaucher's disease are classified into three types based upon the extent and progression of neurological involvement; Type 1 non-neuronopathic, Type 2 acute neuronopathic, and Type 3 subacute neuronopathic (Barranger and Ginns, 1989; Beutler and Grabowski, 1995). However, these subtypes do not adequately reflect the spectrum of symptoms (Martin et al, 1989; Sidransky and Ginns, 1993). Type 1 patients include asymptomatic octogenarians as well as children with extremely debilitating bone and visceral disease. Recently it has become apparent that Type 2 Gaucher's disease is not as stereotypic as previously thought, and while universally devastating with death ensuing by the age of three, it can present prenatally with hydrops, at birth, or after several months of life (Sidransky et al, 1992a). Type 3 Gaucher's disease is also quite variable in presentation. One subgroup has been described with extreme visceral pathology and a specific oculomotor abnormality consisting of slowing and looping of the horizontal saccadic eye movements (Cogen et al, 1981; Sidransky et al, 1992b; Patterson et al, 1993). Other Type 3 patients have been described with epilepsy (Frederickson and Slone, 1972), cardiac calcifications (Abrahamov et al, 1995; Chabás et al, 1995), hydrocephalus (Uyama et al, 1992) and even with Parkinson-like symptoms (Neudorfer et al, 1996). Understanding the factors contributing to this wide range of heterogeneity has been a major challenge.

The gene for glucocerebrosidase was localized to chromosome 1q21 (Ginns et al, 1985) and subsequently characterized and sequenced (Horowitz et al, 1989). There are 11 exons. Approximately 16 kb downstream is a highly homologous sequence that is thought to be a pseudogene (Horowitz et al, 1989). To date, more than 70 mutant alleles resulting in Gaucher's disease have been described, including missense mutations, frame shift mutations, deletions, fusion genes and recombinant alleles (Beutler and Gelbart, 1997). Although several of the mutant alleles are commonly encountered, most are rare. Because many mutant alleles have resulted from recombination events with the nearby glucocerebrosidase pseudogene (Eyal et al, 1990; Latham et al, 1990; Zimran et al, 1990), the identification of mutations can sometimes be complicated. The literature is particularly confusing, because some laboratories have used techniques that would not identify a recombinant or deleted allele (Tayebi et al, 1996a,b).

While genotypic analysis can be useful (i.e. patients with the common N370S mutation do not develop neuronopathic types of Gaucher's disease) (Beutler and Grabowski, 1995; Tayebi et al, 1996c), generally genotype/ phenotype correlation has limited value for determining prognosis (Sidransky et al, 1994a,b, NIH Technology Assessment Conference, 1996).

Groups of patients sharing similar symptoms demonstrate multiple different genotypes. Likewise, patients with the same DNA point mutations, even within the same family, can have a widely different spectrum of clinical manifestations. Thus other, as of yet unidentified factors appear to contribute to the heterogeneity encountered in Gaucher's disease.

There has been great incentive to develop animal models of Gaucher's disease, both to establish the phenotypic consequences of specific mutant alleles and to have a model to test novel therapeutic strategies. No naturally occurring animal model of Gaucher's disease is currently available for study. A canine model of Gaucher's disease was reported in 1982 (Farrow et al, 1982) but not propagated. Mice treated with conduritol B-epoxide (CBE), a glucocerebrosidase inhibitor, demonstrate transient biochemical alterations seen in Gaucher's disease but are of limited usefulness (Kanfer et al, 1982; McKinney et al, 1995). Efforts have been focused toward generating knockout and point mutation models by modifying the glucocerebrosidase gene locus in murine embryonic stem cells and using these stem cells to generate mouse lines with the mutant glucocerebrosidase alleles. This approach has led to new research directions.

THE NULL ALLELE GAUCHER MOUSE

The initial knockout mouse model of Gaucher's disease was described by Tybulewicz et al in 1992. It was generated using a targeting strategy that replaced an approximately 400 bp segment of the murine glucocerebrosidase gene, including parts of exon 9 and 10, with a neomycin resistance cassette (Figure 1A). This alteration of the glucocerebrosidase gene deleted approximately 30 amino acids from the C-terminal portion of glucocerebrosidase (Tybulewitz et al, 1992).

The resultant mice (Figure 2A), homozygous for the targeted null allele, had an unexpectedly severe phenotype and no glucocerebrosidase activity. These mice were underweight, had difficulty feeding, and developed respiratory distress. Shortly after birth, the affected mice were recognized both by their mothers and investigators as abnormal. They were not nutured, became dehydrated, cyanotic, and died after 6–12 hours. A particularly notable feature of the affected mice was their cellophane-like, rugated, dry skin (Sidransky et al, 1992a). Interventions such as supplemental oxygen, feedings and artificial skin barriers did not extend their survival. Thin layer chromatography of lipids extracted from the brains of these newborn homozygote animals, as well as mid gestation affected embryos, revealed a significant elevation of glucosylceramide levels as compared with unaffected and heterozygous littermates (Tybulewitz et al, 1992; McKinney et al, 1995). In addition, HPLC determinations indicate that levels of glucosylsphingosine, a neurotoxin, are also elevated in the brains of affected mice (McKinney et al, 1995) and increased glycosylsphingosine may contribute to the early demise of these animals. Glucosylsphingosine is also elevated in brains from patients with

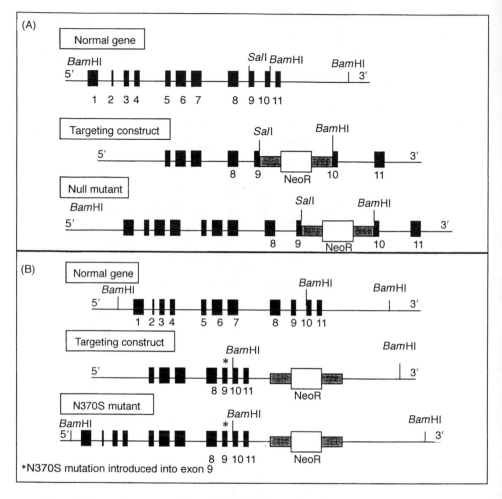

Figure 1. Strategy for gene targeting. (A) Null allele construct. The targeting vector was assembled with a neomycin resistance cassette (NeoR) inserted into the murine glucocerebrosidase gene between the *Sal*I restriction site in exon 9 and the *Bam*HI site in exon 10. The altered null mutant allele lacks portions of exon 9 and 10 and the entire intron 9 as shown. (B) N370S point mutation construct. The targeting vector was assembled with the point mutation N370S (shown by an asterisk). The neomycin resistance cassette (NeoR) was placed downstream to exon 11 of glucocerebrosidase.

Type 2 Gaucher's disease (Nilsson and Svennerholm, 1982). The Twitcher mouse model similarly demonstrated that in Krabbe disease, elevations of another sphingosine derivative, galactosphingosine, was responsible for the observed central nervous system pathology (Suzuki and Suzuki, 1983; Tanaka et al, 1989).

The light microscopic pathological evaluation of the null allele Gaucher mice revealed no Gaucher cells and surprisingly few abnormalities (Tybulewitz et al, 1992). However, electron microscopic studies of tissues

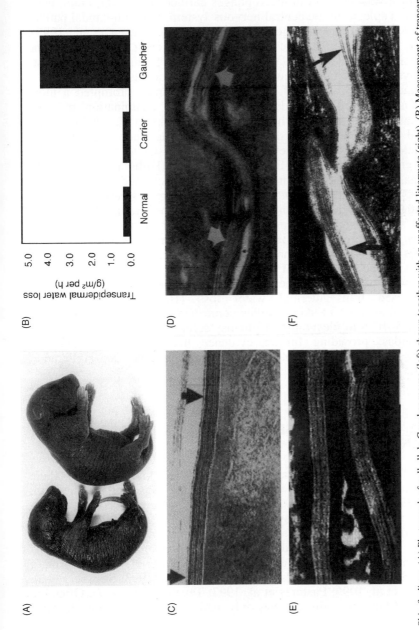

Figure 2. Skin findings. (A) Photograph of null allele Gaucher mouse (left) shown together with an unaffected littermate (right). (B) Measurement of transepidermal water loss measured in normal mice and heterozygous and homozygous null allele Gaucher mice (for details see Holleran et al, 1994). (C) Ultrastructure of skin from a normal newborn mouse demonstrating regularly appearing lamellar body-derived sheets in stratum corneum. (D) Ultrastructure of stratum corneum in Type 2 Gaucher mice revealing immature lamellar body-derived sheets arranged in loose arrays. (E) Skin from patients with Type 1 Gaucher's disease demonstrating normal lamellar bilayer structure. (F) Skin from a patient with Type 2 Gaucher's disease demonstrating unprocessed lamellar body derived sheets in loosely packed arrays.

from these Type 2 mice demonstrated distinct storage in characteristic elongated tubular arrays within the lysosomes of macrophages. The glyco-lipid storage was apparent in macrophages derived from liver, brain, bone marrow and spleen. In the central nervous system, a rostral-caudal pattern of increasing neuronal storage was observed (Willemsen et al, 1995). However, the degree of storage did not appear sufficient to account for the early demise of these animals (Willemsen et al, 1995) and further suggests the involvement of a potent neurotoxin such as glucosylsphingosine.

The unusual appearance of the skin of these mice prompted a more detailed analysis of the epidermis. Histological examination revealed hyperkeratosis and epidermal hyperplasia (Sidransky et al, 1992a). Ultra-structural studies demonstrated that the null allele mice had abnormal, incompletely processed, lamellar body-derived sheets throughout the stratum corneum interstices (Figure 2C and D) (Holleran et al, 1994). Additionally, the null allele mice had greatly increased transepidermal water loss as compared with normal and heterozygote littermates (Figure 2B). Both the sphingolipid content and ratios in the stratum corneum are essential to the maintenance of the epidermal permeability barrier. Normally, glucocerebrosidase is abundant in mammalian epidermis, while ceramides are a major component of the intercellular bilayers (Holleran et al, 1993). The deficiency of glucocerebrosidase in the skin of the null allele mice resulted in both the observed morphological abnormality, and the increased transepidermal water loss (Holleran et al, 1994). Biochemical analysis of skin samples confirmed that the Type 2 Gaucher mice had 5–10 fold elevations in glucosylceramide and decreased levels of ceramides, providing further evidence that glucocerebrosidase is necessary for the generation of competent epidermal barriers (Holleran et al, 1994).

TYPE 2 GAUCHER'S DISEASE: INSIGHTS FROM MICE TO MAN

The rapidly progressive lethal phenotype of the knockout null allele Gaucher mice prompted a new appreciation of a subset of patients with Type 2 Gaucher's disease having a particularly severe course, character-ized by a very early onset of symptoms (Sidransky et al, 1992a). In these patients with Type 2 Gaucher's disease, manifestations are apparent either prenatally or at birth. Several dozen of these fetuses and infants have now been described (Frederickson and Sloan, 1972; Lui et al, 1988; Lipson et al, 1991; Sidransky et al, 1992a, 1996a; Sherer et al, 1993; Strasberg et al, 1994; Ince et al, 1995; Pastores et al, 1997; Tayebi et al, 1997). Often the diagnosis of Gaucher's disease was only made at autopsy or after the birth of a second affected child to a family. It appears that many of the very severe patients with Type 2 Gaucher's disease develop hydrops fetalis in utero, as has also been reported for patients with other lysosomal storage disorders (Gillan et al, 1984; Meizner et al, 1990; Landau et al, 1995;

Vervoort et al, 1996). Mutational analysis of fetuses and infants with severe Type 2 Gaucher's disease reveals significant genotypic heterogeneity even in this subgroup of patients (Strasberg et al, 1994; Sidransky et al, 1996a; Tayebi et al, 1997).

Although there have been several case reports describing the association of Type 2 Gaucher's disease and congenital ichthyosis (Lui et al, 1988; Lipson et al, 1991; Fujimoto et al, 1995), it was the similarity of skin findings and clinical course in these Type 2 neonates with Gaucher's disease and the knockout (null allele) glucocerebrosidase deficient mice that suggested that the enzyme deficiency directly resulted in the phenotype (Sidransky et al, 1996b). Subsequently, skin analyses on patients with Type 1, 2, and 3 Gaucher's disease (Holleran et al, 1993; Sidransky et al, 1996b) demonstrate that only skin samples from infants with Type 2 Gaucher's disease display hyperkeratosis. Ultrastructural analysis of epidermis from patients with Type 1, 2 and 3 Gaucher's disease also show that only in the Type 2 patients do abnormal arrays of loosely packed lamellar body derived sheets replace the normal lamellar bilayer unit structures (Figure 2E and F). Type 1 and Type 3 patients appear to have normal epidermal ultrastructure and function. The changes found in skin in patients with Type 2 Gaucher's disease were seen both in ichthyotic neonates and older non-ichthyotic 'classic' Type 2 children. Biochemical analyses of epidermis from patients with Type 2 Gaucher's disease demonstrated that the ratio of glucosylceramide to ceramide was reversed compared with normal, just as in the knockout mice. No abnormalities in the ratios of glucosylceramide to ceramide were seen in epidermis from patients with Type 1 or Type 3 disease (Sidransky et al, 1996b). The unique skin ultrastructural and biochemical abnormalities in patients with Type 2 Gaucher's disease may provide an early means to discriminate between this uniformly devastating and the other milder Gaucher phenotypes.

Thus the first targeted knockout mouse model of Gaucher's disease has provided an appropriate clinical, biochemical and ultrastructural model for the most extreme Type 2 Gaucher phenotype. This animal model of Gaucher's disease led to the appreciation of a subset of Gaucher patients presenting perinatally with hydrops fetalis and/or congenital ichthyosis, and as a consequence, more recently an increased number of cases of neonatal Gaucher's disease have been recognized and even diagnosed prenatally. The epidermal abnormalities present in both the Type 2 Gaucher mouse and infants with Type 2 Gaucher's disease also have important diagnostic implications, for they may enable the presymptomatic identification of patients with acute neuronopathic (Type 2) Gaucher's disease.

Attempts to rescue these Type 2 Gaucher mice by in utero treatments, including direct intraventricular injections of neuronal progenitor cells and direct in utero injections of glucocerebrosidase, have not been successful (McKinney et al, 1995). However, other strategies including the use of transgenes with epidermal and/or brain specific promoters are being explored. Those therapies that can successfully prolong the life of the knockout mice may have important therapeutic implications for the treatment of Type 2 Gaucher's disease.

GENES CONTIGUOUS TO THE GLUCOCEREBROSIDASE GENE: NEW DIRECTIONS FROM MOUSE MODELS

While the null allele Type 2 Gaucher mouse provided new insights into acute neuronopathic Type 2 Gaucher's disease, efforts have still been directed toward the creation of a longer lived Gaucher mouse that will have a course more analogous to patients with Type I and Type 3 Gaucher's disease. Another targeting construct used in an attempt to generate such a Gaucher mouse model was designed with the point mutation N370S located in exon 9 and a neomycin resistance cassette located immediately downstream of the glucocerebrosidase gene (Figure 1B) (Bornstein et al, 1995). Chimeric mice and heterozygote germline founders were generated from embryonic stem cells correctly targeted with this construct, but no liveborn N370S homozygote mice were observed. This was perplexing because it was anticipated that the phenotype of N370S homozygote mice would be milder, and that the mice would live longer than the Type 2 Gaucher mice. In the human, patients homozygous for the mutation N370S generally have mild disease, and this mutation has not been encountered in patients with neuronopathic Gaucher's disease. Yet this construct appeared to result in early embryonic lethality.

The explanation for this came with the discovery of a new gene, metaxin, located immediately downstream of the murine glucocerebrosidase gene (Bornstein et al, 1995). Targeting of the murine glucocerebrosidase gene with N370S mutation had resulted in a knockout of the murine metaxin gene by the neomycin resistance cassette (Figure 3). Subsequently, it was established that mice without the glucocerebrosidase point mutation, but homozygous for a metaxin gene knockout, also die in early gestation. The genes for murine metaxin and glucocerebrosidase are transcribed convergently with polyadenylation sites that are only 431 bp apart. Metaxin appears to be a component of a preprotein import complex in the outer membrane of mitochondria (Armstrong et al, 1997), sharing sequence identity to the yeast mitochondrial protein, Tom37 (Gratzer et al, 1995).

The discovery of this novel murine gene prompted closer scrutiny of the glucocerebrosidase gene locus. The human metaxin gene was identified (Long et al, 1996). It is 6 kb in length and is organized in 8 exons. The gene for human metaxin is located between the glucocerebrosidase pseudogene and the gene for human thrombospondin 3 and is transcribed convergently

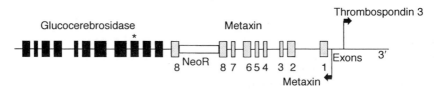

Figure 3. Altered allele initially used to generate a N370S mutant mouse. Note that the neomycin resistance cassette (NeoR) disrupts exon 8 of the metaxin gene. The asterisk shows the site of the N370S mutation.

to the human glucocerebrosidase gene (Figure 4). The gene for thrombo-spondin 3 is transcribed divergently to that for metaxin, although the two genes share a common promoter (Aldoph et al, 1995). A pseudogene for human metaxin, which is not transcribed, is located within the 16 kb of DNA separating the glucocerebrosidase gene from its pseudogene. A fourth gene, polymorphic epithelial mucin I (MUC1), is located immediately downstream to the gene for thrombospondin 3 (Vos et al, 1995). This recent appreciation of the close array of genes downstream from gluco-cerebrosidase has complicated the strategy using targeting constructs for the generation of additional mouse models of Gaucher's disease carrying more subtle mutations in the glucocerebrosidase gene.

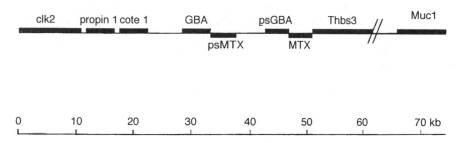

Figure 4. The physical relationship of seven closely arranged genes and two pseudogenes on human chromosome 1q21. GBA, glucocerebrosidase; MTX, metaxin; Thbs, thrombospondin; Mucl, poly-morphic epithelial mucin; ps, pseudogene; clk2, protein kinase.

These findings stimulated a detailed sequence analysis of the region upstream of glucocerebrosidase that has now revealed three additional genes in the 32 kb region upstream of glucocerebrosidase (Figure 4) (Winfield et al, 1997). Of the three genes, that most distant to gluco-cerebrosidase is a protein kinase (clk-2), which was previously described and mapped to chromosome 1 (Hanes et al, 1994). The second gene, propin 1, located 15–21 kb upstream to the glucocerebrosidase gene, encodes a 1.5 kb cDNA with homology to a rat secretory carrier membrane protein (SCAMP 37) (Brand and Castle, 1993). The gene located nearest (only 6–15 kb upstream) of glucocerebrosidase, cote 1, is composed of 12 exons and the corresponding cDNA is predicted to be 3.15 kb in size. The function of cote 1 is unknown. All three genes are ubiquitously expressed in all tissues tested. Zooblot analyses also revealed a conservation of the organization of the glucocerebrosidase gene locus and the proximity of these genes across species (Winfield et al, 1997). Thus, the region surrounding glucocerebrosidase is particularly gene rich, with seven genes and two pseudogenes located in close proximity. All of the genes, except metaxin, are transcribed in the same direction (Figure 4).

Alteration in the expression of these closely arrayed genes may potentially contribute to the phenotypic variation observed in Gaucher's disease. It has been long appreciated that some mutant alleles encountered in Gaucher patients arose by gene conversion, recombination or fusion occurring within the locus. Deletions in the iduronate 2 sulphatase locus that extend into nearby genes (Timms et al, 1997) have recently been reported in patients with Hunter syndrome exhibiting atypical phenotypes. Similarly, the possibility that other genes may have also been interrupted in Gaucher's disease during these recombination events is particularly intriguing.

FUTURE DIRECTIONS

The generation of other knockout and more subtle murine models to help elucidate the function of the genes nearby to glucocerebrosidase is already in progress. The presence of these newly discovered genes has impacted on strategies to generate longer-lived Gaucher mouse models, which will be analogous in course to patients with Type 1 and Type 3 Gaucher's disease. These models are critically needed to facilitate a better understanding of the pathophysiology of Gaucher's disease and to enable the testing of new therapeutic strategies. The location of nearby genes must be taken into account because any alteration of the locus may have phenotypic conse-quences. Thus other strategies to introduce the more subtle mutation changes are being employed to ensure that no unexpected changes in contiguous gene expression occur. The study of animal models of Gaucher's disease has already led to novel insights and research directions. Murine models having the common mutations seen in patients with Gaucher's disease should soon be available, and if our past experience is any indication, these mice may provide other unanticipated findings (Figure 5).

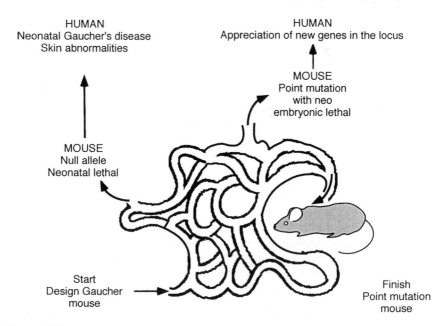

Figure 5. Efforts to create mouse models of Gaucher's disease have led to directions not anticipated.

These new models, with alterations in the glucocerebrosidase gene and in the other genes contiguous to glucocerebrosides may ultimately redefine how we approach Gaucher's disease.

REFERENCES

Abrahamov A, Elstein D, Gross-Tsur V et al (1995) Gaucher's disease variant characterized by progressive calcification of heart valves and unique genotype. *Lancet* **346**: 1000–1003.

Aldoph KW, Long GL, Winfield S et al (1995) Structure and organization of the human thrombospondin 3 gene (THBS3). *Genomics* **27**: 329–336.

Armstrong LC, Komiya T, Bergman BE et al (1997) Metaxin is a component of a preprotein import complex in the outer membrane of the mammalian mitochondrion. *Journal of Biological Chemistry* **272**: 6510–6518.

Barranger JA & Ginns EI (1989) Glucosylceramide lipidoses: Gaucher disease. In Scriver CR, Beaudet AL, Sly WS, et al (eds) *The Metabolic Basis of Inherited Disease*, pp. 1677–1698. New York: Mc Graw-Hill

Beutler E & Grabowski GA (1995) Gaucher disease. In Scriver CR, Beaudet AL, Sly WS, et al (eds) *The Metabolic and Molecular Bases of Inherited Disease*, pp. 2641–2670. New York: Mc Graw Hill

Beutler E & Gelbart T (1997) Hematologically important mutations: Gaucher disease. *Blood Cells, Molecules, and Diseases* **23**: 2–7.

*Bornstein P, McKinney CE, LaMarca ME et al, (1995) Metaxin, a gene contiguous to both thrombospondin 3 and glucocerebrosidase, is required for embryonic development in the mouse: implications for Gaucher disease. *Proceedings of the National Academy of Science, USA* **92**: 4547–4551.

Brand SH & Castle JD (1993) SCAMP 37, a new marker within the general cell surface recycling system. *EMBO Journal* **12**: 3753–3761.

Chabás A, Cormand B, Grinberg D et al (1995) Unusual expression of Gaucher's disease: cardiovascular calcifications in three sibs homozygous for the D409H mutation. *Journal of Medical Genetics* **32**: 740–742.

Cogan DG, Chu FC, Reingold D & Barranger J (1981) Ocular motor signs in some metabolic diseases. *Archives of Ophthalmology* **99**: 1802–1808.

Eyal N, Wilder S, Horowitz M et al (1990) Prevalent and rare mutations among Gaucher patients. *Gene* **96**: 277–282.

Farrow BR, Hartley WJ, Pollard AC et al (1982) Gaucher disease in the dog. *Progress in Clinical and Biological Research* **95**: 645–653.

Frederickson DS, & Sloan HR (1972) Glucosylceramide lipidoses: Gaucher's disease. In Stanbury JB, Wyngarden JB & Frederickson DS (eds) *The Metabolic Basis of Inherited Disease*, pp. 730–759. New York: McGraw-Hill.

Fujimoto A, Tayebi N & Sidransky E (1995) Congenital ichthyosis preceding neurologic symptoms in two siblings with type 2 Gaucher disease. *American Journal of Medical Genetics* **59**: 356–358.

Gaucher P (1882) De l'épithélioma primitif del la rate. MD Thèse, Faculté de Médecine de Paris.

Gillan JE, Path MRC, Lowden JA et al (1984) Congenital ascites as a presenting sign of lysosomal storage disease. *Journal of Pediatrics* **104**: 225–231.

Ginns EI, Choudary PV, Tsuji S et al (1985) Gene mapping and leader polypeptide sequence of human glucocerebrosidase: implications for Gaucher disease. *Proceedings of National Academy of Science, USA* **82**: 7101–7105.

Gratzer S, Lithgow T, Bauer RE et al (1995) Mas 37p, a novel receptor subunit for protein import into mitochondria. *Journal of Cell Biology* **129**: 25–34.

Hanes J, von der Kammer H, Klaudiny J & Scheit KH (1994) Characterization by cDNA cloning of two new human protein kinases: evidence by sequence comparison for a new family of mammalian protein kinases. *Journal of Molecular Biology* **244**: 665–672.

Holleran WM, Takagi Y, Menon GK et al (1993) Processing of epidermal glucosylceramides is required for optimal mammalian cutaneous permeability barrier function. *Journal of Clinical Investigations* **91**: 1656–1664.

*Holleran WM, Ginns EI, Menon G et al (1994) Epidermal consequences of β-glucocerebrosidase deficiency: Permeability barrier alterations and basis for skin lesions in type 2 Gaucher disease. *Journal of Clinical Investigations* **93**: 1756–1764.

Horowitz M, Wilder S, Horowitz Z et al (1989) The human glucocerebrosidase gene and pseudogene: Structure and evolution. *Genomics* **4**: 87–96.

Ince Z, Coban A, Peker O et al (1995) Gaucher disease associated with congenital ichthyosis in the neonate. *European Journal of Pediatrics* **154**: 418.

Kanfer JN, Stephens MC, Singh H & Legler B (1982) The Gaucher mouse. *Progress in Clinical and Biological Research* **95**: 627–644.

Landau D, Meisner I, Zeigler M et al (1995) Hydrops fetalis in four siblings caused by galacto-sialidosis. *Israel Journal of Medical Science* **31**: 321–322.

Latham T, Grabowski GA, Theophilus BDM et al (1990) Complex alleles of the acid β-gluco-cerebrosidase gene in Gaucher disease. *American Journal of Human Genetics* **47**: 79–86.

Lipson AH, Rogers M & Berry A (1991) Collodion babies with Gaucher disease: a further case. *Archives of Disease in Childhood* **66**: 667.

*Long GL, Winfield S, Adolph KW et al (1996) Structure and organization of the human metaxin gene (MTX) and pseudogene. *Genomics* **33**: 177–184.

Lui K, Commens C, Chong R et al (1988) Collodion babies with Gaucher's disease. *Archives of Disease in Childhood* **63**: 854–856.

*McKinney CE, Sidransky E, LaMarca ME et al (1995) Gaucher disease: a tale of two species. *Mental Retardation and Developmental Disabilities Research Reviews* **1**: 79–86.

Martin BM, Sidransky E & Ginns EI (1989) Gaucher disease: advances and challenges. *Advances in Pediatrics* **36**: 277–306.

Meizner I, Levy A, Carmi R et al (1990) Niemann–Pick disease associated with nonimmune hydrops fetalis. *American Journal of Obstetics and Gynecology* **163**: 128–129.

Neudorfer O, Giladi N, Elstein D et al (1996) Occurrence of Parkinson's syndrome in type 1 Gaucher disease. *Quarterly Journal of Medicine* **89**: 691–694.

*NIH Technology Assessment Conference (1996) Gaucher disease: current issues in diagnosis and treatment. *Journal of American Medical Association* **1**: 1–27.

Nilsson O & Svennerholm L (1982) Accumulation of glucosylceramide and glucosylsphingosine (psychosine) in cerebrum and cerebellum in infantile and juvenile Gaucher disease. *Journal of Neurochemistry* **39**: 709–717.

Pastores GM, Ashton-Prolla P, Sogni A et al (1997) Heteroallelisms for acid β-glucosidase mutations L444P and E326K results in severe neonatal Gaucher disease. *Pediatric Research* **41**: 106A.

Patterson MC, Horowitz M, Abel RB et al (1993) Isolated horizontal supranuclear gaze palsy as a marker of severe systemic involvement in Gaucher's disease. *Neurology* **43**: 1993–1997.

Sherer DM, Metlay L, Sinkin RA et al (1993) Congenital ichthyosis with restrictive dermopathy and Gaucher's disease: a new syndrome with associated prenatal diagnostic and pathology findings. *Obstetrics and Gynecology* **81**: 843–844.

Sidransky E & Ginns EI (1993) Clinical heterogeneity among patients with Gaucher's disease. *Journal of American Medical Association* **269**: 1154–1157.

*Sidransky E, Sherer DM & Ginns EI (1992a) Gaucher disease in the neonate: a distinct Gaucher phenotype is analogous to a mouse model created by targeted disruption of the gluco-cerebrosidase gene. *Pediatric Research* **32**: 494–498.

Sidransky E, Tsuji S, Stubblefield B et al (1992b) Gaucher patients with oculomotor abnormalities do not have a unique genotype. *Clinical Genetics* **41**: 1–5.

Sidransky E, Bottler A, Stubblefield BK et al (1994a) DNA Mutational analysis of type 1 and type 3 Gaucher patients: how well do mutations predict phenotype? *Human Mutation* **3**: 25–28.

Sidransky E & Ginns EI (1994b) Phenotypic and genotypic heterogeneity in Gaucher disease: implications for genetic counseling. *Journal of Genetic Counseling* **3**: 13–22.

Sidransky E, Tayebi N, Stubblefield BK et al (1996a) The clinical, molecular, and pathological characterization of a family with two cases of lethal perinatal type 2 Gaucher disease. *Journal of Medical Genetics* **33**: 132–136.

*Sidransky E, Fartasch M, Lee RE et al (1996b) Epidermal abnormalities may distinguish type 2 from type 1 and type 3 of Gaucher disease. *Pediatrics Research* **39**: 134–141.

Strasberg PM, Skomorowski MA, Warren et al (1994) Homozygous presence of the crossover (fusion gene) mutation identified in a type II Gaucher disease fetus: Is this analogous to the Gaucher knock-out mouse model? *Biochemical Medicine and Metabolic Biology* **53**: 16–21.

Suzuki K & Suzuki Y (1983) Galactoceramide lipidosis: Globoid cell leukodystrophy. In Stanbury,

Syngarden JB, Fredrickson DS et al (eds) *The Metabolic Basis of Inherited Disease*, pp. 857–880. New York: McGraw-Hill

Tanaka K, Nagara H, Kobayashi T et al, (1989) The Twitcher mouse: accumulation of galactosyl-sphingosine and pathology of the central nervous system. *Brain Research* **483**: 347–350.

Tayebi N, Cushner SR & Sidransky E (1996a) Differentiation of the glucocerebrosidase gene from pseudogene by long-template PCR: implications for Gaucher disease. *American Journal of Human Genetics* **59**: 740–741.

Tayebi N, Stern H, Dymarskaia I et al (1996b) The presence of a 55 base pair deletion in certain patients with Gaucher disease may complicate screening for common Gaucher alleles. *American Journal of Medical Genetics* **66**: 316–319.

Tayebi N, Herman J, Ginns EI et al (1996c) Genotype D399N/R463C in a patient with type 3 Gaucher disease previously assigned genotype N370S/R463C. *Biochemical and Molecular Medicine* **57**: 149–151.

Tayebi N, Cushner SR, Kleijer W et al (1997) Prenatal lethality of a homozygous null mutation in the human glucocerebrosidase gene. *American Journal of Medical Genetics* (in press).

Timms KM, Bondeson ML, Ansari-Lari MA, et al (1997) Molecular and phenotypic variation in patients with severe Hunter syndrome. *Human Molecular Genetics* **6**: 479–486.

*Tybulewicz V, Tremblay ML, LaMarca ME et al (1992) Animal model of Gaucher's disease from targeted disruption of the mouse glucocerebrosidase gene. *Nature* **357**: 407–410.

Uyama E, Takahashi K, Owada M et al (1992) Hydrocephalus, corneal opacities, deafness, valvular heart disease, deformed toes and leptomeningeal fibrous thickening in adult siblings: a new syndrome associated with β-glucocerebrosidase deficiency and a mosaic population of storage cells. *Acta Neurologica Scandinavica* **86**: 407–420.

Vervoort R, Islan MR, Sly WS et al (1996) Molecular analysis of patients with β-glucuronidase deficiency presenting as hydrops fetalis or as early mucopolysaccharidosis VII. *American Journal of Human Genetics* **58**: 457–471.

Vos HL, Mockensturm-Wilson M, Rood PML et al (1995) A tightly organized conserved gene cluster on mouse chromosome 3 (E3-F1). *Mammalian Genome* **6**: 820–822.

*Willemsen R, Tybulewicz V, Sidransky E et al, (1995) A biochemical and ultrastructural evaluation of the type 2 Gaucher mouse. *Journal of Chemical Neuropathology* **24**: 179–192.

*Winfield S, Tayebi N, Martin BM et al (1997) Identification of three additional genes contiguous to the glucocerebrosidase locus on chromosome 1q21: implications for Gaucher disease. *Genome Research* **7**: 1020–1026.

Zimran A, Sorge J, Gross E et al (1990) A glucocerebrosidase fusion gene in Gaucher disease. *Journal of Clinical Investigation* **85**: 219–222.

7

Pathological features

GREGORY M. PASTORES MD

Assistant Professor of Neurology and Paediatrics
Departments of Neurology and Paediatrics, New York University School of Medicine, Neurogenetics Laboratory, 400 East 34th Street, IRM RR 311, New York, NY 10016, USA

Gaucher's disease is the most common lysosomal storage disease. The pathological features are a consequence of the progressive accumulation of glucosylceramide within mononuclear phagocytes. A wide variety of gross and microscopic anatomical changes are seen, primarily in the bone marrow, liver, spleen and bones. It is probable that cellular reactions to the presence of Gaucher cells ('lipid-engorged' macrophages) contribute to the tissue damage observed in this disease, although only a few investigations have been undertaken to elucidate what, if any, other mechanisms may play a contributory role in defining individual disease outcome. The general clinico-pathological features of Gaucher's disease are reviewed herein, with exclusion of the central nervous system and skin involvement, which are covered elsewhere.

Key words: Gaucher's disease; pathology; macrophage; lysosomal storage.

Gaucher's disease (GD) is characterized clinically by a broad spectrum of clinical features that reflect the systemic burden of disease resulting from deficiency of acid β-glucosidase (glucocerebrosidase) (Beutler, 1995b). The primary pathology in GD is restricted to cells of monocyte/macrophage lineage, wherein the lysosomal storage of the undegraded substrate, glucosylceramide (glucocerebroside; GL_1) results in their transformation to 'Gaucher cells' (Beutler, 1995a). GL_1 is a metabolic byproduct of the catabolism of globoside and gangliosides, and the breakdown of non-neuronal membranes (i.e. senescent leukocytes and erythrocytes) represent the major peripheral substrate source (Kattlove et al, 1969; Grabowski et al, 1990). In neuronopathic forms of GD (i.e. Types 2 and 3), GL_1 in the brain is believed to originate from the turnover of membrane gangliosides of cells in the central nervous system.

The Gaucher cell (~20–$100\,\mu m$ in diameter), a lipid-laden histiocyte, has a characteristic pale blue to grey cytoplasm in Romanovsky stained preparations examined on light microscopy, with a striated, fibrillary or tubular pattern likened to 'wrinkled tissue paper' and an eccentrically located nucleus (Figure 1A) (Parkin and Brunning, 1982). It also stains for tartrate-resistant acid phosphatase (Figure 1B) and iron, and shows

Copyright © 1997, by Baillière Tindall
All rights of reproduction in any form reserved

increased lysozyme activity. Electron microscopy reveals the presence of dilated single membrane-bound vesicles (0.6 to 4 mm) containing characteristic twisted tubular-appearing structures that are postulated to represent the polymerization of GL_1 in a polar head-to-apolar tail manner (Lee, 1968).

THE SPLEEN, LIVER AND LYMPH NODES

Progressive splenomegaly is commonly found in GD patients, resulting in hypersplenism (i.e. thrombocytopenia, anaemia and occasionally leuko-penia).

The general contour of the spleen is preserved and its consistency firm. The splenic surface is often nodular, with a dark purple or brownish-red colour which corresponds to focal collections of Gaucher cells within the red pulp, extramedullary haematopoiesis, and regions of fibrosis or infarctions (Figure 2A and B) (Lee, 1982). Thickening of the splenic capsule and perisplenitis may also be seen. Ultrastructural studies have demonstrated active erythrophagocytosis by Gaucher cells, as well as the release of stored intracellular glucosylceramide into the extracellular spaces resulting in elevated plasma levels (Elleder and Jirasek, 1981). Ultrasonography and magnetic resonance imaging (MRI) of the spleen in GD patients often reveal the presence of nodules that may have a target-like configuration and be misconstrued to be malignant lesions (Aspestrand et al, 1989). Splenic artery aneurysm has been described in an adult GD patient attributed to compression (Colovic, 1989).

The liver is the major organ of GL_1 storage, trapped within the Kupffer cells in the hepatic sinusoids (James et al, 1981). Grossly, the liver can take on a yellow-brown or dark red to purple hue over areas with replacement by Gaucher cells (Figure 3A) or extramedullary haematopoiesis. Histological sections usually demonstrate clusters of Gaucher cells surrounding the central and hepatic veins with increased connective tissue. The portal and hepatic veins are normal. Electron micrograph of liver sections reveal the presence of tubular structures within lysosomes surrounded by fibrosis (Figure 3B). Although liver enlargement is often seen, functional abnormalities, cirrhosis and the formation of varices are rarely reported because the hepatocytes are spared (James et al, 1982). The absence of hepatocyte GL_1 storage has been attributed to its excretion into the bile (Tokoro et al, 1987). Rare cases of GD patients with portal hyper-tension because of increased intrahepatic vascular resistance and a mech-anical block at the pre-sinusoidal level, with ascites and oesophageal varices have been described (Sales and Hunt, 1970; Aderka et al, 1982). In most GD patients, gross liver dysfunction should prompt evaluation for other intercurrent pathology (e.g. hepatitis B or C).

Gaucher cells are frequently found in the lymph nodes, thymus and pharyngeal tonsils. The superficial lymph nodes are rarely enlarged. However, the lymph nodes in the thorax and abdomen may be increased in

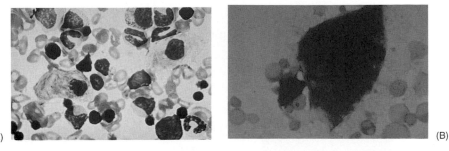

Figure 1. (A) Gaucher cells (at high magnification) with a fibrillary type of cytoplasm ('crumpled tissue paper' appearance) and eccentrically placed nucleus. (B) A Gaucher cell stained for acid phosphatase.

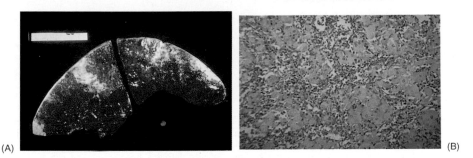

Figure 2. (A) Grossly, areas of fibrosis, often wedge-shaped and subcapsular, are seen in a massively enlarged spleen, (B) Gaucher cells infiltrating the spleen show expansion of the red pulp.

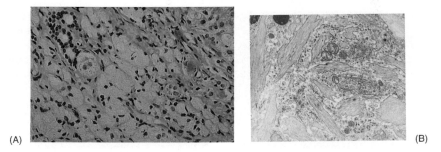

Figure 3. (A) Liver section (under high magnification) showing Gaucher cell infiltration. (B) Electron micrograph of a liver section showing the lysosomal storage of glucosylceramide; hepatocyte architecture is otherwise unremarkable.

size, and take on a dark red, yellowish-red or brownish-black discolouration. Marked retroperitoneal or periportal lymphadenopathy were noted in 11 out of 34 (32%) splenectomized patients (Neudorfer et al, 1997). Gaucher cell infiltration of the medullary portions of lymph node is seen, with minimal cellular reaction. The lymph node capsule and trabecula may be thickened.

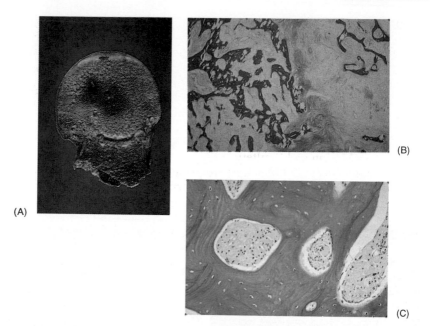

Figure 4. (A) Femoral head obtained at the time of a hip replacement in a patient with Gaucher disease who sustained a fracture at the femoral neck region. (B) Section of bone (under high magnification) showing areas of necrosis and fibrotic changes. (C) Gaucher cells infiltrating the Haversian canal. The subperiosteal oedema, that sometimes occurs during a bone crises and can lead to periosteal elevation ('pseudo-osteomyelitis'), presumably results from microscopic fluid egression through the Haversian systems and Volkmann canals persisting in the devitalized cortex.

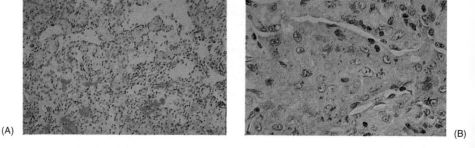

Figure 5. (A) Infiltration of alveolar septa and interstitium with Gaucher cells under low magnification. (B) Higher magnification showing aggregation of Gaucher cells in the pulmonary interstitium.

THE BONE

A broad spectrum of bone changes may be found in GD patients, ranging from osteopenia and focal lysis or sclerosis to infarction (Rosenthal et al, 1989). Although frequently generalized, skeletal disease at various anatomical sites of involvement are often noted to be at different stages of progression. Bone loss is usually most severe in the axial (i.e. spine) and the proximal appendicular (i.e. proximal femoral and humeral) skeleton. In patients with Types 1 and 3 GD, skeletal complications such as femoral (Figure 4A) or humeral head osteonecrosis or vertebral compression fractures represent a major source of morbidity (Stowens et al, 1985). Although involvement of the mandible and maxilla is infrequent, haemorrhage following dental extraction and osteomyelitis secondary to odontogenic infection have been reported (Schubiner et al, 1981; Hall et al, 1985). Pathological fractures in the spine can lead to neurological compression syndromes (Markin and Skultety, 1984).

Gross bone anatomical changes are present, with expansion of the distal third of the femur (Erlenmeyer flask deformity) being the most characteristic feature. The flaring of the long bones is not restricted to the femurs; it can also be found in the tibia and humerus. These changes have been attributed to failure of tubulation of the bone (Orcy, 1953). The cortices of the bone become demineralized, and there is extensive endosteal scalloping. Histomorphometric studies reveal abnormal bone architecture with loss of trabecular connectivity, porous trabeculated cortices, increased cancellous eroded surfaces and increased number of osteoclasts (Figure 4B) (Stowens et al, 1985). Gaucher cells can be found within the Haversian canals (Figure 4C). There is also extensive intramedullary replacement of normal triglyceride with glucosylceramide-containing macrophages as well as other pathological alterations (i.e. fibrosis and infarction). Sclerotic changes caused by dystrophic calcification of the necrotic Gaucher cell mass is also seen. Extraosseous extension with extravasation of Gaucher cells and formation of sinus tracts caused by cortical erosion may occur spontaneously and may mimic a malignant process (Hermann et al, 1994). Changes in the osseous structure may lead to secondary joint disease (osteoarthritis) with and without joint effusion.

Recent bone studies in adult patients with Type 1 GD revealed mean bone density at the spine, hip and forearm that was significantly lower than expected for age and sex (Pastores et al, 1996). The severity of the osteopenia correlated significantly with other clinical indicators of disease severity, including the N370S/84GG genotype, prior splenectomy and hepatomegaly. The bone density measurements also correlated significantly with the severity of skeletal disease as assessed by skeletal radiography. The cause of the osteopenia in Gaucher's disease is not known. It is felt that Gaucher cells do not resorb bone directly, but they may initiate increased bone resorption as suggested by in vitro studies which show that addition of GL_1 to macrophages in culture induced interleukin-1 secretion, a cytokine known to increase osteoclast activation (Gery et al, 1981).

The presence of lytic lesions on X-rays and increased serum gamma globulin levels seen in GD patients can sometimes lead to confusion with multiple myeloma (Benjamin et al, 1979; Burstein et al, 1987). A malignant epithelioid haemangioendothelioma (a rare vascular tumour of bone) that developed in association with a bone infarct in the tibia of a 39-year-old male GD patient has been described (Pins et al, 1995). Osteoblastoma of the humerus associated with Type 1 GD has also been reported (Kenan et al, 1996). In the preceeding two cases, persistent localized bone pain was a prominent feature in the clinical history.

HAEMATOPOIETIC SYSTEM

Displacement of normal bone marrow by progressive Gaucher cell infiltration and splenic sequestration result in anaemia, thrombocytopenia, and less often leukopenia. The peripheral smear of splenectomized patients show severe anisocytosis and poikilocytosis, with many target cells, some nucleated red blood cells and Howell–Jolly bodies.

Bone marrow biopsy reveals the characteristic lipid-engorged macrophages (Gaucher cell), which occur in clumps, surrounded by reticulum fibres. Ocassionally, very similar cells ('pseudo-Gaucher' cells) have been described in a variety of other disorders, including chronic granulocytic leukaemia, thalassaemia, multiple myeloma, Hodgkin disease, plasmacytoid lymphomas, and in the acquired immunodeficiency syndrome (AIDS) and *Mycobacterium avium* infections (Scullin et al, 1979; Zidar et al, 1987; Papadimitriou et al, 1988). These 'pseudo-Gaucher' cells often occur in isolation and do not contain the typical tubular structures of authentic Gaucher cells. Presumably, the increased cell turnover and presentation of GL_1-containing myeloid membranes to macrophages in these disorders lead to the formation of these cells.

Neoplastic disorders are reputed to be more common in patients with GD than in the general population (Shiran et al, 1993). Numerous case reports have documented the co-occurrence of GD and lymphoproliferative disease including chronic lymphocytic leukaemia, multiple myeloma, lymphoma, Hodgkin disease and non-Hodgkin lymphoma (Bruckstein et al, 1980; Garfinkel et al, 1982; Mark et al, 1982). The existence of monoclonal and polyclonal gammopathy has also been documented in a high proportion of GD patients greater than 50 years of age, although the clinical significance of these findings is not known (Benbassat, 1976; Marti et al, 1988; Liel et al, 1991). A discordant haematological profile should prompt evaluations for other causes of blood dyscrasias, such as immune-mediated thrombocytopenia and autoimmune haemolytic anaemia, which have been reported in patients with GD (Lester et al, 1984; Haratz et al, 1990).

PULMONARY AND CARDIOVASCULAR SYSTEM

Clinically significant pulmonary disease occurs infrequently in GD patients, although patients with massive hepatosplenomegaly may be restricted and report dyspnoea on exertion because of limited diaphragmatic excursions. In patients with severe liver dysfunction, cyanosis and clubbing can result from shunting within the lung due to an unidentified humoral factor(s) reported to clear following hepatic transplantation.

Three patterns of pulmonary pathology have been observed: (i) interstitial Gaucher-cell infiltration, that is, Gaucher cells in the perivascular, peribronchial and septal regions, with fibrosis (Lee and Yousem, 1988) (Figure 5A and B), (ii) alveolar consolidation, that is, Gaucher cells filling air spaces that mimic lobar pneumonia, and (iii) capillary plugging; Gaucher cells occluding small capillaries with secondary pulmonary hypertension. In patients with pulmonary involvement, clinical assessments may reveal the presence of interstitial infiltrate on chest radiograph and irregular areas with a ground glass appearance, alveolar filling and a diffuse interstitial infiltrate on high resolution chest computed tomography (CT) (Tunaci et al, 1995). Gaucher cells have also been demonstrated in bronchoalveolar lavage fluid (Carson et al, 1994).

Clinically, less than 5% of patients with Type 1 GD show signs (i.e. clubbing, cyanosis, hypoxaemia) of pulmonary involvement, although intensive investigations may reveal the presence of subclinical changes. In a study of 95 Type 1 GD patients, 68% had some pulmonary function abnormalities, including airways obstruction with reduced expiratory flows, reduction in lung volumes and alveolar–capillary diffusion abnormalities (Kerem et al, 1996).

Pulmonary hypertension in GD can be found in a few cases (<3%), as a result of chronic hypoxaemia in patients with interstitial lung disease, liver dysfunction, and long bone infarction and fracture with pulmonary emboli (Theise and Ursell, 1990). In some cases, it has been suggested that very high levels of serum angiotensin-converting enzyme seen in GD patients may also play a contributory role (Lieberman and Beutler, 1976).

Primary involvement of the heart in GD is extremely rare; an adult female with GD is reported to have Gaucher cell infiltration of the myocardium (Edwards et al, 1983). Haemorrhagic pericardial effusion with cardiac tamponade has been described, although these probably represent complications due to a coagulopathy rather than primary Gaucher cell infiltration (Davies and Foreman, 1970; Mester and Weston, 1992). Other pathological features reported include constrictive pericarditis and calcification of the ascending aorta, and aortic and mitral valves (Benbassat et al, 1968; Casta et al, 1984; Saraclar et al, 1991). None of these cases had genotype information to ascertain whether this rare complication may be unique to a particular subgroup of GD patients, as illustrated in the following case reports of patients with neuronopathic GD and atypical presentations. Three Spanish sisters with GD, born to a non-consanguineous couple, who were homozygous for the D409H mutation had cardiovascular abnormalities consisting of calcification of the ascending aorta and of the aortic and mitral valves (Chabas et al, 1995). In addition, neurological findings (i.e. ophthalmoplegia and saccadic eye movements in two of the siblings and tonic-clonic seizures in the third sibling) were present. Twelve GD patients of Arab (Jenin) descent, also homozygous for the D409H mutation, had calcifications of the aortic and/or mitral valves with oculomotor apraxia and mild systemic signs of glucosylceramide storage (Abrahamov et al, 1995). Severe cardiopulmonary amyloidosis that developed following splenectomy has been described in an adult Type 1 GD patient with the N370S/D409H genotype (Hrebicek et al, 1996).

RENAL AND GASTROINTESTINAL SYSTEM

Clinically, renal and intestinal disease due to GD is rare, even among patients with aggressive systemic problems and massive liver and splenic involvement. Proteinuria, which may result from infiltration of the glomeruli and interstitial capillaries by Gaucher cells can be found occasionally but almost never leads to renal failure. Patients may complain of abdominal pain, although this is more often related to hepatic or splenic infarctions or from gallstones resulting in obstruction or cholecystitis.

Gaucher cells, felt to be derived from circulating macrophages, have been found in the glomerular mesangial and endothelial cells, and in interstitial cells of the kidney (Rosenmann and Aviram, 1972; Chander et al, 1979). A patient with GD, nephrotic syndrome, and systemic amyloidosis has been described, although plasmacytosis in the bone marrow, the presence of light chains in the urine and renal glomeruli, and the finding of low circulating immunoglobulin levels suggest that the amyloid in this patient is related to a plasma cell dyscrasia (Dikman et al, 1978). Death from renal and pulmonary failure was reported in a 33-year-old Japanese male who underwent a splenectomy at age three (Morimura et al, 1994).

Gaucher cells have been found in Peyer's patches and at other sites in the gastrointestinal tract. Reported complications include lower intestinal bleeding attributed to colonic infiltration by Gaucher cells with polyp formation (Henderson et al, 1991). In another case, deposition of brown pigment (ceroid granules) in smooth muscles fibres of the gastrointestinal tract, urinary bladder and prostate were observed (Yamadori et al, 1990).

Acknowledgement

An educational grant was generously provided by Genzyme Therapeutics (European Divison) to cover the expenses for colour reproduction of the figures. The author also would like to acknowledge critical comments provided by Dr Ari Zimran.

REFERENCES

Abrahamov A, Elstein D, Gross Tsur V et al (1995) Gaucher's disease variant characterised by progressive calcification of heart valves and unique genotype [see comments]. *Lancet* **346(8981):** 1000–1003.
Aderka D, Garfinkel D, Rothem A et al (1982) Fatal bleeding from esophageal varices in a patient with Gaucher's disease. *American Journal of Gastroenterology* **77(11):** 838–839.
Aspestrand F, Charania B, Scheel B et al (1989) Focal changes of the spleen in one case of Gaucher disease—assessed by ultrasonography, CT, MRI and angiography. *Radiologe* **29(11):** 569–571.
Benbassat J, Bassan H, Milwidsky H et al (1968) Constrictive pericarditis in Gaucher's disease. *American Journal of Medicine* **44(4):** 647–652.
Benbassat J, Fluman N & Zlotnick A (1976) Monoclonal immunoglobulin disorders: a report of 154 cases. *American Journal of Medical Science* **271(3):** 325–334.
Benjamin D, Joshua H, Djaldetti M et al (1979) Nonsecretory IgD-kappa multiple myeloma in a patient with Gaucher's disease. *Scandinavian Journal of Haematology* **22(2):** 179–184.
Beutler E (1995a) Gaucher disease. *Advances in Genetics* **32:** 17–49.
Beutler E (1995b) Gaucher disease, a paradigm for single gene defects. *Experientia* **51(3):** 196–197.

Bruckstein A.H, Karanas A & Dire JJ (1980) Gaucher's disease associated with Hodgkin's disease. *American Journal of Medicine* **68(4):** 610–613.

Burstein Y, Zakuth V, Rechavi G et al (1987) Abnormalities of cellular immunity and natural killer cells in Gaucher's disease. *Journal of Clinical Laboratory Immunology* **23(3):** 149–151.

Carson KF, Williams CA, Rosenthal DL et al (1994) Bronchoalveolar lavage in a girl with Gaucher's disease. A case report. *Acta Cytology* **38(4):** 597–600.

Casta A, Hayden K & Wolf WJ (1984) Calcification of the ascending aorta and aortic and mitral valves in Gaucher's disease. *American Journal of Cardiology* **54(10):** 1390–1391.

Chabas A, Cormand B, Grinberg D et al (1995) Unusual expression of Gaucher's disease: cardio-vascular calcifications in three sibs homozygous for the D409H mutation. *Journal of Medical Genetics* **32(9):** 740–742.

Chander PN, Nurse HM & Pirani CL (1979) Renal involvement in adult Gaucher's disease after splenectomy. *Archives in Pathological and Laboratory Medicine* **103(9):** 440–445.

Colovic R (1989) Splenic artery aneurysm in a patient with Gaucher's disease. *Srp Arh Celok Lek* **117(1–2):** 107–113.

Davies GT & Foreman HM (1970) Haemorrhagic pericardial effusion in adult Gaucher's disease. *British Heart Journal* **32(6):** 855–858.

Dikman SH, Goldstein M, Kahn T et al (1978) Amyloidosis. An unusual complication of Gaucher's disease. *Archives of Pathology and Laboratory Medicine* **102(9):** 460–462.

Edwards WD, Hurdey HPD & Partin JR (1983) Cardiac involvement by Gaucher's disease documented by right ventricular endomyocardial biopsy. *American Journal of Cardiology* **52(5):** 654.

Elleder M & Jirasek A (1981) Histochemical and ultrastructural study of Gaucher cells. *Acta Neuropathology Supplement Berlin* **7:** 208–210.

Garfinkel D, Sidi Y, Ben Bassat M et al (1982) Coexistence of Gaucher's disease and multiple myeloma. *Archives of Internal Medicine* **142(12):** 2229–2230.

Gery I, Zigler JS, Brady RO & Barranger JA (1981) Selective effects of glucocerebroside (Gaucher's storage material) on macrophage cultures. *Journal of Clinical Investigations* **68:** 1182–1189.

Grabowski GA, Gatt S & Horowitz M (1990) Acid beta-glucosidase: enzymology and molecular biology of Gaucher disease. *Critical Review of Biochemical and Molecular Biology* **25(6):** 385–414.

Hall MB, Brown RW & Baughman RA (1985) Gaucher's disease affecting the mandible. *Journal of Oral and Maxillofacial Surgery* **43(3):** 210–213.

Haratz D, Manny N & Raz I (1990) Autoimmune hemolytic anemia in Gaucher's disease. *Klinische Wochenschrift* **68(2):** 94–95.

Henderson JM, Gilinsky NH, Lee EY et al (1991) Gaucher's disease complicated by bleeding esophageal varices and colonic infiltration by Gaucher cells. *American Journal of Gastro-enterology* **86(3):** 346–348.

Hermann G, Shapiro R, Abdelwahab IF et al (1994) Extraosseous extension of Gaucher cell deposits mimicking malignancy. *Skeletal Radiology* **23(4):** 253–256.

Hrebicek M, Zeman J, Musilov J et al (1996) A case of type 1 Gaucher disease with cardiopulmonary amyloidosis and chitotriosidase deficiency. *Virchows Archiv* **429:** 305–309.

James SP, Stromeyer FW, Chang C et al (1981) Liver abnormalities in patients with Gaucher's disease. *Gastroenterology* **80(1):** 126–133.

James SP, Stromeyer FW, Stowens DW et al (1982) Gaucher disease: hepatic abnormalities in 25 patients. *Progress in Clinical Biological Research* **95:** 131–142.

Kattlove HE, Williams JC, Gaynor E et al (1969) Gaucher cells in chronic myelocytic leukemia: an acquired abnormality. *Blood* **33(2):** 379–390.

Kenan S, Abdelwahab IF, Hermann G et al (1996) Osteoblastoma of the humerus associated with type-I Gaucher's disease. A case report. *Journal of Bone and Joint Surgery B* **78(5):** 702–705.

Kerem E, Elstein D, Abrahamo A et al (1996) Pulmonary function abnormalities in type I Gaucher disease. *European Respiratory Journal* **9(2):** 340–345.

Lee RE (1968) The fine structure of the cerebroside occurring in Gaucher's disease. *Proceedings of the National Academy of Science USA* **61(2):** 484–489.

Lee RE (1982) The pathology of Gaucher disease. *Progress in Clinical Biological Research* **95:** 177–217.

Lee R & Yousem S (1988) The frequency and type of lung involvement in patients with Gaucher disease [Abstract]. *Laboratory Investigation* **58:** 54A.

Lester TJ, Grabowski GA, Goldblatt J et al (1984) Immune thrombocytopenia and Gaucher's disease. *American Journal of Medicine* **77(3):** 569–571.

Lieberman J & Beutler E (1976) Elevation of serum angiotensin-converting enzyme in Gaucher's disease. *New England Journal of Medicine* **294(26):** 1442–1444.

Liel Y, Hausmann MJ & Mozes M (1991) Case report: serendipitous Gaucher's disease presenting as elevated erythrocyte sedimentation rate due to monoclonal gammopathy. *American Journal of Medical Science* **301(6):** 393–394.

Mark T, Dominguez C & Rywlin AM (1982) Gaucher's disease associated with chronic lymphocytic leukemia. *Southern Medical Journal* **75(3):** 361–363.

Markin RS & Skultety FM (1984) Spinal cord compression secondary to Gaucher's disease. *Surgery and Neurology* **21(4):** 341–346.

Marti GE, Ryan ET, Papadopoulos NM et al (1988). Polyclonal B-cell lymphocytosis and hypergammaglobulinemia in patients with Gaucher disease. *American Journal of Hematology* **29:** 189–194.

Mester S & Weston M (1992) Cardiac tamponade in a patient with Gaucher's disease. *Clinical Cardiology* **15:** 766–767.

Morimura Y, Hojo H, Abe M & Wakasa H. (1994) Gaucher's disease, type 1 (adult type), with massive involvement of the kidneys and lungs. *Virchows Archiv* **425:** 537–540.

Neudorfer O, Hadas-Halpern I, Elstein D et al (1997) Abdominal ultrasound findings mimicking hematological malignancies in a study of 218 Gaucher patients. *American Journal of Hematology* **55:** 28–34.

Orcy L (1953) Failure in modeling of bone. *Radiology* **73:** 645–649.

Papadimitriou JC, Chakravarthy A & Heyman MR (1988) Pseudo-Gaucher cells preceding the appearance of immunoblastic lymphoma. *American Journal of Clinical Pathology* **90(4):** 454–458.

Parkin JL & Brunning RD (1982) Pathology of the Gaucher cell. *Progress in Clinical and Biological Research* **95:** 151–175.

Pastores G, Wallenstein S, Desnick R et al (1996) Bone density in type 1 Gaucher disease. *Journal of Bone and Mineral Research* **11:** 1801–1807.

Pins MR, Mankin HJ, Xavier RJ et al (1995) Malignant epithelioid hemangioendothelioma of the tibia associated with a bone infarct in a patient who had Gaucher disease. A case report. *Journal of Bone and Joint Surgery of America* **77(5):** 777–781.

Prence E, Chakravorti S, Basu A et al (1985) Further studies on the activation of glucocerebrosidase by a heat-stable factor from Gaucher spleen. *Archives in Biochemistry and Biophysics* **236(1):** 98–109.

Rosenmann E & Aviram A (1972) Glomerular involvement in storage diseases. *Journal of Pathology* **111(1):** 61–64.

Rosenthal DI, Mayo Smith W, Goodsitt MM et al (1989) Bone and bone marrow changes in Gaucher disease: evaluation with quantitative CT. *Radiology* **170(1 Pt 1):** 143–146.

Sales JE & Hunt AH (1970) Gaucher's disease and portal hypertension. *British Journal of Surgery* **57(3):** 225–228.

Saraclar M, Atalay S, Kocak N et al (1991) Gaucher's disease with mitral and aortic involvement: echocardiographic findings. *Pediatrics and Cardiology* **13:** 56–58.

Schubiner H, Letourneau M & Murray DL. (1981) Pyogenic osteomyelitis versus pseudo-osteomyelitis in Gaucher's disease. Report of a case and review of the literature. *Clinical Pediatrics* **20(10):** 667–669.

Scullin DC Jr, Shelburne JD & Cohen HJ (1979) Pseudo-Gaucher cells in multiple myeloma. *American Journal of Medicine* **67(2):** 347–352.

Shiran A, Brenner B, Laor A et al (1993) Increased risk of cancer in patients with Gaucher disease. *Cancer* **72(1):** 219–224.

Stowens DW, Teitelbaum SL, Kahn AJ et al (1985) Skeletal complications of Gaucher disease. *Medicine (Baltimore)* **64(5):** 310–322.

Theise ND & Ursell PC (1990) Pulmonary hypertension and Gaucher's disease: logical association or mere coincidence? *American Journal of Pediatrics, Hematology and Oncology* **12(1):** 74–76.

Tokoro T, Gal AE, Gallo LL & Brady RO (1987) Studies of the pathogenesis of Gaucher's disease: tissue distribution and biliary excretion of ^{14}C-L-glucosylceramide in rats. *Lipid Research* **28:** 968–972.

Tunaci A, Berkmen YM & Gokmen E (1995) Pulmonary Gaucher's disease: high-resolution computed tomographic features. *Pediatrics and Radiology* **25(3):** 237–238.

Yamadori I, Morikawa T, Kobayashi S et al (1990) Gaucher's disease type I. Report of a case with prominent deposition of ceroid in splenic endothelial cells and intestinal smooth muscle fibers. *Acta Pathologica Japonica* **40(6):** 425–430.

Zidar BL, Hartsock RJ, Lee RE et al (1987) Pseudo-Gaucher cells in the bone marrow of a patient with Hodgkin's disease. *American Journal of Clinical Pathology* **87(4):** 533–536.

8

Enzyme replacement therapy for Gaucher's disease

ERNEST BEUTLER MD

Professor and Chairman
Department of Molecular and Experimental Medicine, The Scripps Research Institute, 10550 North Torrey Pines Road, La Jolla, CA 92037, USA

Modified placental human glucocerebrosidase (alglucerase) and recombinant gluco-cerebrosidase (imiglucerase) are effective means of treating Type 1 Gaucher's disease. Amelioration of hepatosplenomegaly and of haematological manifestations is usually apparent within 6 months. Bone disease responds more slowly but within several years improvement is evident in most patients. Analysis of a large body of data demonstrates that the rate of response of all manifestations of Gaucher's disease is independent of dose over the range of 30 to 260 U/kg body weight per month. Even the response to 15 U/kg per month appears to be equivalent under most circumstances; treatment failures are the same in patients treated with 15, 30 and 130 U/kg per month. Patients with severe manifestations respond more rapidly than those with mild disease, and this, too, is true at all but the 15 U/kg per month dosage level. All available data thus support the administration of no more than 15 to 30 U of alglucerase or imiglucerase per kg/month. Frequent dosing, i.e. three times weekly, appears to be the most effective means of administration.

Key words: Gaucher's disease; glucocerebrosidase; imiglucerase; alglucerase; bone; liver; spleen; blood; central nervous system; pregnancy.

Infusion of exogenous human glucocerebrosidase into patients with Gaucher's disease, enzyme replacement therapy, is a major advance in the management of this disorder. Although the concept that replacing the missing enzymes in patients with lysosomal storage disorders is more than a quarter of a century old (De Duve, 1964; Brady, 1966; Brady et al, 1974), it was only with improved understanding of enzyme trafficking in the late 1970s (Achord et al, 1978) that clinically useful results were achieved (Barton et al, 1991a). The history of the development of enzyme replacement therapy for Gaucher's disease has been reviewed elsewhere in this volume. This chapter will deal with the manner in which enzyme replacement therapy is most efficiently, most effectively, and most safely given.

It is sometimes stated that the dose of enzyme that should be used is 'controversial'. *Controversy* is defined as 'a discussion marked especially

Baillière's Clinical Haematology—
Vol. 10, No. 4, December 1997
ISBN 0–7020–2378–7
0950–3536/97/040751 + 13 $12.00/00

751

Copyright © 1997, by Baillière Tindall
All rights of reproduction in any form reserved

by the expression of opposing views'. Widely divergent views of the proper dosage of enzyme have indeed, been expressed. This is, perhaps, not surprising since the economic stakes are enormous. However, even though views or opinions about the proper enzyme dosage appear to vary widely the actual data that are now available for examination are not only quite extensive but are entirely consistent in most respects. Opinions unsupported by fact play no legitimate role in science whether the question be a clinical or a laboratory one. The focus of this review will, therefore, be what the data show. Where the data are contradictory or inconsistent, this will be pointed out.

PRINCIPLES OF ENZYME THERAPY OF GAUCHER'S DISEASE

Enzyme replacement therapy is based on the principal that exogenous enzyme is targeted to the lysosome of a macrophage that is either in the process of accumulating glucocerebroside or one that has already become engorged with the glycolipid and has therefore become a Gaucher cell. Although in the ultimate analysis it is the results of therapy that must guide us, theoretical considerations have been important in framing therapeutic approaches and are therefore considered here.

Alglucerase and imiglucerase are both processed to increase the amount of mannose exposed with the idea that this will direct the enzyme to the mannose receptor of macrophages. To the extent that this is what accounts for the success of this therapy it is important to consider the density and affinity of the mannose receptors and the intracellular half-life of the enzyme. The development of low-dose high-frequency therapy was based on the assumption that the number of mannose receptors are limited and that they compete with much larger numbers of low-affinity receptors (Beutler et al, 1991). The validity of this assumption was challenged by Barton et al (1991b) based on the plasma clearance rates of alglucerase infused at different levels, showing that the clearance was independent of the amount of enzyme infused. This is, of course, precisely the result that would be anticipated if uptake, particularly at higher levels, was due largely to nonspecific binding sites (Beutler, 1994). Subsequent studies have amply confirmed the concept that the number of specific binding sites is very limited; when large doses of enzyme are infused most of the enzyme is apparently taken up by non-specific sites and is presumably wasted. Alglucerase has been shown to bind not only to the classical mannose receptor but also to a much more prevalent and broadly distributed mannose receptor that is found on all cells tested, including endothelium (Sato and Beutler, 1993). More recently the concept that high affinity mannose receptors do not limit the amount of enzyme that can be taken up by macrophages has been further contradicted by the elegant in vivo studies of Mistry et al (1996) in which radiolabelled enzyme was administered to human subjects. They found that when a subject was given an enzyme dose of 35 U/kg just prior to a dose of 5 U/kg the clearance half-time increased from 4 minutes to 12 minutes.

VARIABLES IN RESPONSE TO ENZYME REPLACEMENT THERAPY

As with any other drug therapy the variables that may affect response to enzyme replacement include (i) frequency of administration; (ii) rate of administration; (iii) total dosage; and (iv) the mode of manufacture. In the case of enzyme replacement therapy two different preparations must be considered. Alglucerase (Ceredase®), is glucocerebrosidase that has been purified from human placenta. It was the first preparation to have been used and thus most of the available data are concerned with this preparation. Fewer data and follow-up information are available with respect to imiglucerase (Cerezyme®), the recombinant form of the enzyme.

In considering the response of patients with a disease as complex as Gaucher's disease one may attempt to determine whether different treatment regimens exert a differential effect on different disease manifestations, especially when considering a disease in which several different organ systems are involved. We will therefore examine the effect of replacement therapy on various organ systems.

VISCERAL CHANGES

The largest body of evidence regarding the response to therapy has been the measurement of the size of the liver and spleen using a number of different imaging techniques. Integration of consecutive organ slice areas measured by either magnetic resonance imaging (MRI) or computerized axial tomography (CAT) scanning provides results that are relatively reproducible. Somewhat surprisingly, measurement of the size of the liver with ultrasound, a much less costly procedure, provides data that correlate very well with those obtained on the same patients with MRI scanning (Glenn et al, 1994).

A liver or spleen that is minimally enlarged or not enlarged at all could hardly be expected to diminish in size with therapy. Thus, the degree to which an enlarged liver or spleen decreases in size bears a relationship to its original volume. Figure 1 depicts the change of liver and spleen size after the first 6 months of therapy as a function of original organ size in all patients in whom measurements were reported in the six major studies of response to various doses that have been published since 1991 (Barton et al, 1991a; Pastores et al, 1993; Zimran et al, 1994; Beutler et al; 1995a; Hollak et al, 1995; Zimran et al, 1995). Earlier studies by the same groups (Beutler et al, 1991; Kay et al, 1991; Figueroa et al, 1992; Hollak et al, 1993) are included in all of the later publications, so that these six studies represent a very complete assessment of all published series. The figure demonstrates not only the relationship between organ size and organ

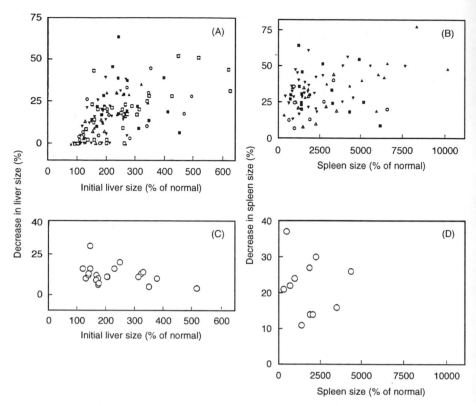

Figure 1. The relationship between initial liver and spleen size and response to 6 months' therapy in doses ranging from 15 U/kg per month to 130 U/kg per month. (A) Liver and (B) spleen show responses to doses between 105 and 130 U/kg per month in solid symbols (▲ 130 U/kg per month: ▲, Barton et al, 1991a; ▼, Grabowski et al, 1995.) and doses of 30 U/kg per month in open symbols (○, Beutler et al, 1995a; □, Zimran et al, 1994; △, Zimran et al, 1995). (C) Liver and (D) spleen show the response to 15 U/kg per month (○, Hollak et al, 1995).

response, but also shows that response is independent of dosage in the range of 30 U/kg per month to 130 U/kg per month. At the level of 15 U/kg per month the relationship between initial organ size and response seems to be lost. At this dose, the response of modest organomegaly is the same as at higher doses, but the few patients with massive hepatomegaly that have been studied seem to have responded less well than those patients who were given 30 U/kg per month or more. At least to the extent that organ size reflects disease severity it provides no support for the suggestion that larger doses of enzyme must be administered for more severe disease.

In one study (Pastores et al, 1993) 30 patients were investigated over an approximately 2.5-fold range of doses. Most of the patients had been splenectomized, and thus only the liver size data are meaningful. These are presented in Figure 2. As pointed out by the authors (Pastores et al, 1993), no effect of dose on the change in organomegaly could be detected.

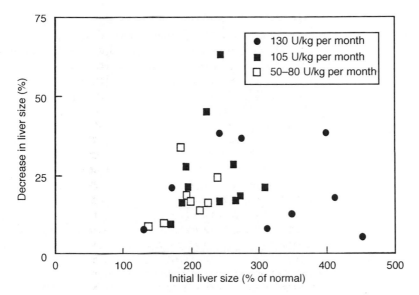

Figure 2. The relationship between initial liver size and response to 6 months' therapy in doses ranging from 50 U/kg per month to 130 U/kg per month in a study reported by Pastores et al (1993). The 105–130 U/kg per month data are included in panel A in Figure 1.

HAEMATOLOGICAL RESPONSE

Haematological data are easy to collect, but valid analysis is much more difficult than that of organ size. Many patients, particularly those that have been splenectomized, are not anaemic or thrombocytopenic at the time that therapy is started. Some patients are even polycythaemic and require phlebotomies because of Gaucher's disease-related lung disease. In such patients it is a decrease, not an increase of the haemoglobin level that represents the desired clinical response. Finally, the age and sex of the patient is a significant factor in assessing the response to treatment. A haemoglobin level of 12.5 g/dl represents anaemia in a male but not in a female.

We have attempted to take all of these consideration into account in analysing the effect of treatment on the haemoglobin level and platelet counts of patients being treated with alglucerase or imiglucerase. Figures 3–4 summarize all of the published data (Zimran et al, 1994; Beutler et al, 1995a; Grabowski et al, 1995; Hollak et al, 1995). It is apparent that there is no significant difference between the response to high and low doses of enzyme with the possible exception of a slightly lower response at a dose of 15 U/kg per month. This finding contradicts a report of the International Collaborative Gaucher Group Registry (International Collaborative Gaucher Group Registry and Genzyme Therapeutics, 1995) of Genzyme Corp. (Boston, MA), which claims a slight advantage for high doses with respect to haematological responses. However, the latter studies failed to

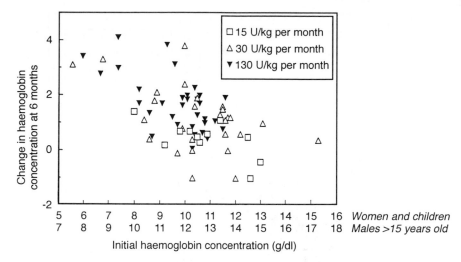

Figure 3. The change in haemoglobin concentration after 6 months treatment of non-splenectomized Gaucher's disease patients with alglucerase or imiglucerase at doses of 15 U/kg per month (Hollak et al, 1995), 30 U/kg per month (Zimran et al, 1994 and Beutler et al, 1995a) and 130 U/kg per month (Grabowski et al, 1995). The latter data are adjusted from 9 months, as tabulated, to 6 months according to the 6-month mean values given by the authors. Some studies (Barton et al, 1991a) could not be included because the time at which blood counts were obtained was not stated. There is a statistically significant negative correlation between initial haemoglobin levels and the rise in haemoglobin concentration.

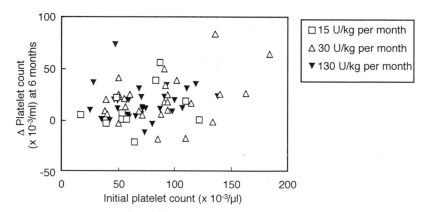

Figure 4. The change in platelet levels after 6-months treatment of non-splenectomized Gaucher's disease patients with alglucerase or imiglucerase at doses of 15 U/kg per month (Hollak et al, 1995), 30 U/kg per month (Zimran et al, 1994 and Beutler et al, 1995a) and 130 U/kg per month (Grabowski et al 1995). The latter data are adjusted from 9 months, as tabulated, to 6 months according to the 6-month mean values given by the authors. Some studies (Barton et al, 1991a) could not be included because the time at which blood counts were obtained was not stated.

stratify results either by severity of cytopenia or by sex; the slight differences observed were probably because the patients with milder haematological manifestations were given lower doses.

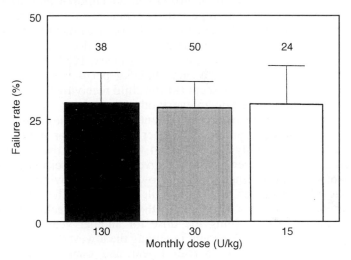

Figure 5. The failure rate at different monthly doses of alglucerase or imiglucerase (Beutler, 1995)
using the criteria of Hollak et al (1995). These criteria are based on a combination of the haematological and visceral response. The analysis is based upon all studies of five or more patients in which
sufficient data were given to allow evaluation of the response at 6 months (Fallet et al, 1992; Zimran
et al, 1994; Beutler et al, 1995b; Grabowski et al, 1995; Hollak et al, 1995). The error bars represent
one standard error of the mean and the numbers above represent the number of patients.

'TREATMENT FAILURES'

Several advocates of high-dose therapy (Moscicki and Van Heek, 1994;
Marodi, 1995) have expressed concerns about 'treatment failures' at low
doses. However, all studies show a broad distribution of results, with
spectacular changes in blood counts and organomegaly in some patients
and little or no response in others. It has often been assumed that such
differences are because of dose sensitivity, some patients requiring higher
doses than others. Indeed, a number of recommendations have been made
for dose adjustment according to response (Hollak et al, 1995; McCabe et
al, 1996) with the underlying assumption that dose and response are related.
There is little doubt that over some range this must be true. In such a dose
range one would anticipate that treatment failures would be less common at
high doses than at low doses. However, using the criteria of Hollak et al
(1995), no such dose-sensitivity is apparent (Beutler, 1995) (Figure 5).

GROWTH RETARDATION IN CHILDREN

Growth retardation is common in children with moderate to severe
Gaucher's disease. When such patients were treated with alglucerase at a

dose of 30 U/kg per month given three times weekly, three of seven patients whose height percentile was less than 10 improved their percentile score after 12 months of therapy (Zevin et al, 1993). Recently (Kaplan et al, 1996) a retrospective analysis of growth in 54 children and adolescents treated with alglucerase was reported. Detailed results were reported in only 18 of these, of whom 12 had a height before treatment that was under the 25th percentile. Among these patients, the initial dose was 240 U/kg per 4 weeks in one patient, 120 U/kg per 4 weeks in six, 108 U/kg per 4 weeks in one, 66 U/kg per 4 weeks in one, 30 U/kg per 4 weeks in one, and 20 U/kg per 4 weeks in two. Except for the child receiving the largest dose, all doses were administered on an every-other-week basis. After 1 year the percentile height had improved in all patients except for the children receiving 240 U/kg per 4 weeks and 108 U/kg per 4 weeks. Surprisingly, even the children who received only 20 U/kg per 4 weeks, a dose that is ineffective in reducing liver and spleen size when given every 2 weeks (Barton et al, 1993), had some improvement in their growth, one improving from << 5 to < 5 and the other from < 25 to 25 percentile. The first of these children had a mid-parental value of < 5, and may therefore have achieved her full potential. Indeed, after tripling the dose for another year the percentile score was still < 5. The other patient receiving the lowest dose increased her percentile score from < 25 to 25 after 1 year, and, continued on the same dose to 50 after 2 years of treatment, exceeding the mid-parental score of < 25. It is difficult to reconcile these data with the authors' conclusions that 'Normal growth ... occurred only in those receiving higher doses (60 to 120 U/kg per 4-week period) of alglucerase'.

SKELETAL DISEASE

Evaluation of the response of bone involvement in the enzyme replacement treatment of Gaucher's disease has proven to be particularly difficult. Rosenthal et al (1995) have carried out detailed imaging studies of the skeleton of 12 patients with Gaucher's disease treated with enzyme at a level of 130 U/kg per month for 2 years and then gradually decreasing doses. Included were MRI examinations, Xenon update and measurement of trabecular bone density and cortical bone thickness. No significant changes were documented until the patients had been treated for 42 months. They confirmed our findings (Beutler et al, 1995b) that delivery of alglucerase to bone was very inefficient and concluded that 'large doses will likely be necessary for this indication, because enzyme delivery to bone marrow is relatively inefficient'. Others (Moscicki and Van Heek, 1994) have attempted to use this study as justification for the use of large doses of alglucerase or imiglucerase in the treatment of patients with skeletal involvement. However, since no studies using smaller doses were performed by Rosenthal et al (1995), no conclusions can be drawn from this study regarding the size of dose required. Moreover, our own studies of bone uptake failed to show a dose effect (Beutler et al, 1995b). In reality, response to treatment with small doses has not differed from the response reported to large doses in all parameters that were studied (Beutler et al, 1995a; Beutler, 1996; Elstein et al, 1996). Specifically, Elstein et al measured the cortical bone thickness of Gaucher's disease patients who were either untreated or treated with 30 U/kg per month. The results, summarized in Figure 6 are indistinguishable from the results of high-dose therapy.

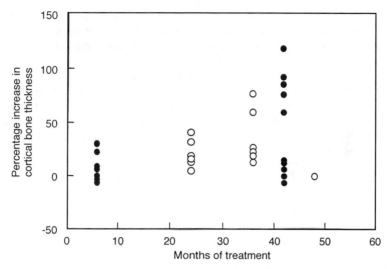

Figure 6. Change in cortical bone thickness before and at intervals after therapy of patients receiving low dose (30 U/kg per month), Elstein et al (1996) = ○ and high dose (130 U/kg per month), Rosenthal et al (1995) = ● therapy with alglucerase.

NEUROLOGICAL DISEASE

Attempts to modify the course of the acute infantile neuronopathic disease (Type 2 Gaucher's disease) have been made, but in spite of relatively heroic measures, such as infusing enzyme directly into the spinal fluid of such infants, their disease has generally progressed to a fatal outcome (Brady et al, 1997). The result of treatment of the chronic neuropathic disease (Type 3 Gaucher's disease) is uncertain (Brady et al, 1997). Visceral manifestations of the disease respond, but oculomotor apraxia has not regressed, and we have observed the development of this early neurological manifestation in one child after several years of enzyme therapy. Since the rate of progression of neurological manifestations in patients with Type 3 disease are quite unpredictable, it is difficult to be certain whether treatment has retarded progression of neurological signs.

PULMONARY DISEASE

The development of pulmonary disease in patients with Gaucher's disease has been recognized for over 60 years (Myers, 1937), but its pathogenesis remains unclear. Indeed, it is possible that there is more than one mechanism. In some instances, particularly when pulmonary shunting is a prominent finding, it may be secondary to the cirrhosis of the liver that these patients develop. In other instances, particularly when pulmonary hypertension is a major manifestation, it may be secondary to embolization of pulmonary vessels or even direct involvement of pulmonary macrophages. Because pulmonary disease occurs in only a small proportion of patients with Gaucher's disease, most probably less than 5%, there are relatively few data regarding the response of these patients to enzyme replacement therapy. A preliminary impression is that shunting of blood from the right side of the circulation to the left improves with enzyme replacement therapy (Pelini et al, 1994; Dawson et al, 1996). However, some patients with shunting have developed pulmonary hypertension while being treated with alglucerase. Indeed, two patients developed progressive pulmonary hypertension and died while receiving enzyme replacement therapy (Harats et al, 1997). Other patients have experienced a stable course or have even improved somewhat while receiving enzyme replacement. We are inclined to believe that the development of pulmonary hypertension in patients with shunting who are treated with alglucerase may be the predictable haemodynamic consequence of closing shunts in a patient predisposed to pulmonary hypertension. Pulmonary hypertension is known to be exacerbated by pregnancy, and indeed, one of the Gaucher's disease patients who died with progressive pulmonary hypertension had become pregnant (Harats et al, 1997). Because of the remote possibility that contaminants in the placental preparation, alglucerase, may play a role, we have switched our patients with pulmonary hypertension to imiglucerase. The long-term outlook of patients with pulmonary hypertension is unknown.

PREGNANCY

Physicians have been reluctant to administer alglucerase or imiglucase to patients who are attempting to become pregnant and who are pregnant. There is no compelling reason not to administer the drug during pregnancy, but contamination of alglucerase with chorionic gonadotropin and the possibility that there may be unknown viral agents in either alglucerase or imiglucerase are reasons for caution. The package insert states 'It is also not known whether Ceredase® can cause fetal harm. . . . Ceredase® should be given to a pregnant woman only if clearly needed'.

Some experience has been gained in the use of Ceredase during pregnancy, and it is generally reassuring. According to data gathered by Genzyme Corp. (Boston Mass) (personal communication), seven patients were treated during the first trimester. One spontaneous abortion and six healthy babies resulted from these pregnancies. In the second trimester of pregnancy seven patients were treated with alglucerase and one with imiglucerase. There was one case of pre-eclampsia with fetal death in this group of patients. Some of this experience has been reported in an abstract (Esplin et al, 1993). Elstein et al (1996) administered alglucerase to an additional five pregnant patients without untoward effects. These studies lead me to conclude that if clearly needed, alglucerase or imiglucerase should be given to pregnant women with Gaucher's disease. If there are not compelling reasons for doing so, it is probably prudent to interrupt therapy during pregnancy.

FREQUENCY OF INFUSION

The commonly used schedule of administering alglucerase or imiglucerase each 2 weeks is convenient for patients, and was probably selected for this reason. Given the very short plasma and intracellular half-life of the exogenously administered enzyme, many investigators (Beutler et al, 1991, 1993; Kay et al, 1991; Zimran et al, 1993a, 1994; Hollak et al, 1995; Mistry et al, 1996) have concluded that more frequent dosing is likely to be more effective. Data regarding the frequency with which enzyme is optimally administered are conflicting. Barton et al observed a suboptimal decrease in organomegaly in patients given 22 U/kg per month (Barton et al, 1993) when compared with the results obtained when 15 U/kg per month (Hollak et al, 1995) or 30 U/kg per month (Figueroa et al, 1992; Beutler, 1993; Zimran et al, 1994; Beutler et al, 1995a) were given thrice weekly. In one study, however, the administration of 30 U/kg per month of imiglucerase to five patients three times weekly and to five patients every 2 weeks showed only minor differences in the response (Zimran et al, 1995). Daily administration did not seem to be strikingly more effective than administration three times weekly (Figueroa et al, 1992). Moreover, fractionated total doses of 120 U/kg per month did not appear to be more effective than the same very large dose given once twice weekly.

Although the question of optimal frequency is an important one, it is not likely to be answered by clinical studies, since the number of new patients now being treated is relatively small. On balance, it seems likely that more frequent administration is more effective at the lower dosage range but not when very large doses are administered. Infusing enzyme three times weekly usually requires placement of a central line. Patients tolerate this well and infuse themselves at home. Most patients appear to prefer this to travelling to a clinic every 2 weeks. Indwelling lines carry a small, but finite risk of infection. Our experience with home therapy has been quite favourable (Zimran et al, 1993b), but occasional episodes of infection do occur, and patients must be made aware of the necessity of treating such infections promptly and vigorously if they occur.

Acknowledgements

This is manuscript 10675-MEM from The Scripps Research Institute. Supported by National Institutes of Health grant RR00833 and the Stein Endowment Fund.

REFERENCES

Achord DT, Brot FE, Bell CE & Sly WS (1978) Human beta-glucuronidase: In vivo clearance and in vitro uptake by a glycoprotein recognition system on reticuloendothelial cells. *Cell* **15:** 269–278.

Barton NW, Brady RO & Dambrosia JM (1993) Treatment of Gaucher's disease. *New England Journal of Medicine* **328:** 1564–1565.

Barton NW, Brady RO, Dambrosia JM et al (1991a) Replacement therapy for inherited enzyme deficiency—macrophage-targeted glucocerebrosidase for Gaucher's disease. *New England Journal of Medicine* **324:** 1464–1470.

*Barton NW, Brady RO, Murray GJ et al (1991b) Enzyme-replacement therapy for Gaucher's disease: Reply. *New England Journal of Medicine* **325:** 1811.

*Beutler E (1993) Modern diagnosis and treatment of Gaucher's disease. *American Journal of Diseases in Children* **147:** 1175–1183.

Beutler E (1994) Economic malpractice in the treatment of Gaucher disease. *American Journal of Medicine* **97:** 1–2.

Beutler E (1995) Treatment regimens in Gaucher's disease. *Lancet* **346:** 581–582.

Beutler E (1996) Effect of low-dose enzyme replacement therapy on bones in Gaucher disease patients with severe skeletal involvement—Commentary. *Blood Cells, Molecules, and Diseases* **22:** 113–114.

Beutler E, Figueroa M & Koziol J (1993) Treatment of Gaucher's disease. *New England Journal of Medicine* **328:** 1567.

Beutler E, Kuhl W & Vaughan LM (1995b) Failure of alglucerase infused into Gaucher disease patients to localize in marrow macrophages. *Molecular Medicine* **1:** 320–324.

Beutler E, Kay A, Saven A et al (1991) Enzyme replacement therapy for Gaucher disease. *Blood* **78:** 1183–1189.

*Beutler E, Demina A, Laubscher K et al (1995a) The clinical course of treated and untreated Gaucher disease. A study of 45 patients. *Blood Cells, Molecules, and Diseases* **21:** 86–108.

Brady RO (1966) The sphingolipidoses. *New England Journal of Medicine* **275:** 312–318.

Brady RO, Murray GJ & Barton NW (1997) Glucosylceramide lipidosis: Gaucher disease. In Rosenberg RN, Prusiner SB, DiMauro S & Barchi RL (eds) *The Molecular and Genetic Basis of Neurological Disease*, 2nd edn, pp. 405–420. Boston: Butterworth Heinemann.

Brady RO, Pentchev PG, Gal AE et al (1974) Replacement therapy for inherited enzyme deficiency. Use of purified glucocerebrosidase in Gaucher's disease. *New England Journal of Medicine* **291:** 989–993.

Dawson A, Elias DJ, Rubenson D et al (1996) Development of pulmonary hypertension after alglucerase therapy in two patients with hepatopulmonary syndrome complicating type 1 Gaucher disease. *Annals of Internal Medicine* **125:** 901–904.

De Duve C (1964) From cytases to lysosomes. *Federation Proceedings* **23:** 1045–1049.

*Elstein D, Hadas-Halpern I, Itzchaki M et al (1996) Effect of low-dose enzyme replacement therapy on bones in Gaucher disease patients with severe skeletal involvement. *Blood Cells, Molecules, and Diseases* **22:** 104–111.

Esplin J, Greenspoon JS, Cheng E et al (1993) Alglucerase infusions in pregnant type I Gaucher patients. *Blood* **82:** 509a.

Fallet S, Sibille A, Mendelson R et al (1992) Enzyme augmentation in moderate to life-threatening Gaucher disease. *Pediatric Research* **31:** 496–502.

*Figueroa ML, Rosenbloom BE, Kay AC et al (1992) A less costly regimen of alglucerase to treat Gaucher's disease. *New England Journal of Medicine* **327:** 1632–1636.

Glenn D, Thurston D, Garver P & Beutler E (1994) Comparison of magnetic resonance imaging and ultrasound in evaluating liver size in Gaucher patients. *Acta Haematologica* (Basel) **92:** 187–189.

*Grabowski GA, Barton NW, Pastores G et al (1995) Enzyme therapy in type 1 Gaucher disease: comparative efficacy of mannose-terminated glucocerebrosidase from natural and recombinant sources. *Annals of Internal Medicine* **122:** 33–39.

Harats D, Pauzner R, Elstein D et al (1997) Pulmonary hypertension in two patients with type I Gaucher disease while on alglucerase therapy. *Acta Haematologica* (Basel) **98:** 47–50.

Hollak CEM, Aerts JMFG, van Weely S et al (1993) Enzyme supplementation therapy for type I Gaucher disease. Efficacy of very low dose alglucerase in 12 patients. *Blood* **82 (supplement 1):** 33a.

Hollak CEM, Aerts JMFG, Goudsmit R et al (1995) Individualised low-dose alglucerase therapy for type 1 Gaucher's disease. *Lancet* **345:** 1474–1478.

International Collaborative Gaucher Group Registry and Genzyme Therapeutics (1995) Dosage regimens of alglucerase in Gaucher disease: a comparison of the rate and extent of clinical response. *ICGG Registry Update*: 1–11.

Kaplan P, Mazur A, Manor O et al (1996) Acceleration of retarded growth in children with Gaucher disease after treatment with alglucerase. *Journal of Pediatrics* **129:** 149–153.

Kay AC, Saven A, Garver P et al (1991) Enzyme replacement therapy in type I Gaucher disease. *Transactions of the Association of American Physicians* **104:** 258–264.

Marodi L (1995) Low-dose versus high-frequency regimens in Gaucher's disease. *Lancet* **346:** 1434.

McCabe ERB, Fine BA, Golbus MS et al (1996) Gaucher disease—current issues in diagnosis and treatment. *Journal of the American Medical Association* **275:** 548–553.

*Mistry PK, Wraight EP & Cox TM (1996) Therapeutic delivery of proteins to macrophages: implications for treatment of Gaucher's disease. *Lancet* **348:** 1555–1559.

Moscicki RA & Van Heek J (1994) Ceredase dosing concerns for Gaucher's disease. *American Journal of Medicine* **4:** 402–403.

Myers B (1937) Gaucher's disease of the lung. *British Medical Journal* **2:** 8–10.

Pastores GM, Sibille AR & Grabowski GA (1993) Enzyme therapy in Gaucher disease type 1: Dosage efficacy and adverse effects in thirty-three patients treated for 6 to 24 months. *Blood* **82** 408–416.

Pelini M, Boice D, O'Neil K & LaRocque J (1994) Glucocerebrosidase treatment of type I Gaucher disease with severe pulmonary involvement. *Annals of Internal Medicine* **121:** 196–197.

Rosenthal DL, Doppelt SH, Mankin HJ et al (1995) Enzyme replacement therapy for Gaucher disease: skeletal reponses to macrophage-targeted glucocerebrosidase. *Pediatrics* **96:** 629–637.

Sato Y & Beutler E (1993) Binding, internalization, and degradation of mannose-terminated glucocebrosidase by macrophages. *Journal of Clinical Investigation* **91:** 1909–1917.

Zevin S, Abrahamov A, Hadas-Halpern I et al (1993) Adult-type Gaucher disease in children: genetics, clinical features and enzyme replacement therapy. *Quarterly Journal of Medicine* **86:** 565–573.

Zimran A, Hadas-Halpern I, Zevin S et al (1993a) Low dose high frequency enzyme replacement therapy for very young children with Gaucher disease. *British Journal of Haematology* **85:** 783–786.

Zimran A, Hollak CEM, Abrahamov A et al (1993b) Home treatment with intravenous enzyme replacement therapy for Gaucher disease: An international collaborative study of 33 patients. *Blood* **82:** 1107–1109.

*Zimran A, Elstein D, Kannai R et al (1994) Low-dose enzyme replacement therapy for Gaucher's disease: Effects of age, sex, genotype, and clinical features on response to treatment. *American Journal of Medicine* **97:** 3–13.

Zimran A, Elstein D, Levy-Lahad E et al (1995) Replacement therapy with imiglucerase for type 1 Gaucher's disease. *Lancet* **345:** 1479–1480.

9

Gaucher's disease: studies of gene transfer to haematopoietic cells

J. A. BARRANGER MD, PhD

E. O. RICE MS, CGC

J. DUNIGAN BS

C. SANSIERI BS

N. TAKIYAMA MD

M. BEELER BS

J. LANCIA BS

S. LUCOT BS

S. SCHEIRER-FOCHLER BS

T. MOHNEY BS

W. SWANEY BS

A. BAHNSON PhD

E. BALL MD

University of Pittsburgh Medical Center, Pittsburgh, PA 15261, USA

Baillière's Clinical Haematology—
Vol. 10, No. 4, December 1997
ISBN 0–7020–2378–7
0950–3536/97/040765 + 14 $12.00/00

765
Copyright © 1997, by Baillière Tindall
All rights of reproduction in any form reserved

Transfer of the gene coding for glucocerebrosidase (GC) via a retroviral vector (MFG-GC) to haematopoietic progenitors results in engraftment and life-long expression of the human protein at high levels in transplanted mice. Studies of human CD34 cells were carried out to evaluate their potential use in a gene therapy approach to Gaucher's disease. High transduction efficiency and correction of the enzyme deficiency was possible in CD34 cells obtained from patients with Gaucher's disease. Based on these results, a clinical trial of gene therapy was designed and initiated. Preliminary results of this study indicate the persistence or engraftment of genetically corrected cells in the transplanted patients.

Key words: Gaucher's disease, glucocerebrosidase, gene transfer.

Gaucher's disease is the most frequently encountered lysosomal storage disorder (Barranger and Ginns, 1989; Zimran et al, 1991). Individuals with Gaucher's disease have inadaquate amounts of a lysosomal enzyme known as glucocerebrosidase (GC). Because of the deficiency of GC, glucosyl-ceramide accumulates in the lysosomes of reticuloendothelial cells, particularly macrophages.

Each of the three types of Gaucher's disease is the result of GC deficiency. The disorders are inherited in an autosomal recessive manner. The classification of the types is based on the presence and progression of neurological complications. Type 1 Gaucher's disease is the most common and has a chronic, non-neuronopathic course. The age of onset and severity of symptoms vary widely. The variability in all types of Gaucher's disease is the consequence not only of different mutations in the GC gene, but also of the influence of one too many so-called modifier genes. The nature of these modifier genes has not yet been identified.

The most common mutations in the GC gene cause Type 1 disease (Barranger and Ginns, 1989; Barranger et al, 1989). This mutation is a single base pair substitution in codon 370. It accounts for approximately 70% of the mutant alleles in Ashkenazic Jewish patients with Gaucher's disease (Zimran et al, 1991). The lysosomal enzyme produced by this allele has reduced activity, but is not diminished in concentration in the lysosome (Ohashi et al, 1991). Most patients with the more severe types of Gaucher's disease (Types 2 and 3), which present with neurological complications, often carry at least one allele with a single base substitution in codon 444. This allele results in an unstable enzyme that leads to little or no enzymatic activity in the lysosome (Ohashi et al, 1991). Of the more than 50 mutations described in the GC gene, most are private alleles occurring in single kindreds.

Enzyme replacement therapy (ERT) has simplified the management of patients with Type 1 Gaucher's disease. This therapy grew out of studies of the properties of GC. While initial biochemical responses to ERT were encouraging, further studies revealed that glucocerebrosidase in its native form was not effectively delivered to the storage macrophages in which glucosylceramide accumulates. Further research established that if the oligosaccharide side chains of the enzyme were partially degraded to expose mannose residues, the enzyme was bound to a mannose-specific receptor on the macrophage (MØ) plasma membrane and endocytosed. Studies in rats revealed more than a tenfold increase in MØ uptake of enzyme was achieved using the modified (mannose-terminated) form of the enzyme, compared with uptake of native enzyme by the same cells, (Furbish et al, 1981) Periodic infusion of mannose-terminated gluco-cerebrosidase in patients with Gaucher's disease is effective in reaching storage macrophages and reversing disease manifestations. Clinical responses include an increase in haemoglobin concentration, an increase in platelet count, a reduction in the size of the liver and spleen, and a gradual improvement in bone manifestations. Enzyme replacement therapy represents the first therapeutic breakthrough for the treatment of persons with lysosomal storage diseases (Barranger et al, 1989; Barton et al, 1991). The pharmacology of mannose-terminated glucocerebrosidase has been incompletely studied, and multiple variables need to be clarified to fine tune and enhance the success of enzyme replacement therapy. The recom-mended dosage is 60 Units per kilogram of body weight every 2 weeks (Barton et al, 1991). The minimum effective dose and the optimal dosage frequency are only beginning to be determined (Barton et al, 1991; Beutler et al, 1991; Fallet et al, 1992). Because of the heterogeneity of Gaucher's disease, predictions that individual responses to enzyme therapy will vary are being borne out. Additional research using cell cultures and transgenic animal models as well as further clinical experimentation are needed to further refine this therapeutic approach. Until then, the prudent physician will adjust the dose based on the patient's responses. Objective criteria of response include organ volumes, magnetic resonance imaging (MRI) images of bone, haematological indices, non-tartrate inhibitable acid phosphatase, serum angiotensin converting enzyme and chitotriosidase levels. Subjective criteria of response include fatigue, bone pain and sense of a high quality of life.

Macrophages are derived from the bone marrow and are the principle storage cells in which glucosylceramide accumulates. It is logical that bone marrow transplantation (BMT) is curative for this genetic disease. Successful BMT has been reported in several patients with Gaucher's disease, who had resolution of enzyme deficiency in circulating white blood cells, regression of organomegaly, and an improvement in general health. The risks of allogeneic transplantation, however, do not justify this approach in patients with milder forms of the disease. Moreover, trans-plant-associated risks increase with the severity of the disease and the age of the patient and the availability of matched donors is very limited. The success and safety of enzyme replacement therapy obviously limits the number of patients who will be considered for BMT. The efficacy of ERT and BMT provide important rationale for the pursuit of gene therapy for Gaucher's disease.

RETROVIRAL TRANSFER OF THE GC GENE

The cloning of cDNA for the glucocerebrosidase gene led to studies of gene transfer as an approach to the treatment of Gaucher's disease (Ginns et al, 1984). Glucocerebrosidase deficiency in cultured fibroblasts of persons with Gaucher's disease was revealed by transfer of the glucocerebrosidase. Initial results with N2 derived vectors demonstrated efficient transduction of murine haematopoietic stem cells in long-term bone marrow cultures (Nolta et al, 1990) and in irradiated syngeneic recipients of transduced bone marrow (Ohashi et al, 1992). In these studies expression of the transgene was observed in vitro but only minimally in vivo in spleen colonies of mice transplanted with bone marrow transduced with the N2-SV-GC vector (Ohashi et al, 1992). In contrast, sustained long-term expression was achieved in animals transplanted with bone marrow transduced with the MFG retroviral vector. The features of the MFG-GC vector are that the GC cDNA is transcribed by the retroviral LTR, and the GC cDNA was placed at the start codon of the deleted envelope gene. There is no internal promoter or dominant selectable marker in the MFG-GC construct (Ohashi et al, 1992).

The MFG-GC vector facilitated effective supernatant transduction of enriched populations of CD34+ cells obtained from normal cord blood, normal bone marrow, peripheral blood of granulocyte colony-stimulating factor (G-CSF) primed leukaemia patients, and from Gaucher patient bone marrow. Enzyme activity in transduced CD34+ cells from Gaucher patients, showed that potentially therapeutic levels of glucocerebrosidase could be obtained (Bahnson et al, 1994).

In initial studies, CD34+ enriched cells were pre-stimulated in medium containing the cytokines, interleukin-3 (IL-3), IL-6 and stem cell factor (SCF) (Bodine et al, 1986), followed by four or five daily exposures to fresh vector-containing supernatants. During the course of these initial studies, experiments indicated that a pre-stimulation period of 1 day and a reduced number of infections over a shorter time period were equally effective (Bahnson et al, 1994; Nimgaonkar et al, 1994). The rapid appearance of myeloid differentiation antigens on the CD34+ cells over time in culture stressed the importance of minimizing the ex vivo period as much as possible if transduced stem cells were to be obtained (Nimgaonkar et al, 1994).

Transduction of CD34+ cells was directly analysed by Southern blot analysis of *Sst*I digests of genomic DNA from expanded transduced CD34+ cells. To estimate copy number, vector proviral DNA hybridization intensity in transduced cells was compared with controls consisting of human DNA quantitatively spiked with DNA from a murine fibroblast clone carrying a known vector copy number. Results showed that low copy numbers of the MFG-GC vector (< one copy/cell) resulted in gluco-cerebrosidase expression levels that more than compensated for the deficiency of this enzyme in Gaucher patient haematopoietic cells in culture. Supporting evidence for gene expression was provided by immunocytochemical staining, which indicated that at least 20% of the expanded CD34+ cells expressed the transgene and displayed a staining intensity equal to or greater than that of normal BM cells (Bahnson et al, 1994).

Centrifugal enhancement of transduction

Despite the encouraging results described above, variability and reports of lower than expected transduction efficiencies have been reported when research procedures were applied to the large number of cells needed for transplantation (Dunbar et al, 1993; Kohn et al, 1993). This problem spurred us to investigate centrifugation as a method to improve the transduction process (R. W. Atchison, personal communication). In part, this effort is based on the assumption that higher transduction in progenitor cells will be found to correlate with a higher probability of transduction in the ultimate target: the engrafting pluripotent stem cells. This assumption is necessary at the present time, regardless of the method, since there are no proven in vitro assays for stem cells.

Initial experiments comparing centrifugal with non-centrifugal transduction of cord blood CD34+ enriched cells demonstrated the potential for improved transduction. In experiments comparing both methods, polymerase chain reaction (PCR) analysis of granulocyte–macrophage colony forming cells (CFU-GM) indicated a transduction efficiency as high as 95% using centrifugation.

Additional experiments in a human haematopoietic cell line (TF-1) indicated that the enhancement achieved by centrifugation is directly related to the centrifugal force up to $10\,000\,g$ and to the time of centrifugation. On the other hand, the effect was inversely related to cell number in a given container, presumably reflecting a requirement for surface area exposure to suspended virus (Bahnson et al, 1995). These variables provide opportunity for further improvement, but for practical application at the present time, we have adopted a procedure using blood transfer bags containing up to 5×10^6 cells per bag centrifuged at $2400\,g$ for 4 hours. A major advantage of the centrifugation protocol is that it reduces to a minimum the time the cells must be kept in culture. This may be particularly important in light of studies by Quesenberry and co-workers showing rapid reduction in engraftment potential with increasing time in culture (Peters et al, 1996).

PRE-CLINICAL STUDIES OF CD34 CELLS FROM GAUCHER PATIENTS

Transplantation of CD34+ cells is advantageous for several reasons (Berenson et al, 1991). First, the number of CD34+ cells required for transplantation is considerably smaller than a whole bone marrow transplant, consequently reducing the side-effects associated with cell transplantation as well as those associated with infusion of the toxic cryopreservant dimethyl sulphoxide (DMSO). Secondly, the amount of viral supernatant and cytokines required for transduction and pre-stimulation are significantly reduced.

We have shown that CD34+ cells can be collected in patients with Gaucher's disease (GD) in amounts adequate for transplantation

(Nimgaonkar et al, 1995). In this study, three patients with GD were entered into an IRB approved study. Patient no. 1 (JH) aged 48 years was diagnosed as having Type 1 GD in 1968. He was started on ERT in September of 1993 and is at present on Ceredase™ 30 U/kg every 2 weeks. Patient no. 2 (RH) aged 35 years was diagnosed with Type 1 GD in 1965 and has been maintained on Ceredase™ 45 U/kg every 2 weeks. The third patient, patient no. 3 (IM) aged 49 years was diagnosed with Type 1 GD in 1954. This patient has been maintained on Ceredase™ since June of 1992 at a dose of 30 U/kg every 2 weeks. All three patients had responded to enzyme therapy as evidenced by a reduction in organ size and an increase in haematological indicies. Each continues to experience skeletal complications of the disease. The different doses of enzyme in these individuals reflect the efforts made to reduce the dose from 60 U/kg every 2 weeks to a lower maintenance dose. All patients gave written informed consent to participate in the study.

Mobilization regimen and leukapheresis

Patient no. 1 and 2 received G-CSF (Neupogen™ (Amgen)) 5 µg/kg per day subcutaneously for 10 days. Patient no. 3 received G-CSF at the dose of 10 µg per day for 10 days. Pre G-CSF laboratory evaluation for each patient included GC activity, genotype, CBC and differential, platelets, uric acid (UA), alkaline phosphatase, lactate dehydrogenase (LDH) and flow cytometric analysis (FACS) for CD34$^+$ cells. Daily evaluation while the patient was on G-CSF included CBC, platelet count and differential, UA, LDH, alkaline phosphatase, and FACS analysis for CD34$^+$ cell number.

Leukapheresis was started in the three patients on day 5. A total of five leukaphereses were done in each patient using the Cobe Spectra Apheresis device. The total volume of the leukapheresis product was recorded and samples were removed for cell counts and further analysis. All cell counts were done on the Coulter Counter ZM to determine the total number of white blood cells in the leukapheresis product. The leukapheresis product was washed with RPMI 1640 on the Cobe 2991. The final volume of the washed cell preparation was approximately 150 ml.

Mobilization of CD34$^+$ cells

Following leukapheresis, the total number of white blood cells (WBC) in the apheresis products averaged 1.6×10^{11} (range 1.0×10^{11}–2.5×10^{11}). Enrichment for CD34$^+$ cells was done using the Ceprate™ column (CellPro, Bothell, WA). The washed leukapheresis product was incubated with the biotin labelled anti-CD34 antibody and 0.1% HSA (25%) for 25 minutes at room temperature for 15 minutes. Following incubation the cells were washed on the Cobe 2991 and resuspended in phosphate buffered saline (PBS) to a volume of 300 ml. Samples were removed for further analysis at this stage, which included cell counts, flow cytometry for CD34 and subset analysis, viability and clonogenic assays. The cells were processed on the Ceprate SC instrument. The enriched and depleted fractions were collected and aliquots were removed for further analysis. Sterility testing was also performed on the enriched fraction. The enriched fraction was centrifuged at 1200 rpm for 8 minutes and the supernatant removed. The enriched CD34+ cells were cryopreserved in Media 199 with DMSO plus 20% autologous plasma using a clinically approved controlled rate freezing protocol.

The number of white cells in the enriched fractions averaged 6.3×10^8 (range 4.5×10^8–7.9×10^8) or 9.6×10^6/kg. Using the clinical Ceprate™ column, enrichments averaging 195-fold (range 4 to 625-fold) were observed. FACS analysis demonstrated up to a sixfold increase in the per cent of CD34+ cells in peripheral blood in the three patients (Table 1). The recovery varied from a mean of 25.6% (range 4.9–48.4%), 61.4% (range 22.4–168.3%) and 36.9% (range 25–59%) in the three patients, respectively. The total number of CD34+ cells collected was 1.2, 3.5 and 2.1×10^6 cells/kg, respectively.

Table 1. White blood cell count and CD34 mobilization in the three patients.

	Patient 1			Patient 2			Patient 3		
	WBC/ml	CD34%		WBC/ml	CD34%		WBC/ml	CD34%	
Days	PB	PB	Enriched	PB	PB	Enriched	PB	PB	Enriched
0	9.8×10^6	0.10		1.1×10^7	−0.12		6.6×10^7	0.05	
1	2.8×10^7	0.10		3.1×10^7	0.08		1.0×10^7	0.01	
2	3.5×10^7	0.27		3.8×10^7	0.04		4.4×10^7	0.03	
3	4.5×10^7	0.17		4.0×10^7	0.04		6.1×10^7	0.11	
4	4.5×10^7	0.21		4.4×10^7	0.11		7.2×10^7	0.12	31.5
5	3.2×10^7	0.26	19.8	4.0×10^7	0.23	37.0	6.8×10^7	0.07	17.3
6	5.0×10^7	0.17	6.1	3.7×10^7	0.30	28.4	8.1×10^7	0.04	
7	4.5×10^7	0.55	19.2	4.2×10^7	0.07	28	6.6×10^7	0.04	25.0*
8	4.8×10^7	0.62	2.9	4.4×10^7	0.12	3.8	1.0×10^7	0.08	16.3
9	4.7×10^7	0.26	5.9	4.4×10^7	0.07	25.9	7.7×10^7		
10				4.5×10^7	0.07				

* Apheresis products from days 6 and 7 were pooled for a CD34+ separation.

Flow cytometric analysis for CD34+ cells

The cell concentration was adjusted to 1×10^7 cells/ml in PBS. An aliquot of 100 µl of the cell suspension was then incubated with the labelled monoclonal antibodies. Dual colour staining was done using the following monoclonal antibodies: CD34 (FITC), combined with either CD38 (phyco-erythrin) (PE), HLA-DR (PE), Thy-1 (PE) or CD33 (PE) and CD34 (PE) combined with CD45 (FITC). Relevent isotype controls were used. A 100-µl aliquot of stained cells was mixed with an equal volume of PBS containing 1% human albumin and 0.1% sodium azide and incubated for 15 minutes at room temperature in the dark. After incubation, 2 ml of FACS lysing solution was added to each tube and the cells incubated for an additional 10 minutes. The tubes were then centrifuged again for 5 minutes at 250 g and the supernatant decanted. The cells were worked in 2 ml of PBS and the pellet resuspended in 500 μl of 1% paraformaldehyde. The suspensions were stored at 4°C in the dark and submitted to flow cytometric analysis in their respective staining solutions.

Transduction of human haematopoietic progenitors

We have previously demonstrated high transduction efficiencies using a centrifugation promoted infection protocol (Bahnson et al, 1995). This method involves centrifugation of small numbers of cells in tubes, which is not feasible in the clinical setting. We have developed a method using blood collection bags for the centrifugation of large numbers of cells applicable to the clinical trial. The patients' CD34+ enriched cells that had been frozen were thawed rapidly while mixing constantly. The cells were washed immediately in long-term bone marrow culture media (LTBMC), counted, and resuspended at a concentration of 2×10^5 cells/ml. Pre-stimulation of the cells was performed using the cytokines IL-3, IL-6 and stem cell factor (SCF) at concentrations of 10 ng/ml for 16–24 hours. The cell concentration was maintained at 2×10^5/ml throughout the pre-stimulation procedure. Following this, the cells were resuspended at 5×10^6–3×10^8 cells in 50 ml of LTBMC. The cytokine concentration was maintained at 10 ng/ml and protamine sulphate was added to achieve a concentration of 4 μg/ml. A 60-ml syringe was used to inject the cell suspension into a 150-ml capacity blood collection bag. An aliquot of 50 ml of viral supernatant was injected into the same blood collection bag. The air pocket was removed, the bag sealed and the excess tubing removed. The blood bags were then centrifuged at 2400 g at 24°C for 4 hours. The bags were removed from the centrifuge and transferred to a 50-ml conical tube. The bag was rinsed with 50 ml of LTBMC to remove any adherent cells. The cells were then centrifuged at 2400 g for 5 minutes, the supernatant removed and the cells resuspended in 25 ml of LTBMCM. The cells were counted and subjected to further analysis.

Analysis of transduction efficiency

Polymerase chain reaction (PCR) analysis of CFU-GM colonies

Clonogenic assays. Transduced CD34+ cells were plated at a concentration of 1×10^4 cells/ml in methyl cellulose with IL-3 and GM-CSF. Individual CFU-GM colonies generated after 14 days were plucked and analysed by PCR for the GC gene in the retroviral vector.

DNA extraction from methylcellulose colonies. Isolated, single colonies were removed by a micropipettor and placed into a sterile, nuclease-free microcentrifuge tube. The DNA extraction method was as follows: The lysis solution consisted of 1.5 μl of glycogen, 10 μl 2M sodium acetate (pH 4.5), 20 μl of sterile distilled water, 100 μl phenol, and 20 μl chloroform. To each tube, 150 μl of this mixture was added and left to incubate for at least 30 minutes at 4°C. The tubes were then spun in a microcentrifuge at 12 000 g for 10 minutes. The aqueous phase was transferred to a clean tube and precipitated with 100 μl isopropanol at −80°C ≥3 hours or −20°C overnight. The samples were spun at 12 000 g for 10 minutes, the pellets were washed in cold 70% ethanol, allowed to briefly air-dry and resuspended in 30 μl sterile distilled water. This sample was then ready for PCR analysis, as described below.

PCR technique. PCR was carried out on genomic DNA samples in a final volume of 50 μl. The reaction mixture contained 200 μM of each dNTP, 1.25 units AmpliTaq (Perkin–Elmer), 2 mM $MgCl_2$, and 0.4 μM of each primer in Amplitaq buffer (Perkin–Elmer). One primer was hybridized within the GC-cDNA and the second within the viral sequence to yield a unique 407 bp amplification product. (AB1: 5′ ACG GCA TCG CAG CTT GGA TA 3′; AB2: 5′ AGT AGC AAA TTT TGG GCA GG 3′). Thermal cycling was performed on a Gene Amp PCR System 9600 as follows: 94°C × 5 minutes for an initial denaturing cycle, followed by 30 cycles of 94°C × 30 seconds, 58°C × 30 seconds, 72°C × 30 seconds. The PCR products were resolved on a 6% acrylamide or 2% agarose gel and the bands visualized by ethidium bromide and UV light.

PCR analysis of LTC-IC

Long-term bone marrow cultures were maintained as previously described (Eaves et al, 1991). Transduced CD34$^+$ cells were placed on pre-formed irradiated allogeneic BM stroma at a minimum concentration of 5×10^5 cells per T25 flask. Half the media was replaced weekly. The cultures were maintained at a temperature of 33°C. Cells were removed after 4–5 weeks and plated in methylcellulose for clonogenic assays. At week 6, non-adherent cells and adherent cells were removed using trypsin plated individually in methylcellulose. Individual CFU-GM were plucked at 14 days and analysed by PCR for the GC gene as described above.

Glucocerebrosidase enzyme assay in expanded cells

The cells were expanded for 6 days in cytokines and assayed for enzyme activity as previously described (Bahnson et al, 1994).

Results in the pre-clinical trial studies

The transduction efficiency was measured in clonogenic cells, and long-term culture initiating cells (LTC-IC). Using the clinically approved viral supernatant LM30.2.7, a mean transduction efficiency of 32% was demonstrated in clonogenic cells. A transduction efficiency of 25% for patient no. 1 and 50% for Patient no. 3 in LTCIC was noted at week 6 (Mannion-Henderson et al, 1995). Cells were maintained in LTBMC media and these cells assayed for their GC enzyme levels at 6 days post-transduction. Up to a 50-fold increase in enzyme levels above deficient levels was noted on day 6.

CLINICAL TRIAL OF GENE THERAPY FOR
GAUCHER'S DISEASE

In this study, we have transduced CD34$^+$ cells obtained from the blood of Gaucher patients using a replication defective retroviral vector called R-GC. The vector carries the human GC cDNA. Genetically corrected CD34$^+$ cells are returned intravenously to the patient who donated the cells. This process is referred to as ex vivo gene transfer and autologous peripheral blood stem cell (PBSC) transplantation. The primary aim of the study is to evaluate the safety of this approach. Other aims include estimating the extent of competitive engraftment of genetically corrected CD34$^+$ cells, measuring the endurance of bone marrow engraftment with CD34$^+$ cells, measuring the ability of these genetically corrected cells to sustain expression of GC, as well as examining the patients for any clinical response.

The hypothesis of this study is that genetically corrected PBSC will engraft and result in the supply of enzymatically competent progeny sufficient to reverse the phenotype in patients with Gaucher's disease. The specific aims to be achieved are:

1. Evaluation of the safety and feasibility of correcting the basic genetic defect of Gaucher's disease by infusing patients with transduced CD34$^+$ cells.
2. Transfer of the human GC gene into PBSC obtained from patients with Gaucher's disease.
3. Autologous transplantation of transduced PBSC to patients.
4. Measurement of the carriage and expression of the transferred gene and its duration in peripheral blood leukocytes (PBL) and bone marrow.
5. Assessment of the clinical effects of transplanting genetically corrected PBSC in patients with Gaucher's disease.

The outcome of the study will influence future plans by providing information about the safety and capability of gene transfer using our proposed method. Further developments could influence our decisions about different vectors, different preparations of haematopoietic stem cells, and different methods of preparation of the patients.

Description of the study

This clinical trial is a phase I study to evaluate the safety and limited efficacy of the gene therapy approach as a treatment for Type 1 GD. A total of five patients with moderate to moderately severe disease were enrolled.

Patients with Type 1 Gaucher's disease were recruited from clinics at the University of Pittsburgh and from referrals. They were counselled and informed of the risks and inconveniences of the study during three separate interviews. They were required to sign a consent form. Both patients who were undergoing enzyme replacement therapy and untreated patients were selected for the study.

G-CSF mobilization (10 µg/kg) was used in patients admitted to the study. Leukapheresis procedures began on day 6 of the G-CSF mobilization and continued until a total of 7×10^8/kg mononuclear cells were obtained. The cells were transduced with the R-GC vector to deliver the GC gene. Patients were transplanted with autologous genetically corrected cells at a dose of ~2×10^6/kg CD34+cells. The patient's white blood cells were assessed for the carriage and expression of the transduced gene. Measurement of GC activity was used to quantify the extent of restoration of enzyme activity in these cells. Patients were studied for the clinical responses to the transplantation.

In this study the extent to which CD34+ cells can engraft without a myeloablative preparative step was assessed. Engraftment of CD34+ cells was rapid and occurred within 1 month. Therefore, assay of peripheral blood leukocytes (PBL) for carriage of the GC gene and GC activity was performed after that interval of time. The results in these patients will determine the approach to be used in subsequent studies during the first year. If the amount of GC leukocytes is not increased twofold above the deficient level, it will be concluded that an inadequate number of corrected CD34+ cells have engrafted, and the procedure will be repeated up to a maximum of four times in the first year. Each time a transplant is performed, the leukapheresis procedure, enrichment of CD34+ cells and transduction of CD34+ cells will be repeated. The same certifications of the transduced cells will be performed prior to their use. A flow sheet summarizing the study is shown in Figure 1.

Three study candidates were entered into the study. One patient experienced a decline in platelet count below 100 000 during G-CSF stimulation. No other unexpected side-effects of the procedure have been noted in the 9-month duration of the study. All of the candidates have been transplanted with genetically corrected CD34 cells at a dose of $2-4 \times 10^6$/kg. The glucocerebrosidase activity of the corrected cells was 2- to 26-fold higher than their deficient level (Table 2). Positive PCR signals for the transgene have been observed in the PBL of each subject and enzymatic activity in circulating white cells has risen to as high as carrier levels. The summary of this study to date is listed below.

1. Ten transplants have been done in three study subjects
2. G-CSF at a dose of 5–10 µg/kg mobilizes CD-34 cells in Gaucher patients with marrow disease.
3. Transduction efficiency of ~10^8 CD34 cells using centrifugation in blood transfer bags averaged 20% (range: 3–38).
4. Glucocerebrosidase activity of the transduced CD34 cells increased to a level of 152 U/mg on average.
5. Following the second transplant of transduced CD34 cells, the GC enzymatic activity in PBL from the first study subject had risen steadily to a level of 14 U/mg (control 17.9 ± 1.0).
6. The GC activity of CD34 cells isolated from all three study subjects after transplantation had increased progressively.
7. These results indicate persistence or engraftment of transduced haematopoietic cells.

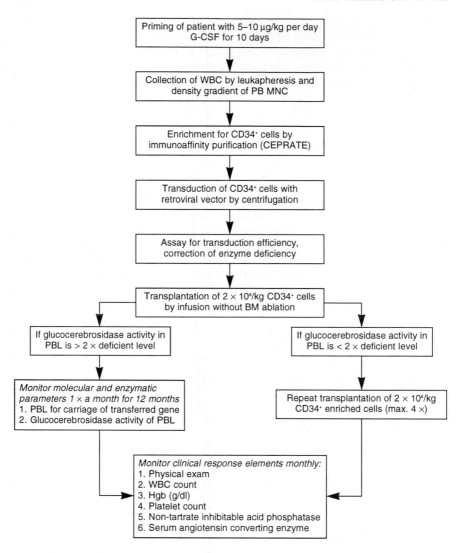

Figure 1. Flow diagram for the clinical trial of gene therapy for Gaucher's disease.

8.   One subject developed thrombocytopenia secondary to G-CSF. Other side-effects were minor, consisting of headache and mild bone pain.

These results are promising and suggest that gene transfer to CD34 cells may result in the persistence or engraftment of genetically corrected cells in the patient. Further study will be required to determine if this biochemical result has clinical value. Two other studies of gene transfer to the haematopoietic cells of Gaucher patients have not produced encouraging results. Both the gene transfer vectors and methods of transduction used by

Table 2.

Transplant no.	Transduction efficiency (CFU-GM)	Glucocerebrosidase activity (at 6 days in culture)
1	16	124
2	3	45
3	31	140
4	26	117
5	20	128
6	9	49
7	8	38
8	38	444
9	33	288
Average	20%	152
		(Deficient level = 15)

Sheuning et al and Karlsson et al differ substantially from those used in our own study. Low transduction efficiency of CD34 cells was seen in these studies and no transgene could be detected in transplanted patients. These studies have been closed.

Acknowledgement

The work reported in this paper was supported by grants from the National Institutes of Health DK43709-06, DK48436-02, DK44935-04, RR00056-35, the National Gaucher Foundation and Genzyme Corporation. The generous gifts of Neupogen® from Amgen Corp. and Ceprate® columns from Cell-Pro-Corp are greatly appreciated. We would like to thank the UPMC, GCRC Nursing Staff for their help, Joseph E. Kiss and the Apheresis Unit, and Nicole Moore for typing the manuscript. The courage and cooperation of the patients involved in these studies have made these contributions possible.

REFERENCES

Bahnson A, Nimgaonkar M, Fei Y et al (1994). Transduction of CD34⁺ enriched cord blood and Gaucher bone marrow cells by a retroviral vector carrying the glucocerebrosidase gene. *Gene Therapy* 1: 176–184.

Bahnson AB, Dunigan JT, Baysal BE et al (1995). Centrifugal enhancement of retroviral-mediated gene transfer. *Journal of Virological Methods* 54: 131–143.

Barranger JA & Ginns EI (1989) Glucosylceramide lipidoses: Gaucher disease. In Scriver CR, Beaudet AL, Sly WS & Valle D, (eds) *The Metabolic Basis of Inherited Disease*, 6th edn pp.1677–1698. New York: McGraw-Hill.

Barranger JA, Ohashi T, Hong CM et al (1989) Molecular pathology and therapy for Gaucher disease. *Japanese Journal of Inherited Metabolic Disease* 51: 45–71.

Barton NW, Brady RO, Dambrosia JM et al (1991) Replacement therapy for inherited enzyme deficiency-macrophage-targeted glucocerebrosidase for Gaucher's disease. *New England Journal of Medicine* 324: 1464–1470.

Berenson RJ, Bensinger WI, Hill RS et al (1991) Engraftment after infusion of CD34⁺ marrow cells in patients with breast cancer or neuroblastoma. *Blood* 77(8): 1717.

Beutler E, Kay A, Saven A et al (1991) Enzyme replacement therapy for Gaucher disease. *Blood* 78: 1183–1189.

Bodine DM, Karlsson S & Neinhuis AW (1986) Combination of interleukins 3 and 6 preserves stem cell function in culture and enhances retrovirus-mediated gene transfer into hematopoietic stem cells. *Proceedings of the National Academy of Science* 86(22): 8897–8901.

Choudary PV, Barranger JA, Tsuji S et al (1986) Retrovirus mediated transfer of the human gluco-cerebrosidase gene to Gaucher fibroblasts. *Molecular Biology and Medicine* **3**: 293–299.

Dunbar CE, O'Shaughnessy JA, Cottler-Fox et al (1983). Transplantation of retrovirally-marked CD34+ bone marrow and peripheral blood cells in patients with multiple myeloma or breast cancer. *Blood* **82(10) supplement 1**: 217a.

Eaves CJ, Cashman JD & Eaves AC (1991) Methodology of long-term culture of human hemato-poietic cells. *Journal of Tissue Culture Methods* **13**: 55–62.

Fallet S, Sibille A, Mendelson R et al (1992). Gaucher disease: enzyme augmentation in moderate to life-threatening disease. *Pediatric Research* **31**: 496–502.

Furbish FS, Steer CJ, Krett NL & Barranger JA (1981) Uptake and distribution of placental gluco-cerebrosidase in rat hepatic cells and effects of sequential deglycosylation. *Biochimica Biophysica Acta.* **673**: 425–434.

Ginns EI, Choudary PV, Martin BM et al (1984) Isolation of cDNA clones for human β-gluco-cerebrosidase using the ht11 expression. *Biochemical and Biophysical Research Communications* **123**: 574–580.

Kohn DB, Weinberg KI, Parkman R et al (1993). Gene therapy for neonates with ADA-deficient SCID by retroviral-mediated transfer of the human ADA cDNA into umbilical cord CD34+ cells. *Blood* **82(10) supplement 1**: 315a.

Mannion-Henderson J, Kemp A, Mohney T et al (1995) Efficient retroviral mediated transfer of the glucocerebrosidase gene in CD34+ enriched umbilical cord blood human hematopoietic progenitors. *Experimental Hematology* **23**: 1623–1632.

Nimgaonkar M, Bahnson A, Boggs S et al (1994) Transduction of mobilized peripheral blood CD34+ cells with the glucocerebrosidase gene. *Gene Therapy* **1**: 201–207.

Nimgaonkar M, Mierski J, Beeler M et al (1995) Cytokine mobilization of peripheral blood stem cells in patients with Gaucher disease with a view to gene therapy. *Experimental Hematology* **23**: 1633–1641.

Nolta JA, Sender LS, Barranger JA & Kohn D (1990) Expression of human glucocerebrosidase in murine long-term bone marrow cultures following retroviral vector-mediated transfer. *Blood* **75**: 787–791.

Ohashi T, Hong CM Weiler S et al (1991) Characterization of mutant glucocerebrosidases from different alleles. *Journal of Biological Chemistry* **266**: 3661–3667.

Ohashi T, Boggs S, Robbins P et al (1992) Efficient transfer and sustained high expression of the human glucocerebrosidase gene in mice and their functional macrophages following transplan-tation of bone marrow transduced by a retroviral vector. *Proceedings of the National Academy of Science* **89**: 11332–113336.

Peters SO, Kittler ELW, Ramshaw HS & Quesenberry PJ (1986) Ex vivo expansion of murine marrow cells with interleukin-3, interleukin-6, interleukin-11 and stem cell factor leads to impaired engraftment in irradiated hosts. *Blood* **87**: 30–37.

Zimran A, Gelbart T, Westwood B et al (1991). High frequency of the Gaucher disease mutation at nucleotide 1226 among Ashkenazic Jews. *American Journal of Human Genetics.* **49**: 855–859.

10

Gaucher's disease: genetic counselling and population screening

EPHRAT LEVY-LAHAD MD Diplomate ABMG

Director, Medical Genetic Services

ARI ZIMRAN MD

Associate Professor of Medicine, Director Gaucher Clinic
Department of Medicine and Gaucher Clinic, Shaare-Zedek Medical Center, Jerusalem, Israel

Genetic counselling for Gaucher's disease requires a comprehensive approach, including accurate diagnosis at both the enzymatic and molecular levels, and assessment of disease severity. These goals are particularly challenging given the great allelic and phenotypic heterogeneity encountered in this disorder. Counselling should address the specific concerns of the counsellee, which may be related to evaluation of an affected person, or to reproductive options in couples at risk. Advances in both diagnosis and treatment have led to increased ascertainment of cases and carriers through population based screening, rather than through affected probands, raising new ethical and medical dilemmas. This chapter outlines practical issues in counselling for the various forms of Gaucher's disease, based on current data and experience.

Key words: Gaucher's disease; genetic counselling; genotype–phenotype correlation; population screening; prenatal diagnosis.

Genetic counselling is a process whereby an individual or family obtains information about a real or possible genetic problem. This includes establishing the diagnosis, assessing recurrence risk, offering information regarding reproductive options (including prenatal testing), and sympathetic counsel regarding medical, economic, psychological and social implications of the disease. In this chapter we will discuss these objectives as they relate to Gaucher's disease.

DIAGNOSIS OF GAUCHER'S DISEASE

Clinical recognition

Clinical recognition of Gaucher's disease obviously depends on the type involved. Type 1 (non-neuronopathic) patients are often diagnosed because

Baillière's Clinical Haematology —
Vol. 10, No. 4, December 1997
ISBN 0–7020–2378–7
0950–3536/97/040779 + 14 $12.00/00

779

Copyright © 1997, by Baillière Tindall
All rights of reproduction in any form reserved

of organomegaly, haematological abnormalities (such as anaemia and thrombocytopenia), or bone disease. All of these findings can be symptomatic but may also be incidental findings on physical examination, laboratory tests or radiography. Because of the extreme variability in disease severity, age at diagnosis can vary from infancy to old age. Type 2 (acute neuronopathic) and Type 3 (subacute neuronopathic) patients, are clinically recognized by the combination of characteristic neurological signs and organomegaly. Type 2 patients are diagnosed in infancy; Type 3 patients are usually diagnosed in early childhood, but diagnosis may be delayed to early adolescence.

Laboratory diagnosis

Laboratory diagnosis of all types of Gaucher's disease is currently based on both enzymatic testing and DNA analysis of mutations in the glucocerebrosidase gene. Historically, diagnosis was histological, based on the presence of the 'Gaucher cell', a characteristic lipid-laden cell of the monocyte-macrophage lineage. The Gaucher cell, however, is not specific for Gaucher's disease, and its demonstration requires invasive testing (biopsy of the bone marrow or other organs). Since enzymatic and DNA testing are both highly specific and require only a simple blood draw, histological diagnosis no longer has a role in confirming a clinical suspicion of Gaucher's disease (Beutler and Saven, 1990).

Enzymatic testing

Low glucocerebrosidase activity (<10% of normal) in leukocytes or fibroblasts is still the diagnostic standard of Gaucher's disease, and enzymatic testing should be performed in all cases. Its major advantages are that it is sufficient to establish the diagnosis in affected subjects, and it does not depend on ethnic origin (see below) or previous knowledge of the specific familial mutation. The limitations of enzymatic testing are lability of enzymatic activity (requiring sample processing within 24 hours), the lack of correlation between in vitro enzymatic activity and the type and severity of the disease, and poor differentiation between heterozygote carriers and normals (homozygotes for the normal allele).

DNA testing

DNA testing involves identification of pathogenic mutations in the glucocerebrosidase gene. Its main limitation is incomplete sensitivity. Since Gaucher's disease is recessive, patients are expected to have two mutated alleles: either the same mutation on both alleles (mutation homozygotes) or a different mutation on each allele (compound heterozygotes). Theoretically, the entire glucocerebrosidase gene could be sequenced in each patient: the glucocerebrosidase cDNA (coding sequence) is 2.5 kb in size, and genomic sequencing of approximately 7 kb would also allow identification of intronic mutations resulting in splicing aberrations

(Beutler and Grabowski, 1995). Sequencing of this magnitude is currently cumbersome for technical reasons, and is rarely performed outside of research settings. In practice, DNA analysis is usually confined to rapid testing of a limited number of known mutations, utilizing PCR-based techniques. Thus, when compared with the complete (100%) sensitivity of enzymatic testing, the actual sensitivity of DNA analysis depends on the scope of mutations tested, and the combined frequency of these mutations in patients from a similar ethnic background.

There are three ethnic groups in which a small number of mutations account for the vast majority of disease alleles, resulting in high sensitivity of DNA testing: Ashkenazi Jews (Jews of Eastern European origin) with Type 1 Gaucher's disease, and Norrbottnian Swedes and 'Jenin Arabs' with Type 3 Gaucher's disease (McCabe et al, 1996). In Ashkenazi Jewish patients, five mutations account for 89% of disease alleles, with two, 1226G(N370S) and 84GG, accounting for 83% of disease alleles (see Chapter 2, Table 2). At the population level, however, these two mutations probably account for approximately 95% of disease alleles (Beutler and Grabowski, 1995). Since DNA-based diagnosis requires identification of both disease alleles, the sensitivity of a five-mutation screen in Ashkenazi Jews is approximately 80%. Swedish Norrbottnian Type 3 patients are all homozygous for a single mutation, 1448C(L444P), so for this type of Gaucher's disease in this particular population, DNA testing is diagnostic. A similar situation exists for Type 3c Gaucher's disease, a rare variant that includes cardiac manifestations and has been described mainly in Palestinian Arabs from a circumscribed geographic area near the town of Jenin (Abrahamov et al, 1995; Mistry, 1995). These patients are all homozygous for the 1342C(D409H) mutation probably as a result of founder effect in a community with a high rate of consanguinity. In all other populations, sensitivity of DNA testing is significantly lower; a five mutation screen detects 74% of disease alleles, with two mutations, 1226G(N370S) and 1448C(L444P), accounting for approximately 70% of all alleles (see Chapter 2, Table 2). Given a 74% detection rate, DNA testing would be diagnostic (i.e. detect both mutated alleles) in only 55% of cases, underscoring the importance of enzymatic diagnosis.

In contrast to enzymatic testing, which does not predict disease type or severity, DNA testing allows some prediction of disease course, based on observed genotype–phenotype correlations (see Chapter 2, and below). Thus, laboratory diagnosis of Gaucher's disease should be based on enzymatic testing, and refined using DNA analysis.

Prenatal testing for Gaucher's disease

Both enzymatic and molecular testing described above can be performed prenatally, either by chorionic villus sampling (CVS) at 8–10 weeks of pregnancy, or by amniocentesis at 15–17 weeks of pregnancy. The same caveats outlined for each form of testing also apply prenatally. In addition, because diagnosis on material obtained by CVS may be complicated by maternal contamination in up to perhaps 6% of cases (Teshima et al, 1992; Smidt-Jensen 1993; Association of Clinical Cytogeneticists Working Party, 1994), it is particularly important to correlate results of molecular and enzymatic testing in these cases. There has been at least one report in the literature of a false negative prenatal diagnosis for Gaucher Type 2 in which some villus cultures had normal enzymatic activity due to maternal contamination (Besley et al, 1988).

Present methods of prenatal diagnosis essentially rely on selective abortions of affected fetuses. Newer methods currently under investigation, such as identification of fetal cells in the maternal circulation, may allow selection at earlier stages (Cheung et al, 1996). Although, this does not completely solve the issue of selective abortion, in the orthodox Jewish community, termination before 40 days of pregnancy (for medical indications) is allowed by most rabbinical authorities. Pre-implantation diagnosis, which has been performed for other recessive disorders (such as cystic fibrosis and Tay–Sachs disease) allows selective pregnancy with unaffected embryos thus avoiding the thorny problem of abortion (Handyside et al, 1992; Delhanty, 1994; Harper, 1996). However, it should be noted that this procedure requires the mother to undergo in vitro fertilization (IVF), which is more invasive than current methods for obtaining fetal tissue for diagnosis.

DIAGNOSIS OF GAUCHER'S DISEASE CARRIERS

Carriers of Gaucher's disease have sufficient glucocerebrosidase activity and are completely healthy in this regard. Thus, determination of carrier status is purely a laboratory diagnosis, and is important only for its reproductive implications. In contrast to its usefulness in diagnosing affected subjects, enzymatic testing does not reliably distinguish between carriers and non-carriers. Although carriers have, on average, half-normal glucocerebrosidase activity in leukocytes and fibroblasts, there is considerable overlap with non-carriers. Despite many attempts to refine the enzymatic assay, about one-third of carriers are still found to have enzymatic activity that is defined as normal and would be falsely diagnosed as non-carriers. In contrast, DNA testing is unequivocal for those mutations tested, so in families with known mutations, DNA testing identifies carriers and non-carriers with complete accuracy. In families where one or both mutations are unknown, carrier detection must rely on enzymatic testing, which may result in misclassification of some carriers as non-carriers, or on identification of the familial mutation by complete sequencing of the glucocerebrosidase gene. Carrier status can also be determined indirectly using polymorphisms in the glucoceberosidase gene and the tightly linked pyruvate kinase gene (Glenn et al, 1994). A number of highly polymorphic markers in this region have recently been described (Sidransky et al, 1997), so most families in which parents and an affected child are available are likely to be informative.

RECURRENCE RISK

The inheritance of Gaucher's disease is autosomal recessive. Therefore there is no risk for an affected child unless *both* parents are carriers. At-risk couples, i.e. couples where both partners are carriers, have a 25% risk for an affected child in each pregnancy. Many at-risk couples are identified only after the birth of an affected child. Others are identified as more distant relatives of affected individuals, or increasingly, as a result of screening in particular ethnic groups, especially Ashkenazi Jews. Healthy children of at-risk couples have a two-thirds chance of being carriers, and a one-third chance of being non-carriers. These a priori risks should be taken into account in families where molecular diagnosis of carrier status is not possible.

It should be noted, however, that these formal recurrence risks are only partially relevant to at-risk couples, who are more concerned with issues of disease severity and, in the case of Gaucher's disease, with the need for and implications of treatment. These issues are usually the main focus of counselling sessions (see genotype–phenotype correlation below).

REPRODUCTIVE OPTIONS

Formally, the reproductive options available to at-risk couples are as follows: (i) cessation of childbearing, with or without adoption; (ii), continuation of childbearing without prenatal testing; (iii), artificial insemination by a donor (AID), (provided the donor is not a carrier); and (iv), prenatal testing (by CVS or amniocentesis) with or without selective pregnancy termination. These options should all be discussed non-directively with at-risk couples. A practical limitation of AID is that in many sperm banks donors are not tested for carrier status, and for reasons of confidentiality (at least in Israel) their sperm cannot be tested either. In such cases, patients choosing AID can use sperm from donors from an ethnic background in which carrier rates are low. It bears mentioning that prenatal testing should not be conditional upon prior acceptance of selective pregnancy termination. At-risk couples can have other legitimate reasons for testing which should be respected (e.g. adequate preparation for the birth of an affected child, or wish for reassurance), and decisions often evolve in the course of pregnancy and may depend on the actual results of prenatal testing. Except for cases in which religious or moral convictions preclude some of the reproductive options, decision making is often based on the perceived severity and implications of disease and treatment. Current diagnostic testing gives an accurate dichotomous result of affected versus non-affected, but is limited in addressing the real concerns of at-risk couples, which are the clinical course and prognosis.

Since enzymatic testing does not even distinguish between the various forms of Gaucher's disease, clinical prediction of disease manifestations is based on the phenotype of previously affected sibs, if such exist, and on known genotype–phenotype correlations. Except for the Norrbottnian Swedish cases, neuronopathic Gaucher's disease is usually the result of rare mutations in the general population (Beutler and Grabowski, 1995). Therefore, at-risk couples are usually identified only after the birth of an affected child. In these cases, if both parents are carriers, all affected offspring can be predicted to have neuronopathic Gaucher's disease. In the rare case where one parent is found to be affected with Gaucher's disease (obviously Type 1), offspring can have different genotypes, and counselling would based primarily on genotypic information.

GENOTYPE–PHENOTYPE CORRELATIONS

Genotype–phenotype correlations in Gaucher's disease are useful primarily for distinguishing between the neuronopathic and non-neuronopathic forms. They are less accurate in predicting severity within the type of disease involved, especially in Type 1 disease, which is both the most prevalent and the most highly variable form of the disease. On one extreme, which is probably the most common in the general population, glucocerebrosidase deficiency within the category of Type 1 disease is asymptomatic, so it is actually a non-disease, and persons with the enzymatic deficiency cannot be strictly regarded as 'affected'. An analogous situation exists in acute intermittent porphyria, which is caused by a 50% deficiency in PBG deaminase. Approximately 90% of subjects with this enzymatic deficiency remain unaffected throughout their lives (Kappas et al, 1995).

Early attempts at genotype–phenotype correlations were made as soon as the first two glucocerebrosidase mutations, 1448C(L444P) and 1226G (N370S), were identified (Zimran et al, 1989). These studies showed that homozygosity for the 1226G (N370S) mutation was associated with relatively mild Type 1 disease with later age of onset, whereas 1226G(N370S)/1448C(L444P) compound heterozygotes tended to have more severe Type 1 disease with earlier age of onset. 1448C(L444P) homozygotes all had neuronopathic disease. With the identification of the second most common mutation in Ashkenazi Jews (the 84GG) and a number of other mutations, including IVS2 + 1, 1297T(V394L), 1342C(D49H) and three 'recombinant' alleles (Beutler and Gelbart, 1996 and Chapter 2), further genotype/phenotype correlations could be made (Sibille et al, 1993, Balicki and Beutler, 1995), but they are still imperfect in predicting within-type variability. In addition, they do not address the majority of more than 100 mutations known today, most of which are private mutations (Chapter 2). Given the extensive allelic heterogeneity in Gaucher's disease, a classification scheme that defines three mutation classes was proposed (Beutler et al, 1995): mild mutations (e.g. 1226G, 1604A), severe mutations (e.g. 1448C) and null mutations (resulting in no protein product, e.g. 84GG, IVS 1 + 2) (Table 1). Specific combinations among the classes are predicted to result in certain phenotypes. This scheme has the advantage of allowing generalization of all known mutations, and prediction of disease type for combinations of known mutations and for some compound heterozygotes of known/unknown mutations. New mutations can be classified as null versus non-null, but among non-null

Table 1. Interaction between different types of Gaucher's disease mutations.

		One allele		
		Null	Severe	Mild
Other allele	Null	Non-viable	Type 2/3	Type 1
	Severe	Type 2/3	Type 2/3	Type 1
	Mild	Type 1	Type 1	Type 1

Reproduced from Beutler (1995, *Blood Cells, Molecules and Diseases* **21(2)**: 20–24), with permission.

mutations severity is still defined on the basis of the known phenotype of an affected person. In general, the presence of a mild mutation predicts Type 1 disease, whereas lack of a mild mutation predicts neuronopathic Gaucher's disease. The NIH Technology Assessment Conference on Gaucher's disease (McCabe et al, 1996) has published similar recommendations on the use of genotype–phenotype correlations in patient care and counselling:

'1. Homozygosity for N370S (1226G) precludes neuronopathic involvement; that is it produces Type 1 disease only. Nevertheless, this genotype is present in individuals with considerable variability in expression, ranging from absence of signs or symptoms, to mild to moderate disease, to, less commonly, severe Type 1 disease.
2. Compound heterozygotes with one N370S (1226G) allele have non-neuronopathic Gaucher's disease. These individuals have generally more severe Type 1 disease than do N370S (1226G) homozygotes.
3. Homozygotes for L444P (1448C) in the Swedish Norrbottnian population generally present with neuronopathic Type 3 disease of variable severity. This same genotype in the Japanese population is associated with non-neuronopathic disease, indicating that genotype–phenotype correlations, to the extent that they exist, may vary with genetic background.'

The original report mentioned that the statement that N370S precluded neuronopathic disease should be tempered by the observation of 'one exception, a child with oculomotor involvement', but this observation has been proven to be erroneous in that the child does not have the N370S mutation (Tayebi et al, 1996).

COUNSELLING AFTER PRENATAL TESTING

Once the genotype is determined, counselling must convey the predicted severity of disease (including limitations of such predictions) and the expected necessity and efficacy of enzyme replacement therapy. Every effort should be made to provide information in a manner that is meaningful to the patient but non-directive.

As discussed above, prenatal testing can usually distinguish between neuronopathic and non-neuronopathic disease. In our experience, couples who feel selective termination is an option usually choose to terminate pregnancies predicted to result in the birth of a child with the neuronopathic form. Enzyme therapy has not been shown to ameliorate neurological manifestations. Type 2 disease is essentially untreatable at this time (Prows et al, 1997), and in Type 3 disease response to therapy is highly variable, unpredictable and essentially limited to the visceral features of the disease (see Chapter 5).

The most common, and most problematic situation is counselling for Gaucher Type 1. In compound heterozygotes for a mild and a null/severe mutation, treatment will be necessary in all likelihood. Although therapy is clearly efficacious and has the potential of preventing devastating clinical complications, it has been in use only since 1991 (for the placental form) and 1994 (for the recombinant preparation) so long-term safety is yet to be determined. In addition, current treatment regimens involve intravenous infusions no less frequently than once every 2 weeks, possibly over the entire lifespan. Therefore, regardless of cost, issues regarding the individual psychosocial implications of such long-term therapy should not be treated lightly even in the context of a benign, treatable disease.

Different issues arise in cases homozygous for mild mutations (most commonly 1226G homozygotes). Based on gene frequency data for each recognized patient, there are four to five asymptomatic/minimally affected individuals who have never come to medical attention. Only a minority of recognized patients with this genotype require therapy (approximately 20% in the Israeli patient population). Therefore, for at-risk couples identified solely through population screening programmes, there is a low (less than 10%) chance, that an affected child would require treatment, which would most probably not be initiated before adolescence/early adulthood. For at-risk couples identified through the birth of an affected child, the phenotype in future affected children will most likely be similar to that of the proband: at the Shaare Zedek Gaucher Clinic, analysis of 19 families with more than one affected child (with the genotype 1226G/1226G) revealed phenotypic concordance in about 75 % of siblings. However, this leaves a 25% chance of discordance, which is worrisome to many couples. If the previously affected child has mild disease, they are faced with the possibility of severe disease in the future sibling, and in the case of a previous child with severe disease, they are faced with the possibility of terminating a pregnancy with what could be a very mildly affected/asymptomatic child.

FAMILIAL EVALUATION

The diagnosis of an affected person raises the issue of familial evaluation. In principle, this involves molecular and enzymatic testing of both parents, and other persons at risk of being either carriers (e.g. the parents' siblings) or affected (e.g. the proband's siblings). Because Gaucher Type 1 can be asymptomatic or unrecognized, it is important to advise families that testing may reveal additional affected persons, not only carriers. This can be advantageous in symptomatic subjects who would benefit from correct diagnosis and perhaps treatment, but can also result in labelling of asymptomatic individuals as being 'ill' when in fact they do not require any medical attention in this regard. It is also important to recognize that in rare cases a parent of a child with Gaucher's disease will be found to be affected with Type 1 disease, so enzymatic testing is warranted in the parents. In such cases recurrence risks are obviously higher (50% for a mating of an affected subject with a carrier). Patients should be advised which relatives beyond the nuclear family are at risk of being carriers. In some cases families are reluctant to notify relatives. For reasons of confidentiality it is the prerogative of the counselled individual to decide whether or not to inform other relatives at risk. In some situations, dependent on the counsellee's consent, such relatives can be informed of their risk by the genetic service, while preserving the proband's anonymity.

POPULATION SCREENING FOR GAUCHER'S DISEASE

Population screening for Gaucher's disease has been advocated for those ethnic groups in which it is common (Ashkenazi Jews, Norrbottnian Swedes, Jenin Arabs at risk for Gaucher's Type 3c). It is discussed in the context of genetic counselling because an increasing number of at-risk couples are being recognized through such programmes, particularly those aimed at Ashkenazi Jews in Israel and the US. Accepted criteria for implementing population-based carrier screening for a disease are as follows:

1. A disorder with significant morbidity.
2. A defined population for screening.
3. A screening test which is accurate (>95% sensitivity, high specificity), reliable, easily performed, and predicts the clinical course of the disease.
4. A public and professional education programme.
5. Informed consent (McCabe et al, 1996).

While it could be argued that there are certain defined populations in which testing is highly sensitive, Gaucher's disease is frequently not associated with significant morbidity, and furthermore, as discussed above, genotyping does not predict disease severity. For these reasons the NIH Technology Assessment Conference did not recommend general population screening (McCabe et al, 1996). In practice, however, carrier testing is often offered as part of an 'Ashkenazi Jewish screen', and at-risk couples identified face difficult dilemmas when a fetus is diagnosed as affected. An exception to problems raised by screening couples is the 'Dor Yeshorim' (DY) programme, which takes advantage of the unique social characteristics of the ultra-orthodox Jewish community (Broide et al, 1993). In this community pregnancy terminations are usually unacceptable and most marriages are arranged by matchmaking. Young adults of marriageable age are tested anonymously by being given a unique ID number at the time of testing. From that point on, they are identified only by this number and their date of birth, so that only the individual tested can associate the ID number with his/her name. In order to avoid stigmatization, individual carrier status is not divulged, but rather when a couple is considering marriage, they call DY and receive a 'genetic compatibility' assessment. If both are found to be carriers they are told they are not compatible for marriage, and are offered genetic counselling. This approach was initiated by DY in 1983 for Tay–Sachs screening and has virtually eliminated this disease in the ultra-orthodox community (Kleiman, 1992); it has the advantage of tailoring genetic testing to the specifications of the community it serves. In addition, issues raised by the limitations of prenatal testing and genotype–phenotype correlations are essentially avoided, since almost all carrier couples choose not to mate.

Current estimates of Gaucher carrier frequencies in Ashkenazi Jews suggest that perhaps 80% of persons with glucocerebrosidase deficiency are asymptomatic. As a result, population screening in this ethnic group would identify not only at-risk couples, as outlined above, but also thousands of asymptomatic persons with a laboratory diagnosis of Gaucher's disease. In a study of 68 asymptomatic/very mildly affected subjects, there was no significant change in disease manifestations or subjective self-report of health status over a mean follow-up period of 2.6 years (Azuri et al, 1997). Given the consistent absence of symptoms and lack of indication for enzyme replacement therapy, the adverse effect of labelling large numbers of asymptomatic people should not be discounted. Genetic discrimination is not theoretical (Billings et al, 1992). To cite a few examples we have encountered: in Israel persons with Gaucher's disease are not drafted into the army, regardless of their clinical status. In a country where military service is the norm, persons, who have not served are often discriminated against in employment and schooling, and are not eligible for many benefits reserved for veterans. An asymptomatic patient's application to medical school was put on hold until her prognosis could be evaluated by the medical school's consultant haematologist. In countries without state-provided medical insurance, such as the US, Gaucher's disease could result in denial of medical insurance. In Israel, supplementary medical and life insurance, which many employers provide gratis to their senior employees, is either denied or provided only at cost to persons with Gaucher's disease, again, regardless of their clinical status.

Despite these problems, and against the recommendations of various panels (McCabe et al, 1996; Zimran et al, 1997), genetic testing for Gaucher's disease in Ashkenazi Jews is commonly practiced at the population level in both the US and Israel, and it behoves such programmes to monitor their psychosocial and medical impact.

ILLUSTRATIVE CASES

Case A

In a pregnancy screening programme for Ashkenazi Jewish couples, a husband and wife were both found to be carriers of the 1226G(N370S) mutation. They had three older children, aged 6, 11 and 13 years, all considered healthy. Since both parents were carriers, their children were also tested, and the asymptomatic 11-year-old son was found to have Gaucher's disease. The woman underwent prenatal testing and the fetus was also found to have Gaucher's disease. At the time of referral, she was 24 weeks pregnant, and was seriously considering pregnancy termination.

This case illustrates many of the problems in population-based testing. The couple was confronted not only with the problems of having an affected fetus, but also with the diagnosis of 'disease' in their healthy, 11-year-old son. Some of the issues raised in counselling were the predictive value of the son's status regarding the fetus' prognosis, guilt at considering termination of a pregnancy that was in essence equivalent to that of a much loved son, and fear of the burden of having a clinically affected child who might require life-long therapy. The couple were advised that there is 75% concordance between sibs, but that there was still up to, but probably less than 25% risk that a future child would be symptomatic. They decided to continue the pregnancy, which is ongoing at the time of this writing.

Case B

A 28-year-old mother of two, of Kurdish Jewish origin, requested prenatal testing during her third pregnancy. One of her children was affected with severe disease, which at the time was considered to be Type 3 (1448C/1448C), but was responding well to enzyme replacement therapy. On amniocentesis, enzymatic testing revealed that the fetus was affected with Gaucher's disease, with the same genotype as his older sibling (Zimran et al, 1995).

The couple were advised that according to the genotype, the fetus would also have severe Gaucher's disease, and that the neuronopathic form could not be ruled out. Issues raised during counselling were the dilemma of terminating a pregnancy for an illness that is most probably treatable, concern about the possibility of neuronopathic disease and the difficulties of caring for another severely affected child. The couple decided to terminate the pregnancy. A year later, the mother became pregnant again, and prenatal testing revealed that the fetus was a carrier. Pregnancy was carried to term, and this child is now a healthy 3-year old.

Case C

A 28-year-old primigravida of Ashkenazi Jewish origin presented with a twin pregnancy. Enzymatic testing revealed that she was a carrier, but not of any mutation known at the time. Her husband, also an Ashkenazi Jew, was known to have moderate Type 1 Gaucher's disease, with hepatosplenomegaly, occasional bone pains and easy bruisability. His genotype was 1226 (N370S)/IVS2 + 1. On amniocentesis, one twin was found to be a carrier of the 1226G(N370S) mutation, and the other was found to be affected, a compound heterozygote of the IVS2 + 1 mutation and the mother's unknown mutation. The couple were advised that unless the unknown mutation was a mild one, presence of the IVS2 + 1 mutation in the affected fetus was consistent with the possibility of neuronopathic Gaucher's disease. Genetic counselling they received at another institution suggested selective fetal reduction based on the fetuses' position at the time of the original amniocentesis (Zimran et al, 1995).

Since it could not be ascertained that the affected, rather than the unaffected fetus would indeed be targeted, and termination of both twins was unacceptable to the couple, they elected to continue the pregnancy. Sequencing of the mother's glucocerebrosidase gene at the Scripps

Research Institute revealed that she was a carrier of the 1604A(R496H) mutation. At the time, there were only three known patients who were compound heterozygotes for this mutation (two with the 84GG mutation and one with the 1226G mutation). Since they were all mildly affected, the couple were counselled that the affected fetus would not have neurono-pathic disease, although this was not certain, given the limited experience with the mutation at the time. The pregnancy was carried to term, and the twins are now 2 years old. One is a healthy carrier, and the other is minimally affected with Gaucher Type 1 disease.

This woman is now pregnant again, and the couple are thinking of forgoing prenatal diagnosis since if the child were to be affected, it would have Type 1 disease.

Case D

A 30-year-old Ashkenazi woman presented during her first pregnancy. Her father was known to have Gaucher's disease, but declined clinical evaluation or genotyping. Based on historical facts known to the daughter, he most probably has moderate Type 1 disease. The woman was tested and found to be a carrier of the IVS2 + 1 mutation. Testing of her husband, also an Ashkenazi Jew, revealed he was a carrier of the 1226G(N370S) mutation. The woman underwent CVS at another institution, and DNA analysis showed the fetus to be affected, with the IVS2 + 1/1226G(N370S) genotype. Enzymatic testing was not performed.

The couple were advised that since there was no enzymatic diagnosis, there was a small, but distinct (perhaps 5%) chance that the fetus was only a carrier of the paternal mutation and the maternal mutation was detected as a result of maternal contamination (Besley et al, 1988). Therefore, if they were seriously considering pregnancy termination, enzymatic testing on the amniocentesis would be warranted to confirm the diagnosis. If the child were affected, it would be predicted to have moderate Type 1 disease, and would most probably require enzymatic replacement therapy at some point. Issues raised during counselling were the parents' concern about the burden and uncertainties of long-term intravenous treatment. As a professional, highly educated couple they also had difficulty confronting their previous expectations of having a 'perfect' baby. However, they were worried that since there was no assurance of having unaffected children in subsequent pregnancies, they might be facing repeat terminations while they were still childless. They elected to continue the pregnancy. The child is now a 4-month-old boy, with mild splenomegaly. He has not had any blood tests performed yet.

This case also highlights the need for enzymatic testing as the gold standard of prenatal diagnosis since PCR-based techniques are more prone to problems of contamination.

FUTURE DIRECTIONS

Neuronopathic Gaucher's disease presents classical counselling issues encountered with severe, recessive disorders. In this arena future developments will on the one hand in the realm of earlier and better preimplantation or prenatal diagnosis, and on the other hand in the realm of new treatments, e.g. gene therapy. However, non-neuronopathic Gaucher's disease is in a sense a paradigm for a treatable, often benign genetic disorder. While scientific and medical issues, such as refining genotype–phenotype correlations and defining optimal therapy will lead to improved patient management, they must be accommodated into a broader social and ethical context, in which genetic variation is accepted, rather than automatically stigmatized as an illness. This goal can only be achieved through public and professional education, and efforts of the medical community to ensure that genetic testing is driven only by patient benefit.

REFERENCES

Abrahamov A, Elstein D, Gross-Tsur V et al (1995) Gaucher's disease variant characterised by progressive calcification of heart valves and unique genotype. *Lancet* **346**: 1000–1003.

Association of Clinical Cytogeneticists Working Party on Chorionic Villi in Prenatal Diagnosis (1994) Cytogenetic analysis of chorionic villi for prenatal diagnosis: an ACC collaborative study of UK data. *Prenatal Diagnosis* **14**: 363–379.

Azuri J, Elstein D, Lahad A et al (1997) Asymptomatic Gaucher disease: Objective and subjective aspects with implications for large scale screening of this disorder in Ashkenazi Jews. *American Journal of Human Genetics* **61**: 248A.

Balicki D & Beutler E (1995) Gaucher disease. *Medicine (Baltimore)* **74**: 305–323.

Besley GT, Ferguson-Smith ME, Frew C et al, (1988) First trimester diagnosis of Gaucher disease in a fetus with trisomy 21. *Prenatal Diagnosis* **8**: 471–474

Beutler E & Saven A (1990) Misuse of marrow examination in the diagnosis of Gaucher disease. *Blood* **76**: 646–648.

*Beutler E & Grabowski GA (1995) Glucosylceramide lipidoses: Gaucher disease. In: Scriver CR, Beudet AL, Sly WS et al (eds) *The Metabolic and Molecular Basis of Inherited Disease*, 7th edn, pp. 2641–2670. New York: McGraw-Hill.

*Beutler E & Gelbart T (1996) Mutation update: Glucocerebrosidase (Gaucher disease). *Human Mutation* **8**: 207–213.

Beutler E, Gelbart T, Demina A et al (1996) Five new Gaucher disease mutations. *Blood Cells, Molecules and Diseases* **21**: 20–24.

*Billings PR, Kohn MA, de Cuevas M et al, (1992) Discrimination as a consequence of genetic testing. *American Journal of Human Genetics* **50**: 476–482

Broide E, Zeigler M, Eckstein J, & Bach G, (1993) Screening for carriers of Tay–Sachs disease in the ultraorthodox Ashkenazi Jewish community in Israel. *American Journal of Medical Genetics* **47**: 213–215.

Cheung MC, Goldberg JD, Kan YW. (1996) Prenatal diagnosis of sickle cell anaemia and thalassaemia by analysis of fetal cells in maternal blood. *Nature Genetics* **14**: 264–268.

Delhanty JD (1994). Preimplantation diagnosis. *Prenatal Diagnosis* **14**: 1217–1227.

Glenn D, Gelbart T & Beutler E. (1994) Tight linkage of pyruvate kinase (PKLR) and glucocerebrosidase (GBA) genes. *Human Genetics* **93**: 635–638.

Handyside AH, Lesko JG, Tarin JJ et al, (1992) Birth of a normal girl after in vitro fertilization and preimplantation diagnostic testing for cystic fibrosis. *New England Journal of Medicine* **327**: 905–909.

Harper JC. (1996) Preimplantation diagnosis of inherited disease by embryo biopsy: an update of the world figures. *Journal of Assisted Reproduction and Genetics* **13**: 90–95.

Kappas A, Sassa S, Galbraith RA & Nordman Y, (1995) The porphyrias. In Scriver CR, Beaudet AL, Sly WS, et al, (eds) *The Metabolic and Molecular Bases of Inherited Disease*, 7th edn., pp. 2103–2160. New York: McGraw-Hill.

Kleinman M (1992) An alternative program for the prevention of Tay–Sachs disease. In, Bonne-Tamir B & Adam A (eds) *Genetic Diversity Among the Jews*, pp. 346–348. New York: Oxford University Press.

*McCabe ERB, Fine BA, Globus MS et al (1996) Gaucher disease—Current issues in diagnosis and treatment. *Journal of the American Medical Association* **275**: 548–553.

Mistry PK (1995) Genotype/phenotype correlations in Gaucher's disease. *Lancet* **346**: 982.

Prows CA, Sanchez N, Daugherty C & Grabowski GA (1997) Gaucher disease: Enzyme therapy in the acute neuronopathic variant. *American Journal of Medical Genetics* **71**:16–21.

*Sibille A, Eng CM, Kim S-J et al (1993) Phenotype/genotype correlation in Gaucher disease type 1: clinical and therapeutic implication. *American Journal of Human Genetics* **52**: 1094–1101.

Sidransky E, Lau EK, Winfield S et al (1997) Identification of two novel polymorphisms in the gluco-cerebrosidase gene region. *American Journal of Human Genetics* (in press).

Smidt-Jensen S, Lind AM, Permin M et al (1993) Cytogenetic analysis of 2928 CVS samples and 1075 amniocenteses from randomized studies. *Prenatal Diagnosis* **13**: 723–740.

Tayebi N, Herman J, Ginns EI & Sidranski E (1996) Genotype D399N/R463C in a patient with type 3 Gaucher disease previously assigned genotype N370S/R463C. *Biochemical and Molecular Medicine* **57**: 149–151.

Teshima IE, Kalousek DK, Vekemans MJ et al (1992) Canadian multicenter randomized clinical trial of chorion villus sampling and amniocentesis. Chromosome mosaicism in CVS and amniocentesis samples. *Prenatal Diagnosis* **2**: 443–466.

Zimran A, Zaizov R & Zlotogora J (1997) Large scale screening for Gaucher disease in Israel—a position paper by the National Gaucher Committee of the Ministry of Health. *Harefuah—Journal of the Israel Medical Association* **133**: 107–108.

Zimran A, Sorge J, Gross E et al (1989) Prediction of severity of Gaucher's disease by identification of mutations at DNA level. *Lancet* **2**: 349–353.

*Zimran A, Elstein D, Abrahamov A et al (1995) Prenatal molecular diagnosis of Gaucher disease. *Prenatal Diagnosis* **15**: 1185–1188.

11

Skeletal involvement in Gaucher's disease

DEBORAH ELSTEIN PhD

Research Coordinator
Gaucher Clinic, Shaare Zedek Medical Center, PO Box 3235, Jerusalem, 91031 Israel

MENACHEM ITZCHAKI MD

Chairman
Department of Orthopaedics, Shaare Zedek Medical Center, Gaucher Clinic, Jerusalem, 91031 Israel

HENRY J. MANKIN MD

Visiting Orthopaedic Surgeon, Massachusetts General Hospital, Director, Harvard Combined Residency Program in Orthopaedics, Harvard Medical School and Edith M. Ashley Professor of Orthopaedics
Department of Orthopaedic Surgery, Massachusetts General Hospital, Boston, Massachusetts, USA

Perhaps the most variable of all the symptoms attributed to Gaucher's disease is that of bone involvement, both in the Type 1 and Type 3 forms of the disease. Expression of skeletal involvement in Gaucher patients ranges from asymptomatic disease, with or without radiological signs, to symptomatic disease, which can be severe and engender considerable pain and disability. Herein we discuss the imaging techniques currently available to document the presence and progression of bone involvement as well as the various forms of medical and surgical management that are employed to help the Gaucher patient cope with skeletal disease.

Key words: Gaucher's disease; avascular necrosis; arthroplasty; dual energy X-ray absorptiometry; magnetic resonance imaging; computed tomography; osteoporosis; enzyme replacement therapy; bisphosphonates.

In a disease that is marked by considerable phenotypic heterogeneity, both among the various genotypes as well as between patients with the same genotype, perhaps the most variable symptom of Gaucher's disease is that of bone involvement. Although infants with Type 2 do not survive long enough to manifest skeletal complications, early surveys in Type 1 patients reported significant orthopaedic problems in 21 to 83% of patients (Matoth and Fried, 1965; Beighton et al, 1982; Kolodny et al, 1982; Zimran et al, 1992), including in 80% of children (Zevin et al, 1993); but in Type 3 patients, the incidence ranged from none in the Arab Type 3c variant patients (Abrahamov et al, 1995) to 100% among the Norrbottnian variant patients (Svennerholm et al, 1982). One feature of Gaucher's disease is the

Copyright © 1997, by Baillière Tindall
All rights of reproduction in any form reserved

failure of correlation of bone with visceral or haematological disease. Asymptomatic bone disease, such as Erlenmeyer flasking of the distal femora, medullary infarcts and diffuse osteopenia may occur in any patient regardless of the extent of the visceral manifestations, and may be present or relatively absent in patients with severe splenomegaly or bone marrow depression. The spectrum of symptomatic bone disease (Stowens et al, 1985; Pastakia et al, 1986), with preferential involvement of the long bones of the large joints and the spine, including pathological fractures, avascular necrosis (AVN) of the heads of femur and humerus, and compression fractures and/or vertebral collapse in the spine, is comparable in Types 1 and 3; but may not be correlated with the severity of any other parameter of Gaucher's disease. Interestingly, asymptomatic involvement may be marked by extensive changes on imaging studies (especially magnetic resonance imaging) of lytic lesions and sclerotic progression (Beighton et al, 1982) whereas the debilitating pain of 'bone crises' may not be easily documented (Yosipovitch and Katz, 1990; Katz et al, 1996).

The purpose of this chapter is to outline the skeletal disease seen in patients with Gaucher's disease, review the modalities currently being employed to diagnose the presence and extent of involvement, and discuss the implications of both surgical management and enzyme replacement therapy. In large measure, we will draw on the experience at Shaare Zedek Medical Center in Jerusalem, Israel, a national referral clinic for Gaucher patients, and from the Orthopedic Services at Massachusetts General Hospital in Boston, MA, which specializes in metabolic bone diseases. It is important to note at the outset that in a cohort of 266 Type 1 patients, comparison between patients homozygous for the N370S (1226G) mutation, the 'mild' genotype most prevalent among Jewish Ashkenazi patients, with those who are compound heterozygotes with the N370S mutation (more often seen in the polyracial patients in the US), showed significant differences in skeletal involvement (Elstein et al, 1997). The degree of disease severity as evaluated by hepatosplenomegaly and haematological abnormalities was underscored by a greater number of splenectomized patients in the compound heterozygote group (38%) than in the homozygous patients (10%). Nonetheless, the incidence of the Erlenmeyer flask deformity in the distal femur, herring bone (chevron sign) in the humerus, and osteoporosis were all comparable in the two groups. However, the incidence of avascular necrosis (AVN) of the hip was three times greater in the compound heterozygote group (26%) than in the homozygous group (9%); similarly, the incidence of vertebral collapse was two times higher in the compound heterozygote group (12%) than in the homozygous group (5.5%). If the genotype N370S/84GG group is considered separately (35 patients), the percentages are even higher: 40% incidence of AVN and 23% of vertebral collapse. Thus, although it is hazardous to suggest that a specific genotype for Gaucher's disease is correlated with a specific phenotype, it appears that patients with the N370S/84GG genotype evince a higher incidence of bone disease, albeit that this may also be related to the greater prevalence of splenectomy in this group (43%), which may be directly correlated with the emergence and/or deterioration of skeletal symptoms (Rose et al, 1982; Zimran et al, 1995). This latter point was reiterated in an analysis of 51 Type 1 patients at the Massachusetts General where AVN of the proximal femora statistically were more frequent in splenectomized patients, in males, and in patients with high platelet counts (unpublished data).

SKELETAL INVOLVEMENT IN GAUCHER'S DISEASE

Infiltration of normal bone marrow by lipid-laden Gaucher cells (Figure 1) results in apparently progressive displacement of the fat-rich marrow proper (and thus contributes to the frequently noted pancytopenia) with a consequent shift in haematopoietic activity from proximal to more distal sites (Rosenthal et al, 1986), albeit with epiphyseal sparing. However, the pathophysiology, particularly the impact of altered numbers and increased activity of osteoclasts (whose progenitors in the marrow are of haemato-poietic lineage) and possibly suppressed osteoblast activity (Figure 2) (Siffert and Platt, 1982; Mankin et al, 1990), is imperfectly understood, as is the mechanism of bone infarction caused by impaired collateral bone micro- and macrovascular supply (Figure 3). These phenomena account for the major elements of Gaucher bone disease, specifically failure to remodel (a failure of osteoclast function); osteopenia and lytic lesions (a failure of osteoblast function); and osteonecrosis (or AVN, a micro- and macro-occlusion in the proximal femora, proximal humera, distal femora and proximal tibial subchondral sites). In addition, the last mentioned is

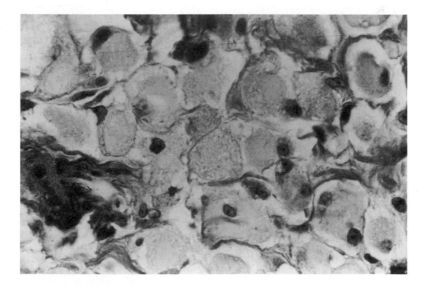

Figure 1. High power photomicrograph of bone marrow containing principally Gaucher cell, histio-cytes containing huge concentrations of glucosyl ceramide (haematoxylin and eosin ×400).

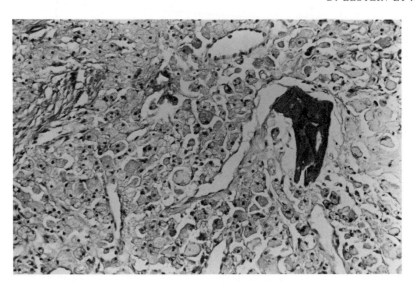

Figure 2. Low power photomicrograph of bone from a patient with florid Gaucher bone disease. Note that the marrow is in large measure replaced by Gaucher cells and that the bone spicule is tiny and has no osteoblasts or osteoclasts present (haematoxylin and eosin ×40).

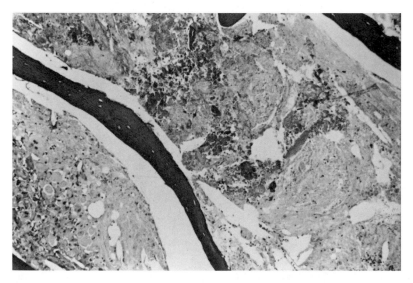

Figure 3. Low power photomicrograph of bone from a patient with osteonecrosis showing thin medullary segments with empty lacunae. The bone is surrounded by Gaucher cells and there is necrotic calcareous detritus present (haematoxylin and eosin ×40).

believed to be the cause of medullary sclerosis, based on the time of avascular cell death, and the release of free fatty acids that form an insoluble 'soap' with calcium ions.

Accumulation of Gaucher cells in the bone marrow is associated with varying degrees of necrosis, fibrous proliferation and resorption of the bony trabeculae, followed by erosion of the endosteal surface of the cortex and modelling deformities. Hermann et al (1986) have formulated a five-stage classification of lesions seen in Type 1 Gaucher's disease, with the range from diffuse osteoporosis (stage 1), to medullary expansion (stage 2), to osteolysis (stage 3), to necrosis/sclerosis (stage 4), to destruction and collapse (stage 5). Thus, among the earliest signs is the Erlenmeyer flask deformity of the distal femur and the proximal tibia (stage 2) (Figure 4), which, although not pathognomonic of the disease, is seen in most patients at presentation. Osteopenia of varying degrees is seen (Figure 5) with concomitant poor osteoblast re-building of bone. Medullary expansion (Figure 6) is often present as is osteolysis, both of which result in lytic lesions (Figure 7) which in fact may lead to slowly healing fractures (Figure 8) (Lee et al, 1982; Siffert and Platt, 1982; Hermann et al, 1986; Mankin et al, 1990; Zevin et al, 1993). Marrow sclerosis is a sign of osteonecrosis (Figure 8) and if present in subchondral sites, such as the

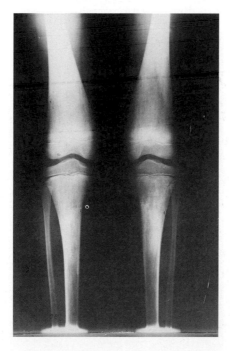

Figure 4. Roentgenogram of the distal femora and proximal tibia showing classic Erlenmeyer flask deformities. characteristic but not pathognomonic for Gaucher's disease. Note the wide metaphysis and unremodelled distal diaphysis. The patient in addition shows some sclerosis (see text and Figure 5).

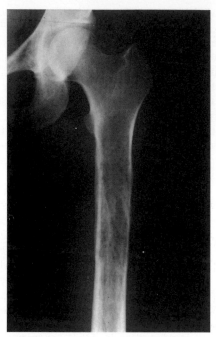

Figure 5. X-ray of the proximal femur showing diffuse osteopenia but in addition the portion of the shaft just below the trochanters shows a mottled, permeative appearance.

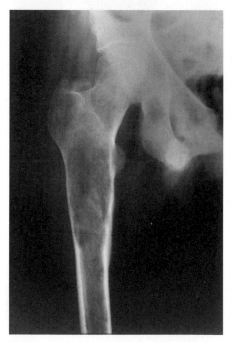

Figure 6. Roentgenogram of the proximal femur showing not only the diffuse osteopenia and the mottled irregular appearance quite characteristic of Gaucher's disease, but an 'expansion' of the shaft, which is quite striking. This area is very subject to fracture.

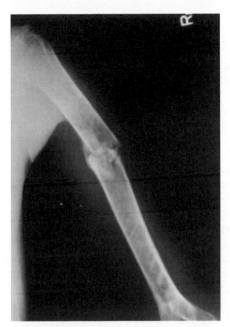

Figure 7. Roentgenogram showing a typical fracture in the humerus of a patient with Gaucher's disease. The fracture is transverse (like breaking a pencil) and is slow to heal even with open reduction and internal fixation.

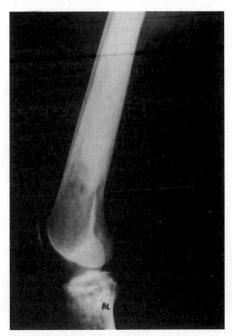

Figure 8. Marrow necrosis causes rather severe degrees of increased density, related to calcium serving as a counterion for released free fatty acid. The calcium 'soap' so produced is insoluble in body fluids.

femoral head, may result in osteonecrosis and collapse, the most severe problem of all (Figure 9). Some patients evince focal involvement wherein radiolucent shadows with geographic or moth-eaten patterns and/or ground glass veiling mimic malignancy (Pastakia et al, 1986), but the more commonly seen bilateral incidence (versus unilateral occurrence of tumors) may help rule out the presence of tumorous lesions (Watanabe et al, 1984). It should be noted, however, that the incidence of myeloma in patients with Gaucher's disease may be higher than in the population at large (Shiran et al, 1993) and that some Gaucher's disease involvement may mimic cancerous processes (Neudorfer et al, 1997).

Infarcts in the long bones are of considerable clinical concern in that they often result in excruciating pain and functional handicap. Areas of sclerosis, the soap bubble pattern on radiographs, implicating bone infarction and/or osteonecrosis, are common in Gaucher's disease probably because of the compression of intraosseous sinusoids and lumina by Gaucher cells. These events may be correlated with 'bone crises' of acute, albeit circumscribed, pain (Noyes and Smith, 1971) and systemic reactions such as elevated temperature. Osteomyelitis, in contradistinction to the historical explanation for bone crises (Sacks, 1971; Kolodny et al, 1982), is rather uncommon, being caused by bacterial proliferation within areas of bone necrosis. Findings during the episodic pain of bone crises (which has been termed 'sterile' or 'pseudo-osteitis'), because of true infections in the bones and joints, either as chronic discharging sinuses or as acute toxaemia, are generally a result of post-surgical or post-drainage complications (Yosipovitch et al, 1965) or because of an adventitious infection in

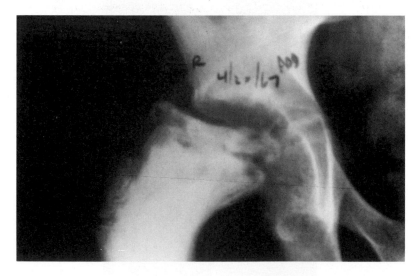

Figure 9. Osteonecrosis has produced collapse and a severe deformity of the proximal femoral epiphysis in this 8-year-old child with Gaucher's disease. The entity is difficult to distinguish from Legg Calve Perthes disease except for the region of marked increase in density in the adjacent metaphysis and diaphysis of the femur.

avascular bone of Gaucher patients who are often prone to infections due to various reasons (Shoenfeld et al, 1982).

Aseptic necrosis has long been known to occur (Arkin and Schein, 1948) in the femoral and humeral heads (Figure 10), tibial plateau (Figure 11), distal femur and rarely, in the small bones such as the talus. Secondary degenerative joint changes may occur because of the irregularity of the articular surfaces, but today it is rarely seen as a presenting sign (Kolodny et al, 1982). Pathological fractures, particularly in weight-bearing bones, and bizarre deformations of the long bones, accompanied by both acute (phasic) and chronic (tonic) pain, are not uncommon in these patients with severe bone involvement. An interesting anecdote is the prevalence of 'romantic fractures' (Elstein et al, 1997), fractures of the ribs after being hugged (seen in seven female and in three male patients at Shaare Zedek), and other evidence of skeletal damage after relatively slight trauma.

Spinal changes may include osteopenia with loss of trabeculae as well as compression fractures (Strickland, 1958; Rourke and Heslin, 1965; Stowens et al, 1985; Hermann et al, 1989) with consequent kyphosis, although this latter finding may be seen without evidence of vertebral abnormalities, especially in Type 3 patients (Erikson, 1986). Vertebrae may become flattened and evince either the typical 'H-type' deformation or the fish-mouth pattern, or they may become completely collapsed, especially in the thoracolumbar spine and involve multiple vertebrae, to form the shape of vertebral plana; however, these defects only rarely result in spinal deformation and do not necessitate immediate surgical intervention unless spinal cord or nerve involvement is present (Raynor, 1962; Markin and

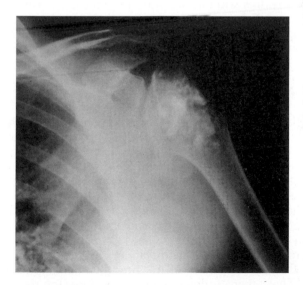

Figure 10. Roentgenogram of the shoulder in a 52-year-old woman with Gaucher's disease showing not only the collapse of the proximal humeral articular surface but extensive necrosis in the subjacent metaphysis. This patient was disabled with this problem which was particularly related to her inability to abduct and forward flex her shoulder.

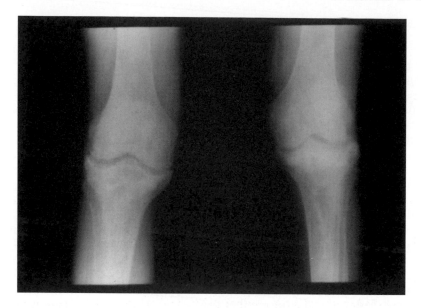

Figure 11. Anterior-posterior views of both knees in a 63-year-old patient with Gaucher's disease showing severe deformity of the tibial surfaces resulting from osteonecrotic collapse.

Skultety, 1984). Findings of vertebra plana as ordinarily seen in Calve's disease is now thought to be correlated with eosinophilic granulosa (Figure 12) and similarly, this will rarely compromise the cord or the cauda.

It should be noted, however, that there is a sub-set of patients, apparently not associated with any specific genotype or other disease parameter, who evince no bone involvement, even in old age.

IMAGING METHODOLOGIES

The use of plain X-rays, minimally, including chest, thoracolumbar spine, all four limbs and pelvis, should be considered part of the routine work-up of a Gaucher patient at presentation (Rademakers, 1995) in order to derive a general status report of the skeletal involvement. Since evidence of skeletal involvement impacts on the course of clinical management in Gaucher patients in that this appears to be a process that probably does not reverse or halt spontaneously, clinicians have attempted to find non-invasive, inexpensive and readily available means of assessing this parameter. In addition, because of the need to frequently monitor the patho-logical progression, in all patients including children, both with and with-out enzyme therapy, the choice of imaging methodology is of non-trivial importance. Thus, there follows a list of options for the task of early diagnosis of the presence and severity of bone involvement (with the caveat that the extent of individual lytic foci may have no diagnostic or prognostic value), as well as their subsequent use in appraisal of the effect of enzyme

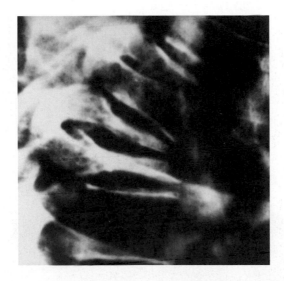

Figure 12. Lateral roentgenogram of the thoracic spine of a patient with Gaucher's disease showing the classic changes of vertebra plana (Calve's disease). Both segments are flattened and water like.

replacement therapy, which have found adherents for inclusion in the follow-up regimen. Nonetheless, it is to be stressed that the ideal tool for sensitive evaluation, which can be employed to predict the advent of skeletal damage and/or correlate with clinically-meaningful changes in bone, is as yet unavailable.

Magnetic resonance imaging (MRI) in Gaucher's disease (Rosenthal et al, 1986; Hermann et al, 1993) accurately depicts marrow and soft-tissue damage secondary to infarction and provides a crude estimate of the burden of Gaucher cells in the marrow (Figure 13). It should be used as a diagnostic adjunct in those patients with pinpointed skeletal involvement, e.g. ascertainment of AVN or spinal compression in anticipation of surgery, in which case, T_1- and T_2-weighted images on both coronal and axial planes, and sagittal planes on images for the spine should be considered (Cremin et al, 1990). MRI estimates the Gaucher cell infiltration with relative accuracy particularly in the lower limbs because of the differential signaling on T_1-weighted images between normal and lipid-laden marrow (Lanir et al, 1986; Rosenthal et al, 1986). Since haemorrhages are easily identified by both T_1 and T_2 signals, or alternatively oedema is clear on T_1-weighted MRI images, MRI has also been used for documentation of bone crises (Horev et al, 1991), although this latter point may be moot in that these secondary changes may resolve and/or remain as asymptomatic artifacts. MRI is particularly valuable in the study of the spinal segments and defining the extent of the impingement on the cord or cauda equina. MRI is very sensitive to osteonecrosis and can define the extent of these changes even in the asymptomatic patient. The test also does not have any radiation hazard and hence is a better study for repeated evaluation to assess disease progress or the results of treatment. As may be intuited, MRI is inappropriate in

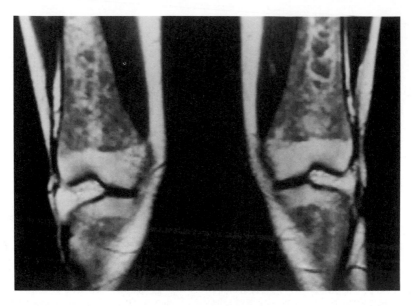

Figure 13. T₁ MRI images of the distal femur showing the changes characteristic of Gaucher's disease. The epiphyses are spared. The distal femur shows the classic 'salt and pepper' pattern but in addition, there are in both femora islands of central osteonecrosis.

patients with surgically implanted metal devices (as well as shrapnel etc.), which disallows many Gaucher patients who have undergone joint replacements, external fixation of fractures, etc. A classification comparing severity of bone disease with marrow infiltration as seen on T_1-weighted MRI images has been suggested (Rosenthal et al, 1986), as has a classification based on comparison of T_1 and T_2 signal intensities to ascertain the presence of necrosis (Esplin and McPherson, 1994), for the purpose of quantifying bone involvement (Terk et al, 1995) in older children and adults (Waitches et al, 1994). However, it is to be conceded (Barton et al, 1996) that this tool may be insensitive to slight changes in marrow composition, and hence, the use of quantitative chemical shift imaging (QCSI) has been suggested (Johnson et al, 1992). The advantage of the QCSI image is that it accurately estimates the displacement of normal marrow by lipid-laden Gaucher cells by comparing the differential (proton) signalling of water to fat (triglyceride fraction), especially in the lumbar spine where infarctions are rare, and has been shown to correlate with splenic enlargement as a measure of disease severity (Rosenthal et al, 1992). However, although non-invasive, this test is only available at present in two centres world-wide, is expensive, and ultimately, it is questionable whether changes in marrow composition, even as a result of enzyme replacement therapy (Barton et al, 1996), reflect clinically relevant events in patients with established skeletal involvement (Rosenthal et al, 1992).

Computed tomography (CT) has also been suggested as a marker of disease severity (Siffert and Platt, 1982; Starer et al, 1987; Rosenthal et al,

1989) based on the ability to track Gaucher cell infiltration and based on studies of improvement following transplant-induced restoration of marrow function; but CT is incapable of quantitative assessment and is associated with significant radiation, making it a less good choice for frequent follow-up examinations. A newer modality is high resolution quantitative CT employing both single (SEQCT) and dual energy (DEQCT) calculations as measures of trabecular and cortical bone density in addition to marrow fat content; however, in a report comparing these results with those of MRI, there was poor correlation (Rosenthal et al, 1989). Similarly, quantitative CT of bone density in children with moderate to severe manifestations of Gaucher's disease was normal, and the progressive decrements with age documented by quantitative CT, both in males and females, was not correlated with Gaucher complications (Rosenthal et al, 1992). Thus, this tool may be equally imperfect as a means to assess bone disease parameters and their deterioration or amelioration over time.

Dual energy X-ray absorptimetry (DEXA) to assess bone density has proven to be valuable in gauging the extent of osteopenia in osteoporosis, and hence has also been investigated as a potentially useful measure to evaluate skeletal involvement in Gaucher's disease (Pastores et al, 1996). The advantages of DEXA include reduced radiation dose, high precision, accessibility to multiple skeletal sites and is an accurate measure of the soft-tissue composition (both lean and fat mass) (Mazes, 1990); although the equipment is more generally available, it is not inexpensive, and may vary with machine, so that studies must be done consistently in the same location. In a group of 61 adult Gaucher patients, the mean bone density (or bone mass) at four skeletal sites, including the lumbar spine and distal radius, was significantly lower than in age- and sex-matched controls; the severity of osteopenia was correlated with the N370S/84GG genotype (see above), splenectomy and hepatomegaly; and the values at the various sites correlated well with each other. Thus, this may be a more sensitive measure of bone disease in adult Gaucher patients, and has the non-trivial attributes of being non-invasive and inexpensive; the one drawback is its relative inaccuracy in the presence of vertebral infarcts or collapse, which in this population are prevalent (Rosenthal, 1995), or in large medullary infarcts (which materially increase the bone density at the site).

Inhalation of radio-labelled lipid-soluble xenon gas (^{133}Xe) in Gaucher patients with direct scintigraphic imaging of fat deposits, has shown increased uptake in the marrow because of an increase in blood flow, but more importantly because of diminished venous return (clearing) on the basis of an infarcted and infiltrated marrow (Castronovo et al, 1993). According to this initial report, the biphasic release of ^{133}Xe from Gaucher deposits in bone can be used as a quantitative measure that reflects the earliest significant 'normalizing' alterations in marrow fat induced by enzyme replacement therapy. However, the method restricts data to images of the knee and, in addition to being restricted to a few centres, is quite demanding technically. Two other radiopharmaceuticals, the cationic complex technetium-99m sestamibi (^{99m}Tc-MIBI) as an indicator of cellular density and metabolic activity, and technetium-99m hexametazime

(^{99m}Tc-HMPAO) as an indicator of fat infiltration, have also been employed recently in a single case report (Mariani et al, 1996). The results demonstrate good uptake in skeletal areas affected by Gaucher cell infiltration, which correlates with those seen on X-ray. ^{99m}Tc-MIBI scintigraphy, representative of the newest class of radio-labelled drugs with tremendous potential for imaging cell biochemistry, evinced fewer technical problems than nobel gas inhalation, and therefore has been recommended in preference to xenon scintigraphy because of its greater availability, easier mode of administration and the need for less equipment to record data. Despite the scientific excitement associated with such techniques, they are sometimes difficult to apply and reproduce, and hence, one must question the value of these modalities, other than as being of academic interest at this time, if the ultimate goal of imaging is diagnosis of severity of bone involvement and/or prognosis of resolution.

THE JAW IN GAUCHER'S DISEASE

The mandible, although a long bone, has heretofore not received much attention as a potential nidus for Gaucher cell infiltration. In a recent study (unpublished data) of 88 Type 1 Gaucher patients who underwent oral examination for the presence of jaw-related findings, 28 agreed to submit a panoramic dental X-ray for evaluation. Despite this inherent bias, since it is to be inferred that this sub-group was more predisposed to dental awareness, 25 of the 28 patients (89%) evinced involvement of the jaw. The mandible alone was involved in 21 patients, and both mandible and maxilla in four patients. Features common to Gaucher infiltration seen in other long bones, including enlarged marrow spaces (in 84%), radiolucencies (24%), endosteal scalloping (8%) and cortical thinning (8%), were reported. Interestingly, root resorption, which was seen in four of these cases, but in the population at large is an extremely rare finding, was associated with frank radiolucencies, and cortical thinning with consequent inferior displacement of the inferior alveolar canals. In addition, in five of the nine children under the age of 20 years, delayed eruption of the permanent dentition (the difference between chronological age and dental age ranged from 1 to 5 years) was noted, which was correlated with other bone involvement, whereas in the four children with normal eruption of permanent dentition, none had evidence of bone involvement. The general dental and gingival condition in all of these patients was good to excellent. Thus, it is to be noted that despite the sampling bias, even if the results of these 25 patients were to be extrapolated to the entire group of 88 patients, the incidence of abnormal findings is considerably greater than in normal patients, and merits consideration as a means of early diagnosis of bone involvement in Gaucher's disease. Parenthetically, it has been the experience of some clinicians that many Gaucher patients, because of concern for low platelet counts, are loath to initiate proper dental hygiene, especially routine dental cleanings. This is clearly an error and patients should be dissuaded from this self-defeating attitude.

POST-MENOPAUSAL OSTEOPOROSIS AND
GAUCHER'S DISEASE

Normally the adult skeleton turns over at a rate of 8% per year and after the age of 20 years most adults (males as well as females) lose approximately 0.3% of their bone annually. These activities are mediated by the osteoblasts that synthesize new bone and osteoclasts that destroy them; ordinarily in the young adult the rates are essentially equal in extent but opposite in direction. Normal bone remodelling is a result of resorption of old bone by osteoclasts and formation or synthesis of new matrix of bone by osteoblasts. In osteoporosis the resorbed cavity is not completely filled with new bone and hence there is a gradual loss of bone, which ultimately leads to an increased risk of fracture (Parfitt, 1982). Bone loss is a universal process but is more pronounced in women than in men (Riggs and Melton, 1986). In men, especially those who exercise regularly, this is of little consequence because of the very low rate of bone loss. In women, bone loss is more serious for several reasons including the fact that they achieve a lower peak bone mass at skeletal maturity, and the fact that they pass through menopause with a concomitant decrease in oetrogen, which accelerates the rate of bone loss (Consensus Development Conference, 1993). Although the actual rate of post-menopausal bone loss may also be affected by many genetic and environmental factors, the impact of a low peak bone mass at maturity is most dramatic since it confers less immunity from risk of fracture at a relatively younger age. One of the positive attributes of early menarche is adequate oestrogen levels in which women achieve their peak bone mass potential; the corollary being that late menarche results in decreased bone mass before the advent of menopause and hence, pre-menopausal amenorrhea is a known risk factor for osteo-porosis and osteoporotic fractures. In a study of 53 Type 1 Gaucher patients, 66% achieved menarche after the age of 14 years; 50% of these patients had mild rather than severe disease (Granovsky-Grisaru et al, 1995). Thus, it appears that in the female Gaucher patient there is the added burden of decreased peak bone mass at menopause in addition to osteo-penia (Pastores et al, 1996), which may result in osteoporosis and increase the risk of fractures of the hip, spine and wrist in this group of patients.

Another factor that may impinge on the severity of osteoporosis is the contribution of cytokine production. In vitro, addition of solvent-solubilized glucocerebroside to cultured macrophages leads to the release of secretory cytokines (Gery et al, 1981) including interleukin-1 (IL-1), which is known to stimulate bone resorption (Pacifici et al, 1987). In a recent study that investigated the role of pro-inflammatory cytokines, including that of interleukin-6 (IL-6), another potent stimulator of bone resorption (Lowik et al, 1989) that may also be involved in the osteoporosis of oestrogen deficiency, and interleukin-10 (IL-10), a growth/differentiation-promoting factor involved in both bone formation (Van Vlasselaer et al, 1993) and resorption, showed that levels of both were elevated in Gaucher patients relative to controls (Allen et al, 1997). IL-6 and IL-10 may work in concert in Gaucher skeletal disease in that osteoclast precursors are stimulated by

IL-6 and osteoblast metabolism is inhibited by IL-10 (Lowik et al, 1989). Thus, this evidence of a connection between cellular regulators produced in response to the presence of pathological macrophages (Gaucher cells) may provide a preliminary theoretical basis for the connection between the biochemical abnormality and bone involvement of Gaucher's disease.

SURGICAL MANAGEMENT OF BONE DISEASE IN GAUCHER'S DISEASE

With the advent of enzyme replacement therapy, and conceivably with new curative approaches such as gene transfer, which will alter the natural history of Gaucher's disease, it is to be hoped that Gaucher patients in the future will no longer be affected by skeletal complications. In the past and even now, however, the morbidity due to severe bone involvement was of primary concern to both the patient and his physician, since, despite the multiplicity of presentations, severe skeletal disease invariably led to appreciably decreased quality of life and in some cases severe disability. Thus, restorative surgery for pathological fractures, large joint replacements, and various non-surgical approaches to alleviate functional and physiological disability were and remain of critical import.

In a report of skeletal complications of Gaucher's disease in 1966 (Amstutz and Carey, 1966), symptomatic avascular necrosis of the femoral head was treated with non-weight-bearing in (three out of three) children particularly with bilateral involvement (but with recurrence of necrosis and pain in adolescence or adulthood), with radiotherapy (in seven patients with equivocal results and consequent adverse effects), or with total hip arthroplasty (THA) in six hips, all of which were complicated by post-surgical infections and slight settling of the prosthesis. Reconstructive surgery, although recommended to ameliorate functional handicaps, was marked universally by infection and in many cases by haemorrhage. A study 20 years later (Goldblatt et al, 1988) reviewed the results in eight patients with 15 THA. With up to 14 years follow-up, the results, as gauged by limb mobility and freedom from pain, were excellent. The recommendation was that joint replacement was the treatment of choice despite the 'resistance among colleagues to perform this operation among Gaucher's disease' (Goldblatt et al, 1988). Among the problems encountered at that time were risk of infection and haemorrhage, the use of a cemented prostheses in a matrix that might be both damaged and likely to continue to disintegrate (Van Wellen et al, 1994), and the inability to predict the outcome, particularly in young patients (Alkali et al, 1979), based on continuous infiltration of Gaucher cells (Lachiewicz et al, 1981; Lau et al, 1981). This led many surgeons to avoid offering surgery despite the apparent destiny of a wheelchair existence, a reality that was difficult for the patients to accept. Nonetheless, more recent experiences (Tauber and Tauber, 1995), including that in Massachusetts General with more than 80 hips in 110 patients, and in Shaare Zedek with more than 25 hips in 17 patients, meticulous attention to antibiotic cover and haematological stability ensure a good outcome in

Gaucher patients, who should be allowed to avail themselves of the surgical option comparable to any other patient with an equal degree of disability and/or pain. This is especially true in patients for whom haematological abnormalities and/or the tendency to infections have been ameliorated by enzyme replacement therapy.

Hips are the principal site of joint replacement surgery and patients are happily restored to markedly improved function as a result (Figure 14A and B). Although not a weight-bearing joint, the shoulder is also often a nidus of AVN and hence, with the development of functional handicap or unbearable pain, total shoulder arthroplasty (TSA) is a viable option for Gaucher patients. Most reports (Tauber and Tauber, 1995) and the authors' experience both at Shaare Zedek and Massachusetts General, underscore the excellent prognosis post-surgery. The knee, although not infrequently involved in Gaucher's disease, is more rarely brought to surgery, with both standard and customized devices of considerable value to the patient despite the complications inherent in the multiple forms of replacement. Of interest is the fact that the majority of patients with serious knee involvement who are candidates for replacement, have

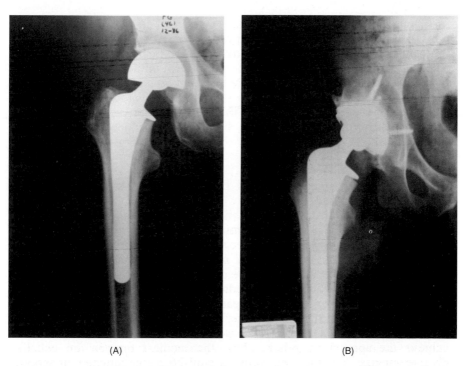

(A)   (B)

Figure 14. Hip replacements in patients with Gaucher's disease are often quite successful in restoring them to excellent function. (A) shows a bipolar arthroplasty in a 19-year-old male 4 years after surgery for severe disability resulting from a painful deformed osteonecrotic hip. (B) shows a total hip arthroplasty in a 55-year-old female 10 years after implantation for necrosis. The device shows no evidence of wear or loosening.

already presented with AVN of a hip joint and most often on the ipsilateral side.

Since Gaucher cell infiltration in the bone may result in compromised vascular supply and consequently decreased oxygen supply to joints, a surgical option that may be suggested as a stop-gap measure in patients with pain but for whom THA or TSA at that point is an unacceptable procedure, is drilling into the femoral/humeral head. Surprisingly, the results of this circumscribed procedure are rather long-term pain relief and improved functional mobility with little added risk for fracture in the experience of the Shaare Zedek group, whereas the Massachusetts General group regards this procedure as of limited value and believe it may increase the risk of fracture in the weakened bone.

The most serious spinal complication of Gaucher's disease is compression fractures, but as suggested above, most are allowed to resolve without surgical intervention (Ruff et al, 1984). Similarly the kyphosis secondary to progression of the skeletal disease is generally treated conservatively, oftentimes with braces appropriate to the spinal location, unless pain or neurological involvement becomes problematic (Hermann et al, 1989). To date there appears to be no survey of a series of patients with either mode of treatment.

When fractures occur in patients with Gaucher's disease, it is essential to treat them just as other individuals in order to restore function. Fractures of the long bones and the neck of the femur must be treated appropriately with hardware to hold the fracture in proper alignment until healing takes place. It should be emphasized that Gaucher patients with severe bone disease and extensive osteonecrosis may be slow to heal. Hardware may cut out from the weak bony cortex and the threat of infection remains a problem just as it does in other anatomical sites that are subjected to operative intervention.

MEDICAL MANAGEMENT OF BONE INVOLVEMENT IN GAUCHER'S DISEASE

Medical treatment of bone complications can be subdivided into the two categories of supportive or palliative, and preventive or prophylactic care; respectively, the various pain-relief regimens, and enzyme replacement therapy or bisphosphonates. It is to be underscored that the Gaucher patient with bone pain may experience episodic but excruciating pain of a crisis, or chronic dull pain, or the acute pain of a sudden fracture or bone infarct/AVN. Each of these situations, and the myriad of variations on the theme of pain seen in Gaucher's disease, require individualized attention to achieve the appropriate relief. Thus, the medical options are equally diverse, ranging from the mild analgesics of the acetaminophen, or aspirin families, as well as the non-steroidal anti-inflammatory drugs (NSAIDs) for mild and/or non-specific and/or chronic pain. The group of recently described NSAIDs directed against the prostaglandin synthase (cyclo-oxygenase) isoform 2 (COX2) implicated in prostaglandin production of inflamed tissues, has an excellent improved safety and similar efficacy profile as compared with the earlier COX1 isoform (Spangler, 1996). In addition, because of the protective effect on platelets, these analgesics may prove to be the treatment of choice in the more chronic forms of skeletal pain, although one is still concerned about the potential to bleed in the patient who is very thrombocytopenic. A single report using high-dose prednisolone in five patients (ages 7–22 years) for relief of the episodic pain of bone crises (Cohen et al, 1996) suggested that the use of narcotic analgesics is sometimes insufficient in these cases. Nonetheless, taking into account the potential multiple adverse effects in children and young adults, this route of pain-relief seems excessive without further studies. Similarly, anecdotal reports of relief of crisis pain using hyperbaric oxygen (Rosenbaum et al, 1997) will require further substantiation prior to recommendation.

The experience with self-administered oral morphine even in children, to relieve pain of both the chronic and acute types associated with the bone symptoms of Gaucher's disease has been very satisfactory, particularly in bone crises that are by definition self-limiting, and hence one may recommend morphine derivatives either in intravenous or oral form as candidates of the first line of analgesics in cases of apparently intractable pain. Nonetheless, the authors remain concerned with the use of narcotics, particularly in children, and would prefer to limit these treatments as much as possible to circumscribed events.

With the advent of enzyme replacement therapy (Barton et al, 1991) which has proven to be safe and effective in improving the haematological parameters and reducing the organomegaly of Gaucher patients, it was hoped that the bone disease would be equally tractable to therapy. However, the universal experience is that the skeletal response lags behind all other symptoms (Hill et al, 1993; Pastores and Einhorn, 1995; Rosenthal et al, 1995; Elstein et al, 1996) and at this point it is unclear whether in fact all the destructive lesions wrought by Gaucher infiltration are reversible. It has been suggested that the two phases of bone, marrow and mineral, be evaluated discretely in order to better monitor the effect of enzyme therapy (Barton et al, 1996). After 42 months of high-dose therapy, the fat-fraction of the marrow was improved on QCSI and quantitative MRI (Hill et al, 1993); similarly, during this follow-up period, trabecular bone as measured by cortical bone thickness increased as well (Rosenthal et al, 1995). Comparable results of improved cortical bone thickness were achieved with the low dose regimen (Elstein et al, 1996). Despite anecdotal reports (Pastores et al, 1996; Ueda et al, 1996) of specific loci that have improved with enzyme replacement therapy, there have also been reports of new AVN or pathological fractures during treatment (Sidransky et al, 1994; Elstein et al, 1996).

Bisphosphonates are potent inhibitors of bone resorption, which act by mechanisms not fully understood, but inhibition of osteoclast activity is implicated (Fleisch, 1991). This family of compounds, characterized by low intestinal absorption and long skeletal retention, have been used successfully to treat various metabolic bone disorders, including vertebral osteoporosis (Watts et al, 1990). In the latter study, vertebral bone mass in the bisphosphonate group increased (4–5%) significantly in the 2-year trial period and the rate of new vertebral fractures decreased by 50%, compared with the control group. The effect of treatment was the greatest in the patients with the lowest bone mineral density. Aside from some gastro-intestinal complaints, mainly in the oesophagus, there were no serious adverse effects, and there was a subjective decrease in pain. Use of various generations of bisphosphonates have also been attempted in Gaucher patients with severe bone involvement and multiple fractures (Harinck et al, 1984; Ostlere et al, 1991; Samuel et al, 1994), and even in a case of a 3-year-old child with Type 3 disease (Bembi et al, 1994), with good results. If these results can be duplicated in random, controlled clinical trials, bis-phosphonates may be a preferred means of dealing with both the pain of bone disease as well as prophylactically deal with the osteopenia and/or osteoporosis seen in Gaucher's disease. The role of calcium and/or vitamin D for Gaucher patients with and without bone involvement has not yet been sufficiently studied. It is quite clear that patients with this disease must not risk a superimposed osteomalacia, and since many Ashkenazi individuals also have a lactose intolerance, addition of calcium to their diet seems to be essential. Vitamin D in relatively high doses have been utilized (at Massachusetts General, 50 000 units once a week) and appear helpful in diminishing some of the bony complications in patients regardless of enzyme therapy. However, priority should be given minimally to maintaining the skeletal status in all patients, possibly based on bone density evaluation at presentation. Thus, as a general recommendation, the level of daily physical activity should be consistent with preservation of the current status, and probably should disallow strenuous activity (e.g. high-impact aerobics) or contact team sports. Bicycle riding is generally acceptable but swimming is still the sport of choice for Gaucher patients of all ages.

CONCLUSION

The clinicians caring for Gaucher patients must become fully familiar with the array of skeletal problems that may present, and be prepared to deal with them early in the medical course in order to reduce disability and complications. Surgeons experienced in the management of patients with Gaucher's disease and the complications that may result from surgery, should be consulted for patients with established skeletal involvement, and be supportive of the patient's needs as well as fully cognizant of the problems that may ensue. It is to be hoped that with the advent of curative approaches to Gaucher's disease and with early diagnosis of patients, the debilitating skeletal involvement, which has been discussed above, will become a historical note. Towards this end, clinicians should attempt a prophylactic attitude to patients with risk factors for bone involvement, e.g. a genotype such as N370S/84GG or an older sibling with bone disease, in order to avert accumulation of lesions, which may prove to be irreversible.

REFERENCES

Abrahamov A, Elstein D, Gross-Tsur V et al (1995) Gaucher's disease variant characterised by progressive calcification of heart valves and unique genotype. *Lancet* **346:** 1000–1003.

Alkali A, Kaufman T & Shazar Y (1979) Bilateral total hip replacement in a young woman with Gaucher disease. *Harefuah* **96:** 480–481.

*Allen MJ, Myer BJ, Khoker AM et al (1997) Pro-inflammatory cytokines and the pathogenesis of Gaucher's disease: increased release of interleukin-6 and interleukin-10. *Quarterly Journal of Medicine* **90:** 19–25.

Amstutz HC & Carey EJ (1966) Skeletal manifestations and treatment of Gaucher's disease. A review of twenty cases. *Journal of Bone and Joint Surgery* **48A:** 670–701.

Arkin AM & Schein AJ (1948) Aseptic necrosis in Gaucher's disease. *Journal of Bone and Joint Surgery* **30A:** 631–641.

Barton NW, Brady RO, Dambrosia JM et al (1991) Replacement therapy for inherited enzyme deficiency: macrophage-targeted glucocerebrosidase for Gaucher's disease. *New England Journal of Medicine* **324:** 1464–1470.

Barton NW, Rosenthal DI, Mankin HJ et al (1996) Skeletal responses to enzyme replacement therapy in patients with Gaucher disease: What are the goals and expectations of treatment? *Gaucher Clinical Perspectives* **4:** 2–7.

Beighton P, Goldblatt J & Sacks S (1982) Bone involvement in Gaucher disease. In Desnick RJ, Gatt S & Grabowski GA, (eds) *Gaucher Disease: A Century of Delineation and Research,* pp. 107–129. New York: Alan R Liss.

Bembi B, Agosti E, Boehm P et al (1994) Aminohydroxypropylidene-bisphosphonate in the treatment of bone lesions in a case of Gaucher's disease type 3. *Acta Paediatrica* **83:** 122–124.

*Castronovo FP, McKusick KA, Doppelt SH et al (1993) Radiopharmacology of inhaled ^{133}Xe in skeletal sites containing deposits of Gaucher cells. *Nuclear Medicine and Biology* **20:** 707–714.

Cohen IJ, Kornreich L, Mekhmandarov S et al (1996) Effective treatment of painful bone crises in type I Gaucher's disease with high dose prednisolone. *Archives of Disease in Childhood* **75:** 218–222.

Consensus Development Conference (1993) Prophylaxis and treatment of osteoporosis. *American Journal of Medicine* **94:** 646–650.

Cremin BJ, Davey H & Goldblatt J (1990) Skeletal complications of type I Gaucher disease: the magnetic resonance features. *Clinical Radiology* **41:** 244–247.

*Elstein D, Hadas-Halpern I, Itzchaki M et al (1996) Effect of low-dose enzyme replacement therapy on bones in Gaucher disease patients with severe skeletal involvement. *Blood, Cells, Molecules and Diseases* **22:** 100–108.

Elstein D, Lebel E, Hadas-Halpern I et al (1997) Skeletal involvement in a cohort of 266 patients with type I Gaucher disease. *Meeting of the Second Working Group of Gaucher Disease.* Maastricht, Netherlands, pp. 61–62.

Erikson A (1986) Gaucher disease—Norrbottnian type (III). *Acta Paediatrica Scandinavica.* **326 (supplement):** S1–S43.

Esplin JA & McPherson EJ (1994) Treatment of bone complications in patients with Gaucher disease. *Gaucher Clinical Perspectives* **2:** 7–11.

*Fleisch H, (1991) Bisphosphonates: pharmacology and use in the treatment of tumor-induced hyper-calcaemic and metastatic bone disease. *Drugs* **42:** 919–944.

Gery I, Zigler JS, Brady RO et al (1981) Selective effects of glucocerebroside (Gaucher's storage material) on macrophage culture. *Journal of Clinical Investigation* **68:** 1182–1189.

Goldblatt J, Sacks S, Dall D et al (1988) Total hip arthroplasty in Gaucher disease. *Clinical Orthopedic and Related Research* **228:** 94–98.

Granovsky-Grisaru S, Aboulafia Y, Diamant YZ et al (1995) Gynecologic and obstetric aspects of Gaucher's disease: a survey of 53 patients. *American Journal of Obstetrics and Gynecology* **172:** 1284–1290.

Harinck HIJ, Bijoet OLM, van der Meer JWH et al (1984) Regression of bone lesions in Gaucher's disease during treatment with aminohydroxypropylidene bisphosphonate. *Lancet* **1:** 513.

Hermann G, Goldblatt J, Levy RN et al (1986) Gaucher's disease type 1; assessment of bone involvement by CT and scintigraphy. *American Journal of Radiology* **147:** 943–948.

Hermann G, Wagner LD, Gendal E et al (1989) Spinal cord compression in type I Gaucher disease. *Radiology* **170:** 147–148.

*Hermann G, Shapiro RS, Abdelwahab F et al (1993) MR Imaging in adults with Gaucher disease type I: evaluation of marrow involvement and disease activity. *Skeletal Radiology* **22**: 247–251.

Hill SC, Parker CC & Brady RO (1993) MRI of multiple platyspondyly in Gaucher disease: response to enzyme replacement therapy. *Journal of Computer Assisted Tomography* **17**: 806–809.

Horev G, Kornreich L, Hadar H et al (1991) Hemorrhage associated with 'bone crisis' in Gaucher disease identified by magnetic resonance imaging. *Skeletal Radiology* **20**: 479–482.

Johnson LA, Hoppel BE, Gerard EL et al (1992) Quantitative chemical shift imaging of the vertebral bone marrow in patients with Gaucher disease. *Radiology* **182**: 451–455.

Katz K, Horev G, Grunebaum M et al (1996) The natural history of osteonecrosis of the femoral head in children and adolescents who have Gaucher disease. *Journal of Bone and Joint Surgery* **78A**: 14–19.

Kolodny EH, Ullman MD, Mankin HJ et al (1982) Phenotypic manifestations of Gaucher disease: clinical features in 48 biochemically verified type I patients and comment on type II patients. In Desnick RJ, Gatt S & Grabowski GA (eds) *Gaucher Disease: A Century of Delineation and Research*, pp. 33–65. New York: Alan R Liss.

Lachiewicz PF, Lane JM & Wilson PD (1981) Total hip repalcement in Gaucher's disease. *Journal of Bone and Joint Surgery* **63A**: 602–608.

Lanir A, Hadar H, Cohen I et al (1986) Gaucher disease: assessment with MR imaging. *Radiology* **68**: 239–244.

Lau MM, Lichtman DM, Hamati YI et al (1981) Hip arthroplasties in Gaucher's disease. *Journal of Bone and Joint Surgery* **63A**: 591–601.

Lee RE (1982) The pathology of Gaucher disease. In Desnick RJ, Gatt S & Grabowski GA (eds) *Gaucher Disease: A Century of Delineation and Research*, pp. 177–217. New York: Alan R Liss.

Lowik CWGM, Vanderpluijm G, Bloys H et al (1989) Parathyroid hormone (PTH) and PTH-like protein (PLP) stimulate interleukin-6 production of osteogenic cells. A possible role of IL-6 in osteoclastogenesis. *Biochemical Biophysical Research Communications* **162**: 1546–1552.

*Mankin HJ, Doppelt SH & Rosenberg AE et al (1990) Metabolic bone disease in patients with Gaucher's disease. In Avioli LV & Krane SM (eds) *Metabolic Bone Disease and Clinically Related Disorders*, pp. 730–752. Philadelphia: WB Saunders.

Mariani G, Molea N, LaCivita L et al (1996) Scintigraphic findings on ^{99m}Tc-MDP, ^{99m}Tc-sestamibi and ^{99m}Tc-HMPAO images in Gaucher's disease. *European Journal of Nuclear Medicine* **23**: 466–470.

Markin RS & Skultety FM (1984) Spinal cord compression secondary to Gaucher's disease. *Surgical Neurology* **21**: 341–346.

Matoth Y & Fried K (1965) Chronic Gaucher's disease. Clinical observations on 34 patients. *Israel Journal of Medical Sciences* **1**: 521–530.

Mazes RB (1990) Dual-energy X-ray absorptiometry for total body and regional bone mineral and soft-tissue composition. *American Journal of Clinical Nutrition* **51**: 1106–1112.

Neudorfer O, Hadas-Halpern I & Elstein D et al (1997) Abdominal ultrasound findings mimicking hematological malignancies in a study of 218 Gaucher patients. *American Journal of Hematology* **55**: 28–34.

Noyes FR & Smith WS (1971) Bone crisis and chronic osteomyelitis in Gaucher's disease. *Clinical Orthopedic Research* **79**: 132–140.

Ostlere L, Warner T & Meunier PJ et al (1991) Treatment of type 1 Gaucher's disease affecting bone with aminohydroxypropylidene bisphosphonate (Pamidronate). *Quarterly Journal of Medicine* **290**: 503–515.

Pacifici R, Rifas L & Teitelbaum S et al (1987) Spontaneous release of interleukin-1 from human blood monocytes reflects bone formation in idiopathic osteoporosis. *Proceedings of the National Academy of Sciences USA* **84**: 4616–4620.

Parfitt AM (1982) Bone remodeling: relationship to the amount and structure of bone, and the pathogenesis and prevention of fractures. In Riggs BL & Melton LJ (eds) *Osteoporosis: Etiology, Diagnosis, and Management*, pp. 74–93. New York: Raven Press.

Pastakia B, Brower AC & Chang VH et al (1986) Skeletal manifestations of Gaucher's disease. *Seminars in Roentgenology* **21**: 264–274.

Pastores GM & Einhorn TA (1995) Skeletal complications of Gaucher disease: pathophysiology, evaluation, and treatment. *Seminars in Hematology* **32**: 20–27.

*Pastores GM, Wallenstein S & Desnick RJ (1996) Bone density in type 1 Gaucher disease. *Journal of Bone and Mineral Research* **11**: 1801–1807.

Pastores GM, Hermann G & Norton KI et al (1996) Regression of skeletal changes in type 1 Gaucher disease with enzyme replacement therapy. *Skeletal Radiology* **25**: 485–488.

Rademakers RP (1995) Radiological evaluation of Gaucher bone disease. *Seminars in Hematology* **32 (supplement 1):** S14–S19.

Raynor RR (1962) Spinal cord compression secondary to Gaucher's disease. *Journal of Neurosurgery* **19**: 902–905.

Riggs BL & Melton LJ III (1986) Involutional osteoporosis. *New England Journal of Medicine* **314**: 1676–1686.

Rose JS, Grabowski GA & Barnett SH et al (1982) Accelerated skeletal deterioration after splenectomy in Gaucher type 1 disease. *American Journal of Roentgenology* **139**: 1202–1204.

Rosenbaum H, Besser M, Brenner B et al (1997) Hyperbaric oxygen therapy for skeletal complications of Gaucher disease. A report of five cases. *Meeting of the Second Working Group of Gaucher disease.* Maastricht, Netherlands, p. 63.

Rosenthal DI (1995) Quantitative imaging of the skeleton in patients with Gaucher disease. *Gaucher Clinical Perspectives* **3**: 4–8.

Rosenthal DI, Scott JA, Barrager JA et al (1986) Evaluation of Gaucher disease using magnetic resonance imaging. *Journal of Bone and Joint Surgery* **68A**: 802–808.

Rosenthal DI, Mayo-Smith W, Goodsitt MM et al (1989) Bone and bone marrow changes in Gaucher disease: evaluation with quantitative CT. *Radiology* **170**: 143–146.

*Rosenthal DI, Barton NW, McKusick KA et al (1992) Quantitative imaging of Gaucher disease. *Radiology* **185**: 841–845.

Rosenthal DI, Doppelt SH, Mankin HJ et al (1995) Enzyme replacement therapy for Gaucher disease: skeletal responses to macrophage-targeted glucocerebrosidase. *Pediatrics* **96**: 629–637.

Rourke JA & Heslin DJ (1965) Gaucher's disease: roentgenologic bone changes over 20 years interval. *American Journal of Roentgenology* **94**: 621–630.

Ruff ME, Weis LD & Kean JR (1984) Acute kyphosis in Gaucher disease. *Spine* **9**: 835–837.

Sacks S (1971) Osteitis in Gaucher's disease. *Suid-Afrikaane Tydskrif vir Chirurgie* **9**: 161–166.

Samuel R, Katz K, Papapoulos S et al (1994) Aminhydroxypropylidene bisphosphonate (APD) treatment improves the clinical skeletal manifestations of Gaucher's disease. *Pediatrics* **94**: 385–389.

Shiran A, Brenner B, Laor A et al (1993) Increased risk of cancer in patients with Gaucher disease. *Cancer* **72**: 219–224.

Shoenfeld Y, Gallant LA, Shaklai M et al (1982) Gaucher's disease: a disease with chronic stimulation of the immune system. *Archives of Pathology and Laboratory Medicine* **106**: 388–391.

Sidransky E, Ginns EI, Westman JA et al (1994) Pathological fractures may develop in Gaucher patients receiving enzyme replacement therapy. *American Journal of Hematology* **47**: 247–249.

Siffert RS & Platt GD (1982) Gaucher disease: Orthopedic considerations. In Desnick RJ, Gatt S, Grabowski GA (eds) *Gaucher Disease: A Century of Delineation and Research*, pp. 617–626. New York: Alan R Liss.

Spangler RS (1996) Cyclooxygenase 1 and 2 in rheumatic disease: implications for nonsteroidal antiinflammatory drug therapy. *Seminars in Arthritis and Rheumatology* **26**: 435–446.

Starer F, Sargent JD & Hobbs (1987) Regression of the radiological changes of Gaucher's disease following bone marrow transplantation. *British Journal of Radiology* **60**: 1189–1195.

Strickland B (1958) Skeletal manifestations of Gaucher's disease with some unusual findings. *British Journal of Radiology* **31**: 246–253.

*Stowens DW, Teitelbaum SL, Kahn AJ et al (1985) Skeletal complications of Gaucher's disease. *Medicine* **64**: 310–322.

Svennerholm L, Dreborg S, Erikson A et al (1982) Gaucher disease of the Norrbottnian (type III). Phenotypic manifestations. In Desnick RJ, Gatt S, Grabowski GA (eds) *Gaucher Disease: A Century of Delineation and Research.* pp. 67–94. New York: Alan R Liss.

Tauber C & Tauber T (1995) Gaucher disease—the orthopaedic aspect. *Archives of Orthopedic and Trauma Surgery* **114**: 179–182.

Terk MR, Esplin J, Lee K et al (1995) MR imaging of patients with type I Gaucher's disease relationship between bone and visceral changes. *American Journal of Radiology* **165**: 599–604.

Ueda T, Fukunaga Y, Migita M et al (1996) Improvement of bone disease with increased dose of glucocerebrosidase in a Gaucher patient who had a bone lesion presenting during low-dose enzyme replacement therapy. *Acta Paediatrica Japonica* **38**: 260–264.

Van Vlasselaer P, Borremans B, Heuvel RVD et al (1993) Interleukin-10 inhibits the osteogenic activity of mouse bone marrow. *Blood* **82**: 2361–2370.

Waitches G, Zawin JK & Poznanski AK (1994) Sequence and rate of bone marrow conversion in the femora of children as seen on MR imaging. *American Journal of Radiology* **162:** 1399–1406.

Watanabe M, Yanagisawa M, Sonobe S et al (1984) An adult form of Gaucher disease with a huge tumour formation of the right tibia. *International Orthopedics* **8:** 195–202.

Watts NB, Harris ST, Genant HK et al (1990) Intermittent cyclical etidronate treatment in post-menopausal osteoporosis. *New England Journal of Medicine* **323:** 73–79.

Van Wellen PA, Haentjens P, Frecourt N et al (1994) Loosening of a noncemented porous-coated anatomic femoral component in Gaucher's disease. A case report and review of the literature. *Acta Orthopedica Belgie* **60:** 119–123.

Yosipovitch Z & Katz K (1990) Bone crisis in Gaucher disease—an update. *Israel Journal of Medical Sciences* **26:** 593–595.

Yosipovitch ZH, Hermann G & Makin M (1965) Aseptic osteomyelitis in Gaucher's disease. *Israel Journal of Medical Sciences* **1:** 531–536.

Zevin S, Abrahamov A, Hadas-Halpern I et al (1993) Adult-type Gaucher disease in children: genetics, clinical features and enzyme replacement therapy. *Quarterly Journal of Medicine* **86:** 565–573.

Zimran A, Kay A, Gelbart T et al (1992) Gaucher disease. Clinical, laboratory, radiologic and genetic features of 53 patients. *Medicine* **71:** 337–353.

Zimran A, Elstein D, Schiffman R et al (1995) Outcome of partial splenectomy in type I Gaucher disease. *Journal of Pediatrics* **126:** 596–597.

12

A practical approach to diagnosis and management of Gaucher's disease

PRAMOD K. MISTRY BSc, PhD, MBBS, MRCP

Senior Lecturer and Honorary Consultant Physician
Hepato-biliary and Liver Transplant Unit, Royal Free Hospital School of Medicine, Pond Street, London NW3 2QG, UK

AYALA ABRAHAMOV MD

Senior Lecturer in Paediatrics
Gaucher Clinic, Shaare Zedek Medical Center, Jerusalem, Israel

The diagnosis of Gaucher's disease is established by demonstration of reduced acid β-glucosidase activity in peripheral blood leukocytes. Genotyping at the glucocerebrosidase gene locus can give additional prognostic information and facilitate carrier detection. However, extreme phenotypic diversity precludes reliable prediction of prognosis in individual patients. Histological diagnosis of Gaucher's disease is unnecessary and can be misleading. A range of clinical, radiological and laboratory parameters are useful for staging disease activity which is central to achieving optimal timing to initiate enzyme therapy. Treatment should be individualized to obtain maximum therapeutic response. The recent introduction of chitotriosidase measurements has provided a valuable indicator of total cellular burden of storage cells. Serial measurements of chitotriosidase activity are useful for monitoring disease progression as well as response to therapy. A number of adjuvant therapies are available for use in conjunction with enzyme treatment. Special considerations apply to management of affected children.

Key words: leukocyte acid β-glucosidase, glucocerebrosidase mutations, mannose-terminated glucocerebrosidase, splenectomy.

The diagnosis of non-neuronopathic Gaucher's disease should be considered in any patient with unexplained splenomegaly with or without bleeding diathesis, skeletal manifestations and hepatomegaly. It should be high on the list of differential diagnosis in any child presenting with hepatosplenomegaly and neurological signs. Another indication for diagnostic investigations includes a positive family history of Gaucher's disease. Screening investigations are not recommended for asymptomatic individuals just because they have Jewish ancestry since a significant number of these individuals have mild disease that would never otherwise

Copyright © 1997, by Baillière Tindall
All rights of reproduction in any form reserved

come to medical attention; however population-based screening is justifiable in some populations like Norrbottnia (Erikson, 1986) and Jenin (Abrahamov et al, 1995) because the disease phenotype is uniformly severe.

ENZYMATIC DIAGNOSIS

Despite the availability of a variety of tests to aid the diagnosis of Gaucher's disease, the definitive investigation remains the demonstration of diminished acid β-glucosidase activity in a variety of tissues (Brady et al, 1965). Mixed leukocytes isolated from peripheral blood harbour abundant acid β-glucosidase activity, and their capacity to cleave gluco-cerebroside is markedly diminished in Gaucher's disease. However, radioactively labelled natural substrate is expensive and difficult to use in routine practice. Under appropriate assay conditions, synthetic, water-soluble substrates are used instead by most routine laboratories. At pH 4, the ability of leukocytes from Gaucher's disease patients to hydrolyse 4-methylumbelliferyl-β-glucosidase is reduced to about 10% of normal (Beutler and Kuhl, 1970a). However it is important to bear in mind that there are other β-glucosidases apart from glucocerebrosidase in cell lysates: for example, at pH 5, 4-methyumbelliferyl-β-glucoside is cleaved almost as well by leukocytes from Gaucher's disease patients as normal controls (Beutler and Kuhl, 1970b). Similar results are obtained under a variety of conditions using different fluorescent substrates and cell lysates with added detergents. Acid β-glucosidase activity in different white blood cell types differs markedly: monocytes > lymphocytes > granulocytes (Beutler et al, 1976). However, in routine diagnosis, enzyme activity in mixed leukocyte preparations is sufficient. The enzyme activity is labile and therefore it is necessary to process blood samples within 24 hours of collection for optimal results. Cultured skin fibroblasts, amniotic fluid cells and chorionic villi can also be used for enzymatic diagnosis (Turner and Hirschhorn, 1978; Beutler and Grabowski, 1995). The majority of individuals with Gaucher's disease demonstrate acid β-glucosidase activity that is ≤15% of mean normal activity. There is a single report of reduced acid β-glucocerebrosidase activity in a patient with Niemann Pick Type C disease and another with chronic non-Hodgkin's lymphoma (Harzer, 1995). In these rare situations ancillary tests like genotyping, histology and serum chitotriosidase activity can collectively confirm or refute the diagnosis of Gaucher's disease.

There are two main limitations of enzymatic assays. On average, the leukocytes and cultured skin fibroblasts of heterozygotes for Gaucher's disease have about half-normal acid β-glucosidase activity. However, enzyme activities in 10–33% of heterozygotes overlap with normal values (Raghavan et al, 1980). Second, enzyme-based diagnosis has not proved to be reliable for differentiating between Type 1, 2 and 3 Gaucher's disease (Grabowski et al, 1985). Thus residual enzyme activity in cell lysates provides limited information of prognostic importance.

MOLECULAR DIAGNOSIS

The major advantage of DNA analysis is that it has the potential to give prognostic information and second, the samples are extremely stable, which allows blood samples (2.5 ml in EDTA tube) to be shipped without haste at ambient temperature. However, although many Gaucher's disease alleles have been identified, others have not (Beutler and Gelbart, 1996). Thus, even when DNA is examined for many different known mutations, a negative result does not guarantee the absence of a Gaucher's disease allele. The mutations N370S (cDNA designation 1226G) and 84GG account for 80–89% of disease-producing alleles in Ashkenazi Jewish patients with Gaucher's disease. The five most prevalent mutations in the Ashkenazi Jewish population (N370S, 84GG, IVS 2(+1), V394L[1297T], R496H[1604A], including L444P[1448C]) account for 88–98% of all disease-producing alleles. Therefore it has been estimated that the probability of detecting only one of the two alleles is 7–8% and the probability that none of the these five most common Gaucher's disease alleles will be present in a Jewish patient with Gaucher's disease is only 0.04–1.4% (Balicki and Beutler, 1995). Thus DNA analysis can be used as a diagnostic test for Gaucher's disease in Jewish patients; it is technically robust and it provides valuable prognostic information for the family in certain situations. It is important to appreciate that in 7–8% of the cases only one disease allele will be found and when this occurs it does not mean that the patient is only a heterozygote carrier for Gaucher's disease. It has been estimated that no abnormal allele will be found in about two in 1000 Jewish patients with Gaucher's disease; thus the absence of one of the five most common alleles in a Jewish patient does not entirely exclude the diagnosis of Gaucher's disease (Balicki and Beutler, 1995). DNA analysis is much less conclusive in non-Jewish patients (Walley et al, 1993). Analysis of DNA for these five mutations as well as XOVR (which includes L444P mutation) identifies only 66–72% of the disease alleles. It has been estimated that in only 42.8% non-Jewish patients will both abnormal alleles be detected, that in 45.2%, one of the two will be detected and that 12% will appear normal even if they have Gaucher's disease (Beutler and Gelbart, 1993). Thus, if Gaucher's disease is suspected clinically in a Jewish patient there is a high probability of being able to confirm the diagnosis by mutation analysis. Patients without Jewish ancestry harbour many more sporadic, uncommon mutations thus reducing the usefulness of mutation analysis in routine practice. Many of these limitations in DNA analysis may be overcome with the advent of DNA microchip technology (Anonymous, 1996); undoubtedly this will be applied to Gaucher's disease in the not too distant future.

A number of polymerase chain reaction (PCR)-based techniques have been developed to facilitate detection of mutations. The gene fragment of interest is targeted with primers that amplify the structural gene but not the pseudogene. Mutations can be detected by restriction digestion (Tsuji et al, 1987), with amplification refractory mutation system (Mistry et al, 1992a), by allele-specific oligonucleotide hybridization (Horowitz et al, 1993) or by 'mismatched' PCR (Beutler et al, 1990). DNA analysis is technically a robust procedure, but rarely, the results can be misleading. In one such case, the gene fragment to be amplified was subsequently found to be deleted from one allele, resulting in erroneous assignment of homozygosity for that allele during initial screening (Beutler and Gelbart, 1995).

Unlike enzyme analysis, mutation analysis has considerable predictive value with respect to disease prognosis although great caution should be exercised in widespread use of genotype–phenotype predictions in routine clinical practice. Patients homozygous for L444P mutation all appear to have severe visceral disease and usually have neurological disease (Tsuji et al, 1987). However, there are exceptions to this and when neurological disease is present there is often striking variability in severity. Homozygosity for L444P mutation can present with Type 3 disease (subtype 3a, late onset form with severe neurological disease but only mild visceral involvement or subtype 3b, early onset form with massive visceral involvement and slowly progressive neurological disease), which is characteristic of the Norrbottnian patients (Dahl et al, 1990) or Type 2 disease or even Type 1 disease (Sidransky et al, 1994). It is likely that L444P homozygosity manifesting as Type 2 disease results from additional mutations derived from the pseudogene (Latham et al, 1990). In contrast, the presence of the N370S mutant enzyme appears to preclude the development of neurological disease. As a group, disease severity is mild in N370S homozygotes compared with N370S/84GG or N370S/L444P compound heterozygotes (Beutler, 1993). However, there is extremely wide variation in disease manifestations and severity within each group, which precludes genotype-based prognosis in individual patients. For example some N370S homozygotes exhibit moderately severe disease while some N370S/L444P and N370S/84GG compound heterozygotes have mild disease. Such variation is seen even within sibships and identical twins further limiting the value of genotype-based prognosis in individual patients (Beutler, 1993; Mistry and Cox, 1995).

DNA analysis is invaluable in detection of heterozygous carrier state. Screening for carriers in the Jewish population is highly reliable because of the high prevalence of the N370S mutation. Many homozygotes for this mutation do not come to medical attention until later in life and often not at all (Beutler, 1993). Thus among the Jewish population over 98% of heterozygotes will be detected by screening for the five most common mutations. In the non-Jewish population a high proportion of heterozygotes will elude detection but, DNA analysis is still very useful for genetic counselling. In sibs of patients in whom the mutations have been identified, genotype identification is virtually 100% reliable.

HISTOLOGICAL DIAGNOSIS

The traditional method for diagnosis of Gaucher's disease was the detection of the characteristic lipid-laden Gaucher cell in the bone marrow aspirate, the liver biopsy or in a spleen that had been removed surgically. However, great caution should be exercised in the interpretation of lipid-laden macrophages that look like Gaucher cells in the bone marrow or other tissues. For example, Gaucher-like cells have been described in chronic granulocytic leukaemia, thalassaemia, multiple myeloma, Hodgkin disease, plasmacytoid lymphoma and in AIDS complicated by *Mycobacterium avium* infection (Beutler and Grabowski, 1995). Up to 70% of patients with Ph positive chronic granulocytic leukaemia have 'pseudo-Gaucher cells' in their marrow, presumably because of massively increased turnover of leukocyte membranes with their abundant glucosylceramide in the macrophage system (Busche et al, 1997). These 'pseudo-Gaucher cells' do not contain the typical tubular structures of authentic Gaucher cells. Therefore, diagnosis on the basis of the demonstration of Gaucher cells in bone marrow aspirate can be misleading, even in combination with the occurrence of clinical symptoms that are usually associated with the disease. Since biochemical and molecular techniques are more specific and less invasive, histological appearances should be a means to diagnose Gaucher's disease only in patients in whom it had not been suspected previously (Beutler and Saven, 1990).

ANCILLARY DIAGNOSTIC TESTS

The activities of a number of macrophage-specific enzymes are elevated in plasma of patients with Gaucher's disease. These include chitotriosidase (Hollak et al, 1994), tartrate-resistant acid phosphatase, angiotensin converting enzyme and β-hexosaminidase (Beutler and Grabowski, 1995). High levels of ferritin (with normal transferrin saturation), hypocholesterol-aemia associated with severe reduction of apolipoprotein A1 and B (Mistry et al, 1997c) and hypergammaglobulinaemia are regularly encountered in patients with Gaucher's disease. When present, these markers support the diagnosis, but are neither required nor sufficient to make a diagnosis of Gaucher's disease. Of these serum markers, chitotriosidase activity is the most specific and sensitive marker of total body Gaucher cell burden as this enzyme is secreted uniquely by glucocerebroside-laden macrophages. Thus, in an individual patient, serial chitotriosidase activity can provide a highly sensitive marker of disease progression and relative tissue pool size of pathological macrophages. However, it is important to bear in mind that ~6% of individuals (normals as well as Gaucher's disease patients) have no detectable chitotriosidase activity because of a null mutation in the cognate gene (Hollak et al, 1994) and elevated chitotriosidase activity can occur rarely in some other pathologies in which macrophages are involved (Young et al, 1997).

CLINICAL STAGING OF GAUCHER'S DISEASE

Once the diagnosis of Gaucher's disease is established, it becomes neces-sary to attempt comprehensive staging of disease severity. There are two main components to assessing disease severity: first, the total mass of cellular glycolipid storage and second, the extent of end-organ damage. The concept of staging severity of Gaucher's disease in terms of cellular burden of storage cells, end-organ damage and symptoms of the disease are now important factors for assessing the timing as well as the response to enzyme therapy. To some extent severity of disease is implicit in the traditional clinical classification of patients according to the rate at which neurological symptoms develop (acute neuronopathic form Type 2 and subacute neuronopathic form Type 3) and those that do not have neurological symptoms (Type 1 disease).

These broad clinical phenotypes have been further refined by sub-classification of Type 3 disease into Type 3a: mild visceral disease but rapidly progressive neurological disease, Type 3b: devastating visceral disease but mild neurological disease and Type 3c: mild neurological and visceral disease associated with cardiac valvular calcification (Brady et al, 1993; Abrahamov et al, 1995; Mistry, 1995). Occasionally it is difficult to assign a definite clinical type; such a conundrum in a severely affected young patient in whom neurological abnormalities cannot be detected by a comprehensive neurological examination can have important therapeutic and prognostic implications. In this regard smooth pursuit eye movement studies can reveal subtle neurological abnormalities, thus changing the designation of a severely affected child from Type 1 to Type 3 (Vellodi, 1997).

A more unifying severity score index (SSI) for Type 1 disease was proposed by Zimran and associates (1989) and has been invaluable for demonstrating the differing clinical impact of various mutations at the glucocerebrosidase gene locus. The SSI is composite of a notional score assigned to the age of presentation, presence of splenectomy, degree of splenomegaly, extent of hepatomegaly and hepatic dysfunction, cytopenia in relation to splenectomy and skeletal disease. While SSI can be used in this way, it is important to remember its limitations. For example it can be mis-leading in those patients who have minimal visceral disease but severe skeletal disease. Also there are no histological correlates in this scoring system and it gives no indication of the extent of fibrosis or infarction in target organs. Specific staging of skeletal disease is extremely important given the morbidity associated with this complication of Gaucher's disease. Recently significant progress has been made in our ability to assess skeletal involvement in Gaucher's disease. Magnetic resonance quantitative chemical shift imaging (MRQCSI) allows a highly sensitive evaluation of cellular composition of the bone marrow and dual-energy X-ray absorptiometry (DEXA) allows a highly accurate determination of cortical and trabecular bone mass; the latter has the advantage of short scanning times and low level of radiation exposure (Johnson et al, 1992; Pastores, 1994). If access to these facilities is limited, it is recommended that dual energy quantitative CT (DEQCT) is performed, which allows quantitative assessment of trabecular bone mass (Rosenthal et al, 1995).

It would be important to evaluate a modified version of SSI incorporat-ing these newer techniques for assessing skeletal disease in the context of genotype at the glucocerebrosidase gene locus as well as chitotriosidase activity for comprehensive staging of Gaucher's disease. Special considerations apply to staging of disease severity in children (*vide infra*). Serial measurements of chitotriosidase levels in individual patients appear to be especially helpful for tracking the relative size of tissue pools of glucocerebrosidase-laden macrophages. A composite database of these parameters may prove pivotal in determining the optimal timing to commence enzyme therapy.

TREATMENT OF GAUCHER'S DISEASE

Before the introduction of enzyme replacement therapy in the early 1990s (Barton et al, 1991), there was only palliative treatment for morbidity associated with Gaucher's disease. Splenectomy was performed to relieve pressure symptoms, cytopenia and growth retardation. The quality of life of patients with Gaucher's disease was greatly improved by appropriate orthopaedic surgical procedures. Now with the availability of enzyme therapy, splenectomy is indicated in only a few special circumstances and it can be argued that no patient should be allowed to develop clinically significant skeletal disease. Thus the central feature of modern management of Gaucher's disease is enzyme therapy for those patients in whom it is indicated and adjuvant therapy to manage end-organ damage.

CANDIDACY FOR ENZYME THERAPY WITH MANNOSE-TERMINATED GLUCOCEREBROSIDASE

A significant number of patients with Type 1 Gaucher's disease have slowly progressive disease that does not require any specific therapy (Zimran et al, 1992). Other patients will have progressive disease resulting in disease manifestations ranging from reversible visceromegaly, bleeding tendency and marrow infiltration to irreversible complications of splenic infarction/fibrosis, liver fibrosis/cirrhosis, pulmonary infiltration and bone infarction. Thus, the key aspect of successful managment of Gaucher's disease is accurate assessment of the candidacy for enzyme replacement therapy and for the clinician to identify the best time to commence treatment. In this context the broad objective of enzyme therapy is to reverse symptomatic disease manifestations and prevent irreversible end-organ damage. Current indications for enzyme therapy for adult patients include symptomatic splenomegaly or skeletal disease, anaemia, bleeding tendency due to thrombocytopenia with or without acquired/coincidental coagulopathy, significant liver infiltration with or without hepatic dysfunction and pulmonary disease. Special considerations apply to children and this is considered in a separate section (*vide infra*).

There is likely to be increasing emphasis on enzyme treatment of asymptomatic patients. This would appear to be a rational approach to prevent undue morbidity and irreversible tissue damage. Development of criteria to identify suitable patients for pre-symptomatic therapy should be studied within the context of a multicentre trial. Some centres use genotype information, serial chitotriosidase levels and comprehensive staging of disease to identify patients who are likely to benefit from such pre-emptive enzyme therapy.

INITIATION OF ENZYME REPLACEMENT THERAPY

There is no simple relationship between severity of disease manifestations, the burden of cellular glcosylceramide storage and the dose of enzyme required for a therapeutic response. The majority of patients worldwide begin alglucerase or imiglucerase infusions at a dose of 30 or 60 IU/kg every other week (Barton et al, 1991; Pastores et al, 1993). When local circumstances dictate that only low doses of enzyme can be administered, clinical as well as tissue pharmacokinetic evidence favours the use of a fractionated low dose therapy ranging from 1–5 IU/kg twice or thrice weekly (Figueroa et al, 1992; Mistry et al, 1992b; Zimran et al, 1994b; Hollak et al, 1995). Patients can be trained to administer these infusions successfully at home. All infusions are administered over 1 to 2 hours in 100 ml normal saline followed by 50 ml flush. In a small number of patients it becomes necessary to establish permanent venous access. There is understandable concern about the risk of infection; however, in practice venous access devices have been remakably free of any such complications (Zimran et al, 1993a). The merits of different dosing regimens have been disccussed in detail in Chapter 5 of this volume.

Nowadays, patients and their physicians understandably express preference for the recombinant mannose-terminated glucocerebrosidase, imiglucerase, when initiating enzyme therapy. Imiglucerase is being phased in and it is expected that within the next 2 to 3 years all patients will have converted to this therapy. The clinical efficacy as well as tissue pharmacokinetics of imiglucerase are very similar to that of alglucerase (Grabowski et al, 1995; Zimran et al, 1995b; Mistry et al, 1996). It is expected that the adverse effect profile of imiglucerase will be better than that of alglucerase; of note imiglucerase is devoid of contaminating mannosylated proteins found in alglucerase (Cohen et al, 1994; Moscicki, 1995). It is recommended that children, especially pre-pubertal boys, women of child-bearing age, and those with a history of allergic reactions to alglucerase should be given priority for conversion to imiglucerase. Patients with coincidental prostatic carcinoma should be treated with imiglucerase because alglucerase is contraindicated in these patients. Imiglucerase comes as a powder for reconstitution and is therefore easier for transportation: this may be an important factor for patients with lifestyles that involve extensive travel.

EVALUATING THE RESPONSE TO ENZYME THERAPY

Enzyme therapy with mannose-terminated glucocerebrosidase is safe and efficacious in reversing many of the manifestations of Type 1 Gaucher's disease. Most patients report an improvement in well-being and amelioration of fatigue. Weight gain is common and is associated with a reduction of resting energy expenditure (Hollak et al, 1997). Abdominal discomfort is relieved as the viscera decrease in size. During the first year of enzyme therapy there is 20–30% regression of hepatomegaly (in patients with baseline liver volume >1.4 times normal i.e. 2.5% of body weight) and 30–50% regression of splenomegaly (Grabowski, 1996). In many patients, the most striking response is observed during the first 6 months of therapy compared with the subsequent 6 months (Pastores et al, 1993). Haemoglobin levels rise and can normalize within 1 year of enzyme therapy. Platelet counts tend to respond more slowly than do haemoglobin levels. The haematological response is most striking in splenectomized patients (Mistry et al, 1992b). It has been noted that a significant number of patients show a poor haematological response during the initial period of 6–9 months, with subsequent rapid improvement even with an unaltered dosage regimen. The slowest organ to respond to enzyme therapy is the skeleton (Rosenthal et al, 1995). However, the symptoms of skeletal disease, i.e., bone pain, can be ameliorated within 3 months of starting enzyme replacement therapy and can result in markedly improved quality of life (Mistry et al., 1992b). Bone marrow responses can be seen at about 6 months with a decrease of glucocerebroside levels and an increase of triglyceride content; this can be assessed non-invasively by MRQCSI (Johnson et al, 1992). Responses of the trabecular and cortical bone are the slowest, taking up to 3 years to document a clear improvement (Rosenthal et al, 1995); this aspect of skeletal involvement can be assessed in a highly accurate way by DEXA (Pastores, 1994). The relatively slow skeletal response to enzyme therapy does not necessarily imply poor delivery of enzyme to the skeleton; in fact tissue distribution studies with tracer doses of radio-iodinated mannose-terminated enzyme show avid uptake in the marrow in proportion to the putative cellular pool of macrophages in this organ (Mistry et al, 1996). Adequate delivery of the enzyme to the marrow is also evident in the brisk haematological response of splenectomized patients who have cytopenia and the rapid reversal of marrow infiltration with enzyme therapy (Mistry et al, 1992b). Thus, the slower response of the skeleton indicates end-organ damage for which adjuvant therapies (i.e. vitamin D, diphosphonates etc; *vide infra*) are necessary in order to achieve a complete response. It is to be hoped that such a degree of end-organ damage will be a rare event with increasing ability of the clinician to identify the best timing to initiate enzyme therapy in the pre-symptomatic stage. When pulmonary involvement is present the response of this organ to enzyme therapy is highly variable, ranging from significant amelioration of disease manifestations (Beutler et al., 1991; Pelini et al, 1994; Zimran et al, 1994a) to an extremely poor response despite large doses of enzyme (Pastores et al., 1993). This may reflect poor ability of the pulmonary macrophages for receptor-mediated endocytosis of mannosylated ligands; in tissue distribution studies with tracer doses of mannose-terminated glucocerebrosidase, little uptake in the lungs was demonstrated in contrast to other sites of disease activity (Mistry et al, 1996).

The response to enzyme therapy can be monitored by serial haematology profile, clotting profile, and serum macrophage markers including chitotriosidase, angiotensin converting enzyme activity and tartarate-resistant acid phosphatase. Of these serum markers, chitotriosidase appears to be most useful for it reflects the total body burden of glucosylceramide-laden macrophages (Hollak et al, 1994). Thus, rising chitotriosidase activity in serial serum samples, despite enzyme therapy, is an indication to review enzyme dose and frequency. Visceral size can be estimated reliably and economically by 6-monthly ultrasonography to determine ultrasound volume index (product of three largest organ dimensions, i.e. longitudinal, transverse at the maximal plane and true anteroposterior), which is highly correlated with volumes determined by CT scanning or MRI (Glen et al, 1994; Elstein et al, 1997). The response of the skeletal disease can be assessed by imaging the marrow and trabecular/cortical bone mass components separately using MRQCSI and DEXA, respectively, or DEQCT. It is important to emphasize that invasive procedures like bone marrow or liver biopsies are not necessary to assess response to enzyme therapy. When pulmonary complications are present, echo-doppler, arterial blood gas measurement, lung function tests and chest radiography or fine cut CT are useful to monitor response of this organ to enzyme therapy. It is not practical to carry out many of these investigations in children but their response can be estimated reliably by using modified criteria (*vide infra*).

THE RESPONSE TO ENZYME THERAPY IS VARIABLE: DETERMINANTS OF POOR RESPONSE

Most patients demonstrate a response to enzyme therapy but there is wide inter-individual variation with a few patients exhibiting poor response. This phenomenon has been observed at all dose regimens (Barton et al, 1991; Zimran et al, 1994b). It has been suggested that variable responsiveness reflects individual dose requirements (Hollak et al, 1995) but such variation is also seen at the highest doses. There is no correlation between genotype at glucocerebrosidase gene locus, disease severity or age and responsiveness to enzyme therapy (Zimran et al, 1994b). Early studies suggested a lack of effect of splenectomy on overall responsiveness to enzyme therapy (Pastores et al, 1993). More recent analysis examining reduction of liver size as a single criterion has demonstrated that regression of hepatomegaly following enzyme therapy is greater in splenectomized patients (Mistry et al, 1997a). On the other hand, there are a number of factors that portend a poor response to enzyme therapy. These include underlying haematological malignancy and massive hypersplenism, both factors that escalate glyco-lipid turnover and presumably overwhelm enzyme supplementation. Other determinants of poor response include multiple splenic infarction with fibrosis (Mistry et al, 1996), liver cirrhosis (R.O. Brady, personal communication; Mistry et al, 1997b) and pulmonary disease especially the form in which pulmonary hypertension is not associated with significant cellular infiltration (Pastores et al, 1993; Dawson et al, 1996; Harats et al, 1997).

Splenectomy may be necessary rarely as an adjunct to enzyme therapy in a patient with massive splenomegaly complicated by extensive areas of infarction and fibrosis. Patients with end-stage cirrhosis also respond poorly to enzyme therapy. Liver transplantation has been performed successfully in patients with decompensated cirrhosis; enzyme therapy is necessary to prevent disease recurrence in the liver allograft (Carlson et al, 1990; Mistry et al, 1997b). High doses of enzyme are required to treat some cases of pulmonary disease (Pastores et al, 1993); this may be related to different kinetics of mannose receptors on the surface of glycolipid-laden macrophages in this organ. An appreciation of the various factors that modulate macrophage mannose receptor activity in vivo can allow the use of enzyme therapy in individual patients to achieve its maximal effect.

CAN ENZYME THERAPY BE TAILORED FOR SPECIFIC ORGAN INVOLVEMENT?

It has been suggested that different enzyme doses may be required to treat specific complications of Gaucher's disease and it has been proposed that effort should be directed to increase the delivery of enzyme to organs believed at present to be poorly accessible to exogenous enzyme, i.e. the bones and the lungs (Grabowski, 1996). There are little data but to some extent this may be true because high doses of enzyme are required in some patients to ameliorate pulmonary complications due to infiltration by Gaucher cells (Pastores et al, 1993). However, at other sites, the distribution of enzyme in vivo shows a remarkable parallel to the distribution of glucocerebroside-laden macrophages in the body (Mistry et al, 1996). Thus at all doses there is evidence to suggest adequate uptake of exogenous enzyme by pathological glycolipid-laden macrophages in the viscera and bone marrow. In order to optimize specific organ responses to enzyme therapy it may be more useful to take account of the intracellular half-life of the enzyme at these sites. Thus increasing dose frequency may help to achieve a consistent restitution of cellular enzyme activity; however, it remains to be seen if this results in greater hydrolysis of tissue glycolipids than when cellular enzyme activity is restored to normal or supra-normal levels intermittently (Mistry et al, 1996).

In order to maximize end-organ response, there is increasing emphasis on adjuvant therapies to reverse tissue damage and/or increase overall effectiveness of enzyme replacement therapy. For example, the use of calcium, vitamin D supplementation and diphosphonates for skeletal complications. Severe fibrosis cannot be reversed by enzyme therapy alone. Rarely, in advanced cirrhosis that results in hepatic decompensation, liver transplantation may be indicated (Carlson et al, 1990; Mistry et al, 1997b). Occasionally, massive splenomegaly can result in hypersplenism and increased glycolipid turnover that is sufficient to overwhelm exogenously administered enzyme and in addition regression of spleno-megaly is hindered because of extensive fibrosis and infarction (Mistry et al, 1996). Under such rare circumstances, splenectomy is indicated as an adjuvant to enzyme therapy.

The pulmonary manifestations of Gaucher's disease are protean including sub-clinical abnomalities of lung function tests, hepatopulmonary syndrome in association with severe liver involvement and pulmonary hypertension with or without cellular infiltration (Lee and Yousem, 1988). Limited experience indicates a favourable response to high-dose enzyme therapy of hepatopulmonary syndrome or pulmonary manifestations associated with extensive cellular infiltration (Beutler et al, 1991; Pelini et al, 1994; Zimran et al, 1994a). However, pulmonary hypertension associated with intra-pulmonary vascular dilatation without cellular infiltration appears not to respond to enzyme therapy and may even progress rapidly to terminal disease during therapy (Dawson et al, 1996; Harats et al, 1997). The cause of this unexpected outcome is not understood but it has been suggested that a contributing factor may be contaminants in the placental enzyme but there is no evidence to support this proposal (Harats et al, 1997). When infiltrative pulmonary disease is life-threatening, despite high-dose enzyme therapy, concomitant administration of corticosteroids may be helpful (J. E. Wraith: personal communication); a possible mechanism of this effect may be corticosteroid-induction of mannose receptor activity in pulmonary macrophages. The recommended dose of prednisolone is 2 mg/kg per day for 1 week and then tapering over a few weeks.

HOW TO DETERMINE THE MAINTENANCE DOSE OF ENZYME THERAPY

After the bulk of tissue glucocerebroside has been hydrolysed, an important aspect of managment is the determination of optimal maintenance therapy. There are no clear guidelines for maintenance therapy to prevent further accumulation of glycolipid. It is important in this respect to bear in mind the magnitude of daily glycolipid turnover. It has been estimated that the major contributors to daily glycolipid turnover are leukocytorrhexis: 380 mg glycolipid per day and erythrocytorrhexis: 10 mg/day (Pentchev et al, 1975). Yet, in the liver of a typical patient with Type 1 Gaucher's disease only 0.19 mg glucosylceramide accumulated each day, presumably the rest being hydrolysed by residual endogenous enzyme activity. Therefore, it is this level of positive balance that has to be abrogated by maintenance therapy. According to one model the dose is reduced by half each year until one quarter of the inital dose is reached and this is deemed to be the maintenance therapy (Beutler and Garber, 1994). In practice it is not so simple and patients require individualized determination of the maintenance dose. The latter could be determined by monitoring clinical symptoms, radiology and laboratory markers. It is likely that serial measurements of chitotriosidase will prove especially valuable, because in the individual patient it seems to be a useful way of tracking the total body pool of glycolipid-laden macrophages. Thus as the enzyme therapy is tapered, if chitotriosidase begins to rise, then this would be an indication to adjust the dose appropriately.

ADVERSE REACTIONS TO ENZYME THERAPY

Over 2000 patients worldwide are receiving long-term enzyme therapy: the longest has been for over 10 years. In general it is extremely well tolerated with little significant toxicity. Apart from minor side-effects related to the route of administration, the most common and significant problem related to alglucerase infusions have been allergic reactions manifesting as immediate hypersensitivity. Some 14% of patients develop IgG antibodies (subclass 1 and 3) to alglucerase at approximately 5 months after treatment commences; de novo antibody formation is rare after 12 months of treatment (Richards et al, 1993). In the majority this is a non-neutralizing antibody. Among patients with detectable antibody levels allergic reactions occurred in 22%, and among patients with allergic reactions 46% were found to have antibodies to alglucerase. In contrast, only 4% of patients without the antibody developed allergic reactions. The most likely mechanism for the allergic reaction involves immunoglobulin (IgG) immune complexes; thus decreasing the rate of infusion is often sufficient to reduce allergic reactions when resuming therapy. To date only three patients have developed neutralizing antibodies. In one such patient, concomitant corticosteroid therapy reduced antibody levels and restored responsiveness to enzyme therapy. The incidence of antibody formation during imiglucerase therapy is similar but it appears to be associated with fewer allergic reactions. There is some evidence that the incidence of antibody formation as well as allergic reactions is lower in patients receiving low dose therapy (Zimran et al, 1994b; 1995b).

Earlier batches of alglucerase were comprised of 4–7% of mannosylated human chorionic gonadotrophin (HCG). Modified HCG is cleared from circulation 30–40 times faster than the native material and thus results in markedly diminished biological effect. However, the HCG may have some biological effect in certain situations. False positive pregnancy tests have occurred because of the excretion of HCG in urine after infusions. In animal studies there has been precocious virilization due to androgen effects of HCG (Moscicki, 1995). Recently, the manufacturing process has been modified to reduce HCG contamination by 15-fold (Genzyme, 1996). When there are any such adverse effects to alglucerase, urgent priority should be given to convert the patient to imiglucerase. To date the recombinant mannose-terminated glucocerebrosidase, imiglucerase, is of comparable efficacy to alglucerase but associated with fewer adverse effects.

Recently, there have been reports of progressive pulmonary hypertension in patients on enzyme replacement therapy with alglucerase (Dawson et al, 1996; Harats et al, 1997). This may reflect intrinsic non-responsiveness of this specific pulmonary complication of Gaucher's disease in which lung disease appears not to be associated with heavy cellular infiltration. It has also been suggested that this phenomenon may be related to contaminants in alglucerase which mediate pulmonary vascular damage, but this is speculative.

MANAGEMENT OF GAUCHER'S DISEASE IN CHILDREN

Special considerations apply to management of paediatric patients because this group includes children with Type 2 and 3 disease as well as severe Type 1 disease. The average age of presentation of Type 2 disease is 3 months usually with heptosplenomegaly and failure to thrive. By 6 months, neurological complications develop with signs indicative of damage to cranial nerve nuclei and pyramidal tract (Barranger and Ginns, 1989). Dysphagia and difficulty in handling secretions develop often resulting in aspiration pneumonitis. Seizures may occur. As neurological disease progresses, the child becomes apathetic and motionless. Death occurs from apnoea or aspiration pneumonia at an average age of 9 months with a range of 1–24 months. It is important to remember that children with Type 1 disease can also present before 2 years of age with rapid progression of hepatosplenomegaly and skeletal disease. Some of these cases have been incorrectly classified as Type 3. It is essential to rigorously document central nervous system involvement prior to making a diagnosis of Type 3 disease. Genotype at glucocerebrosidase gene locus can be an useful ancillary test in this respect, because the presence of N370S mutation in a heteroallelic patient would effectively exclude neurological disease (Beutler, 1993). Conversely homozygosity for L444P mutation would favour neurological disease. In Type 3 disease, hepatosplenomegaly usually preceeds neurological abnormalities, which occur at an older age than in Type 2 disease and are more slowly progressive. Thus, in the Norrbottnian cohort the median age of presentation was about 2 years with a range of 6 months to 14 years (Erikson, 1986). A clinically useful subclassification of Type 3 disease has been proposed into Type 3a: mild visceral disease but rapidly progressive neurological disease, Type 3b: devastating visceral disease but mild neurological disease (Brady et al, 1993) and Type 3c: mild neurological and visceral disease associated with cardiac valvular calcification (Abrahamov et al, 1995; Mistry, 1995) Neurological abnormalities in Type 3 disease include ataxia, spastic para-paresis, grand mal and/or psychomotor seizures, supranuclear ophthalmo-plegia and dementia.

The intake interview of an affected child is similar to that for all sick children but should focus on assessing direct as well as indirect mani-festations of Gaucher's disease. The former should elicit the effects of visceromegaly, skeletal disease, bleeding disorder, tendency to infections, pulmonary involvement and neurological disease if present. There are a number of indirect manifestations of Gaucher's disease in the affected child that also provide important indicator of overall disease activity. These include growth retardation, malnutrition, impaired psychomotor develop-ment, delayed sexual maturation, incapacitating fatigue and school performance. Of these criteria, growth retardation appears to be especially valuable in assessing severity as well as rate of progression of Gaucher's disease in children. For example up to half of paediatric Type 1 patients had anthropometric evidence of growth retardation, which paralleled disease severity as measured by other parameters; furthermore, growth retardation was reversed by enzyme therapy (Kaplan et al, 1996). In some children growth retardation may be the sole overt manifestation of Type 1 Gaucher's disease (A. Abrahamov, unpublished). Investigations to stage disease activity, as described previously, are also applicable to paediatric patients but there are practical difficulties with regard to MRI scanning and the need to minimize radiation during radiological investigations. Thus during the regular follow-up of paediatric patients greater emphasis is placed on a limited battery of laboratory investigations (full blood count, clotting profile, liver function tests, tartarate-resistant acid phosphatase, vitamin D, parathormone and chitotriosidase), serial anthropometric measurements and estimation of visceral size by ultrasonography: it is desirable to use radiology sparingly to monitor skeletal and pulmonary disease. Children with neurological disease should be considered for brain MRI and EEG. These special features of Gaucher's disease in childhood preclude the application of SSI to stage disease severity in this age-group.

Enzyme therapy is highly effective in reversing disease manifestations in children affected with Type 1 Gaucher's disease (Zimran et al, 1993b). Assessing the candidacy of a child for enzyme treatment is usually more straight forward than that for an adult patient. It is indicated without exception in all symptomatic Type 1 and Type 3b (and probably in Type 3a) children but also in otherwise asymptomatic children in whom serial anthropometry indicate growth retardation. The asymptomatic children are usually diagnosed during family screening when a sibling or a parent in a high risk-population is found to have Gaucher's disease. In this setting a strong case can be made for pre-emptive enzyme therapy for the asymptomatic child who is heteroalleic for mutations that are associated with rapidly progessive disease: N370S with L444P, 84GG or IVS2 + 1 (Sibille et al, 1993). However, in a N370S homozygous child, it is wise to adopt an expectant policy. In Type 3 disease, enzyme therapy is highly effective in reversing visceral manifestations and to some extent skeletal disease, but there are conflicting reports with regard to neurological disease (Bembi et al, 1994; Brady, 1994; Zimran et al, 1994a). In Type 2 disease a case report indicated progression of CNS disease, particularly bulbar disease during systemic and intrathecal administration of high dose alglucerase (Bove et al, 1995). However, there is a reason for optimism in this group of patients, because there may be effective combination therapy in the near future in the form of imino sugars to inhibit glucosylceramide synthesis and mannose-terminated glucocerebrosidase (Platt et al, 1997).

Enzyme treatment for the paediatric patient should begin with the recombinant preparation at high dose, i.e. 60 U/kg every other week. Infusions can be facilitated by permanent in-dwelling venous access devices in selected patients. Monitoring of response to enzyme treatment in children is similar to that of the adult patient, as described earlier. However, these young Gaucher patients require more frequent follow-up in the clinic and intensive monitoring of disease activity. In addition, serial anthropo-metric measurements and achievement of puberty are also important end-points of response to enzyme therapy (Kaplan et al, 1996). Special care has to be exercised in conversion of children to maintenance enzyme therapy because premature dose reduction may increase the risk of bone crises or permanent sequelae from growth retardation. A strong case can be made for keeping Type 3 children on high dose therapy on a long-term basis in an attempt to prevent the development of new neurological foci; however, rarity and severity of this type has precluded a systematic study of this question. The long-term outcome of neurological disease appears to be favourable in the Norrbottnian patients following allogeneic bone marrow transplantation (Ringden et al, 1995). However, in considering the candidacy for bone marrow transplantation, the physician has the formidable task to weigh the potential benefits against the high risk of the procedure as well as the degree of established irreversible neurological damage. With the availability of enzyme therapy, bone marrow trans-plantation can no longer be recommended for Type 1 disease.

MANAGEMENT OF SKELETAL COMPLICATIONS OF GAUCHER'S DISEASE

Bone crises

Some 30–40% of all patients will experience bone crises that are most frequent during childhood and adolescence (Yosipovitch and Katz, 1990): Bone crises are most common in the long bones, particularly the distal femur, proximal tibia, humerus, the spine and the pelvis. Recurrent crises are common, occurring once or twice a year and decreasing in the third decade of life. These episodes often occur following a viral infection. The patient is commonly febrile with a temperature of up to 39°C and bed-ridden. It is common to find marked leukocytosis and elevated sedi-mentation rate. Clinical signs may disappear within a few days or can persist for several weeks. The treatment is symptomatic with use of narcotic analgesics, bed rest, hydration and antipyretic agents. Non-steroidal agents may be used effectively in patients but great care should be exercised in patients with thrombocytopenia, coagulopathy or portal hypertension. Antibiotics are sometimes administed as prophylaxis against secondary infection.

Gaucher patients can develop osteomyelitis in osteonecrotic bone, which favours bacterial proliferation (Bell et al, 1986). Multiple blood cultures, serial bone scans and MRI scans can be helpful in establishing the diag-nosis. There is increased uptake of ^{99}Tc-MDP uptake in bone crises but not in osteomyelitis. The involved area should be biopsied and cultured if there is a high index of suspicion. Bone crises have been described in patients already on enzyme therapy, which should be continued; however there appears to be no role for intensifying enzyme therapy in the acute situation (Pastores et al, 1993).

Surgical management

The quality of life of patients with Gaucher's disease may be greatly enhanced by appropriate orthopaedic surgical intervention. However surgical management may be complicated by underlying Gaucher's disease. Thrombocytopenia and coagulopathy can result in problematic per- and post-opertative bleeding jeopardizing the effectiveness of the prosthetic system. Total hip replacement has been performed commonly and successful replacement of the knee joint has also been accomplished in some cases (Goldblatt et al, 1988). It is important to choose the correct prosthesis length and anchoring technique for each patient depending on the extent of bony abnormalities in the affected limb. In patients with very extensive thinning of cortical bone, joint replacement may require special care during surgery because of the lack of sufficient bone structure to support the prosthesis (Mankin et al, 1990). Joint replacement surgery should not be performed in children because it interferes with limb growth, and the prosthesis has a relatively short life.

Adjuvant therapies to improve trabecular and cortical bone mass

In one study a significant number of patients affected by Gaucher's disease were found to be deficient in vitamin D and have a negative calcium balance (Mankin et al, 1990). Clearly, in such patients vitamin D and calcium supplements would be beneficial. In small studies of Gaucher patients, aminohydroxypropylidene biphosphonate administration has been reported to be effective in reversing bone disease as well as in improving calcium balance and bone density (Ostlere et al, 1991; Samuel et al, 1994). Controlled studies of the effect of the effect of this promising class of compounds in Gaucher's disease are planned in several centres. Hormone replacement therapy in post-menopausal women may be helpful but there is little clinical data.

PHYSICAL MANAGEMENT

There are no restrictions on physical activity in patients with mild disease. However, in patients with extensive skeletal infiltration some limitation of physical activity is necessary to maintain the integrity of the skeleton. When pathological fractures occur they often heal slowly or not at all. Collapse of vertebrae or of the femoral head has permanent sequelae. To help prevent these complications, it is advisable to avoid high impact activities and contact sports. However swimming is recommended. Physiotherapy is important to maintain muscle tone and movement.

SPLENECTOMY

With the availability of enzyme therapy, splenectomy should no longer be carried out as a primary therapeutic option for relief of cytopenia, pressure symptoms or growth retardation. It should be considered in the rare instance of failed enzyme therapy when the spleen is deemed to be a contributor to the poor response. It should be reserved for patients who despite enzyme therapy suffer from severe thrombocytopenia (platelet count consistently below 40 000/µl), unremitting abdominal pain secondary to recurrent splenic infarction, growth retardation, and/or mechanical cardiopulmonary compromise. Concern has been expressed about the effect of removal of the spleen on progressive deposition of glycolipid in other organs. It has been argued that removing the major reservoir of glycolipid storage would result in accelerated deposition in other organs such as the skeleton and the liver, and in Type 3 disease, the nervous system. From a review of over 200 patients, it was concluded that the presence or absence of skeletal disease was unrelated to splenectomy (Lee, 1982). However, other investigators have reached opposite conclusions (Fleischner et al, 1991). Also, Norrbottnian patients have been found to accumulate larger amounts of glucosylceramide in their plasma and brains following splenectomy, which correlated with a more rapid clinical deterioration (Conradi et al, 1984). This issue cannot be resolved since it cannot be excluded that patients who require splenectomy have intrinsically the more aggressive type of disease.

When splenectomy in indicated, it is important to provide appropriate prophylaxis to counteract susceptibility to sepsis (Cox and Mistry, 1995). Currently we recommend chemoprophylaxis and routine pre-operative immunization with the available pneumococcal, *Haemophilus influenzae* type B and meningococcal vaccines. Additional measures are recommended for patients who visit regions where the risk of systemic protozoal infections is increased. Many patients with Gaucher's disease have concomitantly acquired or inherited coagulopathy as well as platelet dysfunction. Thus appropriate haemostatic support is essential during surgery.

Partial splenectomy was introduced in an attempt to avoid the hazards of asplenic state in patients with Gaucher's disease. However, recent experience reported rapid regrowth of splenic remnant with recurrence of hypersplenism as well as development of new bone-related complications (Zimran et al, 1995a).

REFERENCES

Abrahamov A, Elstein D, Gross-Tsur V et al, (1995) Gaucher's disease variant characterised by progressive calcification heart valves and unique genotype. *Lancet* **346:** 1000–1003.

Anonymous (1996) To affinity and beyond. *Nature Genetics* **14:** 367–370.

Balicki D & Beutler E (1995) Gaucher disease. *Medicine* **74:** 305–323.

Barranger JA and Ginns EI (1989) Glucosylceramide lipidosis: Gaucher disease. In Scriver CR, Beaudet AL, Sly WS & Valla D (eds) *Metabolic Basis of Inherited Disease*, pp. 1677–1698. New York: McGraw-Hill.

*Barton NW, Brady RO, Di Bisceglie AM et al (1991) Replacement therapy for inherited enzyme deficiency—macrophage targeted glucocerebrosidase for Gaucher's disease. *New England Journal of Medicine* **324:** 1464–1470.

Bell RS, Mankin HJ & Doppelt SH (1986) Osteomyelitis in Gaucher disease. *Journal of Bone and Joint Surgery* **68A:** 1380–1388.

Bembi B, Zanatta M, Carrozzi M et al (1994) Enzyme replacement treatment in type 1 and 3 Gaucher's disease. *Lancet* **344**: 1679–1682.

*Beutler E (1993) Gaucher disease as a paradigm of current issues regarding single gene mutations of humans. *Proceedings of the National Academy of Science USA* **90**: 5384–5390.

Beutler E & Kuhl W (1970a) Detection of the defect of Gaucher's disease and its carrier state in peripheral blood leucocytes. *Lancet* **I**: 612–613.

*Beutler E & Kuhl W (1970b) The diagnosis of adult type of Gaucher's disease and its carrier state by demonstration of deficiency of beta-glucosidase activity in peripheral blood leucocytes. *Journal of Laboratory and Clinical Medicine* **76**: 747–755.

Beutler E & Saven A (1990) Misuse of marrow examination in diagnsosis of Gaucher disease. *Blood* **76**: 646–648.

Beutler E & Gelbart T (1993) Gaucher disease mutations in non-Jewish patients. *British Journal of Haematology* **85**: 401–405.

*Beutler E & Garber AM (1994) Alglucerase for Gaucher's disease. Dose, costs and benefits. *PharmacoEconomics* **5**: 453–459.

Beutler E & Gelbart T (1995) Erroneous assignment of Gaucher disease genotype as a consequence of a complete gene deletion. *Human Mutations* **4**: 212–216.

Beutler E & Grabowski GA (1995) Gaucher disease. In Scriver CR, Beudet A, Sly WS, Valle D (eds) *Molecular and Metabolic Bases of Inherited Disease*, 7th edn, pp. 2641–2692. New York: McGraw-Hill.

Beutler E & Gelbart T (1996) Glucocerebrosidase (Gaucher disease). *Human Mutation* **8**: 207–213.

Beutler E, Gelbart T & West C (1990) The facile detection of nt 1226 mutation of glucocerebrosidase by 'mismatch' PCR. *Clinica Chimica Acta* **194**: 161–166.

Beutler E, Kuhl W, Matsumoto F et al (1976) Acid hydrolases in leucocytes and platelets in normal subjects and in patients with Gaucher's disease. *Journal of Experimental Medicine* **143**: 975–980.

Beutler E, Kay A, Saven P et al (1991) Enzyme replacement therapy for Gaucher disease. *Blood* **78**: 1183–1189.

Bove K, Daughtery C & Grabowski GA (1995) Pathologic findings in Gaucher disease Type 2 patients following enzyme therapy. *Human Pathology* **26**: 104–105.

Brady RO (1994) Enzyme replacement therapy for patients with type 3 Gaucher disease. Fourth National Gaucher Foundation Conference Nov. 6–7. Philadelphia.

*Brady RO, Kanfer JN & Shapiro D (1965) Metabolism of glucocerebrosides. II Evidence of an enzymatic deficiency in Gaucher's disease. *Biochemistry and Biophysics Research Communications* **18**: 221–225.

*Brady RO, Barton NW & Grabowski GA (1993) The role of neurogenetics in Gaucher's disease. *Archives of Neurology* **10**: 1212–1224.

Busche G, Majewski H, Schlue J et al (1997) Frequency of pseudo-Gaucher cells in diagnostic bone marrow biopsies from patients with Ph positive chronic myeloid leukaemia. *Virchows Archiv* **430**: 139–148.

Carlson DE, Bussutil RW, Gindici TA et al (1990) Orthotopic liver transplantation in the treatment of complication of type 1 Gaucher disease. *Transplantation* **49**: 1192–1194.

Cohen Y, Elstein D, Abrahamov A et al (1994) HCG contamination of alglucerase: clinical implication in low dose regimen. *American Journal of Haematology* **47**: 235–236.

Conradi NG, Sourander P, Nilsson O et al (1984) Neuropathology of the Norrbottnian type of Gaucher disease. Morphological and biochemical studies. *Acta Neuropathologica* **65**: 99–109.

Cox TM & Mistry PK (1995) Splenectomy in Gaucher disease. In Aerts JM, Goudsmit R & Tager JM (eds) *Proceedings of the First EWGGD Workshop*. p. 82. Publ Drukkerij Universiteit van Amsterdam.

Dahl N, Lagerstrom M, Erikson A et al (1990) Gaucher disease type 3 (Norrbottnian type) is caused by a single mutation in exon 10 of the glucocerebrosidase gene. *American Journal of Human Genetics* **47**: 275–278.

Dawson A, Elias DJ, Rubenson D et al (1996) Pulmonary hypertension developing after alglucerase therapy in two patients with type 1 Gaucher disease complicated by the hepatopulmonary syndrome. *Annals of Internal Medicine* **125**: 901–904.

Elstein D, Hadas-Halpern I, Azun Y et al (1997) Accuracy of ultrasonography in assessing spleen and liver size in patients with Gaucher disease: comparison to computed tomographic measurement. *Journal of Ultrasound Medicine* **16**: 209–211.

Erikson A (1986) Gaucher disease: Norrbottnian type 3. Neuropathological aspects of clinical patterns and treatment. *Acta Paediatrica Scandinavica* **326**: 1–42.

Figueroa ML, Rosenbloom SE, Kay AC et al (1992) A less costly regimen of alglucerase to treat Gaucher's disease. *New England Journal of Medicine* **327**: 1632–1636.

Fleishner PR, Aufses AH, Grabowski GA et al (1991) A 27-year experience with splenectomy for Gaucher's disease. *American Journal of Surgery* **161**: 69–75.

Genzyme (1996) Circular to treating physicians dated 13.3.96. Genzyme Corp, One Kendall Square, Cambridge, MA 02139, USA.

Glenn D, Turston D, Garner P et al (1994) Comparison of magnetic resonance imaging and ultrasound in evaluating liver size in Gaucher patients. *Acta Haematologica* **92**: 187–189.

Goldblatt J, Sacks S, Dall D et al (1988) Total hip arthroplasty in Gaucher's disease. Long-term prognosis. *Clinical Orthopedics* **228**: 94.

Grabowski GA (1996) Current issues in enzyme therapy for Gaucher disease. *Drugs* **52**: 159–167.

Grabowski GA, Goldblatt J, Dinur T et al (1985) Genetic heterogenity in Gaucher disease: physico-kinetic and immunologic studies of the residual enzyme in cultured fibroblasts from neuronopathic and non-neuronopathic patients. *American Journal of Medical Genetics* **21**: 529–549.

*Grabowski GA, Barton NW, Pastores G et al (1995) Enzyme therapy in type 1 Gaucher disease: comparative efficacy of mannose-terminated glucocerebrosidase from natural and recombinant sources. *Annals of Internal Medicine* **122**: 33–39.

Harats D, Pauzner R, Elastein D et al (1997) Pulmonary hypertension in two patients with type 1 Gaucher disease while on alglucerase therapy. *Acta Haematology* **98**: 47–50

Harzer K (1995) Enzymatic screening for Gaucher disease by assay of beta-glucocerebrosidase in white blood cells. In Aerts JM, Goudsmit R & Tager JM (eds) *Proceedings of the First Workshop of EWGGD* p. 43. Publ Drukkerij Universiteit van Amsterdam.

*Hollak CE, van Weely S, van Oers MHJ et al (1994) Marked elevation of plasma chitotriosidase activity in Gaucher's disease. *Journal of Clinical Investigation* **93**: 1288–1292.

Hollak CE, Aerts JM, Gudsmit R et al (1995) Individualized low-dose alglucerase therapy for type 1 Gaucher's disease. *Lancet* **345**: 1474–1478.

Hollak CE et al (1997) *American Journal of Medicine* (in press).

Horowitz M, Tzuri G, Eyal N et al (1993) Prevalence of nine mutations among Jewish and non-Jewish Gaucher disease patients. *American Journal of Human Genetics* **53**: 921–930.

Johnson LA, Hoppel BE, Gerard EL et al (1992) Quantitative chemical shift imaging of vertebral bone marrow in patients with Gaucher's disease. *Radiology* **182**: 451–455.

Kaplan P, Mazur A, Manor O et al (1996) Acceleration of retarded growth in children with Gaucher disease after treatment with alglucerase. *Journal of Paediatrics* **129**: 149–153.

Latham T, Grabowski GA, Theophilus BDM et al (1990) Complex alleles of the acid beta-glucosidase gene in Gaucher disease. *American Journal of Human Genetics* **47**: 79–86.

Lee RE (1982) The pathology of Gaucher disease. In Desnick RJ, Gatt S & Grabowski GA (eds) *A Century of Delineation*, p. 177. New York, Alan R Liss.

Lee RE & Yousem SA (1988) The frequency and type of lung involvement in patients with Gaucher's disease. *Laboratory Investigations* **58**: 54A.

Mankin HJ, Doppelt SH & Rosenberg AE (1990) Metabolic bone disease in patients with Gaucher's disease. In Avioli LV & Krane SM (eds) *Metabolic Bone Disease*, pp. 730–752. Philadelphia: WB Saunders Co.

Mistry PK (1995) Genotype/phenotype correlation in Gaucher's disease. *Lancet* **346**: 982–983.

Mistry PK & Cox TM (1995) Phenotypic diversity in a pair of identical twins with Gaucher's disease. In Aerts JM, Goudsmit R & Tager JM (eds) *Proceedings of the First Workshop of EWGGD*. p. 62 Publ Drukkerij Universiteit van Amsterdam.

Mistry PK, Wraight EP & Cox TM (1996) Therpeutic delivery of proteins to macrophages: implications for treatment of Gaucher's disease. *Lancet* **348**: 1555–1559.

Mistry PK, Butler P, Elstein D & Zimran A (1997a) Regression of hepatomegaly by mannose-terminated glucocerebrosidase. *Journal of Hepatology* **25 (supplement 1)**: 174A.

Mistry PK, Butler P, Elstein D & Zimran A (1997c) Effect of macrophage targeted glucocerebrosidase on serum lipoproteins in type 1 Gaucher's disease. *Journal of Hepatology* **26 (supplement 1)**: 124A.

Mistry PK, Smith SJ, Ali M et al (1992a) Genetic diagnosis of Gaucher's disease. *Lancet* **339**: 889–892.

Mistry PK, Davies S, Corfield A et al (1992b) Successful treatment of bone marrow failure in Gaucher's disease with low-dose modified glucocerebrosidase. *Quarterly Journal of Medicine* **83**: 541–546.

Mistry PK, Brenton DP, Young E et al (1997b) Liver transplantation in type 1 Gaucher's disease: role of adjuvant macrophage targeted glucocerebrosidase. *Journal of Hepatology* **26 (supplement 1):** 151A.

Moscicki RA (1995) Adverse reaction and development of antibodies during enzyme replacement therapy. In *NIH Technology Assessment Conference: Gaucher Disease, Current Issues in Diagnosis and Treatment*, pp. 123–129. Bethesda: NIH, Continuing Medical Education.

Ostlere L, Warner T, Mennier PJ et al (1991) Treatment of type 1 Gaucher's disease affecting bone with aminohydroxypropylidene biphosphonate (pamidronate). *Quarterly Journal of Medicine* **79:** 503–515.

Pastores GM (1994) Gaucher's disease type 1: clinical assessment of bone disease. *Gaucher Perspectives* **2:** 5–7.

Pastores GM, Sibille AR & Grabowski GA (1993) Enzyme therapy in Gaucher disease type 1: doasage efficacy and adverse effects in 33 patients treated for 6–24 months. *Blood* **82:** 408–416.

Pelini M, Boice D, O'Neil K et al (1994) Glucocerebrosidase treatment of type 1 Gaucher disease with severe pulmonary involvement. *Annals of Internal Medicine* **121:** 196–197.

Pentchev P, Brady RO, Gal AE et al (1975) Replacement therapy for inherited enzyme deficiency. Sustained clearance of accumulated glucocerebrosidase in Gaucher's disease following infusion of purified glucocerebrosidase. *Journal of Molecular Medicine* **1:** 73–78.

Platt FM, Neises GR, Reinkensmeier G et al (1997) Prevention of lysosomal storage in Tay–Sachs mice treated with *N*-butyldeoxynojirimycin. *Science* **276:** 428–431.

Raghavan SS, Topol J & Kolodny EH (1980) Leucocyte beta-glucosidase in homozygotes and heterozygotes for Gaucher disease. *American Journal of Human Genetics* **32:** 158–173.

Richards SM, Olson TA & McPherson JM (1993) Antibody response in patients with Gaucher disease after repeated infusion with macrophage-targeted glucocerebrosidase. *Blood* **82:** 1402–1409.

Ringden O, Groth CG, Erikson A et al (1995) Ten years experience of bone marrow transplantation for Gaucher disease. *Transplantation* **59:** 864–870.

Rosenthal DI, Doppelt SH, Mankin HJ et al (1995) Enzyme replacement therapy for Gaucher disease: skeletal responses to macrophage-targeted glucocerebrosidase. *Paediatrics* **96:** 629–637.

Samuel R, Katz K, Pappapoulos SE et al (1994) Aminohydroxypropylidene biphosphonate (APD) treatment improves the clinical skeltal manifestations of Gaucher's disease. *Paediatrics* **94:** 385–389.

Sibille A, Eng CM, Kim SJ et al (1993) Phenotype/genotype correlation in Gaucher disease: Clinical and therapeutic implications. *American Journal of Human Genetics* **52:** 1094–1101.

Sidransky E, Bottler A, Stubblefield B et al (1994) DNA mutational analysis of type 1 and type 3 Gaucher patients: how well do mutations predict phenotype. *Human Mutations* **3:** 25–28.

Tsuji S, Choudary PV, Martin BM et al (1987) A mutution in the human glucocerebrosidase gene in neuronopathic Gaucher's disease. *New England Journal of Medicine* **316:** 570–575.

Turner BM & Hischhorn K (1978) Properties of beta-glucosidase in cultured fibroblasts from controls and patients with Gaucher disease. *American Journal of Human Genetics* **30:** 346–358.

Vellodi A (1997) Gaucher's disease in children. In *Proceedings of the second EWGGD*, May 1–3, Maastricht (in press).

Walley AJ, Barth ML, Ellis I et al (1993) Gaucher's disease in the United Kingdom: screening non-Jewish patients for the two common mutations. *Journal of Medicine and Genetics* **30:** 280–283.

Yosipovitch Z & Katz K (1990) Bone crises in Gaucher disease—an update. *Israel Journal of Medical Science* **26:** 593–595.

Young E, Lake B, Malone M et al (1997) Gross elevation of plasma chitotriosidase in a patient with normal glucocerebrosidase activity and severe histiocytosis. In *Proceedings of Second EWGGD Workshop*, May 1–3, Maastricht (in press).

Zimran A, Sorge J, Gross E et al (1989) Prediction of severity of Gaucher's disease by identification of mutation at the DNA level. *Lancet* **ii:** 349–352.

Zimran A, Kay A, Gelbart T et al (1992) Gaucher disease. Clinical, laboratory, radiologic and genetic features of 53 patients. *Medicine* **71:** 337–353.

*Zimran A, Hollak CE, Abrahamov A et al, (1993a) Home treatment with intravenous enzyme replacement therapy for Gaucher disease: an international collaborative study of 33 patients. *Blood* **82:** 1107–1109.

Zimran A, Hadas-Halpern I, Zevin S et al (1993b) Low dose high-frequency enzyme replacement therapy for very young children with severe Gaucher disease. *British Journal of Heamatology* **85:** 783–786.

Zimran A, Elstein D, Abrahamov A et al (1994a) Enzyme replacement therapy in type I and type 3 Gaucher's disease. *Lancet* **345:** 451–452.

*Zimran A, Elstein D, Kannai R et al (1994b) Low dose enzyme replacement therapy for Gaucher's disease: effects of age, sex, genotype and clinical features on response to treatment. *American Journal of Medicine* **97:** 3–13.

Zimran A, Elstein D, Schiffmann R et al (1995a) Outcome of partial splenectomy for type 1 Gaucher disease. *Journal of Paediatrics* **126:** 596–597.

Zimran A, Elstein D, Levy-Lahad E et al (1995b) Replacement therapy with imiglucerase for type 1 Gaucher's disease. *Lancet* **345:** 1479–1480.

Appendix: patient associations worldwide

Argentina
Asociación Gaucher Argentina
Leopoldo Marechal 1314—Dto 2
1414 Buenos Aires
Tel: (0054) 1 854 5196
  or 1 782 3439

Australia
Gaucher's Association
6 Logan Street
Capalaba QLD 4157
Tel: (0061) 7 245 1848

Belgium
Gaucher's Association
Kluizestraat 6
B-9100 Knesselare
Tel: (0032) 93 74 02 82
Fax: (0032) 50 44 47 91

Brazil
Associacoa Brasileira dos
  Portadores da Doenca de
  Gaucher
Av. Nilo Pecanha 155
Sobreloja, Centro, CEP 20020-100
Rio de Janeiro
Tel: (0055) 21 220 8633

Canada
National Gaucher Foundation
4100 Yonge Street, Suite 310
North York, Ontario, M2P 2B5
Tel: (00) 1 416 250 2850

Czech Republic
Czech Gaucher Association
Mrs Susan Krajsova
1 Maje No 41
Karlovy 36006
Vary
Tel: 017 48978

France
Vaincre les Maladies Lysosomales
9 Place du 19 Mars 1962
91035 Evry Cedex
Tel: (0033) 1 60 91 75 00

Germany
Gaucher Gesellschaft Deutschland
An der Ausschacht 9
59556 Lippstadt
Tel: (0049) 2941 18870

Israel
Israeli Gaucher Association
Century Tower
124 Iben Gvirol Street
Tel Aviv 62038
Tel: (00972) 3 522 6482

Italy
Associazione Italiana Gaucher
Piazza della Costituzione 7
50129 Florence
Tel: (0039) 55 461 312

Netherlands
Gaucher Vereniging Nederland
Ruitercamp 155
3992BZ Houton
Tel: (0031) 30 637 4417

New Zealand
Gaucher's Association
PO Box 28593
Remuera, Auckland
Tel: (0064) 9 524 9772

South Africa
Gaucher's Society
PO Box 51399
Raedene 2124
Tel: (0027) 11 640 5577

Spain
Fundacion Española para el
    Estudio y Terapeutica de la
    Enfermedad de Gaucher
    (FEETEG)
Apartado 1590
50080 Zaragoza
Tel: (0034) 76 233 646

Sweden
Morbus Gaucher foreningen
Soldatvøgen 19
95531 Røneø
Tel: (0046) 924 10986

UK & Ireland
Gaucher's Association
25 West Cottages
London NW6 1RJ
Tel (UK): 0171 433 1121
Tel: (0044) 171 433 1121

USA
National Gaucher Foundation
11140 Rockville Pike
Suite 350, Rockville
Maryland 20852-3106
Tel: (00)1 301 816 1515

Index

Note: Page numbers of article titles are in **bold** type.